Educational Inequalities

While there is considerable literature on social inequality and education, there is little recent work which explores notions of difference and diversity in relation to "race", class and gender. This edited text aims to bring together researchers in the field of education located across many international contexts such as the UK, Australia, USA, New Zealand and Europe. Contributors investigate the ways in which dominant perspectives on "difference", intersectionality and institutional structures underpin and reinforce educational inequality in schools and higher education. They emphasize the importance of international perspectives and innovative methodological approaches to examining these areas, and seek to locate the dimensions of difference within recent theoretical discourses, with an emphasis on "race", class and gender as key categories of analysis.

Kalwant Bhopal is Reader in Education and Director of Postgraduate Research Degrees at the University of Southampton, School of Education. She has recently edited *Intersectionality and Race in Education* (with John Preston, Routledge 2012) and is currently researching aspects of rural racism in primary schools in England.

Uvanney Maylor is Professor of Education and Director of the Institute for Research in Education at the University of Bedfordshire. She is currently writing a text for Routledge entitled *Teacher Training and the Education of Black Children: Bringing Color into Difference.*

Routledge Research in Education

For a full list of titles in this series, please visit www.routledge.com.

Educational Inequalities

Difference and Diversity in Schools and Higher Education

Edited by Kalwant Bhopal and Uvanney Maylor

Routledge
Taylor & Francis Group

NEW YORK   LONDON

First published 2014
by Routledge
711 Third Avenue, New York, NY 10017

and by Routledge
2 Park Square, Milton Park, Abingdon, Oxon OX14 4RN

*Routledge is an imprint of the Taylor & Francis Group,
an informa business*

Library of Congress Cataloging-in-Publication Data
   Educational inequalities : difference and diversity in schools and higher
education / edited by Kalwant Bhopal and Uvanney Maylor.
      pages cm. — (Routledge research in education ; 102)
   Includes bibliographical references and index.
   1. Educational equalization—Cross-cultural studies.   2. Education,
Higher—Social aspects—Cross-cultural studies.   3. Educational
change—Cross-cultural studies.   4. Educational attainment—Cross-cultural
studies.   I. Bhopal, Kalwant.   II. Maylor, Uvanney.
   LC213.E44 2013
   379.2'6—dc23
   2013012622

ISBN13: 978-0-415-53998-2 (hbk)
ISBN13: 978-1-315-88619-0 (ebk)

Typeset in Sabon
by IBT Global.

SUSTAINABLE FORESTRY INITIATIVE   Certified Sourcing   www.sfiprogram.org   SFI-01234
SFI label applies to the text stock

Printed and bound in the United States of America
by IBT Global.

Contents

Figures and Tables

FIGURES

TABLES

1 Educational Inequalities in Schools and Higher Education

An Introduction

Kalwant Bhopal and Uvanney Maylor

Education in the UK has seen significant changes in the past few years, particularly policy changes introduced by the Coalition government such as the introduction of tuition fees and the introduction of free schools and academies, as well as the eradication of the Education Maintenance Grant (EMA). Such significant changes have affected the poorest students the hardest. Far from creating greater equality, such changes have perpetuated inequality both in schools and in higher education—with greater students from poor working-class backgrounds being further disadvantaged. Recent research suggests, for example, that although the gap between the richest and poorest children has started to fall over the last decade, the gap at the General Certificate of Secondary Education (GCSE) level remains large, with the latest Department for Education (DfE) figures indicating that pupils eligible for free school meals (FSMs) are almost half as likely to achieve five or more A*–C grades at GCSE compared with those who were not eligible (30.9 per cent compared with 58.5 per cent) (Carter-Wall and Whitfield 2012). Furthermore, poorer children are half as likely to go on to study at university compared with their more affluent peers. Educational attainment continues to be strongly associated with socio-economic background (Sutton Trust 2010), despite some signs that social differences in examination results may have started to reduce. There have been some significant changes with the gap in attainment between ethnic groups narrowing, with some previously low-performing groups catching up with the average attainment. Whereas a generation ago almost all the students attending university were White British, today one in five are from Black and minority ethnic (BME) backgrounds (EHRC How Fair Is Britain, 2010). Whereas this change is positive, inequalities in education continue to persist. A recent report by Alan Millburn (2012), MP (member of Parliament), explores how the most advantaged 20 per cent of young people are still seven times more likely than the 40 per cent most disadvantaged to attend the most selective universities, demonstrating how access to university remains inequitable. The report argues that 'there is a strong correlation between social class and the likelihood of going to university generally and to the top universities particularly. Four private schools and one college get more of their students into Oxbridge than the combined efforts of 2,000 state schools and colleges' (2). Furthermore, elite universities such as Oxford and Cambridge are failing to adequately represent BME students and the representation of minority ethnic students at Russell Group universities is unbalanced (*Race into Higher Education* 2010).

A report by the Sutton Trust (2010) found that just 16 per cent of pupils who are eligible for FSMs progress to university, compared with 96 per cent of young people who have been to independent schools. Changes in Coalition government policy outlined earlier, such as the scrapping of the EMA, has had implications for students from low-income backgrounds, affecting their entrance into higher education and consequently their chances of social mobility and future success in the labour market. Inequalities also persist in higher education; research has shown that the majority of the UK professoriate is White and male (Bhopal and Jackson 2013). A report by the Equality Challenge Unit (2011) found that in 2009–2010 only 0.9 per cent of UK staff in professorial roles were from BME backgrounds and 76.1 per cent of professors of UK staff were White males (Equality in Higher Education, Statistical Report 2011).

But these inequalities are not unique to the UK. Michael Apple, in his pioneering new book, *Can Education Change Society?*, starkly reminds us of the disparities and injustices that continue to exist in the US and the significant role that education (particularly schools) play in sometimes perpetuating these inequalities. Schools are 'key mechanisms in determining what is socially valued as "legitimate knowledge" and what is seen as merely "popular". In their role in defining a large part of what is considered legitimate knowledge, they also participate in the process through which particular groups are granted status and other groups remain unrecognised or minimised' (Apple 2013, 21).

As scholars committed to equality and social justice, we are disappointed about the lack of commitment and engagement given to such inequalities not just by politicians, but also policymakers and grant-funding bodies. Consequently, we are committed to examining the discourses of inequalities. *Educational Inequalities in Schools and Higher Education* brings together researchers in the fields of education, class, gender, 'race' and sociology who provide theoretical and empirical understandings of the discourses of educational inequality. The main focus of the collection is to examine difference and diversity, specifically gender, 'race' and class, and how the intersectionalities of these differences work in relation to challenging and also perpetuating inequalities in education.

In particular the collection seeks to locate the dimensions of difference within recent theoretical discourses with an emphasis on 'race', class and gender as key categories of analysis and does so by using theoretical approaches to examine the inequalities and diversities of educational experiences. Whereas there is considerable literature on social inequality and education, there is little recent work which explores notions of difference and diversity in relation to 'race', class and gender. Given the gap in the literature, it becomes all the more important to address the specificity of difference. In this collection, we bring together major research located across the UK and diverse international contexts (such as Australia, the US, New Zealand and Europe). Contributors explore the ways in which dominant perspectives on 'difference', intersectionality and institutional structures underpin and reinforce educational inequality. They also emphasise the importance of international perspectives in such discussions by using innovative methodological approaches to examining these areas. A collection that integrates and interrogates the debates about difference, diversity and inequality in education and theorising such approaches is long overdue.

Educational Inequalities in Schools and Higher Education is based on the premise that education and notions of inequality are controversial subjects in which difficult and contested discourses are the norm. Individuals in education experience multiple inequalities and have diverse identifications that cannot necessarily be captured by one theoretical perspective alone (Gillborn 2008; Ladson-Billings 2003; Reay, David and Ball 2001). The purpose of this collection and the coherence of its arguments are dictated by an examination of controversial grounds, both empirical and theoretical debates, within national and international educational research contexts foregrounding issues of gender identity, 'race', culture and inclusion. As such, the aim of the collection is to do the following:

- Specifically examine areas of discrimination and disadvantage such as gender, 'race' and class within education as well as debating the difficulties of applying such concepts in relation to the experiences of students in education.
- Analyse contesting discourses of identity in different educational cultural contexts.

By combining a mix of intellectually rigorous, accessible and controversial chapters, the collection presents a distinctive and engaging voice, one that seeks to broaden understandings of 'intersectionality' beyond the simple confines of the education sphere into an arena of sociological and cultural discourse. In this way, the collection provides a challenge to current racialised, gendered and classed educational discourse and promotes new ways of thinking about educational practice.

The collection is divided into three specific parts. Part I examines difference, diversity and inclusion and consists of four chapters each of which explores how discourses of difference are understood in different educational contexts. Zeus Leonardo in Chapter 2 interrogates the status of whiteness in American education by exploring two significant camps regarding the uptake of whiteness: White reconstruction and White abolition. In the first, reconstructionists offer discourses—as forms of social practice—that transform whiteness, and therefore White people, into something other than an oppressive identity and ideology. Reconstruction suggests rehabilitating whiteness by resignifying it through the creation of alternative discourses. It projects hope onto whiteness by creating new racial subjects out of White people, which are not ensnared by a racist logic. On the other hand, White abolitionism is guided by Roediger's announcement that 'whiteness is not only false and oppressive; it is nothing but false and oppressive' (1994, 13). In opposition to reconstructing whiteness, abolishing whiteness sees no redeeming aspects of it as long as White people think they are White. This chapter considers White reconstruction and abolition for their conceptual and political value as it concerns not only the revolution of whiteness, but of race theory in general, particularly in relation to educational contexts.

In Chapter 3, Gill Crozier examines the school experiences of secondary-aged young people in England and explores the factors that advantage or disadvantage their academic success. The chapter presents an analysis of existing research of educational under/achievement amongst a cross section of BME, working-class and middle-class, girls and boys in order to investigate the similarities and differences in their school experience. Crozier argues that there is an abundance of research which shows that social mobility between the social classes has remained stagnant for the past twenty years and that the academic achievement of Black Caribbean and Bangladeshi and Pakistani heritage children remains obdurately lower than the rest of the population. By employing theories of ideology, Whiteness and Bourdieu's concept of 'field', the chapter develops insights into why this remains the case in the twenty-first century. As part of this, Crozier considers the role of the school in its challenge to or maintenance of existing stratification and inequalities of outcome. This is followed by Jasmine Rhamie's chapter, 'Black Academic Success: What's Changed?' Rhamie examines whether there have been changes of Black academic success since the new Coalition political climate in England. The chapter begins by reviewing the literature on the academic achievement of Black pupils, focusing on research which identifies and promotes their academic success, it particularly focuses on such research conducted since 2007 (Rhamie 2007). The chapter raises concerns about the education policy direction of the present Coalition government and the implications of some of its key decisions on equality for the inclusion of Black pupils. Rhamie provides a picture of the current situation for Black pupils in terms of (under)achievement and explores some of the theoretical explanations for the continued underachievement of Black pupils. The chapter concludes by emphasising the importance of acknowledging Black academic success and considers the implications of this for educational research and policy making.

In Chapter 5, Robyn Henderson explores intersections of ethnicity, social class and gender based on an itinerant lifestyle identified amongst some Australian students. She does so by deconstructing teachers' narratives in theorising transformative action. Her chapter explores how considerable research has highlighted how social membership—in terms of ethnicity, social class and gender, or combinations of these factors—can influence the successes that children achieve in school literacy learning. Teachers often use these features as points of reference, creating narratives about why some students in the school context succeed and others do not. One result can be narratives of blame—stories that blame students for not bringing appropriate understandings to school, or stories that blame parents for being deficient in caring for their children and negligent in not preparing them for school literacy learning. Such narratives are often based on normative and stereotypical views of families and provide common sense understandings that reinforce educational inequality. The chapter draws on empirical evidence from a two-year research study that was conducted in a school located in a north Australian rural community. It is framed within cultural-critical understandings of literacy, alongside critical discourse and poststructuralist theories. The chapter investigates the intersectionality of social class, ethnicity and gender in teachers' narratives about itinerant farmworkers' children and their successes or otherwise in school literacy learning. In many of the stories, deficit discourses about the children's 'differences' from their residentially stable peers represented commonsense knowledge that regarded children's inappropriate behaviours, actions and underachievement in literacy learning as predictable and 'natural' consequences of families' lifestyles and perceived characteristics. The chapter argues that these taken-for-granted assumptions about the negative impacts of ethnicity, class, gender and an itinerant lifestyle on children's schooling served to narrow the pedagogical options that were available for teachers. As a result, educational inequities seemed to be maintained and there was little opportunity for itinerant children to move beyond underachievement. The chapter further considers possibilities for transformative action, arguing that a reconceptualisation of itinerancy and the supposedly deficient characteristics of itinerant families could disrupt deficit views and help teachers focus on responsive, flexible and enabling pedagogies for children who are often marginalised in school settings.

Part II focuses on 'Understanding Difference: Policy and Practice in Education'. It examines how the effects of educational policy and practice can work to interrogate and understand the discourses of difference in Swedish education. Anne-Sofie Nyström in Chapter 6, 'Negotiating Achievement—Students' Gendered and Classed Constructions of (Un) Equal Ability', explores how educational institutions are structured around achievement and evaluating and comparing students' achievements. The chapter explores how stratification processes are not just about cognition but about social processes such as affect, negotiations of values and causes of achievements. Like other Nordic countries, Sweden has long been associated with equality—not least in education. Many statistics suggest increased differences are primarily based on school and student categories in terms of class and 'race', whereas gender stratification has focussed on policy debates. The chapter examines privilege via analyses of peer-group interactions amongst a student category that is rarely problematised: an ethnographically informed doctoral study on young people's identity negotiations in Swedish upper secondary schools. The focus is on examining a setting structured by high performance and dominated by White, upper-middle-class students. Identification processes such as social categorisations based on gender, class and age and dominance relations are studied as micro-processes and placed in the context of equality/equity and education. The chapter outlines how young men and women in the study draw attention to dominance relations amongst peers in the classroom; it also demonstrates the hierarchies between schools and study programmes. The chapter further explores how students questioned the legitimacy of such identity claims and hierarchies, but these were often reproduced in terms of unequal educational and social ability (resources).

Farzana Shain's chapter, 'Change *and* Tradition: Muslim Boys' Talk about Their Post-Sixteen Aspirations', examines how the neo-liberal restructuring of education has resulted in a relentless pursuit of educational success through policies such as Parental Choice, Beacon and Leading Edge schools, Gifted and Talented (Hey and Bradford, 2007) and, more recently, Academy and Free Schools in England. As Ozga (1999) maintains, these policies are located within a wider framework which ties education to national competitiveness and sees achievement as the solution to social exclusion. Rather than equalising opportunities, analyses (Reay 2008; Tomlinson 2008) suggest that these polices have enhanced middle-class choice and advantage while reinscribing working-class and racialised disadvantage. Despite such observations, policies on citizenship, for example, place the focus on 'helping' individuals navigate their way through a series of individualised 'personalised' choices away from the old certainties of gender, 'race' and class solidarity (Avis 2006). Drawing on a wider empirical study of Muslim (predominantly working-class Pakistani and Bangladeshi) boys' identities and educational experiences (Shain 2011), the chapter argues that class, 'race' and gender remain salient factors which constrain and enable educational outcomes. Following a brief overview of policy and academic debate, the chapter focuses on the boys' orientations to schooling and 'success', their subject preferences and imagined future choices about post-sixteen education and careers. The chapter outlines a range of factors that shape these experiences and 'choices', including school processes such as setting, peer relations, and the boys' economic location in some of the most deprived neighbourhoods in England.

In Chapter 8, Heidi Mirza and Veena Meetoo explore how new and virulent forms of faith-based racism in the form of Islamophobia have gripped Western multicultural societies since the 9/11 and the 7/7 bombings by British-born Muslim (male) youth. In this climate, education has become a key site in the battle against the spectre of the 'Muslim extremist' in our midst. Educational programmes such as the Prevention of Violence and Extremism exemplify this hysteria with its focus on averting the next generation of potential terrorists by combating the ideology which might produce them. However, such programmes are largely aimed at Muslim young men and boys. Ironically, young women in patriarchal Muslim communities, often at risk of domestic forms of violence such as forced marriage, slip through the cracks of educational policy and school practice. In terms of safeguarding and well-being, young Muslim women are effectively caught between the multicultural discourses that focus on issues between communities rather than within communities and the Islamophobia discourse that demonises young Muslim men. Drawing on interviews with seventeen young women in two inner-city schools, this chapter traces the narrative constructions of young Muslim women as they negotiate gendered, 'raced' and classed structures, dominance and power in the classroom and in their everyday lives. Interviews with teachers and policymakers contextualise the young women's subjectivity and social relations with their perspectives on religious identity and gendered discourses of risk, safety and well-being. Using a Black feminist framework of 'embodied intersectionality' (Mirza 2009), the young women's narratives not only demonstrate the fluidity of a collective transcendental ethnic Muslim female identity, but they also express a strong outwardly individualistic neo-liberal career-orientated identity. In effect they were negotiating the traditional wearing of the veil as a means of personal transformation in socially and educationally restrictive circumstances. The chapter concludes that to understand young Muslim women's lived reality in Britain we need to theorise beyond the limitations of the multicultural discourse which invisiblises minority ethnic women and the Islamophobic discourse that visibilises the over determined female Muslim body with its obsession with the 'veil'.

In Chapter 9, Carl A. Grant and Annemarie Ketterhagen Engdahl discuss how the concepts of politics of difference, intersectionality and an understanding of and resistance toward a pedagogy of poverty can be used to help education researchers and teachers to see missed opportunities in the classroom in order to create a culturally relevant instructional environment where all American students are academically engaged and have a meaningful classroom experience that leads to a flourishing life. They conclude the chapter with examples of missed opportunities where teachers did not use a lens of intersectionality or the concept of the politics of difference in their classrooms. The examples used are contrasted with fulfilled opportunities where these lenses and points of view are applied as a counter to the pedagogy of poverty. This chapter is intended to deepen understanding of both academic theory and classroom practice.

Part III of the book, 'Educational Inequalities: Identities, Inclusion and Barriers', specifically examines how educational inequalities persist through an understanding of identities and barriers to inclusion. Alexandra Allweiss, in Chapter 10, 'I Want to Hear You': Listening to the Narratives, Practices and Visions of a Chuj Maya Teacher in Guatemala', examines the progression of educational reform. She argues how in many countries, classroom teachers are on the front line of the reform effort. These education policies, however, are generally devised, implemented and evaluated using a top-down approach. Yet, there is much more that can be learned about the effects of such education policies by discussing these reform efforts with teachers. This chapter documents the experiences of one middle school teacher, who is representative of a sample of thirty-two educators in Xantin, Guatemala, participating in a larger research project designed to shape instructional practices to be responsive to the Intercultural and Bilingual Education (IBE) reforms in Guatemala. At the heart of the teacher's work is the goal of teaching students in a manner that fosters academic, social and personal success. A narrative inquiry approach is used to frame the chapter and investigate the intersections and influences of 'cultural racism', gender inequities and place-based classism on education policy and practice through a teacher's experience. Voices of educators working within the framework of the national reforms provide powerful critiques and visions for change that are not always visible through a top-down approach. The chapter explores how narrative inquiry allows educationalists to view the challenges and possibilities of these reforms using the experiences and insights from one teacher.

Chapter 11, 'What Does It Mean to Be the "Pride of Pinesville"?: Opportunities Facilitated and Constrained', by Amy Johnson Lachuk, Mary Louise Gomez and Shameka N. Powell, presents the life history of one African American woman living in a small rural community in the southern United States. Surpassing many social, economic and contextual barriers, she earned postsecondary degrees and returned to live and work in her community. Using in-depth interviews, the chapter explores factors that facilitate and/or constrain the literacy and educational experiences of this woman. Through examining her life history, the authors present ways that educational pursuit in rural areas is framed by intersecting dimensions of 'race', class, gender and place.

In Chapter 12, Edwina Pio, Ali Rasheed, Agnes Naera, Kitea Tipuna and Lorraine Parker use ethnicity to explore the lived-in and lived-through academic and support staff experiences of Maori and Pasifika peoples in a New Zealand university. Based on staff perceptions of their experiences and hopes around curriculum, students, colleagues and institutional structures, the authors present broad themes on the inscription of ethnicity in the doing and being of who one is in a university. A hermeneutic approach and semi-structured qualitative interviews are used to provide an in-depth understanding of key issues. Using the lens of diversity management, specifically post-colonial scholarship, this chapter examines the enduring impact of ethnicity. The findings point to the coalescence of the historical streams of migration and Indigenous peoples along with newer nuanced ways of handling ethnicity. Creating mana—respect/honour through ethnicity is a prevailing theme, along with the perception that ethnicity is based on stereotypes of Indigenous people which are easily accessible in an environment where there are very few minority ethnic staff. To this end, the chapter explores how government policies seek to positively support Maori and Pasifika staff in universities and develops a model of minority ethnic staff in universities where such policies tend to have a varying impact.

Elżbieta H. Oleksy, in Chapter 13, offers a new approach to pedagogy whilst demonstrating how intersectionality can be experienced, thought and learned. In the wealth of literature on intersectionality as a concept, theory, political option and methodology, little has been published on how intersectionality can be taught. Working with graduate students within the European Commission's Erasmus Mundus Project in Women's and Gender Studies, the chapter demonstrates how such innermost intricate interdependencies as 'race', ethnicity, nationality, gender, sexuality and circumstance can be explored through an audience analysis of intersectional visual products.

In Chapter 14, 'Intersecting Identities: Young People's Constructions of Identity in South-East Europe', Alistair Ross examines a different kind of intersection than that considered elsewhere in this volume: that between potentially conflicting territorial or political identities of the self that arise as young people in Bulgaria and Romania attempt to reconcile their potential memberships of a national community, a regional Balkan identity and a European identity. The educational implications of this analysis relate to young people in a much wider context than these two south-eastern European countries. At the time of writing, they are the most recent members of the European Union, joining in 2007, but they will have been joined by Croatia by the time this book is published and very likely within the next four to six years by six or seven other Balkan states. The chapter explores how some of the implications will resonate much more widely than the Balkan peninsular: The tensions of multiple membership of different and nesting political entities and of being a 'global citizen' are becoming more common and pressing across Europe and beyond. The chapter calls for educators to display sensitivity in understanding and reacting positively to the self-constructions of young people as liminal beings, uncertain of how their mix of identities socially positions them in Western Europe, if they are not to experience inequality in educational settings.

In all these chapters, the authors have aimed to explore how educational inequalities in schools and higher education continue to persist in different social, economic and political climates from national and international perspectives. If we want to work towards achieving equality in education, if we see it as a realisable goal—and as optimists we do—we must continue to question, interrogate and disrupt the discourses of social justice, inclusion and (in)equality; it is only then that we, as educators committed to equality work, can achieve our aims of reaching those on the margins of society who continue to be disadvantaged.

REFERENCES

Apple, Michael. 2013. *Can Education Change Society?* New York: Routledge.
Avis, James. 2008. 'Class, Economism, Individualisation and Post-Compulsory Education and Training'. *Journal for Critical Education Policy Studies* 6 (2): 37–53.
Bhopal, Kalwant. and Jackson, June (2013) *The Experiences of Black and Minority Ethnic Academics: Multiple Identities and Career Progression.* University of Southampton: Engineering and Physical Sciences Research (EPSRC).
Carter-Wall, Charlotte, and Grahame Whitfield. 2012. *The Role of Aspirations, Attitudes and Behaviour in Closing the Educational Attainment Gap.* York: Joseph Rowntree Foundation.
Equality Challenge Unit. 2011. *The Experiences of Black and Minority Academics in HE in England.* London: Equality Challenge Unit.
Equality in Higher Education (2011) *Statistical Report 2010–2011.* London: EHE.
Equality and Human Rights Commission (2010) *How Fair is Britain?* London: EHRC.
Gillborn, David. 2008. *Racism and Education: Coincidence or Conspiracy?* London: Routledge.
Hey, Valerie, and Simon Bradford. 2007. 'Successful Subjectivities? The Successification of Class, Ethnic and Gender Positions'. *Journal of Education Policy* 22 (6): 595–614.
Ladson-Billings, Gloria. 2003. *Critical Race Theory Perspectives on the Social Studies: The Profession, Policies, and Curriculum.* Greenwich, CT: Information Age Publishers.
Millburn, Alan. 2012. *Fair Access to Professional Careers: A Progress Report by the Independent Reviewer on Social Mobility and Child Poverty.* London: Crown Copyright.
Mirza, Heidi Safia. 2009. 'Plotting a History: Black and Postcolonial Feminisms in 'New Times'. *Race Ethnicity and Education* 12 (1): 1–10.
Ozga, Jenny. 1999. 'Two Nations? Education and Social Inclusion-Exclusion in Scotland and England'. *Education and Social Justice* 1 (3): 44–50.
Race into Higher Education. 2010. London: Communities and Local Government.
Reay, Diane. 2008. 'Tony Blair, the Promotion of the "Active" Educational Citizen, and Middle-Class Hegemony'. *Oxford Review of Education* 34 (6): 639–650.
Reay, Diane, Miriam David and Stephen Ball. 2001. 'Making a Difference? Institutional Habituses and Higher Education Choice'. *Sociological Research Online* 5 (4). http://www.socresonline.org.uk/5/4/reay.html. Accessed March 2013.
Rhamie, Jasmine. 2007. *Eagles Who Soar.* Stoke-on-Trent: Trentham.
Roediger, David. 1994. *Toward the Abolition of Whiteness.* New York: Verso.
Shain, Farzana. 2011. *New Folk Devils: Muslim Boys and Education in England.* Stoke-on-Trent: Trentham.
Sutton Trust. 2010. *Education Mobility in England.* London: Sutton Trust.
Tomlinson, Sally. 2008. *Race and Education: Policy and Politics in Education.* Berkshire: Open University Press/McGraw-Hill.

Part I

Difference, Diversity and Inclusion

2 Pale/Ontology
The Status of Whiteness in Education*

Zeus Leonardo

INTRODUCTION

Race scholarship is witnessing a shift. In the past two decades, whiteness studies has penetrated what arguably has been the home of scholars of colour who write for and about people of colour. Circa 1990, whiteness studies burst onto the academic scene with three important publications, written by White scholars about, but not exclusively for, White people. In fact, we would not be far off to characterise whiteness studies as a White-led race intervention. Circa 1990, Peggy McIntosh's (1992) 'Unpacking the White Knapsack', David Roediger's (1991) *Wages of Whiteness* and Ruth Frankenberg's (1993) *White Women, Race Matters* arguably represent the beginnings of a focus on whiteness and White experiences. Since then, there has been a veritable explosion of critical work on whiteness across the disciplines (Morrison 1993; Allen 1994, 1997; Ignatiev 1996; hooks 1997; Winant 1997; Dyer 1997; Aanerud 1997; Lipsitz 1998; Brodkin 1999; Warren 2000; Thompson 2001; Bush 2005; Wise 2007). In education, the impact of whiteness studies has been no less (Sleeter 1995; McLaren 1995, 1997; Giroux 1997a, 1997b, 1997c; Ellsworth 1997; McIntyre 1997; Apple 1998; Kincheloe and Steinberg 1998; Howard 1999; Sheets 2000; Allen 2002; Thompson 2003; Richardson and Villenas 2000; Leonardo 2004; Gillborn 2005; Lee 2005; DiAngelo 2006). It should be noted that scholars of colour previously took up the issue of whiteness, but as a secondary if not tertiary concern (see Du Bois 1989), insofar as studying the souls of White folk was an afterthought to the souls of Black folk. With whiteness studies, whiteness and White people come to the centre in an unprecedented and unforeseen way. This is different from the centring that whiteness is usually afforded in Eurocentric curricula and writing. Indeed it would be problematic to recentre whiteness as a point of reference for civilisation, progress and rationality in order to relegate people of colour to the margins, once again. In whiteness studies, *whiteness becomes the centre of critique and transformation*. It represents the much-neglected anxiety around race that whiteness scholars, many of whom are White, are now beginning to recognise.

Whiteness studies is both a conceptual engagement and a racial strategy. Conceptually, it poses critical questions about the history, meaning and ontological status of whiteness. For example, it contains an apparatus for the precise rendering of whiteness's origin as a social category. In other words, whiteness is not coterminous with the notion that some people have lighter skin tones than others; rather whiteness, along with race, is the structural valuation of skin colour, which invests it with meaning regarding the overall organisation of society. In this sense, whiteness conceptually had to be invented and then reorganised in particular historical conditions as part of its upkeep (Leonardo 2007). Inseparable from the conceptualisation of whiteness, whiteness studies comes with certain interventions or racial strategies. There are two significant camps regarding the uptake of whiteness: White reconstruction and White abolition (Chubbuck 2004). In the first, reconstructionists offer discourses—as forms of social practice—that transform whiteness, and therefore White people, into something other than an oppressive identity and ideology. Reconstruction suggests rehabilitating whiteness by resignifying it through the creation of alternative discourses. It projects hope onto whiteness by creating new racial subjects out of White people, which are not ensnared by a racist logic. On the other hand, White abolitionism is guided by Roediger's (1994) announcement that 'whiteness is not only false and oppressive, it is *nothing but* false and oppressive' (13; italics in original). In opposition to reconstructing whiteness, abolishing whiteness sees no redeeming aspects of it and as long as White people think they are White, Baldwin once opined that there is no hope for them (as cited by Roediger 1994, 13). This chapter will consider White reconstruction and abolition for their conceptual and political value as it concerns not only the revolution of whiteness, but of race theory in general.

Neo-abolitionists argue that whiteness is the centre of the 'race problem'. They go further than suggesting that racism is a 'White problem'. Rather, as long as whiteness exists, little racial progress will be made. In fact, leading abolitionists Ignatiev and Garvey (1996a) argue that multiculturalism and general race theories that accept the existence of races are problematic for their naturalisation of what are otherwise reified concepts. To Ignatiev and Garvey, races are not *real* in an objective and ontological sense and therefore Whites, for example, are not real either. They do not go as far as suggesting that White people do not *exist*, which is a different point. They exist insofar as structures recognise white bodies as 'White people'. But this recognition relies on the reification of a spurious category in order simultaneously to misrecognise certain human subjects as White people. Race treason encourages Whites to disrupt this process by pledging their disallegiance to the 'White club'. Race traitors are white bodies that no longer act like and as White people. The investment in whiteness (Lipsitz 1998) is the strongest form of investment because it is the most privileged racial identification. As long as Whites invest in whiteness, the existence of non-White races will also continue. Hirschman (2004) has argued that as long as race exists, so does racism and it is anachronistic to imagine one without the other. The clarion call for abolitionists asks Whites to disidentify with whiteness, leading to the eventual abolition of whiteness. I would also add that it leads to another consequence, which is the abolition of White people, or the withering away of a racial category and its subjects. In other words, if whiteness disappears, so do White people. I will have more to say about this last point later.

By contrast, White reconstructionists disagree with abolitionists in the former's attempt to recover whiteness. The disagreement falls within two domains: theory and viability. Theoretically, reconstructionists do not accept Roediger's maxim that whiteness is only false and oppressive because there are many examples of Whites who have fought against racism, such as the original abolitionists. Reconstructionists argue that Whites can be remade, revisioned and resignified and are not merely hopelessly racist. Their search is for a rearticulated form of whiteness that reclaims its identity for racial justice. They acknowledge that whiteness is a privilege, but that Whites can use this privilege for purposes of racial justice and therefore contribute to the remaking of whiteness that is not inherently oppressive and false. In schools, reconstructing whiteness includes focusing on White historical figures who have fought and still fight against racial oppression. Reconstructionists consider this strategy as more viable than arguing for the abolition of whiteness, which most Whites will have a difficult time accepting. The discourse of White abolition will only lead to White defensiveness and retrenchment and does not represent much hope for even progressive or anti-racist Whites. To the reconstructionists, abolitionism is tantamount to promoting a certain self-hatred and shame among Whites, guilting them into accepting a movement that does not recognise their complexity. Rather, they prefer to instil critical hope in Whites.

Clearly, there has been a shift in race studies and whiteness has come to the fore much more visibly. It is driven by a complex yet plainly stated question: What to do with whiteness? The debate between White abolition and reconstruction is a fertile educational ground. It represents a neglected aspect in race studies, which is the future of a privileged people and how they can participate in undoing these same privileges. It also poses the question of 'What do Whites become after undoing these said privileges?' Do they become new subjects of whiteness or do they obliterate a racial category beyond recognition when they commit what Ignatiev and Garvey call 'the unreasonable act' of race treason? Just as we may ask what the modern looks like after the postmodern critique (Lyotard 1984), what do Whites look like, in the ontological sense, after the critique of whiteness studies? This chapter hopes to generate not only insights about this process, but a rather needed dialogue. It is less concerned with identifying who is a reconstructionist or abolitionist of whiteness (although one can certainly have a productive discussion that begins there), and more with assessing the interventions that each discourse provides.

WHITE BY ANOTHER NAME: WHITE
RECONSTRUCTIONISM IN EDUCATION

Before we begin, one caveat must be entered. By focusing on whiteness, Apple (1998) warns that scholars of whiteness studies may unwittingly recentre whiteness, insufficiently knocking it off its orbit. He writes:

> We must be on our guard to ensure that a focus on whiteness doesn't become one more excuse to recenter dominant voices and to ignore the voices and testimony of those groups of people whose dreams, hopes, lives, and very bodies are shattered by current relations of exploitation and domination. (1998, xi)

Much useful work has been spent on decentring whiteness from its privileged son-of-God status. When the sun of whiteness has been centred the planets of colour have suffered. However, the centring of whiteness has also been an example of a certain inverted understanding, a geocentric theory that mistakes the real dynamics of social life and development. Not only does whiteness encourage us to be 'flat earthers' (Friedman's phrase), but it constructs a Ptolemaic universe that misunderstands a world it has created after its own image (Mills 1997). As a privileged marker, whiteness assumed that the lives of people of colour depended on White progress and enlightenment, whereas a heliocentric critical theory puts whiteness in its rightful place in racial cosmology, as largely dependent and parasitic on the labour and identity of people of colour. By recentring whiteness here, we counteract what may be dubbed the superstitious beliefs in the rightness of whiteness and institute a more scientific explanation of how the social universe actually functions. In other words, if critical studies of race recentre whiteness, it does not do so in order to valorise or pedestalise it. Quite the opposite. A critical study of whiteness puts the social heavens back in order.

The rearticulation of whiteness is part of an overall emancipatory project that implicates a host of institutions from economic to educational. Discursive interventions in education to transform whiteness attempt to explain the whiteness of pedagogy as they encourage a pedagogy of whiteness. That is, shifting the white racial project from one of dominance to one of justice requires a pedagogical process of unlearning the codes of what it currently means to be White and rescuing its redeeming aspects. Giroux (1997b) writes, '"Whiteness" . . . becomes less a matter of creating a new form of identity politics than an attempt to rearticulate "whiteness" as part of a broader project of cultural, social, and political citizenship' (295). In rescuing whiteness, critical educators insert hope in White people as hermeneutic subjects who may interpret social life in liberating ways and not as hopelessly stuck in the molasses of racism. It recognises the multiple moments of White history as an attempt to complexify racial options for Whites (indeed speak to its existing complexity). In the dialectics of whiteness, Whites search for positive articulations in history as well as facing up to the contradictions of what it means to be anti-racist in a racist society. Seen this way, the current formulations of whiteness are racist, but whiteness itself is not inherently racist. Being White is not the problem; being a White racist is.

Dislodged from the hopelessness and helplessness of having to consider oneself as simply privileged (therefore racist), White students' humanity is affirmed as the ability to choose justice over domination. Here, abolitionists may agree that whiteness is a choice, at least with respect to the kind of White person one chooses to uphold. This new racial project asks:

> How students might critically mediate the complex relations between 'whiteness' and racism, not by having them repudiate their 'whiteness,' but by grappling with its legacy and its potential to be rearticulated in oppositional and transformative terms . . . ways to move beyond the view of 'whiteness' as simply a troupe of domination. (Giroux 1997b, 296)

Questioning the essentialism of identity politics, Giroux projects a third space for Whites, which neither valorises their 'accomplishments' nor overstates their complicity in relations of domination (see also Giroux 1997a, 1997c). Their history is not determined by the originary sin of racism but rather a complex web of contradictions that make up what it means to be White in any given context. As such, educators recognise the anti-racist moments within White hegemony as well as the racist traps of White calls for racial justice. The abolitionist movement of the nineteenth century provides a glimpse into this dualism if we consider the fact that John Brown and his comrades fought to dismantle slavery while their White privilege made their instalment in leadership positions possible over those of Black abolitionists, like Frederick Douglass. A reading of the abolitionists as exceptions to the White rule (so common in history books and lessons) misses the way that White privilege works to favour even White abolitionists; equally, educators note how, by fighting against the institution of slavery, abolitionists were remaking what it meant to be White. It testifies to the fact that '*some* of the time, in *some* respects even when not in *all*, whites empathize and identify with nonwhites, abhor how white supremacy has distorted their social interactions, and are willing to make significant sacrifices toward the eradication of white privilege' (Alcoff 1998; italics in original). In short, they were able to 'rearticulate whiteness in oppositional terms' (Giroux 1997b, 310). To the extent that the abolitionists were racially privileged and that they used these said privileges to edge out Black abolitionists in discursive and institutional positions of leadership, they were anti-racist racists. They were located in the cauldron of whiteness without being entrapped in its determinisms insofar as they were anti-racist without being anti-White.

Within this perspective, social domination is not the sole property of Whites as there have been many examples of non-White forms of domination. As Gary Howard (1999) might put it, whiteness is not the problem, but rather certain interpretations of what it means to be White lead to forms of domination. The theory of social dominance is too deterministic because it fails to recognise the multiple positions that Whites take up in the race struggle. There are different ways to be White: from fundamentalist, to integrationist, to transformationist. Or as Ellsworth (1997) once put it, 'It is more than one thing and never the same thing twice' (266). Just as Christianity is not the source of a religious problem, but interpretations that encourage subjugation of non-Christian peoples, the ultimate meaning of whiteness is up for reinterpretation under concrete conditions of struggle as educators 'disrupt the sanctification of whiteness' (McIntyre 1997, 149). Rather than rejecting whiteness, Howard suggests 'breaking' out of whiteness, 'emerging' from it to become something else. This process should not be underestimated. Just as Lenin once remarked that whereas the proletariat must merely be educated and the bourgeoisie must be revolutionised (see Althusser 1976), so must Whites be transformed or experience a transformative education. In other words, although the social experiences of both the working-class and people of colour provide the basis for understanding the nature of their oppression, we cannot say the same for the bourgeoisie and Whites who must be 'reborn' like the phoenix (Allen 2005; Freire 1993).

Because whiteness is a social construction, a range of possibilities is opened up for White agency. Although durable, racial identity is also fluid and flexible. It fractures into different racial projects, some of which do not merely reproduce and reiterate White power. That said, reconstructionists suggest that struggling with whiteness is well within a racial project, not an attempt to get outside it (see also Omi and Winant 1994). In this sense, *racial ideology has no outside*. As Kincheloe and Steinberg (1998, 8) note, 'As with any racial category, whiteness is a social construction in that it can be invented, lived, analyzed, modified, and discarded', which echoes Omi and Winant's contention that racial projects can be created, modified and even destroyed. For the moment, Ignatiev and Garvey (1996a) agree when they declare that 'what was once historically constructed can be undone' (35). More of an ideological choice than a biological destiny, whiteness is part of a hermeneutics of the self. Although not entirely up to the individual to transform, whiteness represents a constellation of differences articulated to appear as a 'lump-sum' category (Pollock 2004), when in fact 'there are many ways to be White' (Kincheloe and Steinberg 1998, 8). Of course there are masculine and feminine ways to be White, poor and rich ways to be White, straight and gay ways, liberal and radical ways as well, which speak to 'the diverse, contingent racial positions that white people assume' (Giroux 1997b, 309). In this sense, resignifying whiteness leads us to the 'multiple meanings of whiteness' (McIntyre 1997, 4) that, rather than viewing it simply with suspicion for the world it hides, may imagine the world it opens up in front of it (Ricoeur 1981; Leonardo 2003). A hermeneutics of suspicion promotes dis-identification with whiteness as erecting a veil (à la Du Bois) that works against its transparency, whereas a hermeneutics of empathy reserves hope that whiteness may emerge as an authentic worldview. This means that 'making whiteness rather than white racism the focus of study is an important pedagogical strategy' (Giroux 1997b, 309). White racism is inherently oppressive, but whiteness, seen through the prism of reconstructionism, is multifaceted and undecidable.

In rearticulating whiteness, educators offer students discourses that provide not only access to different ways of being White, but also strategies that counter the anxiety associated with current discourses of whiteness. Because essentialist discourses limit the range of possibilities for White students to relate with others, their daily upkeep of whiteness is marked with extreme forms of racial anxiety and inauthenticity (see Leonardo 2004). Whites traverse the social landscape, threatened of being exposed as bogus racial agents as they round every corner. They know few alternative forms of whiteness outside the colonial framework, where they are interpellated as the coloniser. As a result, the unbearable whiteness of their being overcomes their search for alternative subjectivities and they become paralyzed to act. Giroux (1997a) asks:

> What subjectivities or points of identification become available to white students who can imagine white experience only as monolithic, self-contained, and deeply racist? What are the pedagogical and political stakes in rearticulating whiteness in anti-essentialist terms so that white youth can understand and struggle against the legacy of white racism while using the particularities of their own culture as a resource for resistance, reflection, and empowerment . . . a theoretical language for racializing whiteness without essentializing it? (310–311)

The question here is less about students unbecoming White and more about what kind of Whites they will become. It suggests coming to terms with the production of 'white terror', perhaps 'unthinking whiteness', but certainly not the abolition of the self, which comes with obvious contradictions for Whites (McLaren 1995, 1997). It is not a move to promote historical amnesia concerning White atrocities against the Other thereby promoting a certain White 'innocence', but redeeming whiteness in order to come to terms with these crimes and develop a positionality against them. In the process, Whites assert their humanity as beings-in-struggle and beings-for-others, rather than using others-for-their-being. In this search, Giroux is adamant about developing 'power-strategic politics that refuses to accept "whiteness" as a racial category that has only one purpose, which is closely tied to, if not defined by, shifting narratives of domination and oppression' (Giroux 1997b, 306). It is a call for living with difference that is the cornerstone of the pedagogical interaction that Lisa Delpit (1995) coined as 'teaching other people's children'. Because we know that much of the teaching force is comprised by and large with White women, the reinvention of whiteness becomes even more imperative if the educating population not only will reach, but equally teach, the learning population that is increasingly less White.

In articulating a White position against racism, reconstructionists transform White identity from a cul-de-sac formation of endless oppressive histories into a productive, even positive, subjectivity. Anti-racist Whites may still be caught up in the contradictions of their own positionality and the privileges that come with it, but they can actively use their advantages responsibly to create an alternative racial arrangement that is less oppressive. To the extent that Whites are unable to throw off years of racist lessons and are dogged by their racist unconscious, through self-reflection they inhere the possibility of developing into anti-racist subjects. Whiteness is not a hopeless disease and may be rehabilitated (McLaren and Torres 1999). Thus, a:

> key goal of a critical pedagogy of whiteness emerges: the necessity of creating a positive, proud, attractive, antiracist white identity that is empowered to travel in and out of various racial/ethnic circles with confidence and empathy ... Traditional forms of multiculturalism have not offered a space for Whites to rethink their identity around a new, progressive, assertive, counter-hegemonic, antiracist notion of whiteness. (Kincheloe and Steinberg 1998, 12, 20)

Developing a positive racial self for Whites entails that educators open up pedagogical conditions for students to forge an intersubjective space wherein they are able to enter the other without becoming the other. Now it must be noted that Whites already enter racial/ethnic circles with confidence. The phenomenon of racial exoticisation and tourism already encourages Whites to enter non-White spaces in a way that only a coloniser can, who always feels in charge even when outnumbered by the other (Memmi 1965). From Elvis to Eminem, White privilege confers the mobility to travel in and out of communities of colour despite Whites' irrational (and ironic) fears about violence. Moreover, as Ingram (2005) suggests, it is not clear why Whites must develop identities against racism through positive racial affiliations rather than through religious, secular humanist or civic patriotic ones.

The operative concept here is 'empathy'. Rearticulating whiteness reminds Whites that the ghetto and other concentrations of colour were created by Whites in order to fulfil the dictates of segregation, the hallmark of American apartheid (Massey and Denton 1993). Empathy enables Whites to become 'border crossers' (Giroux 1992) with the benefit of critical reflection and recollection. White border crossers understand that transcending boundaries itself is a racial privilege. That is, the policing of people of colour limits their mobility despite the fact that some trickle into White spaces. Border intellectuals recognise the difference between racial fetish-ism that addresses the other as abstract and solidarity that conceives of the other as concrete, albeit a concrete generalised other (Benhabib 1987). Empathy is not a mode of desiring the other to be part of oneself through the process of enfleshment, but rather recognising the completion of the self through the other.

A theory of White reconstructionism comes with certain interventions that make it a viable political movement. To the reconstructionist, it offers a way into whiteness rather than a way out of it. It encourages Whites to own their whiteness rather than disowning it. Reconstructionism is not an idealist politics but a critical, pragmatic one. Kincheloe and Steinberg (1998) put it this way: 'We are not comfortable with the concept of a new oppositional white identity as a "race traitor" who renounces whiteness. It is unlikely that a mass movement will grow around that concept, as oppositional Whites still would have little to rally around or to affirm' (21). Because reconstructing whiteness is likely to provide Whites racial options that are more appealing and imaginable (without understating the difficulties associated with it), reconstructionism may find its way into education as a pedagogical principle. Just as it is becoming increasingly difficult for Whites publicly to oppose multiculturalism insofar as the emerging question asks what kind of multiculturalism will be forged and not if multiculturalism is desirable (Buras 2008), White raciality is becoming more difficult to avoid or deny. The question is no longer whether or not Whites are racial subjects—clearly they are—but rather how this racial project will play itself out.

White teachers and students alike will find their humanity in whiteness rather than denying people of colour of theirs through White deployments of power. Reconstructed White subjects 'develop both theoretical and emotional support' (Kincheloe and Steinberg 1998, 21) rather than wallowing in guilt, which can be paralyzing for even the liberal-thinking White person. In fact, opting out of whiteness is a racial privilege that people of colour cannot enact. Kincheloe and Steinberg punctuate:

> Whites alone can opt out of their racial identity, can proclaim themselves nonraced. Yet no matter how vociferously they may renounce their whiteness, white people do not lose the power associated with being White. Such a reality renders many white renunciations disingenuous. It is as if some race traitors want to disconnect with all liabilities of whiteness (its association with racism and blandness) while maintaining all its assets (the privilege of not being Black, Latino, or Native American). (1998, 22)

Disappearing is not something people of colour can accomplish. To the extent that Whites may desire it, it speaks to their power to make the other disappear and when desirable, make themselves vanish. A project of White reconstruction locates whiteness in order to change it, unlearn much of what passes as White normativity and in the process reappear as transformed Whites.

KILL THE WHITE, SAVE THE HUMAN:
WHITE ABOLITIONISM AND A PEDAGOGY OF ZERO DEGREE

To the extent that White reconstructionism is a more realistic and reasonable option to address the crisis of whiteness, the White abolitionist movement championed by Ignatiev and Garvey (1996a) and Roediger (1991) encourages Whites to commit the 'unreasonable act' of race treason. Committed to the understanding that the 'key to solving the social problems of our age is to abolish the white race . . . so long as the white race exists, all movements against racism are doomed to fail' (Ignatiev and Garvey 1996b, 10), White abolitionism takes its cue from a hybrid strategy melding both the original abolitionist movement's focus on nonparticipation and the inversion of a White supremacist charge that Whites who disown whiteness are 'race traitors'. In other words, neo-abolitionists ask Whites (particularly poignant for poor and working-class Whites) to opt out of their whiteness in search of a more accurate understanding of their social conditions and political interests; strategically, these new abolitionists favour appropriating race treason as their battle cry rather than their badge of dishonour. This is both an empirical as well as a theoretical injunction.

Empirically, Whites have participated in race liberation movements, such as anti-slavery and civil rights, but this does not equate with acts of whiteness but actions by White subjects. In fact, White acts against racism is the very opposite of whiteness as a modus operandi insofar as acting against racism threatens whiteness. One might even go so far as saying that dismantling whiteness and racism leads to the eventual breakdown of White people as a social category. Against reconstructionism, abolitionism suggests that there is little empirical proof of a positive iteration of whiteness and searching for examples of positivity is as elusive as the holy grail. Or as Ingram (2005) puts it, 'The attempt to save whiteness by reducing it to ethnic identity is futile . . . I therefore conclude that, although white persons need not feel guilty about who they are, they should not aspire to a positive ethno-racial identification in the way that blacks and other oppressed racial minorities might' (247). It also leads Ignatiev (1997) to lay down the gauntlet:

> We at *Race Traitor* . . . have asked some of those who think whiteness contains any positive elements to indicate what they are. We are still waiting for an answer. Until we get one, we will take our stand with David Roediger, who has insisted that whiteness is not merely oppressive and false, it is nothing but oppressive and false.

On one hand, this might appear like a performative contradiction and that race traitors want to have their abolitionist cake and eat it too. That is, even when Whites commit morally supportable acts, these do not fall within the domain of whiteness but rather within otherness. Is this a double standard and part of racial entrapment? This is just the kind of fodder that frustrates many Whites who may take it as an instance of 'reverse discrimination'. On the other hand, the sense hinges on a particular conceptualisation of whiteness, which suggests that it cannot be reduced to a deterministic relation between actions and which racialised bodies commit them. Not all acts that Whites commit are categorically part of whiteness. Sometimes, White acts are articulated with histories of colour rather than whiteness.

Historically, transforming whiteness lacks any concrete example. When whites congeal into a skin collective (and people of colour may join them), the results have been predictable. History shows that Irish workers picked race over class by edging out Black workers, Californians voted against affirmative action (a staple of civil rights legislation) and suburbanisation created the hypersegregation of Blacks in ghettos. On the other hand, Whites exist at the intersection of discourses that struggle for supremacy over their subjectivity. They exist in multiple worlds and have had to make decisions about traversing the racial landscape. Here one may insist on the varieties of White people without contradicting the assertion that whiteness exists solely for stratification. In history, Whites may be and have been transformed. But as we shall see, even this assertion needs to be qualified because transforming Whites may lead to their disappearance.

Transforming whiteness also lacks history because it does not come to terms with the function of whiteness—why it was created, where it has been—but rather projects an ideal image of whiteness (what it would like whiteness to be) rather than the concrete history that has constituted it. It wishes away whiteness through a discourse of white positivity that is nowhere to be found. Likewise, one can distinguish between Americanism and Americans, the former an ideology the second a form of citizenship (with all its contradictions). Whereas Americanism has been used in imperialist ways around the globe, Americans may fight against this project and establish some distance from it. Of course, even Americans who fight against American imperialism receive the benefits of being constructed as Americans. However, unlike whiteness, we may argue that Americanism retains false premises and is quite oppressive worldwide, but it is *not only* oppressive and false.

When we define the ideology of whiteness as hopelessly bound up with what it means to be White, then Whites are trapped into a particular way of making sense of their racial experience. Recalling Marx's (1988) words in *Theses on Feuerbach*, today's neo-abolitionists argue that *the point is not to interpret whiteness but to abolish it* (Ignatiev 1997; italics in original). In other words, like the young Hegelians who were satisfied with describing the world rather than changing it, White apostasies short of abolitionism do not pose a real threat to the juggernaut of whiteness. In the same vein that a Marxist would abolish capital rather than reconstruct capitalism, the abolitionist sees little purpose in giving whiteness another chance. There is a difference between White bodies and White people. Beyond a structural determinism which signifies that White bodies are always conceived as White people, one can argue that White bodies (termed 'white' here for convenience) only become White persons when they become *articulated* with whiteness. Certainly White bodies existed prior to race but were interpellated into its discursive structure roughly five centuries ago, articulated to appear a given that White bodies have always been White people. In contrast, White bodies are not always White people *every single moment*, particularly when they are conceived as 'race traitors'. Likewise and with its own specificity, people of colour who side too close with whiteness have been labelled as inauthentic and implicated with whiteness. With a different force and outcome, both have been guilty of racial blasphemy.

In Roediger's (1994) understanding, poor and working-class Whites live a paradoxical relationship with whiteness. Suffering from capitalist exploitation, poor housing, health and substandard education, lacking social and cultural capital, unrealised (as opposed to potential) political power, poor and working-class Whites desperately hang on to 'the public and psychological wages of whiteness' in the face of grim realities (see Roediger 1991; Du Bois 1998). Interested in returning Whites to their full humanity, Roediger opts for a racio-economic perspective and struggle (see also Leonardo 2005). Understanding that class struggle is dependent on, without reducing it to, racial interpellation, Roediger makes sincere attempts to build a race/class analysis. He finds an absence that:

> almost no left initiatives have challenged white workers to critique, much less to abandon, whiteness . . . workers who identify themselves as white are bound to retreat from genuine class unity and meaningful antiracism . . . If it does not involve a critique of whiteness, the questioning of racism often proves shallow and limited. (1994, 13)

In exchange for a more accurate understanding of their class oppression, White proletarians cut themselves off from workers of colour in order to invest in their whiteness, which is often all that they have (Alcoff 1998; see also Willis 1977). They are both oppressed by class exploitation and are beneficiaries of racism. As a result, they cannot galvanise a genuine class movement that fails to establish solidarity with workers of colour, not to mention the problems associated with Whites licking their economic wounds with White privilege.

The race/class problematic has proved to be the thorn in the side of whiteness. Roediger (1994) observes, 'rejection of whiteness is then part of a process that gives rise to both attacks on racism and to the very recovery of "sense of oppression" among white workers' (13). In the end, Roediger observes that their class struggle is intimately bound up with a race struggle; their way out of class is racialised. Ignatiev (1996) agrees:

> It is not black people who have been prevented from drawing upon the full variety of experience that has gone into making up America. Rather it is those who, in maddened pursuit of the white whale, have cut themselves off from human society, on sea and on land, and locked themselves in a masoned walled-town of exclusiveness. (21)

Abolitionists attract suspicion insofar as the dismantling of whiteness becomes a racial means to a Marxist end (Alcoff 1998). In a Marxist project, whiteness is constructed as a distraction to class struggle, preventing White workers from seeing their true objective interests despite the fact that they inhere real, albeit contradictory, racial interests. It seems that a Marxist intervention has failed to galvanise a genuine class struggle because of racial divisions. Therefore, abolishing whiteness (and by implication, race) removes one of the obstacles so that the 'real revolution' can get under way. This position may underestimate White workers' possessive investment in whiteness, which goes against Ignatiev and Garvey's (1996) notion that most Whites would 'do the right thing if it were convenient' (12). Whites of all economic classes cling on to their whiteness, which makes it inconvenient—and to some, inconceivable—to commit racial suicide. That said, and the criticisms notwithstanding, abolitionists question the value of whiteness. Their intentions aside—and one cannot be certain here—race treason is about as disruptive to the established racial code as recently imagined.

Linda Alcoff does not offer textual evidence for her suspicions of the abolitionists' ulterior and Marxist motives, which no doubt would have made her objections more credible. However, it speaks of a history of suspicion from people of colour concerning Whites when it comes to their sincerity in race struggles due to their consistent lack of commitment to racial justice. Derrick Bell (1992) says as much when he writes of 'interest convergence' and explains the fact that racial progress in the US is bound up first with White interests and only second with Black empowerment. In other words, Whites have only accepted racial progress when their overall interest is observed and not threatened. In the case of abolitionists, dissolving whiteness may serve the ultimate end of the impending class abolition. If that is the case, is a movement problematic if it serves more than one end? If abolitionism accomplishes its goal of dismantling whiteness, which in itself is deemed defensible, why should it matter that it contains an ulterior, Marxist motive? If the ultimate goal is objectionable, that seems to be another point altogether, but it does not seem self-evident that an ulterior motive would disrecommend the movement even if one accepts the premise but not the conclusion.

To the abolitionist, it is unconvincing to argue for the 'rearticulation' or 'transformation' of whiteness. Rather than rearticulating whiteness, abolitionists prefer to disarticulate it. Like science's claim to be self-corrective, transforming whiteness assumes that Whites possess enough critical self-reflection and awareness to confront themselves. Searching for an identity that is both White and anti-racist, we may be tempted to conjure up a 'new White American', a 'transformed White global subject'. But this suggestion lacks both empirical support and conceptual legs. It appears as the 'last stand of whiteness' to assert itself into a history that has never existed or provides no example. Arguing for a transformed whiteness is appealing. Its limitation is that it substitutes proxy for praxis. It betrays a conciliatory posture toward the function and purpose of whiteness as a parasitic ideology and social practice. Whiteness exists in order to prey upon its racialised counterparts and *it has always existed in this manner*, according to Roediger. Whiteness has taken different forms in the evolution of societies: official Apartheid there, Jim Crow here and genocide in another. But its face of oppression is unchanging.

On the other hand, White people have made many different choices in life, sometimes working against whiteness but more accurately as vacillating between ideologies of whiteness and the Other, in differing and context-based choices, in various degrees of intensity and commitment. For example, when White teachers and educators question schooling's racial disparities, they are making a choice against whiteness *as* White people. They are not transforming whiteness into something positive because whiteness does not transform to become anti-racist. It is by definition racist. As Whites dismantle racism, they eventually undercut the basis for their existence as supreme people. This signals the end of Whites as we know it. There is no other side out of which to emerge as a different White subject. Just as tinkering with tracking to the point that one may imagine undoing its patterned and patent inequalities is hardly tracking anymore (Oakes 2005), so we may argue that Whites with little to no advantage are hardly White anymore.

Race is a figment of the imagination, a veritable monster in the proverbial hallway closet with whiteness as its most frightening expression. Under these assumptions, even anti-racism is doomed to fail because it acknowledges the existence of races. To Ignatiev and Garvey (1996):

> the task is not to win over more whites to oppose 'racism'; there are enough 'anti-racists' enough already to do the job . . . when there comes into being a critical mass of people who, though they look white, have ceased to act white, the white race will undergo fission, and former whites will be able to take part in building a new human community. (37)

Although Ignatiev and Garvey may be faulted in their overestimation that there are enough anti-racist Whites 'to do the job', their point hinges on questioning the heuristic value of race, and by implication the political value of race struggle designed to perpetuate race. To be fair, Ignatiev and

Garvey do not merely ask Whites to 'put up their hands' in desperation when it comes to racial identification, or to keep their hands down when racial interpellation hails their subjectivity. It is hardly subversive for Whites to announce that they are not White. This is already their inclination. Race treason is not just a transgression involving personal identification, but falls completely within the realm of <u>behaviour</u>. Through oppositional behaviour, race traitors disrupt racial commitments and expectations. Ignatiev and Garvey (1996) write:

> the need to maintain racial solidarity imposes a stifling conformity on whites, on any subject touching even remotely on race. The way to abolish the white race is to disrupt that conformity. (36)

Abolishing the White race does not only mean repudiating membership through annunciation ('I am not White'), but more important through denunciation ('I will not act White'). Denouncing one's whiteness both at the personal and group level suggests acting against its codes. It answers the call to do the work of race, to labour against racial consent. It requires that we 'transform "reverse racism" into an injunction (Reverse racism!)' (Roediger 1994, 17). Again, we see here the ironic strategy of abolitionism to use White logic against itself, of inserting sense into senselessness (e.g. challenging the belief that reverse discrimination exists for Whites).

For most Whites, the opposite of abolitionism is more difficult and resisted: White racial ownership. Reconstructionists have a clearer sense of this first step by recognising the need for belonging and not necessarily in the sense of loyalty to White supremacy, but to some kind of identity. In other words, outside of the call for a universal human identity for Whites, abolitionists do not offer up a specific identity because abolition is precisely the assertion of a non-identity. It is possible that reconstruction may offer the means to an abolitionist end. Alcoff (1998) writes, 'rather than erase these inscriptions as a first step, we need a period of reinscription to redescribe and reunderstand what we see when we see race' at the same time that we may be able to project the emptiness of whiteness, 'which unlike ethnic identities . . . has no other substantive cultural content'. That is, Whites must first come to terms with what whiteness has made of them in order to consider the move towards abolitionism.

It is difficult to imagine Whites, many of whom function through colour-blindness, to take the radical leap of race treason. Because of their colour-blindness, many Whites may find it ironically convenient (and not in the sense that Ignatiev and Garvey predict) to use abolitionism as a way to further mask White privilege. By disabusing themselves of having to take responsibility for White atrocities, White abolitionists do not face up to whiteness, which sounds too familiar. But if after having participated in recognising and then reconstructing whiteness, Whites realise the emptiness of the category, the abolitionist position may not have started the story but would likely end it. So in the final analysis, there is a way that reconstructionism would provide the entrance into whiteness and abolitionism its exit.

*This chapter is reprinted from Leonardo, Z. (2009). Pale/ontology: The status of whiteness in education. In Michael Apple, Wayne Au, and Luis Gandin (Eds.), *Routledge International Handbook of Critical Education* (pp. 123–136). New York: Routledge.

REFERENCES

Aanerud, Rebecca. 1997. 'Fictions of Whiteness: Speaking the Names of Whiteness in U.S. Literature'. In *Displacing Whiteness*, edited by Ruth Frankenberg, 35–59. Durham, NC: Duke University Press.

Alcoff, Linda. 1998. 'What Should White People Do?' *Hypatia* 13. Accessed November 1, 2007, at http://www.msu.edu/-hypatia/White?People.htm. ·

Allen, Ricky Lee. 2002. The Globalization of White Supremacy: Toward a Critical Discourse on the Racialization of the World. *Educational Theory*, 51(4), 467–485.

Allen, Ricky Lee. 2005. 'Whiteness and Critical Pedagogy'. In *Critical Pedagogy and Race*, edited by Zeus Leonardo, 53–68. Malden, MA: Blackwell.

Allen, Theodore. 1994. *The Invention of the White Race*. Vol. 1. London: Verso.

———. 1997. *The Invention of the White Race*. Vol. 2. London: Verso.

Althusser, Louis. 1976. *Essays in Self-Criticism*. Translated by Grahame Lock. London: NLB.

Apple, Michael. 1998. 'Foreword'. In *White Reign*, edited by Joe Kincheloe, Shirley Steinberg, Nelson Rodriguez and Ronald Chennault, ix–xiii. New York: St. Martin's Griffin.

Bell, Derrick. 1992. *Faces at the Bottom of the Well: The Permanence of Racism*. New York: Basic Books.

Benhabib, Seyla. 1987. 'The Generalized and the Concrete Other'. In *Feminism as Critique*, edited by Seyla Benhabib and Drucilla Cornell, 77–95. Minneapolis: University of Minnesota Press.

Brodkin, Karen. 1999. *How Jews Became White Folks and What that Says about Race in America*. New Brunswick, NJ: Rutgers University Press.

Buras, Kristen. 2008. *Rightist Multiculturalism*. New York: Routledge.

Bush, Melanie. 2005. *Breaking the Code of Good Intentions: Everyday Forms of Whiteness*. Lanham: Rowman and Littlefield.

Chubbuck, Sharon. 2004. 'Whiteness Enacted, Whiteness Disrupted: The Complexity of Personal Congruence'. *American Educational Research Journal* 4:301–303.

Delpit, Lisa. 1995. *Other People's Children*. New York: New Press.

DiAngelo, Robin. 2006. 'The Production of Whiteness in Education: Asian International Students in a College Classroom'. *Teachers College Record* 108: 1983–2000.

Du Bois, William Edward Burghardt. 1998. *Black Reconstruction in America, 1860–1880*. New York: Free Press.

———. 1989. *The Souls of Black Folk*. New York: Penguin Books.

Dyer, Richard. 1997. *White*. New York: Routledge.

Ellsworth, Elizabeth. 1997. 'Double Binds of Whiteness'. In *Off White*, edited by Michelle Fine, Lois Weis, Linda Powell and Mun Wong, 259–269. New York: Routledge.

Frankenberg, Ruth. 1993. *White Women, Race Matters: The Social Construction of Whiteness*. Minneapolis: University of Minnesota Press.

Freire, Paulo.1993. *Pedagogy of the Oppressed*. Translated by Myra Bergman Ramos. New York: Continuum.

Gillborn, David. 2005. 'Education Policy as an Act of White Supremacy: Whiteness, Critical Race Theory, and Education Reform'. *Journal of Education Policy* 20:485–505.

Giroux, Henry. 1992. *Border Crossings*. New York: Routledge.

———. 1997a. *Channel Surfing*. New York: St. Martin's Press.

———. 1997b. 'Racial Politics and the Pedagogy of Whiteness'. In *Whiteness: A Critical Reader*, edited by Mike Hill, 294–315. New York: NYU Press.

———. 1997c. 'Rewriting the Discourse of Racial Identity: Towards a Pedagogy and Politics of Whiteness'. *Harvard Educational Review* 67:285–320.

Hirschman, Charles. 2004. 'The Origins and Demise of the Concept of Race'. *Population and Development Review* 30:385–415.

hooks, bell. 1997. 'Representing Whiteness in the Black Imagination'. In *Displacing Whiteness*, edited by Ruth Frankenberg, 165–179. Durham, NC: Duke University Press.

Howard, Gary. 1999. *We Can't Teach What We Don't Know: White Teachers, Multiracial Schools*. New York: Teachers College Press.

Ignatiev, Noel. 1996. *How the Irish Became White*. New York: Routledge.

———. 1997. 'The Point Is Not to Interpret Whiteness but to Abolish It'. Talk given at the Conference on 'The Making and Unmaking of Whiteness', University of California, Berkeley. Accessed July 26, 2009, at http://racetraitor.org/abolishthepoint.html.

Ignatiev, Noel, and John Garvey. 1996a. 'Editorial: When Does the Unreasonable Act Make Sense?' In *Race Traitor*, edited by Noel Ignatiev and John Garvey, 35–37. New York: Routledge.

———.1996b. Abolish the White Race: By Any Means Necessary. In *Race Traitor, edited by* Noel Ignatiev and John Garvey, 9–14. New York: Routledge.

Ingram, David. 2005. 'Toward a Cleaner White(ness): New Racial Identities'. *Philosophical Forum* 36:243–277.

Kincheloe, Joe, and Shirley Steinberg. 1998. 'Addressing the Crisis of Whiteness: Reconfiguring White Identity in a Pedagogy of Whiteness'. In *White Reign*, edited by Joe Kincheloe, Shirley Steinberg, Nelson Rodriguez and Ronald Chennault, 3–29. New York: St. Martin's Griffin.

Lee, Stacey. 2005. *Up against Whiteness*. New York: Teachers College Press.

Leonardo, Zeus. 2003. 'Reality on Trial: Notes on Ideology, Education, and Utopia'. *Policy Futures in Education* 1:504–525.

———. 2004. 'The Color of Supremacy: Beyond the Discourse of "White Privilege"'. *Journal of Educational Philosophy and Theory* 36:137–152.

———. 2005. 'The Unhappy Marriage between Marxism and Race Critique: Political Economy and the Production of Racialized Knowledge'. *Policy Futures in Education* 2:483–493.

———. 2007. 'The War on Schools: NCLB, Nation Creation and the Educational Construction of Whiteness'. *Race Ethnicity and Education* 10:261–278.

Lipsitz, George. 1998. *The Possessive Investment in Whiteness*. Philadelphia: Temple University Press.

Lyotard, Jean-François. 1984. *The Postmodern Condition*. Translated by Geoff Bennington and Brian Massumi. Minneapolis: University of Minnesota Press.

Marx, Karl. 1988. 'Theses on Feuerbach'. In *Marx Selections*, edited by A. Wood, 80–82. New York: Macmillan.

Massey, Douglas, and Nancy Denton. 1993. *American Apartheid*. Cambridge, MA: Harvard University Press.

McIntosh, Peggy. 1992. 'White Privilege and Male Privilege: A Personal Account of Coming to See Correspondences through Work in Women's Studies'. In *Race, Class, and Gender: An Anthology*, edited by Margaret Andersen and Patricia Hill Collins, 70–81. Belmont, CA: Wadsworth Publishing.

McIntyre, Alice. 1997. *Making Meaning of Whiteness*. Albany: SUNY Press.

McLaren, Peter. 1995. *Critical Pedagogy and Predatory Culture: Oppositional Politics in a Postmodern Era*. New York: Routledge.

———. 1997. *Revolutionary Multiculturalism: Pedagogies of Dissent for a New Millennium*. Boulder, CO: Westview Press.

McLaren, Peter, and Rodolfo Torres. 1999. 'Racism and Multicultural Education: Rethinking "Race" and "Whiteness" in Late Capitalism'. In *Critical Multiculturalism: Rethinking Multicultural and Antiracist Education*, edited by Stephen May, 42–76. Philadelphia: Falmer Press.

Memmi, Albert. 1965. *The Colonizer and the Colonized*. Boston: Beacon Press.

Mills, Charles. 1997. *The Racial Contract*. Ithaca, NY: Cornell University Press.

Morrison, Toni. 1993. *Playing in the Dark: Whiteness in the Literary Imagination*. New York: Vintage Books.

Oakes, Jeannie. 2005. *Keeping Track*. 2nd ed. New Haven, CT: Yale University Press.

Omi, Michael, and Howard Winant. 1994. *Racial Formation in the United States: From the 1960s to the 1990s*. 2nd ed. New York: Routledge.

Pollock, Mica. 2004. *Colormute*. Princeton, NJ: Princeton University Press.

Ricoeur, Paul. 1981. *Hermeneutics and the Human Sciences*. Edited and Translated by John B. Thompson. Cambridge: Cambridge University Press.

Richardson, Troy, and Sofia Villenas. 2000. '"Other" Encounters: Dances with Whiteness in Multicultural Education'. *Educational Theory* 50:255–273.

Roediger, David. 1991. *The Wages of Whiteness*. New York: Verso.

———. 1994. *Towards the Abolition of Whiteness*. New York: Verso.

Sheets, Rosa Hernandez. 2000. 'Advancing the Field or Taking Center Stage: The White Movement in Multicultural Education'. *Educational Researcher* 29:15–21.

Sleeter, Christine. 1995. 'Reflections on My Use of Multicultural and Critical Pedagogy When Students Are White'. In *Multicultural Education, Critical Pedagogy, and the Politics of Difference*, edited by Christine Sleeter and Peter McLaren, 415–437. Albany: SUNY Press.

Thompson, Audrey. 2003. 'Tifanny, Friend of People of Color: White Investments in Antiracism'. *Qualitative Studies in Education* 16:7–29.

Thompson, Becky. 2001. *A Promise and a Way of Life: White Antiracist Activism*. Minneapolis: University of Minnesota Press.

Warren, Jonathan. 2000. 'Masters in the Field: White Talk, White Privilege, White Biases'. In *Racing Research, Researching Race: Methodological Dilemmas in Critical Race Studies*, edited by France Winddance Twine and Jonathan Warren, 135–164. New York: NYU Press.

Willis, Paul. 1977. *Learning to Labor*. New York: Columbia University Press.

Winant, Howard. 1997. 'Behind Blue Eyes'. In *Off White*, edited by Michelle Fine, Lois Weis, Linda Powell and Mun Wong, 40–53. New York: Routledge.

Wise, Tim. 2007. *White Like Me: Reflections on Race from a Privileged Son*. New York: Soft Skull Press.

3 How Fair Is Britain?

Addressing 'Race' and Education Inequalities—Towards a Socially Just Education System in the Twenty-First Century

Gill Crozier

INTRODUCTION

During the period of thirteen years (1997–2010) of the New Labour government a raft of education policies specifically targeting 'race' and education were initiated. New Labour also targeted underperforming Black and minority ethnic (BME) groups and improved legislation in order to address racism (including the Race Relations Amendment Act). However, in answer to the question 'how fair is Britain?' the eponymously entitled Equalities and Human Rights Commission (EHRC 2010) report showed that Black Caribbean, Black African and Pakistani heritage children are still the lowest achieving in mathematics and English at sixteen years when they take their General Certificate of Secondary Education (GCSE) examinations and Gypsy, Roma and Traveller (GRT) children do even less well than all these groups (Department for Children, Schools and Families [DCSF] 2008, 2009). In addition, according to the Sutton Trust (2010), privately educated pupils are fifty-five times more likely to go to Oxbridge and twenty-two more times likely to go to a 'top ranked university' than students at state schools who qualify for free school meals (FSMs), whereas only 7 per cent of the population attend private schools. The Race into Higher Education Report (Kerr 2010) showed that even though BME students are proportionately well represented in the university sector, this is not the case across all types of university or all subjects. Moreover, BME students are not succeeding at equal levels to their White counterparts.

More recently under the Coalition government we see that in a period of economic crisis the first to suffer in terms of unemployment, lowering of wages, rescinding of the Education Maintenance Allowance (EMA), cuts in FE (further education) provision for post-sixteen-year-olds and loss of other resources are young, working-class and low-credentialed young people (Blanchflower 2011). Just under half of Black men in Britain in 2011 are reported as unemployed (Ball, Milmo and Ferguson 2012).

Black Caribbean heritage students continue to be disproportionately excluded from school: they are, on average, three times more likely to be excluded from school than White children (Parsons 2009). Consequently, for example, on average one-third of these excluded children is less likely to gain five A*–C GCSEs; they are more likely to be unemployed, more likely to earn less over their lifetime and more likely to commit a crime (Abbott 2009). As Diane Abbott has said, 'the exclusion of our children is not just a one time experience. The exclusion of our children can be a life sentence'. It might be within this group girls do marginally better; middle-class Black Caribbeans do marginally better, but it has been shown that irrespective of class and gender (Gillborn and Mirza 2000; Strand 2011; Vincent et al. 2012), Black Caribbean heritage children are disadvantaged in a range of ways. Similarly children of GRT backgrounds are failed by schools (Derrington and Kendall 2004; Bhopal and Myers 2008). This group is almost invisible in the system.

The August riots (in 2011) across England are arguably a further indication of deep-seated frustration and a sense of injustice amongst BME and also White working-class young people. Social mobility, after all (Hills 2010), has made limited and variable progress in twenty years. With respect to the riots and police stop and search, there is mounting evidence giving concern about police racialised behaviour and attitudes.

All in all, this summary is indicative of the social injustice in the education system in Britain that underpins the concerns of this chapter, and specifically with regard to 'race', the educational experiences of BME children and young people. Within this chapter, I aim to discuss the nature of fairness, which I prefer to call social justice and education; how injustices operate and manifest themselves in education and conclude with an exploration of strategies for change in order to further the achievement of equality of opportunity. The chapter demonstrates the continuation of racism and racial discrimination within education and implicitly challenges the notion of 'post-race/racism'. Although 'race' and racism are foregrounded, it is also recognised that the intersectionality of oppression and, in particular, class and gender with 'race' is essential if we are to achieve equality of opportunity in education. However, firstly I would like to rehearse, or arguably re-rehearse the question 'what is education for?' on the basis that the answer to this underpins the structure and rationale for the education system and points to some fundamental causes for educational injustices.

The purpose of education is a question that has been neglected by sociologists since the wave of New Sociological analyses in the 1970s. One of the most notable contributions to that debate at the time was Bowles and Gintis's (1976) (since contested and rejected by themselves) Correspondence Theory. Put simply, they argued that the education system was designed to prepare the children of the working class for the world of work not only in terms of a skills base, but also, for example, in terms of time management and subjective responses to authority. Although the Correspondence Theory, and particularly the notion of relative autonomy between education and the state, has been contested, the functional role of education providing a skilled and knowledgeable workforce together with the inculcation of societal values is more accepted. The argument that tends to prevail in government and policy is rather the question as to whether schools are adequately fulfilling this role. Bourdieu and Passeron's (1979) theory of social reproduction could be said to be more concerned with the relational dimension of in/justice. They outlined the ways that social class relations were reproduced by an education system that was designed to advantage the middle classes. Others, such as Althusser (2006), have argued that one of the principal purposes of education is to perpetrate hegemonic ideology. All these approaches indicated that education is designed to educate the working class to know and accept 'their place' within society (Moore 2004). The question of the purpose of education may now be coming back onto the policy and academic agendas, particularly in the light of recent financial changes to educational provision. This can be seen particularly with respect to university education and the steep rise in student fees. The criticism of the so-called 'pointless degrees' (e.g. Chapman 2010) and the debate concerning whether universities should be teaching transferable skills as part of the award of an honours degree (Tims 2011) are two examples of this. The refocus on the National Curriculum and the vocational/academic/the English baccalaureate (Stewart 2010) debate is an example in relation to school education.

Although it is difficult to correlate educational opportunity and social mobility, the combination of information about relative working-class examination results, attendance at university and social mobility, all of which show limited change over the past twenty years (Moore 2004), provides an indication that equal opportunities policies have had limited impact on social justice in education. Whereas the general educational achievement of children and young people in albeit narrow assessment terms has improved overall, there has been little narrowing of social class and the BME achievement gap (DCSF 2009; DCSF 2008), as I have already indicated.

SOCIAL JUSTICE AND EDUCATION

Although I have used the term 'fair' in the title, it is arguably another term for 'social justice' given that justice undoubtedly espouses 'fairness and equality'. But all these terms have a multitude of meanings and interpretations and are subjective and value based, and although seemingly the domain of the Left have been and are currently appropriated by the Centre and Right within party politics (in Britain). These ideas therefore are contested. In this chapter I argue that the struggle for a socially just education system is central to challenging racism within education and achieving some fairness and equality of opportunity. I argue that social justice needs to be concerned with tackling structural arrangements that impede equality and fairness. As well as the opportunity to access education, I argue that there needs to be an opportunity to contribute to and shape the very nature of what education is and might be. Built into this position, therefore, is the importance and necessity of agency.

With the current attack, in Britain, on state education, and welfarism in general, as well as the recent report *How Fair Is Britain?* (EHRC 2010) referred to in the preceding, we seem a long way from a socially just society and a socially just education system as part of that. A socially just education system may be impossible in a socially unjust society. However, as Michael Apple (1996) argues:

> schools are not separate from wider society but are part of it and participate fully in its logics and sociocultural dynamics. Struggling in the schools is struggling in society. (107)

Following this sentiment, therefore, social justice is taken here as a generative concept that has to be striven for and worked out through a collective approach as much as through policy initiatives. The idea of social justice has to be understood within the educational community at all levels including the children, in order to work. Arguably, a number of New Labour's educational policies embodied a socially just approach, but they often conveyed contradictory messages and exacerbated the competitiveness between parents, pupils and the schools themselves. The original academies, for example, designed to improve education in some of the poorest areas in effect further contribute to the atomisation of the education system and weaken the involvement and influence of the accountable local authority. They also act as magnets for middle-class parents who tend to be more concerned with the individualistic betterment of their own child rather than contributing to the collective educational change for the common good (Reay, Crozier and James 2011).

Social justice is also a relative concept, relative to contemporary contexts and material conditions. Achieving a socially just education system therefore involves permanent change and adaptation and thus on-going reflection and reflexivity. Although not wholly in tune with Amartya Sen, I do agree with his sentiment that 'a theory of justice . . . must include ways of judging how to reduce injustice and advance justice, rather than aiming only at the characterisation of perfectly just societies' (2009, ix). Sen recognises that societies are forged through human decisions, and humans, he argues, tend not to agree. Therefore, he argues that holding out for absolute, incontrovertible 'justice' is nigh impossible and would in fact impede the immediate need to deal with injustices such as famine, people trafficking and indeed access to education. He goes on to say that in developing justice (policy and processes) it is necessary to be realistic and to take account of the lives people can lead (xi). Sen talks about what is 'more or less just'. I would argue that it is important to strive for something more just than less but recognise that it is an ongoing struggle to achieve this and also it is a dialectic that changes in an ongoing process of reflection and evolving conditions.

A socially just education system has to be concerned with the structures that enable educational opportunity. As we know, these are not merely confined to education because inequalities permeate society and these in turn impact on the educational experience of children and young people. Moreover, a socially just education system cannot take the form of an absolute blueprint, but rather comprises a set of principles to be applied at the various levels of the system: in terms of the national level, school/college/university level and the various dimensions of each of those institutions. Sharon Gewirtz (2002), however, insists on a more precise definition of social justice and, following Iris Marion Young (1990), argues for the combination of a theory of distribution and relational factors attributed to social in/justice. As Young says, injustice is about oppression and domination rather than simply distribution, and, as Halsey (1997, 638) has likewise acknowledged, the 'three giants in the path of equality' are 'race', class and gender, highlighting the need to acknowledge in any struggle against oppression and discrimination, intersectionalities; a point which I will return to in the following. Young (1990) goes on to say that the concept of justice:

> should not only refer to distribution but also to the institutional conditions necessary for the development and exercise of individual capacities and collective communication and cooperation. Under this conception of justice, injustice refers primarily to two forms of disabling constraints, oppression and domination. (39)

The distributional dimension refers to the principles by which the distribution of material resources to power-related resources are linked to the stratification of society and education, and this in turn is based on social class differences and hierarchies. As Rawls (1972) says:

> The subject matter of justice is the basic structure of society . . . the way in which the major social institutions . . . distribute fundamental rights and duties and determine the distribution of advantages from social cooperation. (7)

According to Gewirtz (2002), the relational refers to the nature of relationships that structure society:

> It is about the nature of ordering of social relations and the formal and informal rules that govern how members of society treat each other both on a macro level and at a micro-interpersonal level. Thus it refers to the practices and procedures that govern the organisation of political systems, economic and social institutions, families and one to one social relationships. (140)

If it is accepted that the structures of society and education favour the White middle and upper classes, then the argument follows that the organisations and societal procedures are designed to ensure the maintenance of those inequalities. Although a rather old idea now, Althusser's (2006) concept of education as an ideological state apparatus is still useful. It explains the mechanism for developing and perpetrating hegemonic values which serve to lubricate the system indicated in the preceding. This adds to the complex picture of the struggle for power and access to/control over 'educational goods' taking place in schools, including unintended consequences, contradictory practices and moral ambiguities (Sayer 2005); an example of this is demonstrated by the recent research study into White middle-class parents and identity formations (Reay, Crozier and James 2011). These parents were committed to their local state comprehensive school based on a belief in the welfare state and equal opportunities for all. Nevertheless, in spite of seemingly going against the grain of their privileged class position and the alternative choices available to them, they employed their privilege through their out-of-school cultural cultivation of their children's education in order to position their children's advantage to take on the fierce competition for scarce resources within these relatively disadvantaged urban schools (Crozier, Reay and James 2011). This was demonstrated by these children's success in occupying and dominating the top sets and the gifted and talented scheme (in spite of the parents' disparagement of this scheme). In the London-based section of the study, many of the comprehensive schools had majority BME populations.

Utilising the framework of the interrelationship between distributional and the relational dimensions, I will discuss in the following sections examples of unjust structures and practices and whilst including in this reference to stratification within and between schools, (academic) knowledge hierarchies and cultural knowledge hierarchies, I take assessment as the focus for the discussion. I also discuss how these facets militate against the needs and interests of BME children, and young people in particular.

HOW RACIAL EDUCATIONAL INJUSTICES WORK

Neo-liberal education policies which now permeate the British and many Western education systems were not the beginning of social injustice, but arguably they have intensified and entrenched its effect. Neo-liberal policies have generated individualistic behaviours between parents and between schools (Ball 2003; James et al. 2010). This has resulted in White and middle-class flight from urban comprehensives (Stillwell and Hussein 2010; Sugden 2009; Crowder 2000), giving some support to Trevor Phillips's (Casciani 2005) claim of 'sleep walking into segregation'. Whereas that in itself is of limited significance, the important issue is that successful academic results and the label of 'good school' have tended to follow White middle-class-dominated schools (Butler and Hamnett 2012). Conversely, schools dominated by Black pupils receive negative press and often seemingly struggle to meet the needs of their pupils. The educational assessment requirements for all pupils in English primary and secondary schools at Key Stage 1, 2 and 4 are central to the operationalisation of the market. The intense competition between schools for pupils and for a top place in the league tables has led to a disproportionate focus on achieving these objectives rather than on the needs of the children themselves.

Although the testing regime has seen an increase in credentialing, the parameters are narrow and school education has been much criticised for providing a limited and in some respects sterile educational experience. Although fewer young people leave school without any qualifications at all, which must be a positive development, this is not a justification for maintaining competition or the level of testing as at present. The testing is the mechanism by which schools are ranked as excellent, good, unsatisfactory or failing, and it appears to drive the educational experience. Gillborn and Youdell (2000), for example, have shown how this system has discriminated against Black and working-class children through a process of triage. Through this process of 'rationing education', the children at the borderline of the five A*–C economy, as Gillborn and Youdell termed it, are targeted for extra support. In their study they found that the children labelled as 'hopeless cases whose teachers believe that five higher grade passes is not a credible aim' and therefore do not receive any extra help are overrepresented by Black pupils and those in receipt of FSMs (2000, 163).

Assessment impacts on the organisation and management of the school, the pupils and the teaching itself, manifested through setting or even streaming in both primary and secondary schools. The key problem may not lie entirely in the assessment regime, but rather the use of the tests as sole markers of success both for the individual child and the school. Wells and Serna (1997, 726) argue that 'standardised tests become cultural symbols of intelligence that are used to legitimise the track [streaming and setting] structure '. However, assessment and the much hated (government required achievement) targets have arguably served a useful and socially just purpose in terms of monitoring and accountability both nationally, locally and within schools. These data have clearly demonstrated the underachievement of certain groups, and in some cases this revelation ensured that certain groups of children are not falling behind, as well as providing indicators for the targeting of resources. The competition and the targets have thus, it could be said, raised teachers' expectations of hitherto underperforming groups. Assessment in this respect is a means of calling teachers to account.

Another of the problems with this system of assessment is that even though we have this information, it is not always used to address the issue of the underachievement of the school. Rather it is it is used to patch up the problem rather instead of seeking to transform it: a system of redistribution of sorts or as Sen advocates a 'more or less just system'. However, as Gillborn and Youdell (2000) demonstrated, there were still Black children who always seemed to miss out when the system of triage/educational rationing was employed. Exposing differences in educational performances does not, of course, lead to the right conclusions. In a stratified system which is justified by a view of differential abilities, this is unsurprising. Hence failure is most often blamed on those specific groups or the individual child and their families themselves: They are blamed for their own failure. This has been very apparent with respect to Black African Caribbean boys, for example, and the REACH initiative designed to address putative inadequate role models (Tomlinson 2008) and parenting by single-parent mothers. A similar perspective in relation to low socio-economic groups has also recently been expressed by Frank Field's (2010) report on poverty wherein he argues for the need to compensate for early disadvantage by addressing inadequate parenting skills (see also Machin and McNally 2006).

The assessment regime is integral to the competitive market and all who participate become implicated. More fundamentally it is integral to the stratification of schooling and society. Competition is thus generated for the apparently 'best' resources for learning and gaining the highest possible grades, such as the most experienced and best-qualified and effective teachers as they are distributed to the top subject sets. The evidence against streaming and setting is considerable. It has the effect of undermining learner self-confidence and creating social divisions and antagonisms within the school. It reinforces negative stereotyping and has caused children to give up on their learning (Ireson, Hallam and Plewis 2001). Streaming and setting has been shown to be counterproductive for the learning experiences of young people (Hallam, Rogers and Ireson 2008). It is also discriminatory whereby the lowest sets are dominated by White and BME working-class children; as Wells and Serna (1997) demonstrate, streaming and setting, a form of distributive injustice, leads to class and racial segregation. Likewise, the cycle of low expectations is reinforced (Rist 2000). By contrast, mixed-ability teaching is more likely to generate social mixing amongst pupils because the children will spend most of the school day in the same classrooms, unlike now whereby the top sets of White middle-class children are segregated from the Black and White working classes (Reay, Crozier and James 2011). In this way children and young people are pitted against each other. There is growing evidence of intra-school (and also university) racialised segregation (e.g. Crozier and Davies 2008; Crozier 2012) most often instigated by White young people, but blamed on BME young people creating racial antagonisms and perpetuating racial stereotyping.

Formal educational qualifications play a particularly invidious role whereby the White middle classes acquire the largest proportion of these 'goods', signifying a kind of record of privilege (Wells and Serna 1997). Middle-class success then takes on the appearance of entitlement and superior ability. In marked contrast to this, Collins, Kenway and McLeod explain starkly:

children from different backgrounds achieve different outcomes from school because they do not in fact receive the same schooling . . . they receive a form of schooling that steers them towards the backgrounds they come from. (2000, 135, cited in Moore 2004, 7)

How this plays out in schools is complex and is not simply organisational but is underpinned by and interspersed with the affective, the relational and class competition to ensure social reproduction and educational superiority for the middle and upper classes. Of course the White upper classes tend to send their children to private school and the White middle classes seek out selective state or 'high'-performing state schools. Nevertheless, both of these constituencies set the benchmark, which, given their economic, social and cultural resources, makes it very difficult for the rest to succeed to the same levels. As Bourdieu and Passeron (1979) have clearly demonstrated in their work, economic capital—income, wealth and property—is not the only capital necessary for social reproduction, as important as this is, others are political, social and cultural (Wells and Serna 1997, 720). Bourdieu and Passeron have shown the explicit connection between education, achievement and cultural capital and social capital. The White and BME working class are impeded in the competition for educational resources by the unequal access to these various capitals. The White middle classes embody not only these capitals, but also the capacity and dispositions to operationalise them. White middle-class taste is rewarded by the education system, leading to further rewards. Wells and Serna (1997) and Crozier, Reay and James (2011) identified, from their respective research, the example of those students wealthy enough to travel abroad, whose parents see such experience as part of the job of educational cultivation (Weber 1966). These young people are seen as 'brighter', more 'able' and sophisticated as a result of these trips. When high-status students' taste is seen as valued knowledge in the education system, other students' taste and knowledge that informs it is devalued (Bourdieu and Passeron 1979). A revealing illustration of this in practice is the derision with which Bangladeshi and Pakistani heritage children's visits to Bangladesh and Pakistan are treated by teachers (Crozier and Davies 2007) compared with the (also often in school time) visits White middle-class children take to France, Thailand and the US (Reay, Crozier and James 2011). As Delpit (1995, xv) says: 'the world view of those in privileged positions are taken as the only reality, while the world view of those less powerful are dismissed as inconsequential'. In these ways White middle-class children are ascribed with 'distinction' or put another way 'high-status culture is socially constructed as "intelligence"' (Wells and Serna 199, 720) and White middle-class children are thus rewarded. Hierarchies of knowledge and the availability of certain subject knowledge for some groups and not others is part of this power maintenance and differentiation.

CONCLUSION: CHALLENGING 'RACE' INEQUALITIES IN EDUCATION—TOWARDS A SOCIALLY JUST AND FAIR EDUCATION SYSTEM

The social polarisations referred to in the preceding and neo-liberal competitiveness are counterproductive in achieving equitable educational opportunities. As well as reflecting social anxieties, the social polarisations also reflect the philosophical–sociological dichotomy between redistribution and recognition (Fraser 2007). Whilst acknowledging the strategic importance of essentialism (Spivak 1987), the overarching position in addressing equalities of opportunity is the need for an intersectional approach (hooks 1989; Crenshaw 1995). Moreover, in relation to this is the theoretical principle of addressing the interrelationship between redistribution and recognition (Fraser 1997, 2007). Fraser highlights the problems of 'redistribution' counter-positioned with 'recognition' and identities' politics and, moreover, the shift in sociological research in emphasising 'recognition' alone (ibid). She warns of the negative consequences for social justice of this, in the light of the ever-ascendant neo-liberalism. She points out how the focus on 'recognition' alone can actually undermine the struggle for 'redistribution'. Hence she argues for a 'two-dimensional analysis' which brings together both of these facets. At the same time, this process involves the need to develop understanding of the division of labour and the gendered, classed and racialised nature of this, on the one hand, and, on the other, the danger of decontextualising identity, potentially leading to essentialist and stereotypical constructions. Similar to Fraser, as already outlined, Iris Marion Young (1990) has also argued for the combination of a theory of distribution and relational factors attributed to social in/justice.

The struggle for a socially just and fair education system, therefore, has to come to grips with the race, class and gender discrimination in and oppression by the system, through this interrelationship of the broader structural and policy issues and more localised and individual concerns; redistribution of resources and opportunities is essential but only if this process is related to contextualised identities.

Society needs to redefine or reprioritise the purpose of education. This must involve equal support for children's development and preparation of young people for adulthood. This includes a sense of citizenship and active citizenry, developing an understanding of justice and how injustices work, developing critical thinking, creativity and enjoyment for life. In this model, education has intrinsic value for the individual and also society as a whole. But education also has to prepare young citizens to contribute to society through work and other responsibilities and roles, for the collective well-being of society and their fellow citizens. This model takes into account the individual, but it is not focused in an introspective way on the individual; rather it stands as a challenge to individualism.

Children and young people need to be prepared for their place in a cosmopolitan, diverse, constantly changing and challenging world. They need to be helped to break out of the narrow mind-set of nationalism and be equipped to embrace their own and others' multiple, transnational identities. The model for a socially just education system needs to embed and embody a programme that will promote national and international social justice. Social justice is not about eliminating group differences; rather it demands, in Young's words: 'social equality of groups and mutual recognition and affirmation of group differences' (1990, 191).

A socially just education system needs to challenge contemporary power relations and differentials in the education system and thus the social and cultural reproduction of middle-class values and status. To transform educational provision, process and practice means giving up the maintenance of a White-dominated privileged position. It means addressing the competition for scarce resources and engaging in collaborative, time-consuming activities for the common good. It means being prepared to share educational resources rather than dominate their use and it means contemplating a wider body of valuable knowledge.

Stratification between schools has to be addressed. Rather than generating competition, there needs to be a focus on ensuring all schools achieve highly. By encouraging local schooling rather than school choice, which is only a choice for the privileged, this is more likely to be achieved. The idea of the school as part of the community is important here. Parental involvement has to take on a more realistic meaning, rather than parents acting as appendages to teachers; parents, teachers and children need to develop a relationship to ensure equitable educational experiences. The school as a site of lifelong learning and a space for the whole community is one that has been discussed in the past but undermined by individualistic competitiveness.

As well as the importance of structural change, central to fair practice in education is the teacher. Although teachers have lost a great deal of professional autonomy in the contemporary context and they are strongly bound by policy imperatives and the demands of their respective schools, policy change implementation and pedagogic practice rests with them. As I have said, teachers' attitudes and expectations of BME young people have been cited by many as responsible for their academic underachievement (e.g. Strand 2011). Each year the Teacher Development Agency (now the Teaching Agency) Newly Qualified Teacher (NQT) survey reveals that the NQTs do not feel adequately prepared to teach in ethnically diverse classrooms. Current changes in teacher training basing more of this in schools and moving towards wholly school-based training in many cases, suggest that the necessary professional development to ensure attitudinal change and the development of practice will become even less likely. Teachers need to be helped to support those children who themselves seem to have disengaged and given up on education; they need to be supported to support the young children who start school with limited skills that are necessary for learning in a structured environment. They need to be supported to see beyond 'a type of child', to address their dysconscious racism (King 1991), to raise learning expectations and their own professional pedagogic expectations and to see that given the 'right conditions' all children can learn and progress beyond what the education system is currently achieving.

Research has shown that many young people become disenchanted by school in their teenage years (e.g. Shaughnessy 2012). They feel it is irrelevant and a sense of dislocation. A socially just education system needs to address this by inculcating a sense of belonging and mutual commitment and investment into the school and school/learning experience and developing an understanding of forms of oppression: Whiteness, racism, sexism and classism, in particular, are fundamental to this. But it is fundamental for all young people and not just BME young people. An intersectional approach is essential in order to avoid hierarchies of oppression and avoid racialised, classed and gendered antagonisms.

Many schools now have student councils which enable students to 'have a say'. This is important, but I am suggesting something more far reaching along the lines of the democratic schools advocated by Apple and Beane (1999), for example. Achieving a democratic school involves addressing the democratisation of the structures and organisation and also of the curriculum itself. As Apple and Beane say, all those involved in the school should have the right to be involved in the decision making, including the young people. Given the strong state intervention over the past two decades into curriculum, monitoring, assessment and pedagogic practice, teachers no doubt would also argue that they, too, would like a greater say and greater professional autonomy. Apple and Beane refer to democratic schools as communities of learning which in most cases will be very diverse in a wide range of respects; they involve participation in the engagement and struggle towards 'fairness' and an agreement of what that means in terms of educational experiences, opportunities and access. They also sound a note of caution with respect to the need for local democratic school communities need to abide by a broader, nationally based set of socially just principles. There also therefore needs to be built in some form of external accountability and monitoring.

Finally, access to a broad curriculum for all—an entitlement curriculum—is a prerequisite for a socially just education system. The National Curriculum, albeit criticised for its traditional and hegemonic orientation, has now been whittled away and its entitlement aspect has been undermined with only privileged pupils getting access to the study of modern foreign languages or physics and chemistry: subjects highly valued by society. The issue about which knowledge to teach and what is useful knowledge and valued knowledge is complex and problematic, and it has to be underpinned by a critical understanding of hegemonic values. Part of this involves the shift away from an overly simplistic distributional approach to knowledge and diversity as is often displayed through tokenistic multicultural education, for instance, towards a concern for an education for citizenship as outlined earlier and the development of an understanding of the challenge to discriminatory and oppressive practices.

The term *social justice* has and is an overused term and consequently has become rather meaningless. However, it also seems to be such an important term that it is worth trying to reappropriate it and refashion it. I have outlined some suggested basic principles for doing this in terms of developing aspects of a model for a socially just education system. Some of this may seem idealistic, but there is a precedent for democratically working towards socially just schools in the US through the Rethinking Schools Movement and those discussed by Apple and Beane (1999). Also it is not a case of having to start from a blank canvas, as I have indicated. There is an abundance of reports, recommendations and research analyses that has already been undertaken and can be built on within the parameters of my suggestions here. Crucially, though, to succeed where hitherto this has not happened, there is the need for a major shift in attitude away from the highly stratified and competitive system that we currently have and a willingness to embrace alternative ways of seeing, being and doing.

As this book goes to press, new education policies are being implemented which are likely to narrow rather than expand opportunities. These include the changes to the curriculum, further polarising vocational and 'academic' subjects; the changes to the GCSE examinations at sixteen years, which will mark a return to a two-tier examinations system; and the state funding of 'Free Schools' and academies, which will obviate the responsibility of the local, accountable, authorities.

In this chapter I have attempted to illuminate the nature and purpose of the education system. I have demonstrated how injustices operate and their relationship to wider society. In particular if we are to move towards a socially just, fairer education system, then we need to locate an understanding of the education system within an analysis of the structure and purpose of wider society.

REFERENCES

Abbott, Diane. 2009. Keynote Address, *London Schools and Black Children's Conference*: London.

Althusser, Louis. 2006. 'Ideology and Ideological State Apparatuses'. In *The Anthropology of the State. A Reader*, edited by Aradhana Sharma and Akhil Gupta, 86–111. Oxford, MA: Blackwell.

Apple, Michael.1996. *Cultural Politics and Education*. Buckingham: Open University Press.

Apple, Michael, and James Beane.1999. Eds. *Democratic Schools*. Buckingham: Open University Press.

Ball, James. Dan Milmo and Ben Ferguson. 2012. 'Half of UK's Young Black Males are Unemployed'. *Guardian*, March 9.

Ball, Stephen. 2003. *Class Strategies and the Education Market*. London: RoutledgeFalmer.

Bhopal, Kalwant, and Martin Myers. 2008. *Insiders, Outsiders and Others: Gypsies and Identities*. Hertfordshire: University of Hertfordshire Press.

Blanchflower, David. 2011. Scrapping the EMA and Cutting Young People Adrift. *The Guardian*, 20 January.

Bourdieu, Pierre and Jean-Claude Passeron. 1979. *Reproduction in Education, Society and Culture*. London: Sage.

Bowles, Samuel, and Herbert Gintis. 1976. *Schooling in Capitalist America*. London: Routledge and Kegan Paul.

Butler, Tim, and Chris Hamnett. 2012. *Ethnicity, Class and Aspiration*. Bristol: Policy Press.

Casciani, Dominic. (2005) Analysis: Segregated Britain? BBC News Community Affairs http://newsvote.bbc.co.uk/mpaps/pagetools/print/news.bbc.co.uk/1/hi/uk/4270010.stm Accessed 21/5/13

Chapman, James. 2010. 'Ministers Declare War on Degrees'. *Telegraph*, November 3.

Collins, Cherry, Jane Kenway and Julie McLeod. 2000. *Factors Influencing the Performance of Males and Females in School and Their Initial Destinations after Leaving School*. Melbourne, Australia: Deakin University.

Crenshaw, Kimberlé. 1995. 'Mapping the Margins: Intersectionality, Identity Politics, and Violence against Women of Color'. In *Critical Race Theory. The Key Writings That Formed the Movement*, edited by Kimberlé Crenshaw, Neil Gotanda, Garry Peller and Kendall Thomas, 357–383. New York: New Press.

Crowder, Kyle. 2000. 'The Racial Context of White Mobility: An Individual-Level Assessment of the White Flight Hypothesis'. *Social Science Research* 29 (2): 223–257.

Crozier, Gill. 2011. 'Black and Minority Ethnic Students Negotiating White "Norms", Managing Exclusion: Ethical Challenges in Higher Education'. Presented at the *SRHE Annual Conference*, Newport Wales, December.

Crozier, G. (2012) 'In or Out of the (Social) Mix'?—Developing Multiple Identities to Negotiate Cosmopolitan Educational Settings'. *Keynote Lecture : Education, Identities and Social Inclusion research group seminar, Brunel University*, London, April 19 2012.

Crozier, Gill, and Jane Davies. 2007. 'Hard to Reach Parents or Hard to Reach Schools? A Discussion of Home–School Relations, with Particular Reference to Bangladeshi and Pakistani Parents'. *British Educational Research Journal* 33 (3): 295–313.

———. 2008. 'The Trouble Is They Don't Mix: Self-Segregation of Enforced Exclusion. Teachers' Constructions of South Asian Students'. *Race, Ethnicity and Education* 11 (3): 285–301.

Crozier, Gill, Diane Reay and David, James. 2011. 'Making It Work for Them: White Middle Class Families and Working Class Schools'. *International Studies in Sociology of Education* 21 (3): 199–216.

Crowder, Kyle (2000) 'The Racial Context of White Mobility: An Individual-Level Assessment of the White Flight Hypothesis'. *Social Science Research* 29:2 223–257

Delpit, Lisa. 1995. *Other People's Children: Cultural Conflict in the Classroom*. New York: New Press.

Department for Children Schools and Families. 2008. Attainment by Pupil Characteristics in England. The Poverty Site. Accessed January 30, 2011, at http://www.poverty.org.uk/25/index.shtml?2.

———. 2009. Secondary School Achievement and Attainment Tables. Accessed January 30, 2011, at http://www.poverty.org.uk/25/index.shtml?2.

Derrington, Chris, and Sally Kendall. 2004. *Gypsy Traveller Students in Secondary Schools*. Stoke-on-Trent: Trentham Books.

Equality Human Rights Commission. 2010. *How Fair Is Britain? The First Triennial Review*. London: HMSO.

Field, Frank. (2010) *The Foundation Years: Preventing Poor Children Becoming Poor Adults. The Report of the Independent*. London: HM Government, Cabinet Office

Fraser, Nancy. 1997. *Justice Interruptus: Critical Reflections on the 'Postcolonialist' Condition*. New York: Routledge.

———. 2007. 'Feminist Politics in an Age of Recognition: A Two Dimensional Approach to Gender Justice'. *Studies in Social Justice* 1 (1): 23–35.

Gewirtz, Sharon. 2002.*The Managerial School*. London: Routledge.

Gillborn, David, and Heidi Safia Mirza. (2000) *Educational Inequality: Mapping Race, Class and Gender*. London: HMSO

Gillborn, David, and Deborah Youdell. 2000. *Rationing Education*. Buckingham: Open University Press.

Hallam, Sue, Lynne Rogers and Judy Ireson. 2008. "Ability Grouping in the Secondary School: Attitudes of Teachers of Practically Based Subjects". *International Journal of Research and Method in Education* 31 (2): 181–192.

Halsey, A. H. 1997. 'Trends in Access and Equity In Higher Education: Britain in International Perspective'. In *Education, Culture and Society*, edited by A. H. Halsey, Hugh Lauder, Phillip Brown and Amy Stuart Wells, 638–645. Oxford: Oxford University Press.

Hills, John. 2010. *An Anatomy of Inequalities in the UK*. London: Government Equalities Office.

hooks, bell. 1989. *Talking Back*. Boston, MA: South End Press.

Ireson, Judy, Sue Hallam and Irene Plewis. 2001. 'Ability Grouping in Secondary Schools: Effects on Pupils' Self-Concepts'. *British Journal of Educational Psychology* 71 (2): 315–326.

James, David, Diane Reay, Gill Crozier, Phoebe Beedell, Sumi Hollingworth, Fiona Jamieson and Katya Williams. 2010. 'Neoliberal Policy and the Meaning of Counter-Intuitive Middle Class School Choices'. *Current Sociology, Special Issue on Education in a Globalizing World* 4 (2): 623–641.

Kerr, Sandra, (2010) *Race into Higher Education. Today's Diverse Generation into Tomorrow's Workforce*. London: Business into Community.

King, Joyce. 1991. 'Dysconscious Racism: Ideology, Identity, and the Miseducation of Teachers'. *Journal of Negro Education* 60 (2): 133–146.

Machin, Stephen, and Sandra McNally. 2006. *Education and Child Poverty*. York: Joseph Rowntree Trust.

Moore, Robert. 2004. *Education and Society*. Cambridge: Polity Press.

Parsons, Carl. (2009) 'Explaining Sustained Inequalities in Ethnic Minority School Exclusions in England—Passive Racism in a Neoliberal Grip'. *Oxford Review of Education*. Vol. 35, No. 2, April 2009, pp. 249–265

Rawls, John. 1972. *A Theory of Justice*. London: Oxford University Press.

Reay, Diane, Gill Crozier and David James. 2011. *White Middle-Class Identities and Urban Schools*. London: Palgrave.

Rist, Ray. 2000. 'Student Social Class and Teacher Expectations. The Self-Fulfilling Prophecy'. *Harvard Education Review* 70 (3): 257.

Sayer, Andrew. 2005. *The Moral Significance of Class*. Cambridge: Cambridge University Press.

Sen, Amartya. 2009. *The Idea of Justice*. London: Allen Lane.

Shaughnessy, Julie. 2012. 'The Challenge for English Schools in Responding to Current Debates on Behaviour and Violence'. *Pastoral Care in Education: An International Journal of Personal, Social and Emotional Development* 30 (2): 87–97.

Spivak, Gayatri. 1987. *In Other Worlds: Essays in Cultural Politics*. London: Methuen.

Stewart, William. 2010. '"English Bac"? You'll Have to Pay Children to Do It'. *Times Educational Supplement*, October 29.

Stillwell, John and Hussain, Serena. (2010) 'Exploring the Ethnic Dimensions of Internal Migration in Great Britain using Migration Effectiveness and Spatial Connectivity'. *The Journal of Ethnic and Migration Studies*, 36(9):1381–1403.

Strand, Steve. 2011. 'The Limits of Social Class in Explaining Ethnic Gaps in Educational Attainment'. *British Educational Research Journal* 37 (2): 197–229.

Sugden, Joanna. 2009. 'Report: "White Flight" Causes Growing School Segregation'. The Times Online, July 11. Accessed January 27, 2011, at www.thetimes.com.

Sutton Trust. 2010. 'Private School Students 55 Times More Likely to go to Oxbridge than Poor Students'. Accessed January 27, 2011, at www.sutton.com/news.

Tims, Anna. 2011. 'Courses that Put Corporate Studies on the Curriculum'. *Guardian*, January 15.

Tomlinson, Sally. 2008. *Race and Education*. Berks: Open University-McGraw-Hill.

Vincent, Carol, Nicola Rollock, Stephen Ball and David Gillborn, 2012. 'Being Strategic, Being Watchful, Being Determined: Black Middle Class Parents and Schooling'. *British Journal of Sociology of Education* 33 (3): 337–354.

Weber, Max. 1966. *The Sociology of Religion*. London: Methuen.

Wells, Amy Stuart, and Irene Serna. 1997. 'The Politics of Culture: Understanding Local Political Resistance to Detracking in Racially Mixed Schools'. In *Education, Culture and Society*, edited by A. H. Halsey, Hugh Lauder, Phillip Brown and Amy Stuart Wells, 718–735. Oxford: Oxford University Press.

Young, Iris Marion.1990. *Justice and the Politics of Difference*. Princeton, NJ: Princeton University Press.

4 Black Academic Success
What's Changed?

Jasmine Rhamie

INTRODUCTION

In my book *Eagles Who Soar: How Black Learners Find Paths to Success* (Rhamie 2007), I identified a paucity of research focused on academic achievement amongst Black groups and a glut of research focused on their (under)achievement. One of my key recommendations was for a shift from concentrating on Black (under)achievement to raising the profile of their accomplishments. I suggested that the over-focus on (under)achievement had led to Black pupils being stereotyped as academic failures. However, I argue that there is a growing proportion of Black pupils who do achieve academically and this group needs a higher profile in order to combat the negative stereotypes that exist in education about Black pupils. It is also necessary to provide a fuller and more balanced picture of the achievements of the Black community for two purposes; firstly, to provide role models, a sense of pride, motivation and encouragement for those who are currently and will in the future navigate the school system and. secondly, to disrupt the persistent perception of failing Black pupils and families (Rhamie 2007). Since my research was published, immense changes have taken place across the educational landscape with a new Conservative and Liberal Coalition government introducing changes in education policy and equality legislation. Within academia new theoretical understandings of race equality and social justice have been developed which provide new ways to examine, analyse and interpret the complexities of race, education and in/equality.

This chapter aims to review the literature on the academic achievement of Black pupils, focusing on research which identifies and promotes their academic success since 2007. It will raise concerns about the education policy direction of the Coalition government and the implications of some of its key decisions on equality for and inclusion of Black pupils. It will provide a picture of the current situation for Black pupils in terms of (under) achievement and survey some of the theoretical explanations for the continued (under)achievement of Black pupils. The chapter will conclude by emphasising the importance of acknowledging Black academic success and considering the implications for education and educational research. The term *Black* is used in this chapter to denote those groups that fall within the categories of Black Caribbean, Black African and Black Other, Mixed Black Caribbean and White and Mixed Black African and White. However, where literature utilises a particular term, such as Black Caribbean, this term will be used in that context.

'Intersectionality' is used to describe dimensions of difference that cannot be separated into separate strands. That a consideration of gender, for example, cannot fully convey the multifaceted experiences that intersect with ethnicity and social class and the structural inequalities experienced within each facet including the differential power relations associated with each strand (Brah and Phoenix 2004). The multiplicity of facets results in multiple disadvantages which must be considered when discussing any single strand. However, it is important to note that these intersections do not have the same effect or impact, as some are more politicised than others and the historical developments, experience and understanding of some of these facets impact differently due to the different ways in which they are framed (Verloo 2006). Thus 'race' has been politicised and positioned historically in such a way as to generate emotional and often irrational reactions when raised that it cannot be treated in the same way as social class, for example (Phoenix and Pattynama 2006). This chapter will examine academic achievements through the lens of 'race' but acknowledges the multiple disadvantages experienced in terms of 'gender', social class and multiple discriminations (Verloo 2004).

POLITICAL CLIMATE

The political and educational policy landscape within the UK has changed significantly since the Conservative/Liberal Democrat coalition government came into power in 2010. With it there has been a definite policy shift away from New Labour's attempts at combating social exclusion, promoting community cohesion and tackling racism. Recent policy initiatives such as the Education Act 2011 and the change in the Office for Standards in Education (OFSTED) inspection framework have raised concerns about the government's commitment to genuine inclusion and challenging racism. A number of wide-reaching educational reforms have been introduced which make clear that the breadth and depth of understanding of inclusion has become diluted into a focus on poverty whilst ignoring the impact of 'race', ethnicity, class and gender. There is also a tendency for policymakers, politicians and others to make reference to a 'post racial society' (Race on the Agenda 2012, 12) suggesting a return to a colour-blind agenda (Tomlinson 2011). The absence of a focus on 'race' and the impact of racial discrimination are evident in a range of policies. But three key Coalition policy changes that have specific implications for Black pupils are the Education Act 2011, changes in the OFSTED framework for inspections and the removal of 'race' and equality from the new Teachers' Standards.

Firstly, the Education Act 2011 has given schools new powers to search pupils and takes away the requirement for schools to give twenty-four hours notice to parents prior to issuing a detention (Department for Education [DfE] 2012a). Schools are able to exclude pupils with the removal of the independent appeal panels convened in the case of exclusions. These have been replaced with review panels which can only reinstate a pupil when the head teachers' actions are deemed unlawful. Given the disproportionate number of Black young people being permanently or 'unofficially' excluded from school for trivial reasons, real concerns are raised about the levels of protection in place for pupils at risk of exclusion, particularly Black pupils.

The second key change that has implications for Black and minority ethnic (BME) groups are the changes to the OFSTED inspection framework, which has resulted in the removal of the requirement to inspect for 'race' equality and the duty to promote community cohesion. Throughout their work in the past, OFSTED has produced a number of useful evidence-based reports highlighting good practice in secondary and primary schools that have been successful in raising the attainment of Black pupils and examining 'race' equality in education (OFSTED 1999, 2002a, 2002b, 2005). Given that research has identified that Black pupils continue to experience racism in schools, the shift in OFSTED's role will create a major gap in monitoring 'race' equality in schools (Maylor et al. 2009). Although government and therefore schools will focus much more on addressing poverty, this cannot justifiably be done without considering other facets of intersectionality, such as 'race' and gender. Furthermore, performance tables will no longer collect data on pupils' 'race' and ethnicity. Without this information it will be difficult to determine the impact of institutional racism and policy decisions by pupil characteristics (DfE 2011a). It will also make it difficult to monitor differential outcomes for pupils and identify good and poor practice in relation to vulnerable groups of pupils who may experience multiple discriminations due to the intersections of particular characteristics, such as 'race', ethnicity, social class, gender and special educational needs (SENs), for example. To seek to provide data only on gender and those eligible for free school meals (FSMs) portrays a naive approach to the complex and multiple challenges faced by disadvantaged and (under) achieving pupils.

Finally, the new Teachers' Standards have omitted explicit references to 'race' equality and now includes a section relating to personal and professional conduct which requires that 'teachers uphold public trust in the profession and maintain high standards of ethics and behaviour, within and outside school, by showing tolerance of and respect for the rights of others; not undermining fundamental British values, including democracy, the rule of law, individual liberty and mutual respect, and tolerance of those with different faiths and beliefs' (DfE 2012d, 10). On the face of it, this seems reasonable, but some of the language used in this part of the Standards is problematic. It is quoted directly from the counter-terrorism Prevent Strategy, which was introduced after the 7/7 London bombings. The strategy explicitly aims to 'establish a set of standards for teachers, which clarifies obligations regarding extremism' (Prevent Strategy 2011, 71). In a joint conference held in October 2012 by the Race Ethnicity and Education special interest group (SIG) and the Teacher Education and Development SIG of the British Educational Research Association (BERA) called 'What Are Fundamental British Values?' it was highlighted that there is no agreed definition of what 'fundamental British values' are and serious concerns were raised about the use of the term 'undermine'. But also how do we know when they are being undermined if we do not know exactly what they are? Without the opportunity to discuss what teachers understand by British values and ensure parity of meaning and understanding, it will be difficult for teachers and student teachers to know how to address and achieve this standard. In part 2 of the Standards it states that 'Teachers uphold public trust in the profession . . . by showing tolerance of and respect for the rights of others'. The reference to 'tolerance' has been contested. *Webster's New Collegiate Dictionary* defines 'tolerance' as the 'capacity to endure pain or hardship' and as such has negative connotations (http://www.merriam-webster.com/dictionary/tolerance). Smythe (2012) suggested that the use of the term 'tolerance' in the Teachers' Standards implies that teachers have to 'put up with' other cultures, faiths and 'races'. She further stated that minorities are never expected to tolerate, but to integrate or assimilate. Furthermore, the implications of the term are that a dismissive approach is adopted rather than one supporting engagement and shared understanding. It is against the backdrop of these major policy and legislative changes that I reflect on Black academic achievement.

CURRENT SITUATION

The Black pupil population was 5.4 per cent of all pupils in state funded primary schools and 4.8 per cent of all pupils in state funded secondary schools in January 2012 (DfE 2012c). Whereas this is a relatively small proportion of the pupil population as a whole, it is a significant number of pupils who, based on statistical evidence, are underperforming at every level of schooling in comparison to their White peers. Furthermore, Black groups continue to feature disproportionately more highly in the data for having Social Emotional and Behavioural Difficulties (SEBDs); receiving statements of SENs (Strand 2012a); being excluded from school (DfE 2011b); and having poorer performance in examinations and tests across compulsory schooling (DfE 2011a, 2011c, 2012b). This situation has changed little in the past few decades with further detailed analyses being undertaken on larger data sets revealing further disproportionate experiences for Black groups. These analyses on large data sets reveal a range of interesting patterns in the data.

After analysing school census data, Strand (2012a) found that Black Caribbean pupils were more than twice as likely, and Mixed White and Black Caribbean pupils almost twice as likely, to be identified as having SEBDs than White pupils, whereas Black African pupils were less likely than their White counterparts to be identified as such even when taking social class into account. Black Caribbean pupils and Pakistani pupils were also more likely to be identified as having moderate learning difficulties (MLDs) than other groups; however these differences disappeared when social class was considered (Strand 2012b). The identification of SEBDs and MLD in all cases is greater amongst boys than girls. Furthermore, in cases of MLD socio-economic disadvantage accounted for much but not all of the overrepresentation of Black Caribbean boys. There are a number of key points arising from this research. The first is that using broad ethnic groupings masks the complexities and differences within and between ethnic groups, which is necessary in aiding our understanding of ethnicity and achievement, SEN or other measures, including gender and social class factors. Breaking down the Black group reveals important differences between Black Caribbean and Black African pupils in this research and highlights the need for refining these categories further. Secondly, it raises questions about the criteria teachers use for identifying SEBDs and MLDs, the power of teacher expectations and stereotyping and highlights the extent to which teachers do not fully understand the children they are working with and the challenges they face. Furthermore, it may be that teachers fail to understand or recognise resistance strategies, such as challenging perceived unjust treatment, personalisation of school uniform or making prominent subcultural signifiers influenced by fashion, music or language, to maintain an identity and sense of control. These strategies are employed by Black groups as a means of countering the way they are negatively constructed in order to survive school (Sewell 1997). Teachers then interpret and use it as evidence of Black pupils having social emotional and behavioural difficulties and consequently mild learning difficulties. Moreover, given the high levels of these groups being excluded from school, it is not surprising that they would be identified more frequently as having SEBDs.

The current situation with school exclusions is that Black Caribbean pupils continue to be nearly four times more likely to be permanently excluded from school than other pupils. Only Traveller children of Irish heritage experienced more permanent exclusions (DfE 2011b). Given the UK's commitment to the United Nations Convention on the Rights of the Child (UNCRC), this matter has been deemed so serious that the Office of the Children's Commissioner (OCC) undertook an investigation into school exclusions. Taking multiple factors into account, the OCC revealed that a Black Caribbean boy with SENs and receiving FSMs in 2009–2010 was 168 times more likely to be excluded from school than a White female from an affluent background without SENs (OCC 2012). There is a continuing trend for both Black Caribbean boys and girls and mixed White and Black Caribbean pupils to be excluded more than other groups (Parsons et al. 2005; DfE 2011b). Moreover, since 2000 the proportion of excluded Black pupils has increased at a greater rate and number than other groups (Department for Education and Skills 2006). The OCC report highlighted that the UK school exclusion system was not compliant with the principles of the UNCRC in ensuring that children's interests are the primary consideration and taking children's views into account in decisions that might affect them (OCC 2012). School exclusion continues to be a highly emotive and contested issue that is largely ignored by government and local authorities. Patterns of school exclusion are highly gendered, classed and racialised. The issue of exclusion goes beyond official permanent cases with unofficial, informal and illegal exclusions possibly accounting for some of the twelve thousand children who are reported to be 'missing from education' despite being registered on local authority databases (Domokos 2012).

Where pupils remain in school and are successful at avoiding exclusion, attainment is an area where disproportionate Black underachievement is evident. Statistical attainment data are only available for the broad ethnic groupings Black, White, Asian, etc., for Key Stage (KS) 1 and KS 2. Black groups were reported to be underperforming in primary schools. At KS 1 Black pupils were reported to have made the greatest improvement in attainment over a three-year period from 2007 to 2010 but still lagged behind all other groups across reading, writing, science and maths, the exception being in speaking and listening, where Black groups and Chinese groups both achieved 83 per cent compared with 88 per cent for White groups and 84 per cent for Asian groups (DfE 2011c). At KS 2 only 69 per cent of Black groups achieved the expected level in English and maths, falling below the national average by five percentage points (DfE 2011a). However, whereas these data indicate that pupils on FSMs and girls do better in general, this is not broken down by ethnicity. Examining the data in KS 1 and KS 2, one could argue that most Black pupils *are* achieving to expected levels in primary school, which should be acknowledged as an indication of academic success. The gap between their attainment and the national average could be explained by social class differences.

At KS 4 Black pupils overall continue to perform below other groups with 54.3 per cent achieving 5 General Certificate of Secondary Education (GCSE) A*–C (including mathematics and English) grades below results for White pupils (58 per cent), but equal to pupils of any other White background (54.3 per cent). Black African (57.9 per cent) and mixed White and Black African (57.6 per cent) do better than Black Caribbean (48.6 per cent) and Mixed White and Black Caribbean (49.1 per cent) pupils (DfE 2012b). However, the gender gap is greatest between Black Caribbean girls and boys, with girls performing at 12.5 percentage points better than boys. The national average is only 7.3 per cent. The equally low results for pupils of any other White background may relate to new migrants to the UK, such as those from Eastern Europe and Poland who have been reported as facing high levels of discrimination, but this category needs to be dismantled into its composite groups to enable more detailed analysis (Janta et al. 2011).

The general picture for Black pupils and particularly Black Caribbean and mixed Black Caribbean and White pupils in education, particularly secondary education, looks grim. It suggests real challenges for Black groups featuring highly in all the negative education statistics in relation to achievement. But there have been issues with the concept of (under)achievement and the effectiveness of making group comparisons, which often leads to simplistic interpretations and understandings of particular ethnic groups and their abilities.

(UNDER)ACHIEVEMENT

The concept of 'underachievement' was questioned by a number of researchers from as early as the 1980s. Tomlinson (1986) regarded it as being a problematic concept, the definition of which varied according to who was measuring it and for what purpose. The variety of definitions of (under)achievement range from those that equate it to scores on reading tests, intelligence quotient (IQ) tests and standard assessment tests (SATs) to those that link it to the failure of acquiring particular qualifications, such as GCSE results or failing to achieve a university place. Gillborn and Youdell (2000, 133) suggested that the utilisation of a benchmark of five GCSE grades A*–C as the signifier of achievement resulted in an A–C economy which contributed to the de-personalisation of the education system and the introduction of practices which served to focus resources on a limited number of pupils who could maximise their scores and contribute to raising a school's position in the league tables. These pupils were inevitably seen to be White and middle class. The development of the de-personalisation of schools is being demonstrated in the rapid expansion of Free Schools and academies.

Gillborn (1990), for example, suggested that the term 'underachievement' is counter-productive as it implies that the problem lies within the individual while ignoring the possible influence of the education system. This has implications which negatively influence the way Black children are perceived and defined. It has been argued that it would be more accurate to conceptualise the position of Black children in the UK in terms of 'educational disadvantage' or 'inequality' rather than (under)achievement (Wright 1992).

(Under)achievement is a term that continues to be contested in the research literature. One challenge of using the term lies in the way in which particular groups of pupils based on group average scores are perceived to be capable of achieving or not. Gillborn (2008) challenges the use of assessment to determine children's ability suggesting it creates and reinforces inequalities.

Other researchers challenge the legitimacy of making inter-group comparisons, for instance, in the case of research concluding that Black pupils underachieve 'in relation to their peers' or 'in comparison to other groups' (Troyna 1984). Troyna (1984) suggested that this implies that comparisons are being made between two similar groups of children and young people. However, the experiences of Black children in British society as a whole are fundamentally different to the experiences of White children or pupils from Asian backgrounds. Furthermore, it appears that the experiences of Black African communities, who are more recent migrants to the UK, and the more settled and established Black Caribbean communities are also very different. These differential experiences affect pupils' motivation and attitudes to school and teachers' and society's perceptions of them, which in turn have an impact on their educational performance and achievement. Where Black Caribbean pupils experience the rejection and 'othering' of their position within British society despite believing they have a legitimate claim to what British society has to offer (particularly as many are now second and third generation born in the UK) makes them more vulnerable. Furthermore, the strong religious, cultural and family bonds found within some Asian and African communities provide a powerful sense of belonging on a number of levels: religious, cultural, familial and historical. These multiple levels of belonging create a tight community from which these pupils engage with society and create buffers for them. The older, more established Black Caribbean community has strong family bonds but variable cultural bonds. The strong religious and cultural bonds held by the first generation seem to be diminishing in importance with the second and third generation, who appear to be creating different, fluid and possibly less robust bonds that are more remote from their parents' or grandparents' cultures. Thus, the buffering effect is less effective, leaving them more vulnerable to negative experiences within society, such as high levels of unemployment, high levels of deprivation and poverty and a greater risk of involvement with the criminal justice system. These factors potentially feed into pupils' attitudes and motivation at school.

Gillborn (2008) examined how statistical data that are used to compare different ethnic minority groups mask further complexities, such as the social class of Chinese and Indian pupils seen as traditionally high-performing groups. He suggests that these pupils are typically middle class whose home backgrounds are different in terms of socio-economic status and, for Indian children, they are often privately educated. However, despite the fact that social class is a determinant of high achievement, being Black and middle class does not protect Black children from experiencing racism in all its forms (Vincent et al. 2012).

Understandings of BME achievement have developed over the years from a simple comparison between the examination results of minority ethnic groups with the majority White group to a more sophisticated exploration of the complexities of differential attainment levels amongst these groups. Research has sought to explain some of the structural and underlying inequalities that affect Black attainment, particularly the ways in which teachers label, stereotype and have lower expectations of Black groups than other pupils.

LABELLING, STEREOTYPING AND TEACHER EXPECTATIONS

Historically, Black families have had to fight hard against the perception of their children as being incapable of achieving. Academics have suggested that low teacher expectations, labelling and stereotyping of Black pupils has contributed to Black pupils' underachievement. Over fifty years ago, Rosenthal and Jacobson's classic 1968 study gave rise to an interest in teacher expectations and their effects. It is now acknowledged that teachers influence the self-concepts of pupils by their implicit as well as overt actions. Since the 1960s, research continued to find teachers' perceptions of pupils, prior performance, pupil behaviour, knowledge of siblings achievements, previous grouping allocation and even pupil's physical appearance affected teachers' decisions about ability group placement (Troman 1988; Ireson and Hallam 2001). Teachers have reported that they treat all pupils equally, but there were subtle but persistent differences in how they treated Black pupils (Eggleston, Dunn and Anjali 1986; Gillborn 1990; Gillborn and Gipps 1996; Sewell 1997). Whereas this has historically been the case, what is becoming clear is that despite a plethora of past research in the area, current research is returning to the same fundamental themes of labelling, stereotyping and low teacher expectations which now provide sophisticated interpretations and understandings of these attitudes which are manifested in subtle ways in school.

Youdell (2006, 33) considered the ways in which school processes serve to define particular groups of pupils as 'impossible learners'. In her examination of neo-liberal policies, such as the marketisation of education, she acknowledged the ways in which Black Caribbean pupils are constructed through their subcultural identities to be undesirable learners. The embodiment of different types of learners associated with particular ethnic and gendered identities is demonstrated in the ways in which school discourses constitute Black Caribbean pupils as 'unacceptable learners' (Youdell 2003, 21). These negative constructions of Black learners are informed by and reinforce stereotypes of Black pupils which serve to impact their school interactions, thus leading to their academic failure.

Archer (2008) describes the way in which perceptions of groups of pupils serves to label them as attractive or desirable learners. She refers to the concept of the 'ideal' pupil, typically White and middle class, and the way in which this operates as a powerful means to identifying certain groups of pupils as desirable and others as undesirable. The continued use of GCSE group and SAT scores as a means of tracking academic success is problematic as it results in certain groups being perceived as high achievers and others as not. This has resulted in powerful stereotypes being generated and nurtured about particular groups of pupils; Chinese and Indian pupils seen as hardworking, high achievers, and Black and Traveller pupils as lazy, low achievers. Gillborn (2008, 146–161) refers to 'model minorities' who, because of their high achievement, are used as a yardstick against which other minority ethnic groups are measured. The implication of this is that institutional racism is dismissed as a factor in the underachievement of other minority ethnic groups. It then follows that the problem does not lie within the school, but within the family releasing schools from their responsibility to address inequalities and raise the attainment of those groups deemed to be low achieving.

Rollock's (2007) research suggests that teachers construct two levels of success: 'inclusive success', where GCSE grade D and below were regarded as being an indicator of a broader definition of success, and 'exclusive success', which included pupils who were expected to achieve 5 GCSE A*–C grades. These two types of success were attributed and attached to particular groups of pupils. What is worrying about this research is the impact of this view on Black pupils. For example, when undertaking an education workshop with a group of Black teenage boys and their parents for a community organisation, I found that the boys were adamant that a D grade at GCSE was a pass. They had been led by teachers to believe that this was an acceptable and respectable grade for them. They believed what teachers had told them but were not aware that a D grade was not considered a pass by employers and would not allow them to take A-levels in those subjects. Rollock has suggested that teachers regard Black pupils as being capable of only achieving a D grade, deeming it as 'success', and as such we can see how it can be used to justify the failure of Black pupils or, as Rollock (2007, 275) puts it, 'legitimising Black academic failure'.

What is interesting about Rollock's work is that she demonstrates through analysis of teacher interview data that teachers' judgements about which students are deemed to be part of the 'exclusive success' group and those who are not are based on pupils' dress and appearance. Teachers' descriptions of students wearing 'hoodies' or Nike-labelled clothing were associated with an anti-school attitude. Furthermore, reference to these items of clothing were gendered and racialised and referred specifically to African Caribbean boys, who were then excluded from access to the 'exclusive success' group (Rollock 2007, 281).

It is important to consider how pupils are perceived by teachers and academics as this can have a significant impact on how they are valued and treated in schools and also how pupils see themselves. Average group achievement scores serve to position groups of pupils within a hierarchy of value and importance within the education system and potentially restrict the possibility for these pupils to break out of perceived norms and the expectations of their positioning or to break free from the labels, stereotypes and expectations of teachers. So, for example, Chinese pupils perceived by teachers to be high achieving will constantly be seen as valuable and desirable pupils. However, the assumptions about Chinese pupils' high achievement continue to mask the inequalities and racism they experience (Archer and Francis 2007). Furthermore, they are narrowly stereotyped and homogenised as a group, which results in the diversity of their identities being ignored. Black pupils, on the other hand, with their consistent low performance in attainment tables, occupy subordinate positions in terms of value and experience as (under)achievers.

Strand (2012b), using data from the Longitudinal Study of Young People in England, found that Black pupils from traditionally middle-class family backgrounds with the associated characteristics of success—high parental expectations and support, high educational aspirations—made less progress than expected. He suggests that low teacher expectations were responsible for slowing their potential achievements.

Recent research suggests that teacher assessments may not be a true reflection of pupils' ability. Bradbury's (2011) research showed how minority and disadvantaged pupils were assessed by teachers as achieving above expectations; however, when external advisors monitored their assessments, teachers reported feeling pressured to reduce the assessment levels in line with expectations of different groups based on social class and 'race'. Pupil attainment was not an indication of teachers' assessments of pupils' actual abilities, but a representation of the perceptions and constructions of certain groups of pupils, based on class and race, as (under)achievers.

There is now ample research evidence to suggest that stereotyping, low teacher expectations and labelling have become embedded within teacher discourse despite teachers' inability to recognise or perceive it. Research continues to suggest that Black pupils' 'underachievement' is due to teachers' negative discourses, constructions and stereotyping of Black pupils' behaviour.

Decades of research, discussion and debate around the issue of underachievement, and more sophisticated interpretations and understandings of what are fundamentally low teacher expectations, stereotyping and labelling, have resulted in painting a dismal picture of Black pupils' experiences and achievements. It has created a situation which leads to a sense of hopelessness as these attitudes appear deep rooted and unchangeable. Moreover, with the dismantling of government structures designed to support Black pupils, they contribute to creating a helpless and lost generation who appear to be losing the battle against discrimination and underachievement. It is against this background that I believe a focus on academic success and achievement is important and has the potential to be more effective in challenging negative perceptions of Black pupils.

BLACK ACADEMIC SUCCESS

DfE data on pupil attainment for five- and six-year-olds indicate that although there are gaps between Black pupils and White pupils that Black pupils are performing well with high percentages of pupils performing at level 2 or above (the expected attainment level for children of this age); in teacher assessments the scores are broadly in the 80 per cent region, just below national averages in reading (84 per cent), writing (79 per cent), speaking and listening (83 per cent), maths (86 per cent) and science (84 per cent) (DfE 2011c). Whereas there is value in examining differences between ethnic groups in order to monitor and raise achievement, the results as they stand do indicate that most Black five- to six-year-olds are achieving in the region of expected attainment levels. An acknowledgement and recognition of these children's achievements by schools, local authorities and education policy leaders is critical in encouraging and motivating Black pupils and changing the persistent negative perceptions and stereotypes of them.

For too long the academic success of Black pupils has been overshadowed, ignored or made invisible by the focus on 'underachievement'. If we use the GCSE measure of success 54.3 per cent of Black pupils achieved five GCSEs including English and mathematics at grades C or above in 2011 (DfE 2012b). This means that over half (54.3 per cent) of all Black pupils attained the government's measure of academic success at the end of compulsory schooling, that is 5 GCSEs A*–C grades. The successful achievements of Black pupils are often ignored by academics, statisticians and teachers to the extent that Black academic success has been rendered invisible. However, there have been some attempts, over the past fifty years, to focus on the academic successes of Black pupils. Studies prior to 2004 have been discussed elsewhere (see Rhamie 2004). Since the publication of my book *Eagles Who Soar: How Black Learners Find Paths to Success* in 2007, which focused on Black academic success and recommended that more studies focusing on Black achievement needed to be undertaken, there have been very few further studies focusing on Black academic success. Exceptions include Byfield (2008), who investigated the experiences of Black boys who attended universities in the US (Harvard and Central Florida) and the UK (Oxford and Wolverhampton). Her qualitative study found that Black boys from different social class backgrounds were able to achieve and attend university due to a range of factors. The range of practical support and help with school work varied for these students, yet they all achieved. The traditional attributes of a 'good' parent—attending parents evenings and parent–teacher events and spending time helping with homework—were challenged in that the study found that some of the Black parents provided a pro-education value system in the home but also utilised alternative strategies to support their children's education by capitalising on extended family networks and the church community for support. Byfield's work, similar to my study, also identified some teachers, students' individual characteristics and community projects as significant in enabling these Black boys to achieve. There have also been some attempts to develop Black children's attainment through the use of supplementary schools (Maylor et al. 2010), small-scale community projects such as Black Boys Can and Generating Genius (Sewell 2009) and larger-scale government-funded projects such as the Black Children's Achievement Programme (Maylor et al. 2009).

Tony Sewell's book *Generating Genius*, based on his project of the same name, outlines the aim and success of the project in reversing the underachievement of Black boys from Jamaica and the UK. Sewell (2009) suggested that the focus of this project on identifying and generating genius was successful because of its premise that genius is not an innate gift but can be generated with the right environment and support. His research identified the importance of three principles—ritual, love and schooling—to enable success. He considers rituals as actions, rooted in Greek mythology and ancient traditions; in fact, it seems that Sewell's modern rituals are simply a means of controlling boys through guidance by supportive adults. Thus suggesting that Black boys need more control. Love is defined as 'caring, fatherly love that has no sexual content' (2009, 15). Sewell linked this need for love to the lack of Black fathers in the home and boys' need of a loving relationship with their families, evidenced in the prevalence of Black boys in gangs due to the 'loving family' environment created within gang culture. Finally, schooling referred to hard work and more time being educated, which results in academic success. These principles suggest that Black boys need rituals through order and control, love manifested in support and nurturing along with more hours of education/schooling and hard work. Sewell states that these principles support resilience, which is necessary for enabling Black pupils to succeed at school. This link between academic success and resilience identified in my own work is important (Rhamie 2007). But Sewell locates the power to achieve firmly within the Black community. Whereas he does not completely ignore the impact of institutional racism in schools, low teacher expectations and social class, he challenges the belief that the solution to the (under)achievement of Black boys lies outside the Black community. He suggests there is a need to create an 'eco-system of success' to enable 'genius to flourish' (Sewell 2009, 10), meaning that all the environments within which Black boys live should be focused on success. This was achieved by taking groups of boys away to a university campus for intensive summer schools in his project. Although the success of Generating Genius cannot be denied, it is naive to think that major improvements in the academic attainment of Black pupils can be achieved on a larger scale without change taking place within schools.

More recent research has identified high levels of success attained by Black groups in one London borough. Demie (2012) found that Black Caribbean and Black African pupils were achieving above national averages in Lambeth. He further identified differences within Black groups in his research. His findings suggest that certain African groups were being overlooked in their achievements due to a failure to distinguish between the diverse groups from the African continent represented in schools in the UK. In case study schools, 83 per cent of Black African pupils were achieving 5 A*–C grades at GCSE level compared to 71 per cent within Lambeth generally and 58 per cent nationally. African pupils were performing better than all Lambeth students (61 per cent).

Demie (2012) further breaks down the Black African category into African-language groups and found that particular language groups achieved more highly than other African language groups and White-English-only-speaking British groups. One example is of Black African Ibo-speaking (largely spoken in Nigeria) pupils who did better than Black African Twi/Fante-speaking (largely spoken in Ghana) pupils. In line with OFSTED's finding, Demie's research highlights the importance of school factors in the academic success of Black students. He demonstrated that with strong leadership amongst the senior management team, a strong commitment to raising standards and effective monitoring of the curriculum, with an inspirational head teacher who developed trust between staff and parents, the educational aspirations and achievements of Black African families were raised (Demie 2012). Another key factor identified in his research not highlighted elsewhere was having a diverse teaching and support staff team which was utilised effectively. High-quality staff were recruited who identified with and supported the inclusive ethos of the school, as well as ensuring the ethnic makeup of staff reflected the local community. There are few studies highlighting the academic success of Black groups; this study emphasised good practice that is successful in raising the achievement of Black pupils. It emphasises what schools do rather than what Black parents, families and communities fail to do in raising the achievement of Black children.

CONCLUSION

The aim of this chapter was to review the literature relating to Black academic success. It has highlighted the development of Black academic success research studies which promote and foreground the academic achievements of Black children. The acknowledgement of Black children's academic successes substantiates the belief that Black children can achieve. This is important given the prevalence of negative perceptions of Black children and their perceived lack of engagement with academic learning.

Whereas there remains research evidence of the failure of schools in raising the attainment of Black pupils, the focus on schools, particularly in the London Borough of Lambeth, that demonstrate very successful outcomes for Black pupils is an important one. It highlights the potential for schools to raise the attainment of Black pupils where there is strong leadership and a will to do so. Promoting research that demonstrates successful outcomes for Black pupils in schools that are determined to raise their attainment is a positive step. However, getting the message out there remains a difficult one, particularly as media representations of Black communities remain largely stereotyped and negative. The evidence of high Black achievement is important for reminding academia, educators and Black communities of the reality and achievability of Black academic success.

Although comparatively few studies that have focused on Black academic success have been undertaken, the vast majority of studies that have explored the reasons for the persistent (under)achievement of Black groups—ranging from racisms, institutional racism and stereotyping to the 'othering' and positioning of Black pupils as 'underachievers', problematic, anti-school and undesirable or impossible learners—have done little to change the situation. Theoretical understandings of the barriers faced by Black pupils strongly suggest structural and individual racisms within school structures and teachers' interactions within these structures and the decline in processes and policies to ensure Black children are supported in school. Although these theoretical developments are important in aiding our understanding of the underlying discrimination faced by Black pupils, they also serve to reinforce the perception of a hopeless situation for a group of helpless pupils.

One obvious place to start raising the profile of research highlighting success factors that contribute to ensuring Black pupils achieve highly, particularly the contribution of school success factors, is in teacher training. Despite government changes to teacher training and the invisibility of 'race' equality, it is incumbent upon academics and teacher educators to ensure matters relating to 'race' remain an important and valuable aspect of teacher education provision and that the findings from success research are made accessible to teachers and trainee teachers.

The current common belief that Black pupils are underachievers remains, and without greater efforts to counter this view it will continue to prevail, resulting in sustained negative outcomes. Black pupils do achieve highly as demonstrated in the literature; what is needed now is a renewed emphasis on their positive achievements and academic successes to promote the possibility for success and ensure their full potential is realised.

REFERENCES

Archer, Louise. 2008. 'The impossibility of minority ethnic educational 'success?' An examination of the discourses of teachers and pupils in British secondary schools'. European Educational Research Journal 7: 89–107.
Archer, Louise, and Becky Francis. 2007. *Understanding Minority Ethnic Achievement: Race Gender Class and 'Success'*. London: Routledge.
Bradbury, Alice. 2011. 'Rethinking Assessment and Inequality: The Production of Disparities in Attainment in Early Years' Education'. Journal of Education Policy 26:655–676.

Brah, Avtar, and Ann Phoenix. 2004. 'Ain't I a Woman? Revisiting Intersectional-ity'. *Journal of International Women's Studies* 5:75–87.

Byfield, Cheron. 2008. *Black Boys Can Make It: How They Overcome the Obsta-cles to University in the UK and USA.* Stoke-on-Trent: Trentham Books.

Demie, Feyisa. 2012. 'The Achievement of Black African Students in British Schools: An Ethnographic Study of Success Factors'. Paper presented at the annual conference of the British Educational Research Association, University of Manchester, Manchester, September, 4–6.

Department for Education. 2011a. *First Statistical Release National Curriculum Assessments at Key Stage 2 in England (Revised).* London: DfE.

———. 2011b. *First Statistical Report: Permanent and Fixed Period Exclusions from Schools and Exclusion Appeals in England, 2009/10.* London: DfE.

———. 2011c. *Statistical First Release National Curriculum Assessments at Key Stage 1 in England.* London: DfE.

———. 2012a. *Exclusion from Maintained School, Academies and Pupil Referral Units in England.* London: DfE.

——— 2012b. *Statistical First Release: GCSE and Equivalent Attainment by Pupil Characteristics in England, 2010/11.* London: DfE.

———. 2012c. *Statistical First Release: Schools, Pupils, and Their Characteristics.* London: DfE.

———. 2012d. *Teachers' Standards.* London:DfE

Department for Education and Skills. 2006. *Exclusion of Black Pupils Priority Review. Getting It Right.* London: DfES.

Domokos, John. 2012. 'Illegal School Exclusions How Pupils Are Slipping through the Net'. *Guardian,* November 15. Accessed December 18, 2012, at http://www.guardian.co.uk/education/2012/nov/15/illegal-school-exclusions.

Eggleston, John, David Dunn and Madhu Anjali. 1986. *Education for Some: The Educational and Vocational Experiences of Young Black people.* London: Runnymede Trust.

Gillborn, David. 1990. *Race and Ethnicity.* London: Unwin.

———. 2008. *Racism and Education Coincidence or Conspiracy?* London: Routledge.

Gillborn, David, and Caroline Gipps. 1996. *Recent Research on the Achievements of Ethnic Minority Pupils.* London: HMSO.

Gillborn, David, and Deborah Youdell. 2000. *Rationing Education: Policy, Prac-tice, Reform and Equity.* Buckingham: Open University Press.

Ireson, Judy, and Susan Hallam. 2001. *Ability Grouping in Education.* London: Sage.

Janta, Hania, Adele Ladkin, Lorraine Brown and Peter Lugosi. 2011. 'Employment Experiences of Polish Migrant Workers in the UK Hospitality Sector'. *Tourism Management* 32:1006–1019.

Maylor, Uvanney, Sarah Smart, Kuyok Abol Kuyok and Alistair Ross. 2009. *Black Children's Achievement Programme Evaluation.* London: DCSF RR177.

Maylor, Uvanney, Emily Tanner, Steven Finch, Katie Glass, Tozun Issa, Natalie Low, Sarah Minty, Susan, Purdon, Anthea Rose, Alistair Ross, Eleanor Taylor and Sarah Tipping. 2010. *The Impact of Supplementary Schools on Pupils' Attainment: An Investigation into What Factors Contribute to Educational Improvements, Research Report 210.* Nottingham: Department for Children Schools and Families.

OCC (Office for the Children's Commissioner). 2012. *They Never Give Up on You: Office of the Children's Commissioners School Exclusions Inquiry.* Lon-don: OCC.

Office for Standards in Education. 1999. *Raising the Attainment of Minority Eth-nic Pupils: Schools and LEA Responses.* London: HMSO.

———. 2002a. *Achievement of Black Caribbean Pupils: Good Practice in Secondary Schools.* London: HMSO.

———. 2002b. *Achievement of Black Pupils: Three Successful Primary Schools.* London: HMSO.

———. 2005. *Race Equality in Education: Good Practice in Schools and Local Authorities.* London: HMSO.

Parsons, Carl., Godfrey, Ray. Annan, Gill., Cornwall, John. Dussart, Molly., Hepburn, Simon. Howlett, Keith. And Wennerstrom, Vanessa. 2005. *Minority Exclusions and the Race Relations (Amendment) Act 2000.* Nottingham: DfES Research Brief 616.

Phoenix, Ann, and Pamela Pattynama. 2006. 'Intersectionality'. *European Journal of Women's Studies* 13:187–192.

Prevent Strategy. 2011. Accessed December, 16, 2012, at http://www.homeoffice.gov.uk/publications/counter-terrorism/prevent/prevent-strategy/.

Race on the Agenda. 2012. *Racism in the Classroom: An Alternative Inquiry into Education in London.* Race on the Agenda. Accessed 26 May 2013, *http://www.rota.org.uk/content/race-agenda-autumn-2012-agenda-36*

Rhamie, Jasmine. 2004. 'A Study of the Educational Experiences of African Caribbeans in the UK'. PhD thesis, Institute of Education, University of London.

———. 2007. *Eagles Who Soar: How Black Learners Find Paths to Success.* Stoke-on-Trent: Trentham.

Rollock, Nicola. 2007. 'Legitimising Black Academic Failure: Deconstructing Staff Discourses on Academic Success, Appearance and Behaviour'. *International Studies in Sociology of Education* 17:275–287.

Rosenthal, Robert, and Lenore Jacobson. 1968. *Pygmalion in the Classroom.* New York: Holt Rinehart and Winston.

Sewell, Tony. 1997. *Black Masculinities and Schooling.* Stoke-on-Trent: Trentham Books.

———. 2009. *Generating Genius: Black Boys in Search of Love, Ritual and Schooling.* Stoke-on-Trent: Trentham Books.

Smythe, Geri. 2012. 'Being Tolerant about Intolerance'. Paper presented at a conference of the British Educational Research Association, 'What Are Fundamental British Values?', University of Chichester, Sussex, October 31.

Strand, Steve. 2012b. 'The White British–Black Caribbean Achievement Gap: Tests, Tiers and Teacher Expectations'. *British Educational Research Journal* 38:75–101.

———. 2012a. 'Disproportionate Identification of Ethnic Minority Students with Special Educational Needs (SEN) Recent National Data from England'. Paper presented at the annual conference of the British Educational Research Association, University of Manchester, Manchester, September 4–6.

———. 1986. *Ethnic Minority Achievement and Equality of Opportunity.* Nottingham: University of Nottingham: School of Education.

———. 2011. 'More Radical Reform (But Don't Mention Race) Gaps and Silences in the Government's Discourse'. *Race Equality Teaching* 29:25–29.

Tomlinson, Sally. 1986. Ethnic Minority Achievement and Equality of Opportunity. Nottingham: University of Nottingham: School of Education.

———. 2011. 'More Radical Reform (But Don't Mention Race) Gaps and Silences in the Government's Discourse'. Race Equality Teaching 29:25–29.

Troman, Gary. 1988. 'Getting It Right: Selection and Setting in a 9–13 Years Middle School'. *British Journal of Sociology of Education* 9:403–422.

Troyna, Barry. 1984. 'Fact or Artefact? The "Educational Underachievement" of Black Pupils'. *British Journal of Sociology of Education* 5:153–160.

Verloo, Mieke. 2006. 'Multiple Inequalities, Intersectionality and the European Union'. *European Journal of Women's Studies* 13:211–228.

Vincent, Carol, Nicola Rollock, Stephen Ball and David Gillborn. 2012. *The Educational Strategies of the Black Middle Classes*. London: Institute of Education.

Wright, Cecile. 1992. *Race Relations in the Primary Classroom*. London: David Fulton Publishers.

Youdell, Deborah. 2003. 'Identity Traps or How Black Students Fail: The Interactions between Biographical, Sub-Cultural and Learn Identities'. *British Journal of Sociology of Education* 24:3–20.

Youdell, Deborah. 2006. *Impossible Bodies, Impossible Selves: Exclusions and Student Subjectivities*. Dortrecht: Springer.

5 The Intersections of Ethnicity, Gender, Social Class and an Itinerant Lifestyle

Deconstructing Teachers' Narratives and Thinking about the Possibilities for Transformative Action

Robyn Henderson

INTRODUCTION

School literacy learning is regarded highly in today's climate of accountability. International measures, including PISA (Programme for International Student Assessment; see Organisation for Economic Co-operation and Development n.d.) and PIRLS (Progress in International Reading Literacy Study; see Lynch School of Education, Boston College 2010), provide comparative measures of educational achievement across nations. In Australia, the results of national literacy tests (Australian Curriculum, Assessment and Reporting Authority 2010) are reported on the My School website (Australian Curriculum, Assessment and Reporting Authority 2011), which provides data that allow schools to 'compare themselves with other schools that serve similar students'.

The specific focus on schools 'that serve similar students' highlights the way that contextual factors, such as socio-economic status, cultural background, linguistic background and gender, are implicated in students' literacy achievement levels. As Makin (2007, 5) noted, 'children from cultural minority groups or minority language backgrounds and children living in poverty' are 'at particular risk of low literacy achievement in schools'. There is certainly evidence that these 'gross demographics', to use the term that Kalantzis, Cope and the Learning by Design Project Group (2005, 44) coined for these dimensions, influence how teachers make sense of their students and their capabilities to learn school literacies. The 'persistent problem of inequitable outcomes' (Comber 2007, 18) is one that warrants ongoing investigation, if we are serious about ensuring equitable opportunities and educational trajectories for all students.

We have known for a long time that social membership, in terms of ethnicity, social class, gender, or combinations of these factors, can influence the successes that children achieve in school literacy learning. The term *ethnicity* is, according to Bhopal (2004, 442), an 'imprecise and fluid' term based on the Greek word *ethnos*, meaning a nation. It refers to 'the group to which people belong, and/or are perceived to belong', generally referring to ancestral origins, geographical origins, cultural traditions, such as customs, beliefs and religion, and language/s (Bhopal 2004, 441; Tsolidis 2001). In the Australian context, the term *ethnicity* is used in preference to *race*.

Teachers often use ethnicity, social class and gender as points of reference, creating explanatory narratives about why some students in the school context succeed and others do not. One result can be narratives of blame—stories that blame students for not bringing appropriate understandings to school, or stories that blame parents for being deficient in caring for their children and negligent in not preparing them for school literacy learning. According to Henderson and Woods (2012, 116), 'deficit stories are often beliefs: the belief that poor people are lazy, that girls are better than boys at English, or that a child wearing dirty clothes cannot learn'. Yet beliefs or stories like these can help to perpetuate stereotypical views and assumptions about children and families, particularly those who are poor or culturally diverse. As Comber (2007, 13) pointed out, such stories become 'the "truth" about "these kids"'. The consequences of such stories are often negative, because they provide commonsense understandings which reinforce educational inequality.

The prevalence of deficit discourses has been acknowledged in the considerable body of research that has attempted to find ways to 'turn-around' (Kamler and Comber 2005) and move beyond (Henderson 2001) these discourses (e.g. Comber and Kamler 2005; Gonzales, Moll and Amanti 2005; Henderson and Woods 2012). This chapter, however, looks more closely at deficit discourses and how they work to discursively construct students who seem to be marginalised within the context of a particular school.

The chapter begins with a discussion of literacy learning and its relevance to the children of itinerant farmworkers. It then draws on empirical evidence from a research study that was conducted in a primary school located in a rural community in Australia's north-east. Through examining three small stories and the discourses that teachers use when talking about itinerant farmworkers' children and their successes or otherwise in school literacy learning, the chapter investigates the intersectionality of social class, ethnicity and gender in the teachers' narratives. The chapter concludes by considering some possibilities for transformative action. It argues that a re-conceptualisation of itinerancy could help to disrupt deficit views and assist teachers to focus on responsive, flexible and enabling pedagogies that will work for all students, and that intersectionality is a useful tool in that process.

ITINERANT FARMWORKERS' CHILDREN
IN THE AUSTRALIAN CONTEXT

This chapter builds on research conducted over a number of years to investigate the literacy learning of itinerant farmworkers' children (e.g.

Henderson 2004, 2005, 2007, 2009, 2012). In Australia, as in other countries, many workers who undertake manual farm labour travel from location to location to pick crops. The size of the country means that families sometimes travel large distances and work during winter harvesting seasons in the north and summer harvesting seasons in the south. Many farmworkers bring their families with them, and their children move in and out of schools in various locations. As part of these relocations, many children cross state borders and have to fit into different education systems in different states. These present a range of differences that often translate into difficulties for itinerant children, including different school starting ages, different curricula and even different handwriting styles.

Little information is available about the number of itinerant farmworkers in Australia or the number of children who travel with parents who are farmworkers (Hanson and Bell 2007; Henderson 2005). However, the seasonal movement of agricultural workers appears to be one of the 'most prominent and enduring forms of population movement in rural areas' (Hanson and Bell 2007, 101). The itinerant workforce that contributes to harvests in farming areas comprises 'regulars' who follow seasonal circuits, students, immigrants, backpackers and retirees, often called grey nomads (Mares 2005; National Harvest Trail Working Group 2000). Even though these groups have a particular type of work in common, they represent a diverse range of experiences and patterns of mobility (Hanson and Bell 2007; Henderson 2005).

According to Hanson and Bell (2007, 108), 'the overseas-born element in the Australian seasonal labour force is made up of (mostly legal) permanent immigrants'. Predominantly negative stories about farmworkers seem to circulate, at least in some communities (Henderson 2005, 2008b). Some aspects of these stories seem to reflect an 'entrenched racism and discrimination experienced in the labour force' more generally (Missingham, Dibden and Cocklin 2006, 135), while others have been identified as reflective of societal stories about people with low socio-economic status (Henderson 2005). In school sites where the children of itinerant farmworkers are enrolled, negative and deficit stories have also been reported, paralleling community discourses that construct farmworkers as criminals, illegal immigrants, untrustworthy citizens and inadequate parents (Henderson 2005, 2008a, 2009).

ITINERANT CHILDREN AND LITERACY LEARNING

Research (e.g. Henderson 2005; Henderson and Woods 2012) has shown that many itinerant farmworkers' children underachieve in literacy learning. Indeed, as an example, data from one school that enrols up to sixty itinerant farmworkers' children each winter indicate that up to 75 per cent of this particular group of children perform in the lowest 25 per cent of the school population (Henderson 2005). Such low results suggest that there is a need to further investigate the relationships and interactions between an itinerant lifestyle and literacy learning in the school context.

Since the early 1980s, research in the literacy field has given us a way of understanding why children from particular backgrounds do not achieve as well as other children in the classroom. Shirley Brice Heath's (1983) seminal study in the US, which investigated two small working-class communities located on the edge of a middle-class cotton milling town, indicated that children's language socialisation at home influenced their success or otherwise at school. As Heath explained, some children arrive at school having had 'hundreds of thousands of occasions for practicing the skills and espousing the values the schools transmit' (1983, 368), whereas others 'fall quickly into a pattern of failure' (349). In other words, Heath's work highlighted the advantage that can occur when children have had opportunities to engage with the particular social practices and the specific 'ways with words' of schools and institutions (343).

Similar explanations have been evident in more recent literacy research, where understandings about literacy are grounded in a cultural-critical perspective. From this viewpoint, literacy is understood as a plural concept and the learning of literacies is about access to, and participation in, particular social and cultural practices. As Freebody (2007, 3) highlighted, 'what passes for effective literacy education can differ depending on the culture, history and technologies of social groups, and . . . represents only one possible scholarly tradition'. To be successful in school literacy learning, children need to display culturally-preferred ways of engaging in literacy practices, including talking, listening, speaking, reading and writing. This suggests that group membership, in terms of gender, social class, ethnicity, geographical location or combinations of these factors, can determine the types of literacy that are accessed in homes and communities, and this can therefore influence the successes available to children in the school context. Indeed, it often means that there is 'a wealth of literacy practices in the lives of those often considered by the educational establishment to be "deprived" of literacy' (Gregory and Williams 2000, 203; see also Carrington and Luke 2003; Gonzales, Moll and Amanti 2005; Purcell-Gates 2008).

This way of thinking about literacy learning suggests that schools valorise, and 'measure and reward, a certain set of family and personal attributes' (Gilbert 2000, 10). This becomes an important point when we consider the literacy learning of children who belong to minority cultures and are culturally or linguistically different from what might constitute the 'norm' of a particular school. Tsolidis (2001, 13) noted that ethnicity and its associated traits, including 'language, customs, beliefs, religion or generally those characteristics which create and reproduce a cultural identity' are often tied to incidents of racism and social exclusion. Despite the way that *'everyone* has an ethnicity' (Santoro 2007, 86), it appears that members of ethnic minorities are often noticed because of their difference from others (Whitehouse and Colvin 2001).

CONSIDERING EQUITY

What, then, does this mean in relation to school literacy learning and opportunities for children to achieve equitable learning outcomes? Thomson (2002, 1) used the metaphor of a virtual schoolbag to indicate that children bring to school a bag 'full of things they have already learned at home, with their friends, and in and from the world in which they live'. Yet, schools often seem to operate in ways that result in some children being unable to unpack the contents of their virtual schoolbag for use in the classroom. When children's strengths are invisible, their weaknesses are highlighted, thus allowing stories about 'these kids', 'these parents' and 'these neighbourhoods' (Henderson and Woods 2012, 126) to become taken-for-granted 'truths'.

Unfortunately, deficit discourses are prevalent in school contexts (e.g. see Comber 2007; Comber and Kamler 2004; Harris 2008; Henderson and Woods 2012; Honan 2006). When some families are regarded as 'lacking what society deems to be the educational, social and cultural basics', schools often respond by offering a redistributive justice (Gale 2000, 255). This involves the shifting of resources so that students have opportunities for equitable access and participation in schooling (Fraser 1997). In the case of literacy learning, those who are underachieving might be provided with remedial instruction or intervention programmes. Indeed, these compensatory efforts to 'reform the children' seem to make sense when 'the source of the trouble is seen to lie outside of the parameters of "schooling as usual"' (Alloway and Gilbert 1998, 254). A problem with such approaches is that school processes are left unquestioned.

Currently, Australian schools are under enormous pressure to improve student outcomes on national literacy tests (Woods 2012). Although many Australian students are achieving well on these tests and there has been an ongoing focus on equity issues in policy and practice, it seems that 'our poorest and most disadvantaged children are being left behind' (Henderson and Woods 2012, 113). As Comber (2007) explained, the effects of schooling can be differential and this suggests that further investigation is warranted as a way of understanding how inequities and inequalities are established and sustained. We need to understand the 'how' before we look for ways of ensuring equitable outcomes. According to Woods (2012, 191), this task is both necessary and important, 'teaching in socially-just ways to produce a quality and equitable literacy programme has never been more difficult—or more vital'.

THE STUDY AND ITS CONTEXT

This section returns to data that were collected as part of a larger study that investigated the literacy learning of itinerant farmworkers' children. The study was conducted in a primary school located in a rural community in the north-east of Australia. The community was surrounded by a farming area which attracted a large itinerant workforce during the winter harvesting season. At that time of the year, up to sixty children who accompanied their farmworker parents to the town were enrolled at the school. This influx of students impacted on the school in a variety of ways; it often meant that classes had to be rearranged and that extra staff and teachers were required. Additionally, there was a noticeable change to the ethnicities that were evident in the student population.

Because the focus of the original study related to itinerant children enrolled at one school, access to children and their families was obtained through the school itself. The school's principal acted as the gatekeeper. Because itinerant children were identified as generally having low academic achievement, the principal was keen for research that would assist understandings about the itinerant population that arrived in the community for the harvesting season of each year. In particular, he hoped that the research would feed into the school's attempts to enhance achievement levels.

The study used ethnographic techniques for data collection and required extended periods of time in the school for observations and conducting interviews. As described elsewhere (e.g. Henderson 2008b), ethical considerations were ongoing throughout the study. Of particular concern were issues around maintaining confidentiality and anonymity in a single research site, and the difficulties of writing polyvocal (re)presentations of data, especially when stories from teachers and itinerant families were often very different. My concern was that 'I was responsible for the re(construction) of "reality" . . . and therein lay ethical concerns' about how to represent such diverse and sometimes conflicting stories (Henderson 2008b, 219). However, because the study did not set out to evaluate school practices, it was possible to keep the focus on discursive constructions and how particular constructions occurred in particular contexts. This approach, as is evident in this chapter, enabled an examination of commonsense assumptions and how they are taken up in particular contexts, in this case the school.

The school's population was diverse and the school was known for its willingness to recognise this diversity. Indeed, approximately 20 per cent of the school's students identified as Indigenous students and every morning three flags were raised: the Australian, Aboriginal and Torres Strait Island flags. As farmworker families arrived in the town for the winter harvesting season, children of Turkish, Tongan, Samoan and Korean backgrounds, along with children from White ethnic backgrounds, joined the school. Between 70 and 80 per cent of the itinerant farmworkers' children were learning English as an additional language. There was no doubt that the children's arrival increased the cultural and linguistic diversity of the school's student population. Some of these children were 'regulars' who returned to the school in the winter of each year; some children came from families who mixed periods of itinerancy with intervening periods of residential stability and had attended the school sometime in the past; others had enrolled for the first time in this location.

In thinking about issues of equity and how they relate to literacy teaching, this chapter revisits teachers' discursive constructions of itinerant children and, in particular, identifies interviews where teachers discussed children's ethnicity. This enables an exploration of how teachers talked about particular children they taught and how the points of reference that they used could represent children in particular ways. A specific interest is the way that itinerancy and ethnicity intersect with gender and social class in the teachers' stories. If teachers are to provide quality literacy teaching, then we need to know how their representations of children enable and constrain particular ways of teaching, to begin a process of thinking about how teachers might best work towards a socially just pedagogy. As Woods (2012) highlighted, it is important that teachers provide both high-quality and high-equity teaching practice in classrooms: high quality in relation to students' achievement levels, and high equity in terms of ensuring that all students have fair and equitable opportunities to reach their potential.

THE REANALYSIS OF DATA

To begin this process, the data from the previous research were reviewed. The review searched for sections of the teachers' interview data that told a story of ongoing or past events (Bamberg and Georgakopoulou 2008) and included some consideration of the children's ethnicity. It is widely recognised that people tell stories to represent the world, to explain their experiences and to position themselves in relation to others. When stories are collected as data, they provide evidence of how people have constructed their own versions of 'meaningful selves, identities, and realities' and have made 'sense of personal experiences' (Chase 2011, 422). From the data were identified what could be called three small stories (Bamberg 2006) that had been told by teachers about itinerant children. These stories—Narratives 1, 2 and 3—provided a small data set that could be reanalysed.

The reanalysis of the three narratives is framed within cultural-critical understandings of literacy and has as its starting point the text-interaction-context model from Fairclough's (2001) critical discourse analysis approach. This model interweaves social, discourse and linguistic theories and highlights the way that language use is a form of social practice. The analysis of the selected narratives, then, can investigate both the linguistic and the social, as well as the relationship between individuals and social structures.

This seems particularly relevant to understanding school literacy learning and its valorisation of particular practices.

One aspect of the teachers' narratives noted for particular exploration was the interaction of ethnicity, social class, gender and itinerancy as points of reference. It seemed that issues of social class and gender might be of interest to teachers, as farmworkers do manual labour and many people in the community surrounding the school seemed to regard farmwork as a masculine occupation. Additionally, the interrelationship or intersectionality of ethnicity, social class and gender has been a particular topic of discussion in feminist literature since the work of Crenshaw (1991) and draws attention to 'the simultaneous and interacting effects' of these as 'categories of difference' (Hancock 2007, 63).

Intersectionality provides a useful concept for examining and thinking about teachers' representations of itinerant farmworkers' children and the complexity of those representations. McCall (2005, 1771) identified the utility of intersectionality in women's studies as a way of overcoming 'the limitations of gender as a single analytical category' and recognising 'the relationships among multiple dimensions and modalities of social relations and subject formations'. In light of McCall's argument that there has been little discussion in the literature about methodological approaches appropriate for studying intersectionality, critical discourse analysis is presented here as a way of examining the complexity of social life and identifying the discourses that teachers' use in their descriptions and constructions of particular children.

Although the data used here are limited—only three small stories out of a much larger data set—the aim is to indicate the points of reference used by teachers as they discursively constructed itinerant children as literacy learners. It is important to note that most of the teachers in the school were female and the school staff did not have the ethnic diversity of the students who were enrolled. Indeed, the teachers were representative of the White middle class, and these characteristics are likely to have an influence on the narratives they told about the itinerant children. Additionally, such characteristics are likely to have a 'normative sense' about them and they can therefore remain 'largely unexamined by those whose lived experiences are centred within this space' (Allard and Santoro 2006, 124).

In the sections that follow, the three teachers' narratives are presented, along with analyses that identify how the teachers discursively constructed itinerant children they taught. The intersectionality of the teachers' points of reference is of particular interest.

Narrative 1: A Boy Who Mightn't Read at Home

Narrative 1 comes from an interview with a male teacher who talked about Mustafa (pseudonym), a student who identified himself as Turkish.

Well he [Mustafa] mightn't be exposed to much written material at home, might spend a bit of time in front of the box instead of reading. His parents mightn't supply him with any reading books. His only reading might be at school, so that would slow him down. It might mean that his parents aren't helping him choose books in English. If they're not shooting down to the library to get books themselves, because there's probably not many Turkish books in the library here, and also, because they're itinerant, I imagine what they bring is what they can fit in the car. So you don't bring your library, if you fill one up. So yeah, perhaps there's limited books at home, maybe two or three books period, the Turkish bible or whatever, so that could be it. And then, you know, like so many kids, I think he's into computer games and TV and stuff like that, not reading.

The teacher's narrative highlights the possibility that Mustafa is a boy who might not read at home. Mustafa's ethnicity is named throughout the story as 'Turkish' with mention of 'Turkish books' and 'the Turkish Bible'. However, Mustafa's family is also described in terms of what the teacher thinks it is not doing; in particular, the teacher suggests that the family is not 'helping him choose books in English'. In doing this, the teacher taps into a normative understanding of what parents should be doing for their children. He seems to be suggesting that the parents should be behaving as White middle-class parents do. In other words, acceptable behaviours include reading in English, owning books or borrowing books from a library and privileging book reading over television and computer games. This implies a distinction between Mustafa's parents and other parents, and suggests that Mustafa's parents were 'bad' parents who did not care about their son's education.

The teacher's description of Mustafa's family is also couched in negatives: 'mightn't be exposed to much written material at home', 'mightn't supply him with any reading books' and '[perhaps there's limited books at home'. Whereas many of the teacher's comments are speculations, as indicated by the use of the words *mightn't* and *perhaps*, they suggest that the teacher's points of reference include both cultural practices and linguistic characteristics. The teacher implies that there are differences between Mustafa's family and other families and that these are constraining his success at school. Yet, the teacher also suggests that Mustafa is like 'many kids', because he seems to like 'computer games and TV and stuff like that'. In the teacher's description, Mustafa has been categorised as being a member of a particular ethnicity, but that membership seems to intersect with his being a 'kid'.

Although this is but one small story from the teacher's interview where he talked about itinerant children in his class, it appears that he drew on multiple points of reference and that at times he made what might be construed as contradictory statements about Mustafa's similarity or otherwise to other children in the class. The narrative suggests that Mustafa and his family need to take on the behaviours of White middle-class families, with their Turkish ethnicity being different from what was considered 'normal'.

The teacher also referred to the family's itinerant lifestyle when he said that 'because they're itinerant, I imagine what they bring is what they can fit in the car'. Overall, what seems to be evident is that Mustafa's literacy difficulties in the classroom can be attributed to his family, their ethnicity and their non-residentially stable lifestyle, along with the fact that Mustafa is a 'kid' and likes activities other than reading. According to the teacher, the family is deficient. It is assumed that the family does not have printed materials in the home, does not carry books in the car and does not help Mustafa to choose books in English to read. It is also suggested that he is allowed to watch too much television and to play too many computer games. Mustafa's perceived differences from children and families regarded as mainstream are regarded as significant.

The analysis of Narrative 1 suggests that the teacher drew on discourses about ethnicity and itinerancy, moving from one point of reference to another in his story of blaming Mustafa's parents for what they did 'not do' for their child and his education. It was clear that the discursive construction of Mustafa and his family relied on intersecting characteristics.

Narrative 2: Boys at the Lower End of the Scale

Narrative 2 is a small story told by a female teacher who had several itinerant farmworkers' children enrolled in her class. The teacher's story refers particularly to Zafer (pseudonym), a student who identified as Turkish, and Sepi (pseudonym), a student whose parents were Tongan.

> They're at the lower end of the class scale, but they're not the bottom. You'd expect them, second language, talking another language at home, then coming to school, but they're not the bottom . . . The moving around has to influence, and the coming across states, has to influence, because we don't have the same standard in each state. They come to school regularly. I don't know if that's the same down south. But up here they rarely have any days at home. So both, I assume that their parents see education as important, which puts them one step above some of the others in the class . . . They both want to do well. They both want to please, probably more so Sepi than Zafer. But both want to do well. They have all the right attitudes to help them with learning. They're not sitting saying I've missed the boat. I've never heard them say, 'it's too hard or I can't do it'. They're not sitting there waiting for you to come. Maybe that's because they have had so much moving from a young age, so that every time they come in, they find it so much easier to survive. I think Zafer is much more reluctant, probably because of nationality, with their view on female teachers or on females, yeah, having a female teacher. And Zafer doesn't want to be seen as having difficulty. Even when you ask him, 'are

you alright, are you having a problem there?' He says he's 'fine', whereas you'd ask Sepi if he's having a problem, and he looks at you and says 'yes'. Can you just, just giving him that prompting. It's hard, it could be just personality or it could be cultural.

The teacher emphasised that both Zafer and Sepi were 'at the lower end of the class scale' in terms of their academic achievement in literacy learning, but she stressed that they were 'not the bottom' in her class. She did not fully articulate her academic expectations about the two boys, but she implied that their second language learner status would influence their achievement levels and that they were doing better than she would have expected. Many of her comments are positive, identifying the boys' 'right attitude' towards learning.

Towards the end of the small story, the teacher commented on a difference between Sepi and Zafer. She has noticed that Zafer 'doesn't want to be seen as having difficulty', whereas Sepi does not seem to be concerned by this. She conjectures some possible explanations: 'it could be just personality, or it could be cultural'. This follows statements that grouped the two boys into the one category of 'second language' learners, and it suggests that one attribute alone did not provide a point of reference for the teacher.

Instead, the teacher moves across a range of points of reference. She highlights Zafer as being a 'much more reluctant' learner with a clear link to his nationality (Turkish) and 'their view on female teachers and females'. It appears that ethnicity—in this case, called 'nationality', even though Zafer was born in Australia—intersects with gender in the teacher's discussion. Although there is little elaboration of this point, the teacher seems to consider gender—a male student 'having a female teacher'—to be an important influence on Zafer's behaviour.

The teacher also identifies itinerancy as a point of reference in relation to the boys' schooling. This is stated in a matter-of-fact way: 'moving around has to influence, and the coming across states has to influence'. The teacher returns to itinerancy later in the story and suggests that moving regularly—'they have had so much moving from a young age'—might have built characteristics that helped them integrate into new classrooms. For example, she highlights that both want to do well and are capable of seeking assistance from others. It is evident that the teacher moves between several points of reference, weaving explanations about the boys' literacy learning as being linked to ethnicity, gender and itinerancy. As with Narrative 1, the intersectionality of these characteristics informed the teacher's construction of the itinerant children.

Narrative 3: The ESL Teacher's Small Story about Rough and Tumble Boys

Narrative 3 was told by the school's English as a Second Language (ESL) teacher, who was female. She provided individual language instruction for many of the itinerant students.

We find that a lot of the Samoan and Tongan boys are very aggressive in the playground . . . I talked to [the deputy principal] and he said even the older boys [in a particular family] have terrible aggression levels and after school they fight kids in the playground. And the two young boys are the same. In their culture, I think, I don't know how to put it, they're not defensive, but in their personalities they're aggressive. I think it's part of their communication as well . . . The boys have this aura of rough and tough. They seem to ooze that, whereas the girls don't . . . I think they're fairly rough and tumbly in the playground. [Student's name] is really over the top.

The ESL teacher's story focuses almost exclusively on Tongan and Samoan boys. Although the conversation establishes her understanding about the role of ethnicity, she identifies what she regards as a clear difference between Tongan and Samoan boys and their female counterparts. The teacher describes the boys as 'aggressive' and 'rough and tumbly', but she does not see those characteristics in the girls. Thus, ethnicity and gender are linked, with the teacher's description indicating that boys of a particular ethnicity—Tongan and Samoan—are behaving differently from girls of 'their culture'.

When referring to the children's ethnicity, the teacher looks towards both cultural and linguistic attributes as evidence of the students' differences from other children in the school. In particular, she identified the children's physicality of 'rough and tumbly' aggressive behaviours as evident in their actions as well as their communication with other students and staff. Her descriptions worked to 'other' the Samoan and Tongan boys from the rest of the school population. They were described as being different and not fitting the normative view of how school students should behave.

In naming the boys and including the 'two young boys', the teacher refers to gender differences. However, her description of the girls is a simple statement saying that 'the girls don't'. Nevertheless, those few words set up a binary between the boys and the girls. In particular, the binary is between boys and girls who identify as Tongan or Samoan, although the narrative implies that there is also a binary between Samoan and Tongan boys and all girls in the school.

A legitimacy is given to the story through the link to a conversation with the school's deputy principal. This seems to enable the teacher's construction of some Samoan and Tongan boys to be generalised to the whole group. The generalisation is evident in the way the teacher names 'a lot of the Samoan and Tongan boys', 'their culture' and 'part of their communication'. In this way, the Samoan and Tongan boys are established as not fitting the expected behaviour of school students and they are confirmed as different from all other students within the school.

The teacher's narrative draws on discourses that relate to gender and ethnicity. As the analysis shows, the intersectionality is important to defining the Samoan and Tongan boys as different from Samoan and Tongan girls, as well as different from the school population more generally. One point of reference alone does not explain the teacher's narrative. Indeed, the interweaving of the two points of reference illustrates the need to analyse the complexity of such stories of blame. As with Narratives 1 and 2, this narrative demonstrates the interweaving points of reference, the complexity of social lives and the nuanced meanings that result.

READING ACROSS THE NARRATIVES

Although only three small narratives were examined, it was evident in the analysis that teachers used points of reference that included much more than the children's ethnicity. In particular, the narratives indicated intersections of ethnicity, gender and itinerancy. When considered within the context of the larger study from which the narratives were drawn, the teachers' stories set these particular children apart from the mainstream population of the school. The students were identified as 'different' from the White ethnic and Indigenous students; they were itinerant rather than residentially stable, and in some cases specific gender characteristics also highlighted them as 'different'.

It was evident that teachers did not rely on one category of difference alone in their descriptions. A complex intersectionality of a range of categories—ethnicity, gender and itinerancy—provided the foundations for the teachers' narratives. Whereas it was clear that teachers referred explicitly to aspects of ethnicity, gender and itinerancy, it seemed that they may also have been linking to characteristics that related to economic status and social class. Although not named in a direct or explicit way, teachers' assumptions about the effects of occupation, lifestyle, perceived low incomes and limited family resources may represent references to economic status and social class.

In drawing on multiple points of reference, some directly and others indirectly, the teachers' discursive constructions are complex. Narratives 1 and 3 were predominantly negative, setting up narratives of blame, where a family or particular ethnic group was blamed for not providing appropriate educational support or for encouraging particular behavioural characteristics that were deemed inappropriate in the school context. In contrast, Narrative 2 presented a more favourable description of two itinerant students. However, despite the positives in this story—that Zafer and Sepi wanted to achieve academically and that their parents appeared to support education—they were described as low achievers. Their second language status and their itinerancy seemed to be regarded as taken-for-granted reasons for underachievement in literacy learning.

All three narratives suggest that the teachers had low expectations of the students' academic abilities. The teachers implied that low literacy results at school were predictable consequences of an itinerant lifestyle and of other factors related to the children's circumstances, including ethnicity and the attendant cultural and language backgrounds. These stories had become 'the truth' about itinerant students who attended the school and their underachievement had been normalised. In all three stories, teachers linked to factors which were seen to lie outside of the school's control—parents, culture and lifestyle.

However, these discursive constructions of itinerant farmworkers' children and their families as deficient did not stand alone. They were reminiscent of the negative stories about farmworkers that were circulating in the community that surrounded the school, as identified in the data from the larger study, and to a certain extent they acknowledge historical accounts of mobile peoples who have been ostracised and even persecuted (e.g. Frankham 1994; Staines 1999). They are also reminiscent of stories about low socio-economic families that have been reported in other educational research (e.g. Carrington and Luke 2003; Hamilton and Pitt 2009; Hicks 2002; Lewis 2001). The effect of these stories was to construct itinerant children and their families as different and outside what is considered mainstream.

WORKING TOWARDS EDUCATIONAL EQUALITY

If we are serious about ensuring educational equality and equitable outcomes for all students, then the analysis of this very limited data set provides food for thought. The teachers' narratives demonstrated the complex ways that the itinerant students were constructed as literacy learners. Itinerancy, cultural backgrounds, linguistic backgrounds and gender all provided direct points of reference for the teachers' explanations. It was evident that students and parents who were culturally and linguistically different—those whose languages, customs and religions were dissimilar from hegemonic practices—were blamed for not fitting perceived social norms. It also seemed that economic status and social class were also woven into the teachers' narratives, even though references to these characteristics were less explicit.

The deficit stories demonstrated taken-for-granted understandings that the itinerant children's lack of achievement in literacy learning was a commonsense result of their backgrounds and lifestyles. The cultural and linguistic diversity of the children and their experiences of moving from location to location were not identified by the teachers as starting points for the children's learning at school, nor were they seen as resources that could benefit the literacy learning of other children. Indeed, it appeared that the narrow focus of the stories meant that other characteristics of the children were rendered invisible. The children were conceptualised in terms of what they could not do and their strengths—which included their bilingualism and specific knowledges of their home languages, experiences of travelling across states and moving in and out of schools—had become irrelevant in the school context.

In other words, the teachers' discursive constructions of the children constrained other ways of thinking and seemed to prevent them from thinking about a socially just pedagogy for literacy learning. There was certainly evidence in the other data that were collected that one consequence of these representations of the children was a narrowing of teachers' pedagogical approaches. Because the students were understood to be 'deficient', then teachers drew on remedial or 'top-up' approaches to learning, with the aim of 'fixing' problems located in individual children.

If schools are serious about equity issues, then it is important to find ways of overcoming what Gutiérrez, Morales and Martinez (2009, 238) called 'the default scripts of risk, difference and deficiency'. However, this is not about moving blame from children and families to teachers. It is about rethinking the defaults that are normalised within our society, as evidenced by the discourses circulating in schools and those circulating in the broader community and the media. And it is not suggested for one moment that this is easy to do. As Henderson and Woods (2012, 123) noted, 'this is a difficult task, especially for teachers as they engage in the day-to-day, minute-by minute business of doing school'. Yet, change is necessary if we are to have any chance of ensuring that students' outcomes are both high quality and high equity.

One recommendation is that we need to think about a re-conceptualisation of itinerancy in relation to literacy learning. We need to know much more about the lived experiences of being itinerant and about the diversity of those experiences. This should help to move us away from stereotypical understandings of itinerancy as 'an unfortunate "problem" that must be "solved" or "escaped"' (Danaher and Danaher 2000, 28). A re-conceptualisation would require school personnel to address the difficult issue of how taken-for-granted school practices might change in light of the experiences of itinerant families. As Hicks (2002, 152) pointed out, a re-conceptualisation like this requires 'a moral shift, a willingness to open oneself up to the possibility of *seeing* those who differ from us' and this is 'very hard work'. To contest deficit assumptions and to construct a different school culture requires strong professional learning communities. It also relies on strong school leadership and teachers' willingness to take on intellectually challenging work that is likely to be long-term (Alloway and Gilbert 1998; Comber and Kamler 2004, 2005; Henderson and Woods 2012; Luke 2003).

Some strategies for beginning this change have been identified elsewhere (see Comber and Kamler 2004, 2005; Henderson 2004; Henderson and Woods 2012). Recommendations include widening our view of children to include a broad range of contexts where children learn literacies, including home, communities and schools; avoiding deficit discourses and looking for positive ways of discursively constructing literacy learners; questioning assumptions about students and families; identifying students' strengths;

and forming partnerships with students, their families and communities (see Henderson and Woods 2012, 123–127).

These possibilities for transformative action would help to disrupt deficit views and assist teachers to focus on pedagogies that would be responsive, flexible and enabling. Approaches that build on students' strengths and 'turn around' deficit discourses (Comber and Kamler 2004, 2005) can offer more options for encouraging learning and are likely to be more productive (Gutiérrez, Morales and Martinez 2009; Henderson 2007; Henderson and Woods 2012; Janks 2005). It is through this type of work that we are likely to have some chance of ensuring that our pedagogies will work for students who are currently marginalised in school settings.

CONCLUSION

As has been demonstrated in this chapter, critical discourse analysis proved useful for examining the teachers' representations of itinerant farmworkers' children and showing that teachers shifted across a range of discourses. In revealing the multiple points of reference used by teachers and highlighting the intersectionality in teachers' discursive constructions of the children as literacy learners, the approach fore-grounded complexity and the 'interacting effects' of several 'categories of difference' (Hancock 2007, 63). This chapter, then, has responded to McCall's (2005) call to build knowledge about methodologies suitable for studying intersectionality.

However, it also seems that the notion of intersectionality might be useful for helping us to think beyond what Ladson-Billings (2012, 118) referred to as 'crude measures to sort and slot people into categories'. The data presented in this chapter showed how the teachers' discursive constructions drew on ethnicity, gender, social class and itinerancy and possibly linked to economic status and social class. A focus on multiple categories and their intersections provides a starting point for unpacking the discursive connections that construct students as deficit and for moving beyond deficit discourses.

REFERENCES

Allard, Andrea C., and Ninetta Santoro. 2006. 'Troubling Identities: Teacher Education Students' Constructions of Class and Ethnicity'. *Cambridge Journal of Education* 36 (1): 115–129.

Alloway, Nola, and Pam Gilbert. 1998. 'Reading Literacy Test Data: Benchmarking Success?' *Australian Journal of Language and Literacy* 21 (3): 249–261.

Australian Curriculum, Assessment and Reporting Authority. 2011. *My School*. Accessed October 16, 2012. http://www.myschool.edu.au/.

———. 2010. *NAPLAN: National Assessment Program Literacy and Numeracy*. Accessed May 20, 2012. http://www.naplan.edu.au/.

Bamberg, Michael. 2006. 'Biographic-Narrative Research, *Quo Vadis*? A Critical Review of "Big Stories" from the Perspective of "Small Stories"'. In *Narrative,*

Memory and Knowledge: Representations, Aesthetics and Contexts, edited by K. Milnes, C. Horrocks, N. Kelly, B. Roberts and D. Robinson, 63–79. Huddersfield: University of Huddersfield Press.

Bamberg, Michael, and Alexandra Georgakopoulou. 2008. 'Small Stories as a New Perspective in Narrative and Identity?' *Text and Talk* 28:377–396.

Bhopal, Raj. 2004. 'Glossary of Terms Relating to Ethnicity and Race: For Reflection and Debate'. *Journal of Epidemiology and Community Health* 58 (6): 441–445.

Carrington, Vicki, and Allan Luke. 2003. 'Reading, Homes, and Families: From Postmodern to Modern?' In *On Reading Books to Children, Parents and Teachers*, edited by Anne van Kleeck, Steven A. Stahl and Eurydice. B. Bauer, 231–252. Mahwah, NJ: Lawrence Erlbaum Associates.

Chase, Susan E. 2011. 'Narrative Inquiry: Still a Field in the Making'. In *The Sage Handbook of Qualitative Research*, 4th ed., edited by Norman K. Denzin and Yvonna S. Lincoln, 415–434. Thousand Oaks, CA: Sage.

Comber, Barbara. 2007. 'The Work of Women Teachers in Primary Literacy Education: Knowing and Doing'. *English in Australia* 41 (2): 7–26.

Comber, Barbara, and Barbara Kamler. 2004. 'Getting out of Deficit: Pedagogies of Reconnection'. *Teaching Education* 15 (3): 293–310.

———, eds. 2005. *Turn-Around Pedagogies: Literacy Interventions for At-Risk Students*. Newtown, NSW: Primary English Teaching Association.

Crenshaw, Kimberle. 1991. 'Mapping the Margins: Intersectionality, Identity Politics, and Violence against Women of Color'. *Stanford Law Review* 43 (6): 1241–1299.

Danaher, Patrick Alan, and Geoffrey Radcliffe Danaher. 2000. 'Flight, Enmeshment, Circus and Australian Youth: From Itinerancy as Educational Deficits to Floating Signifiers'. *Youth Studies Australia* 19 (1): 26–30.

Fairclough, Norman. 2001. *Language and Power*. 2nd ed. London: Longman.

Frankham, Eli. 1994. 'The Persecution of Travellers'. Paper read at Land, People and Freedom Conference, Peterborough. Accessed March 3, 2005. http://www.geocities.com/Paris/5121/travellers.htm.

Fraser, Nancy. 1997. *Justice Interruptus: Critical Reflections on the 'Postsocialist' Condition*. New York: Routledge.

Freebody, Peter. 2007. *Literacy Education in School: Research Perspectives from the Past, for the Future*. Camberwell: Australian Council for Educational Research.

Gale, Trevor. 2000. 'Rethinking Social Justice in Schools: How Will We Recognize It When We See It?' *International Journal of Inclusive Education* 4 (3): 253–269.

Gilbert, Pam. 2000. 'The Deepening Divide?: Choices for Australian Education'. Professorial inaugural address, Southbank Convention Centre, Townsville, March 22.

Gonzales, Norma, Luis C. Moll and Cathy Amanti, eds. 2005. *Funds of Knowledge: Theorizing Practices in Households, Communities, and Classrooms*. New York: Routledge.

Gregory, Eve, and Ann Williams. 2000. *City Literacies: Learning to Read across Generations and Cultures*. London: Routledge.

Gutiérrez, Kris D., P. Zitlali Morales and Danny C. Martinez. 2009. 'Re-Mediating Literacy: Culture, Difference, and Learning for Students from Nondominant Communities'. *Review of Research in Education* 33:212–245.

Hamilton, Mary, and Kathy Pitt. 2009. 'Changing Policy Discourses: Constructing Literacy Inequalities'. Paper presented at the *Conference on Literacy Inequalities, East Anglia University, Norwich, UK, September*. Accessed October 4, 2012. http://www.uea.ac.uk/polopoly_fs/1.140653!HamiltonandPitt_UEA%20Conference.pdf.

Hancock, Ange-Marie. 2007. 'When Multiplication Doesn't Equal Quick Addition: Examining Intersectionality as a Research Paradigm'. *Perspectives on Politics* 5 (1): 63–79.

Hanson, Jayde, and Martin Bell. 2007. 'Harvest Trails in Australia: Patterns of Seasonal Migration in the Fruit and Vegetable Industry'. *Journal of Rural Studies* 23 (1): 101–117.

Harris, Fleur. 2008. 'Critical Engagement with the Historical and Contemporary Deficit Construction of Maori Children'. *Critical Literacy: Theories and Practice* 2 (1): 43–59.

Heath, Shirley Brice. 1983. *Ways with Words: Language, Life, and Work in Communities and Classrooms*. Cambridge: Cambridge University Press.

Henderson, Robyn. 2001. 'Student Mobility: Moving beyond Deficit Views'. *Australian Journal of Guidance and Counselling* 11 (1): 121–129.

———. 2004. 'Recognising Difference: One of the Challenges of Using a Multiliteracies Approach?' *Practically Primary* 9 (2): 11–14.

———. 2005. 'The Social and Discursive Construction of Itinerant Farm Workers' Children as Literacy Learners'. Doctoral thesis, James Cook University, Townsville, North Queensland.

———. 2007. 'Looking at Learners: Making Sense of Observations'. *Literacy Learning: The Middle Years* 15 (1): 43–48.

———. 2008a. 'A Boy Behaving Badly: Investigating Teachers' Assumptions about Gender, Behaviour, Mobility and Literacy Learning'. *Australian Journal of Language and Literacy*, 31 (1): 74–87.

———. 2008b. 'Dangerous Terrains: Negotiating Ethical Dilemmas'. In *Troubling Terrains: Tactics for Traversing and Transforming Contemporary Educational Research*, edited by Robyn Henderson and Patrick Alan Danaher, 211–222. Teneriffe, Qld: Post Pressed.

———. 2009. 'Itinerant Farm Workers' Children in Australia: Learning from the Experiences of One Family'. In *Traveller, Nomadic and Migrant Education*, edited by Patrick Alan Danaher, Mairin Kenny and Judith Remy Leder, 47–58. New York: Routledge.

———. 2012. 'Teaching Literacies: Principles and Practices'. In *Teaching Literacies in the Middle Years: Pedagogies and Diversity*, edited by Robyn Henderson, 3–17 South Melbourne: Oxford University Press.

Henderson, Robyn, and Annette Woods. 2012. 'Teaching for Quality and Equity: (Re)focusing the Lens to make Diversity and Difference Visible'. In *Teaching Literacies in the Middle Years: Pedagogies and Diversity*, edited by Robyn Henderson, 113–131. South Melbourne: Oxford University Press.

Hicks, Deborah. 2002. *Reading Lives: Working-Class Children and Literacy Learning*. New York: Teachers College Press.

Honan, Eileen. 2006. 'Deficit Discourses within the Digital Divide'. *English in Australia* 41 (3): 36–43.

Janks, Hilary. 2005. 'Deconstruction and Reconstruction: Diversity as a Productive Resource'. *Discourse: Studies in the Cultural Politics of Education* 26 (1): 31–43.

Kalantzis, Mary, Bill Cope and the Learning by Design Project Group. 2005. *Learning by Design*. Melbourne: Victorian Schools Innovation Commission and Common Ground Publishing.

Kamler, Barbara, and Barbara Comber. 2005. 'Designing Turn-Around Pedagogies and Contesting Deficit Assumptions'. In *Turn-Around Pedagogies: Literacy Interventions for At-Risk Students*, edited by Barbara Comber and Barbara Kamler, 1–14. Newtown, NSW: Primary English Teaching Association.

Ladson-Billings, Gloria. 2012. 'Through a Glass Darkly: The Persistence of Race in Education Research and Scholarship'. *Educational Researcher* 41 (4): 115–120.

Lewis, Cynthia. 2001. *Literary Practices as Social Acts: Power, Status and Cultural Norms in the Classroom*. Mahwah, NJ: Lawrence Erlbaum Associates.

Luke, Allan. 2003. 'Making Literacy Policy and Practice with a Difference'. *Australian Journal of Language and Literacy* 26 (3): 58–82.

Lynch School of Education, Boston College. 2010. *TIMSS and PIRLS*. Accessed October 4, 2012. http://timss.bc.edu/.

Makin, Laurie. 2007. 'Surveying the Landscape'. In *Literacies in Childhood: Changing Views, Challenging Practice*, 2nd ed., edited by Laurie Makin, Criss Jones Diaz and Claire McLachlan, 3–14. Sydney: MacLennan and Petty.

Mares, Peter. 2005. 'Seasonal Migrant Labour: A Boon for Australian Country Towns?' Paper presented at the 2nd Future of Australia's Country Towns Conference, Bendigo, Vic., July 11–13.

McCall, Leslie. 2005. 'The Complexity of Intersectionality'. *Signs: Journal of Women in Culture and Society* 30 (3): 1771–1800.

Missingham, Bruce, Jacqui Dibden and Chris Cocklin. 2006. 'A Multicultural Countryside? Ethnic Minorities in Rural Australia'. *Rural Society* 16 (2): 131–149.

National Harvest Trail Working Group. 2000. *Harvesting Australia: Report of the National Harvest Trail Working Group*. Canberra: Department of Employment, Workplace Relations and Small Business.

Organisation for Economic Co-operation and Development. n.d. *Programme for International Student Assessment (PISA)*. Accessed October 4, 2012. http://www.pisa.oecd.org/.

Purcell-Gates, Victoria, ed. 2008. *Cultural Practices of Literacy: Case Studies of Language, Literacy, Social Practice, and Power*. New York: Routledge.

Santoro, Ninetta. 2007. '"Outsiders" and "Others": "Different" Teachers Teaching in Culturally Diverse Classrooms'. *Teachers and Teaching: Theory and Practice* 13 (1): 81–97.

Staines, Steve. 1999. *Travellers and the Built Environment*. Accessed June 6, 2011. http://mondodesigno.com/travel.html.

Thomson, Pat. 2002. *Schooling the Rustbelt Kids: Making the Difference in Changing Times*. Crows Nest, NSW: Allen and Unwin.

Tsolidis, Georgina. 2001. *Schooling, Diaspora and Gender: Being Feminist and Being Different*. Buckingham: Open University Press.

Whitehouse, Marianne, and Carolyn Colvin. 2001. '"Reading" Families: Deficit Discourse and Family Literacy'. *Theory into Practice* 40 (3): 212–219.

Woods, Annette. 2012. 'What Could Socially-Just Literacy Instruction Look Like?' In *Teaching Literacies in the Middle Years: Pedagogies and Diversity*, edited by Robyn Henderson, 190–207. South Melbourne: Oxford University Press.

Part II

Understanding Difference

Policy and Practice in Education

6 Negotiating Achievement
Students' Gendered and Classed Constructions of Un(Equal) Ability

Anne-Sofie Nyström

INTRODUCTION

Educational institutions are structured around achievement: improving, evaluating and comparing students' achievements (Covington 1998). However, such stratification processes are not just about cognition but about emotion and social processes and about negotiations of values and causes of achievements (Lynch and Baker 2005; Sadovnik and Semel 2010). Along with parents and teachers, peers are important inter-actors who facilitate both academic 'success' and 'failure', for example, via group cohesion and peer influence (Jackson 2003, 2006; Kelly 2009; Hattie 2009).

Previous research on the sociology of education and pedagogy has primarily examined subordinated groups and processes of oppression (Delamont 2000; Ball 2003; Archer 2011). However, as Pease (2010) underlines, this is not sufficient to understand processes of dominance and inequality. It is equally vital to study how privilege is constituted and maintained, that is, by processes of normalisation and naturalisation. An analysis of identity negotiation among privileged students identified as 'ideal students' could therefore be seen as complementary to research on 'risk groups' or subordinated students, such as working-class or minority ethnic students (Delamont 2000; Lynch and Lodge 2002; Ball 2003; Archer 2011).

The aim of this chapter is to examine privileged young peoples' gendered and classed constructions of achievement and ability. The analysis draws from an actor-oriented study of two upper-secondary-school classes in Sweden (Nyström 2012a). Like other Nordic countries, Sweden has long been associated with equality—not least in education. Many statistics now point to a negative change in respect to equality in education both over time, and compared with other countries: 'Sweden is one of the few countries where both average scores and equity in the system have decreased' (Skolverket 2010, 10). Although gender stratification has been more of a focus for national policy debates, increased inequalities are primarily concerned with school and student categories in terms of class (intersecting with 'race'). This relative decline is not primarily due to other countries catching up. The main reason is that the level of equality in Sweden has declined during this period. Not only has the gap between high- and low-performing students increased, but differences between high- and low-performing schools have also increased, and the socio-economic background of students has become more important.[1] The main focus of the analysis presented in this chapter is a group of White upper-middle-class young men and the question of how their identity as 'superior' or 'bright' was negotiated via peer group interactions.

DISRUPTING THE LINKAGE BETWEEN ABILITY AND ACHIEVEMENT

In the social psychology classic *Pygmalion in the Classroom* (Rosenthal and Jacobson 1992), it was concluded that students' educational achievement was significantly related to teachers' expectations. Students who were 'falsely' categorised by the teachers as cognitively gifted improved their academic results, whereas the trend was reversed in cases where students were labelled as less intelligent. A UNESCO (2008, 82) report, *Education for All by 2015*, argued that 'once they have access to school, girls tend to do better than boys'.[2] Taking this into account we might expect that male students would be perceived as less able, but, on the contrary, teachers and students are more likely to associate 'great potential' or 'being gifted' with boys (Jones and Myhill 2004; Wernersson 2006; Barnes 2011). In the policy debates on 'underachieving boys' it is noticeable that boys' shortcomings have been primarily interpreted as due to lack of effort, not to their intrinsic cognitive capacity, although explanations for this differ (Epstein et al. 1998; Walkerdine 1998; Foster, Kimmel and Skelton 2001; Lahelma 2005; Younger and Warrington 2007; Kimmel 2010). Consistent with Plewis's (1991) conceptual inquiry, 'young men' as a social category are in most parts of the world *structurally underachieving* in school,[3] although we can assume they have a better chance than young women of being perceived as *individually underachieving*, that is, they have greater individual potential than their academic accomplishments show.

Ability, Achievement and Identity

Education-relevant abilities can be studied from various perspectives, but from the approach of social identity theory that Jenkins (1998, 2004) sets out, cognitive ability (intelligence or educational potential) is seen as something to be accomplished in interaction. It is teachers or peers that identify an individual as 'bright' or 'knowledgeable', for example, via tests or the way teachers' questions are answered. The reputation of a school or ability groupings (Lynch and Lodge 2002) can be seen as important prerequisites for creating the situations in which identity negotiations about student ability take place. For instance, the chances of encountering positive academic expectations as a fast-track student are huge in schools rated higher achieving, making it easier to accomplish an identity as 'brainy' (Hattie 2009; Kelly 2009).

If cognitive ability is analysed as a cultural feature, it would be expected to signify various qualities, and, therefore, the resources that actors (students) need in order to be identified as 'gifted' change depending on the context. Jenkins (1998; cf. Lynch and Lodge 2002), however, emphasises that the features are generally considered, both by the actor and the inter-actors, as an authentic 'part of' or a 'consequence' of the actor's natural personality and not something that can be acquired. Test results and grades are features related to ability within schooling and, as a consequence, are expected to be influential over young peoples' self-image and the identity others ascribe to them (Covington 1998). As Jackson (2003, 2006) and Covington (1998) argue, being defined as someone who 'fails in school' is a threat to one's self-worth:

> Successful achievement within schools is signaled primarily by marks or grades. Covington argues that nothing at school can boost feelings of self-worth like a good grade, or devastate self-worth so completely as a poor report card; at school you are only as good as your grades. [. . .] There are two obvious ways to protect self-worth. One is to avoid failure, which is not always possible. The second is to avoid the *implications* of failure. (Jackson 2003, 585)

Because schooling is a competitive system, many will inevitably fail. Even if externally defined school failure is not necessarily defined as failure from the student's own perspective (cf. Henriksson 2004). To protect one's self-worth, and to avoid negative feelings such as shame (Bergman Blix 2010), students may use different strategies to manage others' interpretations of their achievements (cf. self-verification strategies, Burke and Stets 1999; self-hindrance strategies, Urdan and Midgley 2001; Hirt, McCrea and Boris 2003). Previous research has implied that students fear making mistakes in front of teachers and peers (Hattie 2009). If one fears failure, withdrawal of effort could be used as a strategy to prevent others linking a potential 'underachievement' to one's ability (Urdan and Midgley 2001; Leondari and Gonida 2007). This theory explains low student effort, not in terms of low motivation, but in terms of how the risk of appearing structurally underachieving can elicit students' use of self-management strategies that disrupt the learning process and reduce the chances of high achievement.

What is considered as educational 'failure' is not necessarily related to institutional goals (such as grading criteria); instead it should be understood as a subjective assessment of what constitutes an adequate level, low or high, in relation to the individuals' or groups' identity. Intragroup processes are thus the analytical focus (Urdan and Midgley 2001). A test result that is seen as inferior in a certain context may be regarded as exceptional in another, and what is considered to represent 'failure' at an institutional level and/or by an individual/group must be taken into account.

Assessments of ability, whether formal or informal, are informed by processes of gendering, classing or racialising (cf. Walkerdine 1998; Francis and Skelton 2005; Hällgren 2005; Alter et al. 2010; Barnes 2011). To understand how students and teachers negotiate identity, we need to know about the discourses that constitute the institutions in which the interactions take place (Collins 2004; Jenkins 2004). From the micro-perspective, student identity is informed by both contemporary discourses about schooling (Devine 2002) and by the narratives that constitute the particular school and education programme one is attending (Mac an Ghaill 1994).

METHODS AND ETHICS: THE EMPIRICAL STUDY

The analysis in this chapter is part of a larger research project. The aim of the study was to examine the significance of schooling on young men's identities by studying features that denote achievements, ability and effort in peer-groups (Nyström 2012a). Of particular interest was how such features were negotiated among privileged students in Swedish upper secondary schools among White upper middle-class young men and women.

The design was inspired by ethnographic methodology (Gordon et al. 2005) and combined participant observation with semi-structured individual and group interviews as well as a background questionnaire. The fieldwork was conducted in two classes, a natural science class and a vehicle programme class, in two different schools during the students' first year at upper secondary school. The selection of the educational contexts (both of which had masculine connotations and although significantly different in terms of class and educational policy[4]), was theoretically informed (Fenstermaker and West 2002; Jenkins 2004) and grounded in previous research (e.g. Foster, Kimmel and Skelton 2001; Frosh, Phoenix and Pattman 2002; Ball 2003; Lynch and Baker 2005; Warrington and Younger 2006).

The study enrolled a total of fifty-six students, aged sixteen to seventeen. In the latter part of the fieldwork, all students were offered the opportunity to participate in group interviews (cf. mini-focus groups; Munday 2006). Thirty-eight students accepted, and among them twenty-five natural science students, divided into seven (self-formed) interview groups. Fifteen participants, among them eight natural science students, were thereafter asked, and gave their consent to be interviewed individually. Participants were interviewed in Swedish and quotations in this text have been translated into English.

The access to conduct fieldwork was negotiated with the principals at each school. They allowed the teachers to decide whether they were willing for their students to participate in the research. Ethical considerations, before, during, and after the field study, were crucial, not least because of the participants' young age, but also as the research was conducted during the school day (see also Nyström 2012a, 2012b). Subsequently, the study was presented to the students and each was asked to state (in writing) whether they were interested in participating. Two natural science students declined to participate in the study.[5]

The analysis in this text is based on the responses of the natural science students; fifteen young men and fourteen young women who were beginning a gender-balanced upper secondary programme which is dominated by students from the upper middle class and is perceived as one of Sweden's most academically challenging, partly, but not exclusively, due to the status of natural sciences (Lidegran et al. 2006). In accordance with the theoretical approach outlined earlier, gendered and classed identities were analysed as interactional accomplishments (Fenstermaker and West 2002; Jenkins 2004).

GENDERED AND CLASSED CONSTRUCTIONS OF (UN)EQUAL ABILITY

Among the participants, higher education was seen as a natural extension of upper secondary school, and, as John concluded: 'You choose natural science [programme] if you're ambitious [. . .] If you're not super uninterested in science'. Their choices of school and education programmes were dominated by upper middle-class young people and associated with excellence. These have been categorised as classed institutionalised resources (Jenkins 2004; cf. Lynch and Lodge 2002; Pease 2010). Although the programme, in all the interviews, was described as one of the nation's and the town's most demanding, for the vast majority of the students a 'good grade' was equivalent to the highest grade, independent of subject:

Sara: It feels as if the girls in our class strive for . . .
Julia: But the guys try, well they . . . they want top grades in everything, the guys I talk to.
Sara: Doesn't everyone want that?!
Julia: Yes, but, it's like they want . . . they truly really, really want it. Then again, I don't know.
Sara: But it's more like the girls struggle more.
Julia: Yeah, we . . . it's . . . it's like girls . . . (Maria: Mm.) But we don't know if they're home studying like crazy. But I've never seen any guys studying. In maths, for example, the guys rarely focus on work. Not really. Although, some work less than others.

But whereas the goal was the same for the young men and women, the road to achieving it was constructed differently. The young women's learning process was characterised by diligence and uncertainty. The young men's route, on the other hand, was associated with indolence and confidence, an effortless realisation in spite of the unique position of the programme:

Linus: It feels as though the girls have more difficulty in especially . . . (Fabian: Mm, mm.) everything, even though they study pretty much.

Nils: Yes, I absolutely believe that the girls in our class study more than boys. (Linus: Yes, very much more) But I still think they . . . I do not know if it has to do with ability to learn or something, but they are (. . .) not as good, in all cases.

Fabian: I have read that . . . (uh) I do not know if one can generalise so much, but the intelligence of girls is pretty even (.) while among men there are some really stupid ones and some that are really smart.

Anne-Sofie: Like one of these? [*Depicting a bipolar curve with hands.*]

Fabian: Yeah right, one of those, yeah: not many guys in the middle range. But if you think about this kind of programme that counts as (huh) 'tougher', maybe there're many . . . (. . .) it's not many of the 'stupid guys' who apply for those programmes, it's those fast learners. While the girls are mostly in the middle range, one could imagine. But maybe it's . . . [Looks at the interviewer questioningly.]

Anne-Sofie: Well, the achievement statistics don't match up, the range is actually less among guys.

Fabian: Hrm, okay, even within (. . .) Natural science, IB [the International Baccalaureate Programme], the more demanding ones? (Anne-Sofie: Uh . . .) It's hard to imagine.

As argued elsewhere (Walkerdine 1998; Jones and Myhill 2004), the young men's high achievements were found to be primarily gained as a result of intrinsic abilities and 'brilliance', as a way of individualising and naturalising their inherited family cultural resources. In the interview quoted in the preceding, Fabian suggested that genetic sex differences may explain the perceived pattern of boys' and girls' abilities and thereby naturalise and extend the distinction to men and women in general (Pease 2010). He also suggested that intelligence could be more unequally spread amongst men than women (cf. variability hypothesis, Shields 1982). Additionally, this 'hypothesis' complemented the differences that were commonly noted between young men as students; that is, successful and 'relaxed' *and* 'intelligent' university preparatory students, and unsuccessful, 'sloppy' *and* 'stupid' vocational students. Implicitly, if one takes the classed structure of educational programmes into account (Lidegran et al. 2006), this could as well be interpreted as Fabian (and others) constructing upper middle-class versus working-class young men in terms of high and low 'intrinsic' ability (see also discussion in the following of 'upper middle-class masculinity').

Disrupting the Established Constructions of 'Superiority'

Young women portrayed a gendered ambivalence towards their identity. Firstly, even if the young men's self-image as 'bright' or as 'extremely bright' was validated by the young women, the dominant young men's self-presentations were described as 'arrogant':

Anne-Sofie:	But, are they 'swots'? [Reverts to a discussion about the young men as being very ambitious.]
Agnes:	No. [*Laughter*] (Moa: No.) I don't think so.
Moa:	It's more about 'doing well without effort'.
Agnes:	Yes, exactly. A bit like that. (Moa: Quite so.) Yes.
Helen:	But really, I think they study pretty much, although they don't want to show it.
Agnes:	Well that could also be: 'One [young men] shouldn't study much'. But then I wouldn't say that . . . Well in fact, I also believe that they think of themselves as much better than they really are.

Similar discussions were also found with interviews with young women and some with young men. However, none of the young women made claims of being superior, either in the classroom or in interviews, although they firmly contested the idea that they had inferior ability. Secondly, the young women had reservations about the accuracy of the young men's claims to have studied for a short amount of time. The young men's supposed understatement of their preparation time was constructed as a strategy to accomplish the aspired identity as 'effortless high-achievers' (cf. Frosh, Phoenix and Pattman 2002).

NEGOGIATING EFFORTLESS HIGH ACHIEVEMENT

Explicit categorisations of students as 'bright', 'ambitious' (diligent) or 'swots' were frequently used in peer interactions, particularly by the dominant young men. Many students were afraid to lose face in front of the class. As John said, 'Like in ninth grade, then it wasn't cool to be a "swot" . . . but now it's worse . . . if you get an answer wrong, you're labelled as "stupid", almost'. High educational achievement such as test results was a required criterion to pass as 'bright'. The most common understanding of proving oneself to be 'bright' was to 'get a perfect score in the test without studying much', as Linus put it. The standards of test results within respected educational contexts and the (assumed) amount of preparation via schoolbooks were critical aspects displaying intelligence, although classroom activity, as well as analytical and societal knowledge, was also important. Inherited cultural resources and quality of prior schooling was vital in this respect.

Trust: Interactional and Institutional Structures

Trust was important to have individual identity claims validated. Important prerequisites for this were to be included in a peer group, and not to be perceived as disloyal by young men who were ascribed high status (Nyström 2012a). Marginalised students were at risk of being labelled "swots", as Julia says:

Julia: If you're alone and don't have many friends in the class and keep to yourself, then—if you have good grades—then you become a 'swot'. But if it's a guy who knows everyone and is like nice, talking to all (Emma: Mm.) and has high grades, like, then nobody says 'Oh, he's like a "swot"'. (Emma: No.) One might say it anyway but mean nothing negative then. (My: Yes.) Yes. It has quite a lot to do with who your friends are—if you have friends—then it will be more positive or more negative. Like, for both girls and guys.

When individuals were regarded as full members of a group and if they were ascribed a high status, there was less risk of being interrogated (Tajfel 1978). When doing homework or preparing for upcoming tests, trust of others was crucial:

Frederick: Bright, you notice it pretty quickly.
Anne-Sofie: How?
Sebastian: Good at tests.
Frederick: Raises his hand, talking. But you can't know how much he's studied before.
John: Only from what he says. (Anne-Sofie: Hm.)
Frederick: You'd have to trust what he says. And if you ask: 'Do you want to do something tonight?' 'No, I'm going to study'. It could mean . . .

One implication of trusting each other is the significance of in-group favouritism (Tajfel 1978). The informal sex division in student interactions was seen as a key factor in how achievements and ability were negotiated, for example, the lack of raised queries of claimed 'superiority' in the group of young men and their negative reviews about the young women. Such social processes have been explained by how the group identity informs the individual member's identity; if the in-group is ascribed a desirable identity, such as 'effortless high-achievers', this reflects on the individual and vice versa. The young women, however, had little to lose by assessing the young men critically in their in-group.

Another aspect of trust is the degree of consistency between claimed identity and the institutional or prior individual identity ascribed to the student. The institutional identity as a natural science student facilitated individual identities as being 'bright' (positive) or 'ambitious' (mediocre), and downplayed being seen as 'stupid' or 'messy' (negative). So, in the case that a student usually participated in joint leisure activities and informal classroom 'chats', a positive student identity was usually ascribed and mediocre or negative identities dismissed (Jackson 2006; Frosh, Phoenix and Pattman 2002). But, once again, the prerequisite for access was in-group member status.

Time-Accounting Practice

It is in light of the foregoing reasoning that the second example of the young men's explicit check of preparation time was analysed.

Anne-Sofie: But is it commonly discussed how much you are studying, or how little?

John: Yes, that is, before each test everyone says how much exactly they have studied. How many minutes that is. [*The group laughs*]

Anne-Sofie: Okay. [*Laughter*] There is a small time-accounting . . . ?

Frederick: I started at eleven o'clock last night and sat until two o'clock. (Anne-Sofie: Okay.) [*We all laugh*] Then, you're perhaps not a 'swot'; if you start at eleven o'clock and end at two o'clock.

John's remark encouraged laughter from the group. This could be perceived as a way of making fun of the interviewer, but as my field notes demonstrate, the young men reported their preparation time to the minute on test-related occasions. Their self-reflections helped illuminate my understanding of a practice that they recognised as a way of distinguishing 'the brightest' from 'the swots'. This repeated peer-group interaction was termed *time-accounting practice* and found to be a collective routine of drawing upon self-worth protective strategies. Through this practice the young men exchanged 'knowledge' about the (limited) amount of time that they had used for studying, from which they could assess their own and their peers' achievements and abilities. Hence, the practice enabled the young men to present themselves as self-confident procrastinators, 'avoiding the appearance of working and promoting the appearance of effortless achievement' (Jackson 2003, 585; cf. Leondari and Gonida 2007; Urdan and Midgley 2001), and could be interpreted as providing a scenario in which they displayed upper middle-class masculinity (Pease 2010). This was also a matter of trust:

Siri: I still think guys, they'd like to appear as if they study as little as possible, and maybe they do, too. Then they take it lightly. (Maia: Mm.) It's when you have exams or something—then I feel that I can say, 'Ah, but hell when you studied biology, it was really difficult'. They are more like, 'Ah, biology in two days, then maybe you need to start studying tomorrow'. Like, really don't tell anybody that you've studied.

The young men's accounting could also be understood as 'bragging' among peers, avoiding exposing vulnerability. In contrast, young women were identified as students who were not put at risk if they publicly spoke about the difficulties they experienced in school and consequently were perceived as more disciplined students. The interactional structure and the circumstance of (some) young men ridiculing peers in public due to academic mistakes prevented the young women using self-worth-protecting strategies. A suggested interpretation of why this practice was maintained among the young men but not among the young women was that 'natural' ability was more valued and withdrawal of effort was more accepted in the former group than in the latter (Urdan and Midgley 2001; Hirt, McCrea and Boris 2003).

Questioning the System from Within

Hindrance in achieving high grades was at times acknowledged in the group of young men and often linked to remaining attentive in lessons:

Olof: I think it [upper secondary school] ought to be a bit more like university, where you can choose whether to go to lessons. (Fabian: Yes.) Sometimes, I think it's . . . like, 95 per cent of all classes are just a waste. You just sit there in order to be like—what we said earlier—to prove that you're ambitious. I think that none of the lessons are really important. Sometimes they cover something important coming up in a test, but it's not so . . .
Linus: Yes, all classes, except for the ten before the test. If you . . .
Olof: I think I'd get better grades if I stayed home and just got the books before the test, and studied . . . three days before.
Fabian: You'd totally fail in every subject, just because they don't assess knowledge, but you'd certainly do better in tests.
Olof: I would do much better in tests.

In the interview interaction, the participants jointly established Olof as individually underachieving, although 'bright', and in control, by questioning pedagogy and grading practices. By presenting themselves as knowledgeable about the education system and referring to a dysfunctional grading system, as favouring effort instead of 'real' knowledge, the young men established a division between (other's) rewarded 'unimportant ability' and (their) overlooked 'genuine ability'.

This argument can also be interpreted in light of the young men's routines of reading newspapers and politically informed collective (classed) identity (Nyström 2012a). The critique of the non-relation between knowledge and grades, gained from the societal educational policy critique of the Social Democratic egalitarian education policy, has been described as promoting a 'Knowledge School' as opposed to the 'Fuzzy School' (Liedman 2011; author's translation).[6] Whereas the latter describe an orientation away from education learning goals, these young men highlighted the importance of higher education (for their future) and criticised their 'overtly egalitarian' schooling from dominant (neo-liberal) educational policy perspectives.

CONCLUSION

This chapter has examined how constructions of gender and class inform privileged students' negotiations of ability and achievement via peer inter-actions. The study outlines social processes where young men's ability was naturalised as intrinsically superior to that of young women, and to that of young men in less privileged, and often racialised, educational settings. The students were well aware that the local school and educational programme gained respect from a Swedish societal perspective, for example, with refer-ence to rankings in newspapers and so on. But, even though some students reflected on the group's (upper-middle) class and (White) 'race' privilege, most did not; they all described themselves as 'normal' young people, that is, as mainstream in terms of youth culture (cf. Pease 2010). Consistent with Jones and Myhill's (2004) research, achievement due to intrinsic cognitive resourcefulness was more valued among the young men than achievement due to disciplined school work. Moreover, the young men dis-identified themselves with diligent students at large and some constructed lessons as pointless in general, which is not dissimilar in several ways to findings associated with 'anti-school culture', 'laddish culture' or 'anti-swot culture' (Frosh, Phoenix and Pattman 2002; Jackson 2006). However, the natu-ral science students' institutional identity, along with average or high test results, effectively prevented the young men from being considered edu-cational 'losers' or 'students at risk' even if they downplayed the value of diligence (cf. Lynch and Lodge 2002; Hällgren 2005).

In the gender-divided interactional structure of the school, class had important implications for how ability intersected with 'race' and was nego-tiated by the White upper-middle-classes. The practices by which 'superior ability' was accomplished were exclusive to young men as the young women never participated in the young men's peer group interactions or vice versa. Practices such as 'time accounting' normalised 'effortless high achievement' among the young men, but was, from time to time, contested by the young women. Still, the difficulties for marginalised young men in controlling how others interpreted their (past, present or future) accomplishments were also significant. In conclusion, being given group member status was criti-cal for upper-middle-class White boys in avoiding negative inquiries about their ability, especially as such membership provided access to the informal interaction spaces where upper-middle-class boys' 'effortlessness' or external hindrances were validated among their peers.

NOTES

1. One explanation for the increase in inequality is that the social stratification of schools has increased significantly since the mid-1990s, which has resulted in students' class background becoming more homogeneous within classes and schools, whereas the differences between schools has become polarised. The independent school reform has acted as a catalyst in this process (Broady 2011).
2. There is no reason to doubt the general veracity of this, not least due to the ever-increasing production of (trans)national comparisons of young people's academic achievement supported by neoliberal discourses (Francis and Skelton 2005; Alexiadou 2007; Grek et al. 2009). It could be noted that in Sweden, where this particular study is located, the only school subject in which boys as a student category exceed girls' achievements is Physical Education (Delegationen för jämställdhet i skolan 2009). However, the pattern is more complex, and the differences within the categories of young men and young women, are greater than between the two categories.
3. Structural (or sociological) underachievement refers to individuals' or collectives' performance below a specified standard, whether this has to do with the similarity between student categories (gender, class, etc.) or a learning objective.
4. Swedish upper secondary schools are structured as a unitary organisation and since the 1990s all programmes are college-preparatory, even if this has recently been challenged (EACEA P9 Eurydice 2010).
5. Primarily, the participants declined because they posed this 'audience' (i.e. readers of the book chapter) as the most threatening to anonymity (Nyström 2012b), because even if the names of persons, schools and the town are changed, they argued it was difficult to ensure anonymity when the research is published in an international book which has a wide circulation. For this reason, I chose to publish the research after the students had finished upper secondary school.
6. That is, advocating neo-liberal ideas of individualism, marketism and measurability rather than social and equality objectives (Nóvoa 2007).

REFERENCES

Alexiadou, Nafsika. 2007. 'The Europeanization of Education Policy: Researching Changing Governance and "New" Modes of Coordination'. *Research in Comparative and International Education* 2 (2): 102–116.

Alter, Adam, Joshua Aronson, John Darley, Cordaro Rodriguez and Diane Ruble. 2010. 'Rising to the Threat: Reducing Stereotype Threat by Reframing the Threat as a Challenge'. *Journal of Experimental Social Psychology* 46 (2): 166–171.

Archer, Louise. 2011. 'Constructing Minority Ethnic Middle-Class Identity: An Exploratory Study with Parents, Pupils and Young Professionals'. *Sociology* 45 (1): 134–151.

Ball, Stephen J. 2003. *Class Strategies and the Education Market: The Middle Classes and Social Advantage*. London: Routledge Falmer.

Barnes, Cliona. 2011. 'A Discourse of Disparagement'. *Young* 19 (1): 5–23.

Bergman Blix, Stina. 2010. *Rehearsing Emotions: The Process of Creating a Role for the Stage*. Stockholm: Acta Universitatis Stockholmiensis.

Broady, Donald. 2011. 'Skolan, Medelklassen Och Statsprogressivismen'. *Kritisk Utbildningstidskrift* 142–144:73–89.

Burke, Peter J., and Jan E. Stets. 1999. 'Trust and Commitment through Self-Verification'. *Social Psychology Quarterly* 62 (4): 347–366.

Collins, Randall. 2004. *Interaction Ritual Chains*. Princeton, NJ: Princeton University Press.

Covington, Martin V. 1998. *The Will to Learn: A Guide for Motivating Young People*. Cambridge: Cambridge University Press.

Delamont, Sara. 2000. 'The Anomalous Beasts: Hooligans and the Sociology of Education'. *Sociology* 34 (1): 95–111.

Delegationen för jämställdhet i skolan. 2009. *Flickor och Pojkar i Skolan: Hur Jämställt är det?: Delbetänkande*. Statens offentliga utredningar. Fritze.

Devine, Dympna. 2002. 'Children's Citizenship and the Structuring of Adult–Child Relations in the Primary School'. *Childhood* 9 (3): 303–320.

EACEA P9 Eurydice, 2010. *Gender Differences in Educational Outcomes: Study on the Measures Taken and the Current Situation in Europe*. Bryssel: European Commission.

Epstein, Debbie, Jannette Elwood, Valerie Hey and Janet Maw, eds. 1998. *Failing Boys?: Issues in Gender and Achievement*. Buckingham: Open University Press.

Fenstermaker, Sarah, and Candace West. 2002. '"Doing Difference" Revisited: Problems, Prospects, and the Dialogue in Feminist Theory'. In *Doing Gender, Doing Difference: Inequality, Power, And Institutional Change*, edited by Sarah Fenstermaker and Sarah West, 205–216. New York: Routledge.

Foster, Victoria, Michael S. Kimmel and Christine Skelton. 2001. '"What about the Boys?" An Overview of the Debates'. In *What about the Boys?: Issues of Masculinity in Schools*, edited by Wayne Martino and Bob Meyenn, 1–23. Buckingham: Open University Press.

Francis, Becky, and Christine Skelton. 2005. *Reassessing Gender and Achievement: Questioning Contemporary Key Debates*. London: Routledge.

Frosh, Stephen, Ann Phoenix and Rob Pattman. 2002. *Young Masculinities: Understanding Boys in Contemporary Society*. Basingstoke: Palgrave.

Gordon, Tuula, Janet Holland, Elina Lahelma and Tarja Tolonen. 2005. 'Gazing with Intent: Ethnographic Practice in Classrooms'. *Qualitative Research* 5 (1): 113–131.

Grek, Sotiria, Martin Lawn, Bob Lingard, Jenny Ozga, Risto Rinne, Christina Segerholm and Hannu Simola. 2009. 'National Policy Brokering and the Construction of the European Education Space in England, Sweden, Finland and Scotland'. *Comparative Education* 45 (1): 5–21.

Hällgren, Camilla. 2005. '"Working Harder to Be the Same": Everyday Racism among Young Men and Women in Sweden'. *Race, Ethnicity and Education* 8 (3): 319–342.

Hattie, John. 2009. *Visible Learning: A Synthesis of over 800 Meta-Analyses Relating to Achievement*. Abingdon: Routledge.

Henriksson, Carina. 2004. *Living away from Blessings: School Failure as Lived Experience*. Växjö: Växjö University Press.

Hirt, Edward R., Sean M. McCrea, and Hillary I. Boris. 2003. '"I Know You Self-Handicapped Last Exam": Gender Differences in Reactions to Self-Handicapping'. *Journal of Personality and Social Psychology* 84 (1): 177–193.

Jackson, Carolyn. 2003. 'Motives for "Laddishness" at School: Fear of Failure and Fear of the "Feminine"'. *British Educational Research Journal* 29 (4): 583–598.

————. 2006. *Lads and Ladettes in School: Gender and a Fear of Failure*. Maidenhead: Open University Press.
Jenkins, Richard. 1998. *Questions of Competence: Culture, Classification and Intellectual Disability*. Cambridge: Cambridge University Press.
————. 2004. *Social Identity*. London: Routledge.
Jones, Susan, and Debra Myhill. 2004. 'Seeing Things Differently: Teachers' Constructions of Underachievement'. *Gender and Education* 16 (4): 531–546.
Kelly, S. 2009. 'Social Identity Theories and Educational Engagement'. *British Journal of Sociology of Education*, 30 (4): 449–462.
Kimmel, Michael S. 2010. *Boys and School: A Background Paper on the 'Boy Crises'*. SOU. www.regeringen.se/sb/d/108/a/149504 (accessed January 2012).
Lahelma, Elina. 2005. 'School Grades and Other Resources: The "Failing Boy"' Discourse Revisited'. *NORA—Nordic Journal of Feminist and Gender Research* 13 (2): 78–89.
Leondari, Angeliki, and Eleftheria Gonida. 2007. 'Predicting Academic Self-Handicapping in Different Age Groups: The Role of Personal Achievement Goals and Social Goals'. *British Journal of Educational Psychology* 77 (September): 595–611.
Lidegran, Ida, Mikael Börjesson, Ingrid Nordqvist and Donald Broady. 2006. *I Korsningen mellan Kön och Klass: Gymnasieskolan i riket, i Uppsala och i Gävle*. www.skolverket.se/publikationer?id=1653 (accessed 10 December 2011).Liedman, Sven-Eric. 2011. *Hets!: En bok om skolan*. Stockholm: Bonnier.
Lynch, Kathleen, and John Baker. 2005. 'Equality in Education: An Equality of Condition Perspective'. *Theory and Research in Education* 3 (2): 131–164.
Lynch, Kathleen, and Anne Lodge. 2002. *Equality and Power in Schools: Redistribution, Recognition, and Representation*. London: RoutledgeFalmer.
Mac an Ghaill, Máirtín. 1994. *The Making of Men: Masculinities, Sexualities and Schooling*. Buckingham: Open University Press.
Munday, Jennie. 2006. Identity in focus: The Use of Focus Groups to Study the Construction of Collective Identity. *Sociology 40* (1): 89 -105.
Nóvoa, Antonio. 2007. 'The "Right" Education in Europe. When the Obvious Is Not So Obvious!' *Theory and Research in Education* 5 (2): 43–51.
Nyström, Anne-Sofie. 2012a. 'Att synas och lära utan att synas lära. En studie om underprestation och privilegierade unga mäns identitetsförhandlingar i gymnasieskolan (To Be Seen and to Learn, without Being Seen to Learn. A Study of Under-Achievement and Identity-Negotiation among Privileged Young Men in Upper-Secondary School)'. Diss., Uppsala, Acta Universitatis Upsaliensis. Studia Sociologica Upsaliensia 59: Uppsala universitet.
————. 2012b. 'Mellan empati och kritisk granskning?: forskningsdeltagande som risk' In *Etiska dilemman: forskningsdeltagande, samtycke och utsatthet*, edited by H. Kalman and V. Lövgren, 71–86. Malmö: Gleerups.
Pease, Bob. 2010. *Undoing Privilege: Unearned Advantage in a Divided World*. London: Zed.
Plewis, Ian. 1991. 'Underachievement: A Case of Conceptual Confusion'. *British Educational Research Journal* 17 (4): 377–385.
Rosenthal, Robert, and Lenore Jacobson. 1992 [1968]. *Pygmalion in the Classroom: Teacher Expectation and Pupils' Intellectual Development*. New York: Irvington.
Sadovnik, Alan R., and Susan F. Semel. 2010. 'Education and Inequality: Historical and Sociological Approaches to Schooling and Social Stratification'. *Paedagogica Historica* 46 (1): 1–13.
Shields, Stephanie A. 1982. 'The Variability Hypothesis: The History of a Biological Model of Sex Differences in Intelligence'. *Signs* 7 (4): 769–797.

Skolverket. 2009. *Beviljade spets*utbildningar. www.skolverket.se/sb/d/2635/a/14878 (accessed January 2012).

——. 2010. *Rustad att möta framtiden? PISA 2009 om 15–åringars läsförståelse och kunskaper i matematik och naturvetenskap—Skolverket*. Rapporter. Skolverket. www.skolverket.se/publikationer?id=2473 (accessed January 2012).

Tajfel, Henri, ed. 1978. *Differentiation between Social Groups: Studies in the Social Psychology of Intergroup Relations*. London: Academic Press.

UNESCO. 2008. *Education for All by 2015: Will We Make It?* Paris: UNESCO Publishing. unesdoc.unesco.org/images/0015/001548/154820e.pdf (accessed January 2012).

Urdan, Tim, and Carol Midgley. 2001. 'Academic Self-Handicapping: What We Know, What More There Is to Learn'. *Educational Psychology Review* 13 (2): 115–138.

Walkerdine, Valerie. 1998. *Counting Girls Out: Girls and Mathematics. Studies in Mathematics Education Series*. London: Falmer.

Warrington, Molly, and Mike Younger. 2006. 'Working on the Inside: Discourses, Dilemmas and Decisions'. *Gender and Education* 18 (3): 265–280.

Wernersson, Inga. 2006. *Könsskillnader i Skolprestationer: En Text som Kartlägger de olika Ideologiska Förändringarna som Inträffat under de Senaste Åren. Bilaga till Könsskillnader i Måluppfyllelse och Utbildningsval*. Stockholm: Skolverket.

Younger, Mike, and Molly Warrington. 2007. 'Closing the Gender Gap? Issues of Gender Equity in English Secondary Schools'. *Discourse: Studies in the Cultural Politics of Education* 28 (2): 219–242.

7 Change and Tradition
Muslim Boys Talk about Their Post-Sixteen Aspirations

Farzana Shain

INTRODUCTION

This chapter explores educational inequalities through an analysis of the post-sixteen aspirations of a group of working-class school boys living in England. I draw on research conducted for a wider project (Shain 2011) on the educational experiences of twenty-four working-class boys who self-identified as Muslim. One of the key aims of the wider study was to explore the resources the boys were able to draw on in constructing their identities. This analysis was set against the backdrop of rising youth unemployment and job insecurity in England as a result of the decline of manufacturing since the 1970s, and global and national concerns about 'security' following 9/11 and the July 2005 London bombings. National policy concerns about social cohesion following the inner-city disturbances in England in 2001 as well as new patterns of immigration as a result of the wars in Afghanistan and Iraq and the enlargement of Europe were also significant factors shaping the analysis of the boys' identities.

Against the background of the economic, political and cultural change referred to in the preceding, dominant sociological accounts (Giddens 1991; Beck 1992) have posited an increasing trend towards individualisation. It is argued that the neo-liberalisation of labour markets, the decline of heavy industry and the growing casualisation of work have led to a weakening of the old bonds of tradition, class and neighbourhood. These are said to have given way to increasingly individualised choices, aspirations and life trajectories. Young people's transitions to adulthood are therefore thought to be less classed and gendered than they were in the 1950s and 1960s and more individualised as they face increasingly risky and uncertain futures without the support of the traditional structures of family and community. Conversely, in relation to some categories of young people—most notably those from disadvantaged Pakistani and Bangladeshi backgrounds—policy and political concerns have continued to centre on the dominance of family, culture and tradition in shaping life trajectories (Alexander 2004). Discourses of deficit and blame still frame references to Pakistani and Bangladeshi communities, and to boys in particular, as 'at risk' of 'extremism' or 'social exclusion' because of their 'over-traditional' upbringing. For example, instead of the external factors such as changing labour markets, the rise of feminism and improving girls' performance, which are often cited as reasons for the apparent educational underachievement of White working-class boys, explanations for the underachievement of Pakistani and Bangladeshi boys have tended to focus on 'race' and culture (Archer 2003, 23). Following the 2001 disturbances in north England, official explanations of the causes of the 'riots' followed this trend of emphasising culture over structure. The widespread disadvantage suffered by Pakistani and Bangladeshi communities in the northern towns was sidelined in favour of arguments that emphasised a lack of aspiration as the reason for the residential and social 'stagnation' of Pakistani and Bangladeshi communities. The Cantle report, for example argued that 'expectations are . . . very low in some areas and some occupations seem to be outside the knowledge and aspirations of some cultures' (Cantle 2001, 44). The tone of the report is reflective of the neo-liberal language of individualisation which heavily inflected New Labour policies from 1997 to 2010. Throughout this period, policy discourses such as lifelong learning placed the onus on individuals to engage in self-improvement or betterment as a way to make themselves more employable. Rather than 'expecting' the state to either create employment opportunities or to provide for them, individuals were encouraged to be more aspiring (Gewirtz 2001; Raco 2009).

In the light of the somewhat contradictory theoretical and policy concerns referred to in the preceding, the current chapter focuses on boys' aspirations in relation to education, employment and family life; drawing on a reanalysis of empirical data from a wider study which reported on Muslim boys' accounts of schooling (Shain 2011). The current chapter addresses the extent to which the boys' accounts reflect narratives of individualisation, that is to say, a shift away from the influence of traditional structures of family and community cultural life or the continued significance of structures of class, race and gender in shaping the boys' current educational choices and their imagined futures. A related aim in this chapter is to assess the extent to which the boys' aspirations support fixed and static conceptions of traditional cultures as expressed in policy discourses emphasising segregation and 'parallel lives', or 'change' in the sense of a reworking of traditional cultural influences. The chapter also offers a fresh perspective on the relationship between educational choices and expectations around marriage for young Muslims by exploring the accounts of boys on these topics. In much of the academic literature and policy and public discourses, marriage is constructed as constraining on the educational choices of girls and considerably less attention has been focused on the relationship between educational choices and the future aspirations of Muslim boys.

The chapter is structured around three sections: the first reviews theoretical debates on young people's choices and aspirations; the second offers a brief summary of the empirical study on which this chapter is based; in the third part I discuss the boys' aspirations in relation to (i) education and employment and (ii) future family life. In the case of the latter, the focus is specifically their views on, and expectations in relation to, marriage.

THEORETICAL CONTEXT: CHOICE, ASPIRATION AND INDIVIDUALISATION

According to theories of 'risk' (Beck 1992) individualisation (Giddens 1991) and the neo-liberalisation of subjectivities (Rose 1996), traditional social structures such as class, gender and race have lost their significance as young people are required to navigate their way through a series of individualised life trajectories. Young people in Western societies are said to face increasingly 'complex and contested' and 'non-linear' pathways into adulthood as the result of the significant restructuring of industrialised economies, the rise of the (largely feminised) service sector and increased flexibility and insecurity in labour markets. In the 1950s and 1960s working-class boys were assumed to experience predictable age- and class-related mass transitions from school to manual work (Furlong and Cartmel 1997; Cohen and Ainley 2000). However, since the 1970s, economic changes, widespread unemployment and job insecurity alongside the consequent extension of education and training have resulted in delayed transitions, diminished young people's engagements with the labour market and significantly weakened collective work-based identities (Roberts 1995; Furlong and Cartmel 1997).

Although the extent to which young people did indeed experience such smooth transitions prior to the 1970s is debated (Goodwin and O'Connor 2005; Vickerstaff 2003), it is now widely accepted that work plays less of a role in shaping the identities of young people, especially those from disadvantaged backgrounds, where people may live in households in which an entire generation has not experienced work. This dismantling of the old bonds of collectivism impacts on all areas of life. As Giddens argues, we live in a world 'where one can no longer simply rely on tradition to establish what to do in a given range of contexts, people have to take a more active and risk-infused orientation to their relationships and involvements' (2003, 4).

The discourse of individualisation has dominated and underscored neo-liberal policy responses to youth unemployment since the 1980s. A range of measures, including modern apprenticeships, internships and the expansion of post-compulsory education, has been introduced to compensate for the decline in the ready availability of unskilled manual work. Under the New Labour government (1997–2010), policy discourses such as 'lifelong learning' and 'widening participation' were ostensibly introduced to help young people navigate their way through a series of 'complex choices' and transitions. These discourses enabled individual success, aspiration and achievement to be set up as the solution to social exclusion and a means by which to improve the national competitiveness of Britain in the global economic marketplace. However, critics have argued that discourses such as lifelong learning and the more recent proposals to extend the compulsory school-leaving age represent state attempts to contain and manage potentially dangerous 'workless' populations of young people (Brine 2006). This view is supported by the research evidence, which shows that young people and disadvantaged groups have fared the worst in recent recessions and that unemployment rates for ethnic minorities are consistently higher than for the Whites (Stafford and Duffy 2009).

As mentioned earlier, sociological claims about individualisation sit uneasily with dominant policy discourses that position minority groups as overly traditionalised, culturally fixed and incapable of change (Cantle 2001; Home Office 2002). The individualisation thesis has also been challenged in the sociological literature. Mythen (2005) for example, has criticised Beck and Giddens 'for shying away from empirical engagement' (4.3) and instead offering an abstract theory of individualisation that makes little connection with peoples lived realities. Empirical research conducted by Smart and Shipman (2010) with members of transnational families supports Mythen's observations. The authors found that traditional values around arranged marriage held out for family members and that these were an important and positive source of identity. They argue that the version of individualisation put forward by Giddens and Beck is not only abstract but also 'culturally monochrome' in that it envisions White Western family norms and values (Smart and Shipman 2010).

Another contradiction that has been identified as inherent in the individualisation thesis is that young people are expected to individually mould and steer their pathways to adulthood. However, traditional gendered social expectations of adulthood continue to prescribe 'what "responsible adulthood" entails, [all] within a myriad of structural uncertainties and inequalities, that may be classed or gendered in their impact, that affect their choices' (McDonald et al. 2011, 70). McDonald et al. (2011) argue that through consumer culture, individualisation supports a 'have it all' approach, but girls and young women continue to be the focus of social and political anxieties around falling fertility rates. At the same time, the impact of structural factors, such as paid maternity leave and childcare flexibility, that may affect fertility choices often go unacknowledged. In this way, traditional gendered and heteronormative expectations of what it means to be an adult are reinforced. Critics of individualisation (Furlong and Cartmel 1997; Savage 2000; Skeggs 2004; Mythen 2005) therefore argue that although class, race and gender as the foundations of social life may have become less dominant, they remain salient features, constraining or enabling young people's transitions from school to college and university and their life chances.

Within the educational literature, arguments linking educational choice and the reproduction of classed, gendered and racialised inequalities are now well established (Ball, Reay and David 2002; Reay, David and Ball 2001; Ball 2003; Archer and Yamashita 2003; Archer and Francis 2006; Crozier and Davis 2006). Much of this educational literature has been underpinned by the theoretical tools offered by Bourdieu, most notably his concepts of social and cultural capital. Research on transitions to higher education has consistently shown that choices are shaped by the availability of resources (material and cultural), which can enhance or constrain aspiration, achievement and ambition (Skeggs 1997; Wright, Standen and Patel 2010), leading to the reproduction of existing classed, gendered and racialised inequalities. Ball (2003), for example, argues that the White middle classes are 'adept at taking up and making the most of opportunities of advantage that [marketised] policies present to them' (261). These White middle-class families have the capacity to maintain competitive advantage due to their possession of embodied forms of social capital (the links and networks that support what might be possible or what can be done) and cultural capital (the possession of understandings, knowledge, ways of behaving and attitudes which can either help or impede a person to progress) (Hodkinson 2004). Although research on working class students shows that a complex array of factors impacts on their aspirations and choices, many working class students, regardless of academic ability, tend to define traditional universities as simply out of their reach. They either lack the resources required or possess the 'wrong' sort of capital for success in elite higher education institutions (Reay, David and Ball 2001).

Whereas this 'social reproduction' literature has addressed intersections of class, race and gender in the reproduction of inequalities, its underlying Bourdieuian framework has recently been criticised as overly class based and unable to 'explain educational success among individuals who lack class-related resources for mobility (both economic and cultural capital)' (Thapar and Sanghera 2010, 9). Other research has drawn on notions of 'family capital' (Archer and Francis 2006, 7) or 'ethnic capital' (Modood 2006) to explain the success of working-class Chinese and Asian students relative to their peers. From a Critical Race Theory perspective, Yosso (2005, 76) challenges traditional interpretations of Bourdieuian cultural capital theory, which she argues tend to privilege White middle-class standards as the norm against which other forms and expressions of culture are judged as culturally wealthy and culturally poor. As a result, the working class in general and racialised minorities in particular are assumed to 'lack' cultural capital rather than possessing other valued forms of capital. Yosso introduces the alternative concept of 'community cultural wealth' to refer to 'an array of knowledge, skills, abilities and contacts possessed and utilized by racialised communities to resist the impact of macro and micro forms of oppression' (2005, 77). Among the six forms of capital that are central to community cultural wealth, Yosso includes aspirational and resistant capital. Aspirational capital is defined as 'the ability to maintain hopes and dreams for the future, even in the face of real and perceived barriers' (77).

Yosso argues that this form of capital promotes resilience and a 'culture of possibility' (78) in the face of a multitude of structural inequalities and racial hostility. It is the supportive networks, primarily the extended family and neighbourhood/kin, that carry a sense of community (79), which in turn provides individuals with the resources needed to deal with the impact of structural oppression. Yosso's argument therefore presents a challenge to the individualisation thesis by emphasising the continued significance of community cultural networks in supporting young people's aspirations and decision making.

Yosso's notion of 'resistant capital' refers to 'those knowledges and skills fostered through oppositional behaviour that challenges inequality' (2005, 80). Whereas Yosso refers to the US context, researchers in the UK (Sivanandan 1982; Gilroy 1987; Mirza and Reay 2000) have also documented collectivised struggles and strategies that emerged directly as a response to the structural racism experienced by Black parents in the 1960s and 1970s. Campaigns against racism and other 'social movements' such as the setting up of Black supplementary schools (Mirza and Reay 2000) could be argued to demonstrate the significance and operation of both aspirational and resistant capital. In my own research (Shain 2011), the boys were able to draw on social histories of local and national collective anti-racist struggle. This collective resistance against racism included Black and Asian youth-led campaigns in the 1980s (Ramamurthy 2006; Shain 2009) to support the defence of their neighbourhoods against physical racist attack. As I have argued in more detail elsewhere (Shain 2011) these local and national anti-racist struggles have had a lasting legacy in urban areas and have proved to be valuable for the boys in the absence of the availability of work as an identity resource. It is against the background of these theoretical debates that the current chapter explores the boys' talk about their aspirations in relation to education, employment and family life. My overall aim is to identify the resources (ethnicity, family, gender or individualised) that the boys draw on in relation to their current educational choices and imagined futures and, specifically, to explore the extent to which their aspirations and choices reflect *change* (away from the significance of traditional family, class influences) and/or *tradition* (the continued significance of family and community).

BACKGROUND TO THE EMPIRICAL STUDY

The analysis presented in this chapter draws from a wider project on Muslim boys and education that is reported in Shain (2011). The study drew on research with twenty-four working-class boys and young men who self-identified as Muslim. The research—conducted between May 2002 and October 2003 in Oldwych in the West Midlands—consisted of group and individual interviews with boys aged between twelve and eighteen.[1] At the time of the research, Oldwych had a population of around 250,000 with the proportion of ethnic minorities (including Irish) around 6 per cent. However, in line with other ethnically diverse areas, the younger (under sixteen) ethnic minority population was larger at around 8 per cent. Ethnic minorities were also overwhelmingly concentrated in two wards: Newtown and Belstone, where they accounted for almost 50 per cent of the population. Like many of the wards in the northern towns, these areas were also severely economically deprived, with higher than average numbers of children in them claiming free school meals (FSMs) and high rates of unemployment. At the time of the research, unemployment was around 5.9 per cent—against an average of 4.9 per cent for Britain overall. In Newtown this figure was far higher: 8.6 per cent.

Fieldwork was conducted across two sites: a youth group located in Newtown where boys met once a week and a mixed comprehensive secondary school, Leyton High, located near Newtown. Access to both sites was negotiated over a considerable period of time. Permission was granted from the teacher of Leyton High to conduct the interviews on the school premises, but the active consent of the boys was negotiated via Mrs. James, a teacher at the school who worked closely with the boys and their parents. Access to the youth group was gained via the Youth Service, but again staff of the centre acted as gatekeepers and Yacoub, one of the youth workers, was instrumental in gaining the active consent of the boys to engage in the interviews and focus groups. Being an 'insider' (a visible ethnic minority and Muslim) played a large part in the recruitment of the boys for the research. However, in other respects I was also an 'outsider' (an older, middle-class female researcher) and, as discussed in Shain (2011), some of the boys were reluctant to engage in talk about their relationships and were also more guarded in their talk about women and girls more generally.

Of the twenty-four boys who took part in the research, seventeen were Pakistani, including one who described himself as mixed-race White English and Pakistani; four were Bengali; two were Afghani; and one was Turkish. The boys' experiences of schooling were shaped in part by their location in Oldwych, which was characterised by significant disadvantage. A number of schools in the area were identified as 'failing' and success rates (5 A*–C grades) in General Certificate in Secondary Education (GCSE) examinations was low at Leyton—just under 30 per cent, compared with a national average of 52 per cent at the time. At Greenbank school, around 39 per cent of students achieved 5 A*–C GCSE grades in the year in which the research was conducted, again lower than the national average. Fixed-term exclusions were high across both schools with, for example, 133 incidents of exclusion involving seventy-eight pupils and three permanent exclusions in Leyton in the year prior to the research.

As the analysis offered in the following of the boys' accounts reveals, traditional structures and intersections of class, gender, ethnicity and neighbourhood remain highly significant in their construction of current and future choices and life trajectories. The boys fiercely defended local identities and placed a strong emphasis on loyalty, backup and 'being there' for friends and family. These constructions drew on a collective working-class community ethos but also reinforced masculine discourses, particularly through notions of 'protecting' girls. Struggles over local territory between groups of boys reinforced traditional gender boundaries and supported a masculine colonisation of public space. As argued in Shain (2011, 2012), these struggles involved the differential positioning of White and Asian girls as respectively predatory and in need of protection, but collectively as symbols of masculinity. Within their schools the boys invested heavily in a 'tough' collective Asian male peer group identity that was constructed in relation to the classed, gendered and racialised order of schooling (Shain 2011, 2012).

TALKING ABOUT POST-SIXTEEN CHOICES: EDUCATIONAL INEQUALITIES REVISITED

Research on educational outcomes (Mirza 1992; Gillborn and Mirza 1998; Gillborn and Youdell 2000) shows that class and ethnicity remain the biggest predictors of educational success and failure; however, as Gillborn (2008, 59–60) maintains, statistics on ethnicity and achievement confirm a complex picture with girls performing better than boys across the board. Since 1992, the achievements of Pakistani and Bangladeshi young people have varied considerably, showing that existing inequalities are not fixed. All groups have enjoyed some improvement over the period but the Black–White gap has remained fairly constant and both Bangladeshi and Pakistani students have experienced a period of growing inequality (Gillborn 2008, 60). There are few detailed trends for other Muslim minorities, but research on Turkish youth by Enneli, Modood and Bradley (2005) and by the Department for Communities and Local Government (DCLG 2009) indicate that Turkish Cypriots perform better academically than students from mainland Turkey, whose educational performance is similar to that of Pakistanis and Bangladeshis.

The picture of 'Muslim underachievement' is somewhat muddied by the research evidence on educational choices, particularly in the context of university application (Modood and Shiner 1994; Modood and Acland 1998; Ahmad 2001; Ball, Reay and David 2002; ; Reay, David and Ball 2001; Abbas 2004: Modood 2006; Shah, Dwyer and Modood 2010; Bhopal 2010). This body of research suggests that Muslim Pakistani and Bangladeshi students, often the poorest and most marginalised of English students, are nonetheless more likely than White working-class youth to submit applications to university.

However, there has remained a 'troubling racial divide' (Reay, David and Ball 2001; Mirza 2009) in students choices, between 'old' (pre-1992 established universities) and 'new' universities or those former polytechnics accorded university status following the 1992 Further and Higher Education Act. Modood (2006) argues that ethnic minorities are less likely to enter the more prestigious 'old' universities and are more likely to withdraw from university. Those who last the course are less likely to gain a high-grade degree. Modood argues that all these factors apply less to Indian and Chinese students than other groups. Ethnic minority students are more likely to be part-time or mature students—which often means that they are less likely to obtain more prestigious and better-paid jobs (see also Bhattacharyya, Ison and Blair 2003). They are also more likely to feature disproportionately in medicine, and health-related subjects, law and business, engineering and ICT but are underrepresented in the pure sciences and the humanities; as Modood (2006) argues, only a few universities and not all disciplines can truly claim to be multiethnic. Universities attended by Muslim students have also, since 2005, been the targets of anti-terror policing via the Preventing Violent Extremism strategy (Home Office 2009) and so the classed experiences of Muslim students have intersected with race (albeit recoded through faith and extremism) (Kundnani 2009). University vice-chancellors have, since 2005, faced pressure to release confidential information to counter-terrorist officers about Muslim students' membership in Islamic societies. Universities were also at one stage advised to consider curtailing their Muslim student populations in response to policy concerns about 'extremism' (Glees and Pope 2005). Such practices have been justified through a 'security' discourse and the widespread surveillance of Muslim students continues under the hugely unpopular Prevent Strategy (Home Office 2009; Kundnani 2009).

Only two of the boys in my study showed 'uncertain aspirations' (Ball, Reay and David 2002; Hodkinson 2005). Nadim, for example, said about his exams, 'I don't think about it', whereas another asked 'what's careers?'(Ibrahim). However, the majority of the boys, even those in the lower and middle sets within their schools, had given consideration to their future choices. Most had career plans, and this concurs with the findings of wider research showing that Muslim students 'aim high' (Ahmad 2001; Abbas 2004; Archer and Francis 2007; Shah, Dwyer and Modood 2011). However, the lack of readily available employment opportunities and the extension of education through schemes such as lifelong learning and widening participation also meant that there was little alternative to further study. Engineering was the most popular of the future career choices listed by the boys, other choices included electronics, medicine, law and race equality work. Three of the boys wanted to be pilots. Two boys did not know what they wanted to do (Rafiq and Nadim) and Aziz saw himself working in a shop. Two others were already at college (Malik and Arshad) studying business. A further two boys were working in restaurants near school (Sajid and Ibrahim), and Malik was working the clubs as a DJ during his college course.

The boys' choices contradict dominant policy discourses that position Muslim Asian communities as lacking aspiration but support much of the research evidence that notes a preference for 'traditional' professional subjects among some ethnic minorities. The preference for subjects such as law, medicine and business can lead to an over-representation of minority students on such degree courses and increased competition for jobs and higher education places in these fields (Hussain and Bagguley 2007; Tackey, Barnes and Khambhaita 2011). As stated, the boys were located in one of the most materially deprived locations in Oldwych in a school in which racial tensions and the prospects of unemployment were high. Although they were often preoccupied with fighting and gaining status through the Asian peer group, the majority of the boys also had strong aspirations for academic success (McDowell 2002). Although, for some of the boys, career choices were not yet well-defined, post-sixteen study featured heavily in their talk about their futures. A number of the boys who invested heavily in masculine identities via the Asian peer group also described their reoriented strategies for achieving successful transitions to college. One of these was Hamid:

FS: So, which set are you in now then?
Hamid: Middle . . . I used to be in top yeah, but I was naughty and they put me down.
FS: Why were you being naughty?
Hamid: Cos I got this homework that I couldn't do . . . I had difficulties doing it yeah and . . . cos I didn't know what to do and I started answering back to the teacher and I swore at her and she like put me down saying I couldn't do the homework . . . After that I started being naughty but recently I started behaving and that . . . I've got to concentrate now exams are coming up.

(Leyton High)

Hamid explains here how his 'bad' behaviour had initially started because of a difficult piece of homework which he did not want to admit to not being able to do. He was moved down a set but because exams are now approaching he has made a conscious decision to concentrate on his work and leave behind the 'naughty' behaviour (Archer and Yamashita 2003). As Renold (2005) found in her study of primary schooling, high-achieving boys bought into dominant modes of masculinity in active ways, but they also knew when it was necessary to 'knuckle down' to hard work.

For the boys who were most successful within the Asian boys' peer group, career or university was not an option. Aziz, for example, had 'not even thought about it'. He admired other 'clever' boys but did not buy into neo-liberal individualised notions of success. For Aziz, collective community spirit, expressed as 'being there' for friends and 'having fun' was valued above individual academic success (see Shain 2011). Asad had been identified by the school as a high achiever but following a racist attack had lost momentum. The incident had apparently undermined his confidence and teachers reported being concerned about his progress.

Asad:	I'd say I'm doing quite good—with all this stuff going on. They've been talking about my grades slipping.
FS:	You were in the higher sets—I gather from Mrs. James.
Asad:	Yeah I have to concentrate on my work. Well before, if they said one thing that made you feel bad . . . one little thing will kick off into a big thing. Well, now I'm going to ignore the little things.

**

FS:	Can I ask you what you see yourself doing in the future?
Asad:	Probably going to university. I was going to be a pilot you know . . . but all this . . . you know terrorist attack, they'd probably get scared shitless . . . probably won't work out will it?
FS:	Why not?
Asad:	There are lot of racist people in this world . . . you might get another attack or something and I'd get the blame for it—Asians always get the blame. I haven't seen any White person . . .
FS:	So if you weren't to be pilot?
Asad:	I'll get a mechanics job.

(Leyton High)

Here Asad talks about how his grades had slipped in recent months and vows to leave behind, if only temporarily, the aspects (readiness to fight, standing up for mates and respect for peers) that were highly valued by the collective Asian boys' peer group. The peer group was the prime source of identity for many of the boys in the context of schooling. Asad sets out his determination to ignore the 'little things', the mundane racism that is embedded in schooling, and to focus on individual academic success. However, this aspiration is mediated by the impact of 9/11 and the 'war on terror' in his own imagined future: 'Asians always get the blame', and says that because of racism he will most likely not be able to pursue the career of his choice. Asad's adoption of a fatalistic attitude here is arguably a reflection of his working-class location but his re-orientated aspirations also reflected the powerful impact of racism in shaping the boundaries of what was imagined to be possible. Asad had engaged in a process of self-exclusion, lowering his expectations because of perceived structural racism. Farood also experienced structural racism—but through his sisters' experiences. Both his older sisters had received top A-level grades but had been denied a place at the medical school of their choice with no formal reason given other than competition. This had impacted upon Farood's own aspirations and he had consequently set his sights on a lower-status university. Given that education remains a positional good, Farood's case highlights the contradiction inherent in policy talk aimed at creating a nation of aspirational individuals. This is supported by evidence presented by Modood (2006), who shows that all things being equal, a Muslim student is 57 per cent likely to be offered a place at an 'old' university, against 75 per cent of White candidates with similar qualifications. Modood argues that racism plays a part in the process of institutional filtering that leads to the disproportionate rejection by higher education institutions of ethnic minority students. In Farood's case, this racism had apparently been experienced second-hand but had led to him to lower his expectations and to opt for his local university.

Staying Local: 'It's Too Far to Travel out of my Neighbourhood'

Research on the post-sixteen choices of working-class students (Taylor 1992; Modood and Shiner 1994; Reay, David and Ball 2001; Ball, Reay and David 2002; Archer and Yamashita 2003) notes that a disproportionate number of students make applications to higher education institutions where family and community relations are positively valued and local choices also reflect this. Researchers have argued that staying at home may offer a solution to the potential isolation reported by an earlier generation of ethnic minority students about their higher education experiences. Archer and Yamashita (2003) found that boys they interviewed as part of their study on 'inner-city masculinities' invested heavily in their local identities and could not imagine moving away from their local area for study or work. Reay, David and Ball (2001) also found that this localism was more prominent in the accounts presented by working-class students than in the narratives of more economically privileged higher-education students. Reay, David and Ball (2001) found that material constraints of travel and finance often meant students were operating within very limited spaces and a few extra stops on the bus or train could place an institution beyond the boundaries of conceivable choice, whereas Ball, Maguire and Macrae (2000) discuss the issue of possibly not 'fitting in' as a further constraint on minority students' choices. But this localism also needs to be placed in the context of the New Labour government's widening participation policies through which 'local place became a convenient proxy for social class. It facilitated the targeting of interventions on those young people deemed to have inappropriately low aspirations without ever directly acknowledging their social class' (Brown 2012, 103). As Brown also argues, to some extent the research evidence on the localism of working class students' decision-making enabled policy discourses:

> to present the lives of poorer young people as being fixed in place in order to justify the prioritisation placed on enabling their social and spatial mobility. . . . Specific scalar orientations became attached to different expressions of aspiration in this policy discourse. 'High' aspiration (for future professional careers) were presented as expansive, mobile and operating at the national and global scales while 'low' (or 'inappropriate') aspirations were considered insular and fixed at the local and domestic scales. (2012, 103)

Asad, who had contacts in London, confirmed this localism by indicating that he would most likely stay in Oldwych, but at the same time he imagined moving away. Like a number of the boys. including Sajid and Tariq, Asad expressed both 'high' and 'low' aspirations. Tariq, who wanted to become a medical consultant, also imagined leaving his local area for a university elsewhere: 'I'd just like to see how it is'. Aziz, however, confirms localised aspirations in his talk about a nearby college, just two miles from his home, as 'too far':

FS: Will you go to college?
Aziz: Probably Ryton, Camton . . . or Tipton . . . but it's too far . . .
FS: Too far?
Aziz: Yeah it's too far . . . I can't be bothered catching a bus in the morning. Ryton's just a walk . . . Tipton's too far and I know some people at Ryton.

Yet, Aziz also imagined moving away from the area in the longer term, not for university but simply to escape the boredom of the local area:

Aziz: It's really boring. I want to move away.
FS: Move away? Why?
Aziz: I don't know. I want to move to London.
FS: What's in London?
Aziz: I go there a lot . . . Near Greenwich.
FS: Is it an Asian area?
Aziz: No, quite a lot of Sikhs . . . quite a lot of *goray* [White people]. In the six weeks holidays I go; all the six weeks and every half term. Sometimes I go on the weekends on the train.
                                                                        (Leyton High)

At first sight this suggests a contradictory positioning. Aziz seems to crave localism and mobility. The local college is considered by Aziz to be too far away, yet he also imagines himself leaving the area to live in London. However, the constant factor across the two extracts is the significance of an existing community or social network. In Aziz's case this community was not necessarily co-ethnic (Thapar and Sanghera 2010) but familiar. Aziz was prepared to travel to London because of 'knowing people there'. Without this 'backup' of a social network, the decision to move out of the area would be 'too risky' (Ball, Reay and David 2002; Hodkinson 2004).

Significant Others: Family and Community Role Models

Abbas (2004) found that the final choices for young South Asian women were still strongly influenced by parents, especially fathers. The boys in my own study also reported a number of local influences in respect to their future career choices. For example, Ibrahim wanted to be a car mechanic, influenced by a family member: 'My uncle used to fix cars so like I learned off him so I could do work there . . . when I finish school I want to learn more'.

The boys who were most instrumental about subject choices mentioned their families as strongly influential in helping them to make these choices. For example, Abid's mother was a teaching assistant in a local school and at the time of the research, his sole parent. Farood, too, was in a single-parent household at the time of the research and spoke about his mother's influence over him in relation to his choice of subjects and career: 'First I wanted to be a pilot but my mum said, "no you don't want to be a pilot, you want to be a doctor"'. These experiences represent, to some extent, feminised choice making, resonating with research on Asian girls which showed that mothers played a significant role in nurturing their daughters' ambitions (Mirza 1992; Bhachu 1991; Dwyer 1999, Ahmad 2001; Abbas 2004), but they also challenge the notion that young people's decision making is less classed and traditional compared with how it was in the 1970s.

Family and community also played a significant role in Hamid's future choice of career, which centred on youth and race equality work. The older Aziz, who worked in both fields, was a significant role model for Hamid: 'Er, like there's this guy his name's Aziz . . . he's my role model'. Zahid also couched his future career in terms of community need and was keen to rationalise his own orientation to success, with reference to a strong justice ethic and 'giving something back to the community':

> I've always wanted to do law since I was young and I want to be a barrister or something like that. [I'd like to] go off to Pakistan and help the people who are poor and because what happens in Pakistan is the law . . . the poor people always get blamed for everything and I don't think that's fair, plus if I went to Pakistan and I killed someone I know I could get away with it . . . because I've got money and I can give it . . . to everybody . . . some poor people can't do that . . . so I want to go to Pakistan to help them. (Zahid) (Leyton High)

Zahid's strong articulation of a justice ethic here appeals to notions of community, but this community service discourse is called on to legitimate his own 'high' aspiration to enter an esteemed and well-paid professional occupation. He positions himself as privileged in relation to 'poor people' in Pakistan and in doing so reinforces Western constructions of a lawless and corrupt Pakistan in which people can literally get away with murder. Zahid's construction of poor people as 'in need of saving' reworks colonial discourses about Asian and 'Arab' lands as the bearers of backward cultures that were in need of Western civilisation. As I argue elsewhere (Shain 2011), the Englishness of the boys often came to the fore in their discussions of other Pakistanis and Muslims 'over there' living abroad.

IMAGINED FUTURES: MARRIAGE AND FAMILY LIFE

As with post-sixteen choices, the boys' discussions of marriage reflected complex interactions between structure and agency and change and tradition as well as the intersection of race/ethnicity, class and gender. The boys did not straightforwardly accept or reject traditional family structures or practices in relation to marriage. However, they did buy into heterosexual discourses around marriage and family and the need to maintain family approval for marriage. The boys' talk about marriage therefore reflected both change *and* tradition. Families were constructed as still central to future choices. However, the boys also displayed confidence in their ability to change their parents' expectations, drawing on religious discourse to support their 'changed' preference and choices for non-Muslim girls as future spouses.

Marriage within Asian communities has been the focus of media and political debate since the 1970s, when stories of runaway brides and honour killings, escaped or forced marriages, dominated public discourses on Asian families and it remains high on policy and political agendas today. In relation to schooling, research (Brah and Minhas 1985; Parmar 1988; Dwyer 1999; Shain 2003) has challenged policy and academic accounts that positioned Asian youth, especially girls, as caught between two cultures and facing a future of forced tradition and marriage. This research instead highlights that racist assumptions about Pakistani and Bangladeshi communities are often embedded in schools, that Asian and Muslim girls in particular will be expected to marry after leaving school (Parmar 1988). In the aftermath of the July 2005 bombings and in discourses on the 'war on terror', arguments about arranged (often used interchangeably with forced) marriages have also been used to justify intense policing of Muslim communities (Wilson 2006; Bhopal 2010).

The boys talked openly about the topic of arranged marriage, but virtually all of them rejected the idea of arranged marriages when talking about their own futures. Only one boy, Yasser, who described himself as 'mixed-race Pakistani and White English', defended the practice of arranged marriage 'because you want people from your family'. Yasser was the only mixed-race boy in the study and he also attended a different ('successful' [Catholic] school) than the other boys. His attendance at the youth group offered him a rare opportunity to mix with other Pakistani boys, and I would suggest that his need to fit in with the other boys and prove his Pakistani credentials was a possible factor in his defence of arranged marriages.

While disagreeing with the idea, Rafiq said he would consider going along with an arranged marriage, 'because parents look after us for how long and they give me whatever I want', so in return for parental support, Rafiq felt obliged to consider his parents' proposals regarding his future. However, Malik appeared to support discourses of tradition and cultural pathology when he talked about a 'backward mentality' among Asian communities:

Malik: What I'm saying is that there's this backward mentality . . . you've got to recognise that you can't force your children to spend their lives . . . because at the end of the day it's the next person's life yeah, and from the Islamic point of view, we've all got to understand that as long as they're Muslims and they accept the Sharia like you do, well there would be no problem there. Okay, your mum and dad do get a say in it but they should just be happy with you . . . because that doesn't resolve nothing. I mean if I was to send my friend Nadim here and not bring him back until he's married . . . and if he's not happy . . . Then what's the point?

Mushtaq: He might come back hating you.

FS: Is there anyone here who could see themselves marrying a non-Muslim?

Nadim: Omer . . . he's got a . . .

Omer: I would marry her but I would turn her into a Muslim.

Nadim: His mum will say to him . . .

Malik: If you marry a non-Muslim and you want children with a non-Muslim then those children are classed as *haraam* [illegitimate] anyway . . .

(Newtown)

* * *

My parents, on the whole yeah, my parents are chillin'. Well not chillin', because at the end of the day, yeah, I'm out and about MC'ing in all clubs all over the country and now my mum won't say this that bla, bla, bla, she'll say, 'mate go out, do it'. But she knows that I won't drink and I won't bring a girl home and have a kid before I'm married because these are the sort of things that basically we've been brought up that you don't do.

(Malik) (Newtown)

Malik initially draws on a discourse of tradition, suggesting there is a 'backward mentality' among Asian communities which leads them to force their children to marry against their will. However, he then goes onto to draw on an Islamic discourse to argue that change is not permitted under Sharia law, through drawing on the example of mixed-faith marriage. Later, he contrasts his own experience of being allowed to travel freely and being trusted with the 'backward mentality' of more traditional Asian families. In doing so he both challenges and supports the stereotypical notion that Asian Muslim families are constrained by a 'backward mentality' or repression. However, the gender specificity of his response needs to be acknowledged: it is not clear whether this freedom is or should, in Malik's view, be applied equally to boys and girls. In this way traditional gendered expectations around marriage are maintained.

Despite disagreeing with the notion of arranged marriage in relation to their own futures boys spoke positively about their families and defended them. In some cases the boys suggested that older generations were more relaxed and lenient than the boys were. 'As far as these two go, their dad's more chilled out than them two' (Malik). However the family and tradition were central to the boys' imagined futures, as Abid's and Sajid's accounts reveal:

Abid:	Er this sounds a bit funny but . . . I want to get married before my grandparents pass on.
FS:	What kind of person would that have to be?
Abid:	A Muslim . . . not sure yet. I'm too young to think about that sort of stuff.
FS:	But would you marry an English person?
Abid:	I don't know maybe . . . don't really matter as long as they're Muslim.

* * *

Sajid:	I'd marry someone who I know. I don't want an arranged marriage. I'd prefer a love marriage.
FS:	Would you marry an English girl?
Sajid:	Would I? It depends really, miss. If I've known her for a long time but it depends on the parents.

(Leyton High)

For Abid, marrying before his grandparents passed on was important, but he did not imagine necessarily marrying somebody from the same ethnic group. Marrying somebody of the same faith, however, was important. While disagreeing with the notion of arranged marriage, Sajid nonetheless sees his family as critical in the final decision over his choice of partner.

The boys expressed a range of views about their families on marriage. Compared with Muslim and Asian girls they were far more confident about their own agency in choices, whereas the girls in my earlier research (Shain 2003) were also confident but reported having to work hard at persuading parents to accept the role of education in their future. The majority of the girls (especially lower-achieving girls) expected their families to play a large part in the decision, and lower-achieving girls expected their families to choose their husbands for them. The boys, on the other hand, took it for granted that they would have a choice about when and who they would marry.

Asad:	Well I've had a bit of a chat with my parents anyway . . . and they said we won't force you to do anything you don't want to do. So if you don't want to marry the person we choose you can marry

someone else. If you've found someone you tell us and we'll see. So they're quite good about it. You see the people round here . . . I got a choice so that's all right.

Such discussions reveal narratives of both change *and* tradition. Arranged marriage still holds value for boys like Asad, but he and the other boys in the study expressed agency in relation to their own imagined futures.

'I Would Marry a White Girl'

A number of boys saw themselves marrying White English girls, but they drew on Islamic discourse to justify these choices. Even Zahid, who distanced himself from 'Western' habits of drinking and going out, said he would marry an English girl and drew on religious discourse to defend this choice.

Zahid: It's not in Islam . . . in the *Quran* or *Hadith*, it says nothing. In the religion it says that . . . love marriage . . . if someone loves someone I believe they should get married no matter what they are because people nowadays are after *Choudhurys* and *Rajas* [high-status clans] you know all these and I think that's a bit pathetic, and that's not in our religion anyway. People talk things about *Isla* but they don't realise they're making a big issue of it. If someone loves someone they should just get married.

FS: So do you see yourself getting married in a few years? What kind of a person would that be then?

Zahid: Basically I don't know like . . . what my parents views is, my mother's, and it's not necessary that I'll listen to them, if it feels wrong . . .

FS: Would you marry someone who is not a Muslim?

Zahid: Yeah, if they turned to Muslim.

FS: Okay . . . so they could be English?

Zahid: In our religion it's very big *Suwab* [divine blessing] if you make someone into a Muslim.

FS: What about of girls? Is it okay for them to do it, too?

Zahid: Yeah. Girls and boys. Like nowadays people a make a big issue that girls can't go to college, they can't do this, can't go out. But erm, it is wrong for them to go out and do bad things you know against their religion but they can always go to college to get their education . . . Education doesn't do harm at all. Because my sister. My older sister she couldn't do her GCSEs because she was ill and the doctor said she couldn't do them so that was the reason otherwise she was all right. She's going to college next September *inshallah*. But I know some people who say they are at college, they going to be like this or that. They just ruin their lives aren't they, by doing that?

FS: Doing what?

Zahid: Like having boyfriends.

(Leyton)

Zahid asserts that there is no law in Islam preventing Muslims from making their own choice in relation to marriage and that converting a future spouse to Islam earns *Suwab* or divine blessing. But he strategically avoids the question of whether this blessing would be equally applied to girls. For Zahid, girls have an equal right to be educated, as his own sisters have, but as long as they behave modestly and avoid romantic relationships. If they do not and are removed from college, they only have themselves to blame. Zahid is drawing on what Hopkins (2006) calls a discourse of sexist equality, suggesting that girls and women are equal but also displaying double standards around sex and relationships.

Like Zahid, other boys also argued that marrying a non-Muslim was not only permissible but particularly condoned within Islam. Asad, for example, said, 'being Muslim . . . cos when you're Muslim, you don't think about she's a White person, I won't marry her. As long as you like her . . . if you turn her into a Muslim that's good enough for Islam'. Arif also drew on a religious discourse to legitimate his potential choice of a non-Muslim future wife, 'in our religion you've got to impress your parents . . . if you impress your parents, then Allah will be pleased with you and you've more chance of going to paradise'. However, Wahid drew on a discourse of integration: 'I'm not bothered what the background is as long as they're Muslim . . . better if they're not cos then you can be more mixed'. Such accounts represent the continued significance of the tradition in decision making. Family and tradition were cited by the boys as significant factors in their future decisions about marriage. However, the boys' choices did not reflect fixed traditions. Their expressed preferences for White girls as future marriage partners reflected not only change in their narratives, but also a greater degree of integration into Western society than currently suggested by dominant discourses on Muslim and Asian families.

CONCLUSION

This chapter has focused on the future aspirations in relation to education, employment and marriage of a group of working-class boys who self-identified as Muslim. The analysis of the boys' accounts has demonstrated the need to take account of the intersectionality of class, race, ethnicity and gender in shaping the boys' current educational choices and their imagined futures.

Most of the boys showed marked preferences for vocational subjects in relation to post-sixteen academic choices, which resonates with wider research and statistical evidence on the choices made by Muslim and ethnic minority students. Boys in the higher sets within their schools were more instrumental and demonstrated 'high' aspiration towards careers in medicine or law. However, virtually all the boys expressed a strong desire to continue their studies after compulsory schooling, which reflected to some extent the success of widening participation and life-long learning policy discourses. A significant factor here is the absence of the ready availability of unskilled manual work, unlike in the 1970s when working-class boys generally left school and entered into manual labour. Policies centring on lifelong learning and widening participation have produced what some refer to as 'delayed transitions' and in this context the desire to stay on for further study after compulsory schooling could be seen as somewhat inevitable and reflective of the classed location of the boys. However, there is also an added layer of cultural complexity that challenges dominant theorising on risk and individualisation. The boys showed both 'high' and 'low' aspirations, sometimes simultaneously, displaying what seemed to be contradictory ambitions. As in the wider research on working-class students, the need to stay local was a strong constraining factor, but some boys also talked confidently about moving away from the local area or imagined that they would. In one sense these contradictory pulls cohere with the discourses inherent in government policies aimed at disadvantaged young people in urban areas. As Brown (2012) notes, the policies depend on and indeed confirm the localism of the choice making of working-class young people at the same time as they call on young people to aspire to 'better' and more mobile futures.

The boys' accounts presented in this chapter did not, however, simply reflect the individualised choice making associated with sociological theories of individualisation and neo-liberal discourses of risk but rather the continued significance of the influence of family and community. Contrary to theories suggesting that individual biographies are tied less to tradition and social structures of class, race and gender, the boys' choices reflected strong ties with community and tradition at the same time that the boys were challenging some of those traditions. Exploring the boys' educational aspirations alongside their imagined futures confirms the importance of taking an intersectional approach to the analysis. Marriage has often been constructed in media, policy and academic discourses as an inhibiting factor in girls' educational choices, and especially in relation to their participation beyond compulsory education. Less attention has been given to the relationship between boys' educational aspirations and future expectations for marriage and the boys' accounts show marriage was not constructed as a hindering factor to educational choice. This chapter has highlighted the cultural and structural complexities underpinning the decision-making and educational aspirations of young people. The boys largely imagined a heterosexual future and expected to have a strong say in their future choice of marriage. They also drew on religion to legitimate and defend choices that might otherwise have been considered unacceptable. These choices therefore reflect both tradition *and* change, so presenting a challenge both to dominant policy and political discourses which position Muslim communities as lacking aspiration and overly determined by tradition and culture. At the same time they challenge theories of individualisation which suggest that young people's choices are now less influenced by tradition and social structures of class, race and gender. Muslim boys' educational aspirations and their future expectations around career and marriage are shaped by complex intersections of race, ethnicity, gender, sexuality and religion as well as culture, structure and agency.

NOTES

1. All names and places are replaced with pseudonyms to protect the anonymity of the participants.

REFERENCES

Abbas, Tahir. 2004. *The* Education *of British South Asians: Ethnicity, Capital and Class Structure*. London: Palgrave Macmillan.

Ahmad, Fauzia. 2001. 'Modern Traditions? British Muslim Women and Academic Achievement'. *Gender and Education* 13 (2): 137–152.

Alexander, Claire, E. 2004. 'Imagining the Asian Gang: Ethnicity, Masculinity, and Youth after "the Riots"'. *Critical Social Policy* 24 (4): 526–549.

Archer, Louise. 2003. *Race, Masculinity and Schooling*. Buckingham: Open University Press.

Archer, Louise and Hiromi Yamashita. 2003. 'Theorising Inner-City Masculinities: "Race", Class, Gender and Education'. *Gender and Education* 15 (2): 115–132.

Archer, Louise and Becky Francis. 2006. 'Challenging classes? Exploring the role of social class within the identities and achievement of British Chinese pupils'. *Sociology, 40*(1), 29–49.

Archer, Louise and Becky Francis 2007. *Understanding minority ethnic achievement: race, gender, class and 'success'*. Routledge.

Ball, Stephen. 2003. *Class Strategies and the Educational Market: The Middle Classes and Social Advantage*. London. RoutledgeFalmer.

Ball, Stephen, Meg Maguire and Sheila Macrae. 2000. *Choice, Pathways and Transitions Post-Sixteen*. London: Routledge.

Ball, Stephen, Diane Reay and Miriam David. 2002. '"Ethnic Choosing": Minority Ethnic Students and Higher Education Choice'. *Race Ethnicity and Education* 5 (4): 333–357.

Beck, Ulrich. 1992. *Risk Society: Towards a New Modernity*. London: Sage.

Bhachu, Parminder. 1991. 'Culture and Ethnicity amongst Punjabi Sikh Women in 1990s Britain'. *New Community* 17 (3): 401–412.

Bhattacharyya, Gargi, Liz Ison and Maud Blair. 2003. *Minority Ethnic Attainment and Participation in Education and Training: The Evidence*. London: Department for Education and Skills.

Bhopal, Kalwant. 2010. *Asian Women and Higher Education: Communities of Practice*. Stoke-on-Trent: Trentham.

Brah, Avtar, and Rehana Minhas. 1985. 'Structural Racism or Cultural Difference'. In *Just a Bunch of Girls*, edited by Gaby Weiner, 14–25. Buckingham: Open University Press.

Brine, Jacky. 2006. 'Lifelong Learning and the Knowledge Economy: Those That Know and Those That Do Not—The Discourse of the European Union'. *British Educational Research Journal* 32 (5): 649–665.

Brown, Gavin. 2012. 'The Place of Aspiration In UK Widening Participation Policy: Moving Up or Moving Beyond?' In *Critical Geographies of Childhood and Youth*, edited by Peter Kraftl, John Horton and Faith Yucker, 97–113. London: Policy Press.

Cantle, Ted. 2001. *Community Cohesion*. London: Home Office.

Cohen, Phil, and Patrick Ainley. 2000. 'In the Country of the Blind? Youth Studies and Cultural Studies in Britain'. *Journal of Youth Studies* 3 (1): 79–95.

Crozier, Gill and Jane Davis. 2006. 'Family matters: a discussion of the Bangladeshi and Pakistani extended family and community in supporting the children's education'. The Sociological Review, 54(4), 678–695.

DCLG . 2009 The Turkish and Turkish Cypriot community in England: understanding Muslim ethnic communities. London: Department for Communities and Local Government

Dwyer, Claire. 1999. 'Veiled Meanings: British Muslim Women and the Negotiation of Differences'. Gender, Place and Culture 6 (1): 5–26.

Enneli, Pinar, Tariq Modood and Harriet Bradley. 2005. *Young Turks and Kurds: A Set of Invisible Disadvantaged Groups*. York: Joseph Rowntree Foundation

Furlong, Andy and Fred Cartmel. 1997. *Young People and Social Change: Individualization and Risk in Late Modernity*. Buckingham: Open University Press.

Gewirtz, Sharon. 2001. 'Cloning the Blairs: New Labour's Programme for the Re-Socialization of Working-Class Parents'. *Journal of Education Policy* 16 (4): 365–378.

Giddens, Anthony. 1991. *Modernity and Self-Identity*. Cambridge: Polity Press.

———. 2003. 'Risk and Responsibility'. *Modern Law Review* 62 (1): 1–10.

Gillborn, David. 2008. *Racism and Education: Coincidence or Conspiracy*. London: Routledge.

Gillborn, David, and Heidi Mirza. 2000. *Educational Inequality: Mapping Race, Class and Gender*. London: OFSTED.

Gillborn, David, and Deborah Youdell. 2000. *Rationing Education: Policy, Practice, Reform, and Equity*. Buckingham: Open University Press.

Gilroy, Paul. 1987. *There Ain't No Black in the Union Jack: The Cultural Politics of Race and Nation*. London: Hutchinson.

Glees, Anthony, and Chris Pope. 2005. *When Students Turn to Terror: Terrorist and Extremist Activity on British Campuses*. London: Social Affairs Unit.

Goodwin, John, and Henrietta O' Connor. 2005. 'Exploring Complex Transitions: Looking back at the Golden Age of from School to Work'. *Sociology* 39 (2): 201–220.

Hodkinson, Phil. 2004. 'Career Decision-Making, Learning Careers and Career Progression'. Nuffield Review paper given at Working Day II, February 23.

Home Office. 2002. *Building Cohesive Communities: A Report of the Ministerial Group on Public Order and Community Cohesion. (Denham Report.)* London: Home Office.

———. 2009. *Pursue Prevent Protect Prepare: The United Kingdom's Strategy for Countering International Terrorism*. London: HMSO

Hodkinson, Phil. 2005. 'Learning as cultural and relational: Moving past some troubling dualisms'. *Cambridge Journal of Education*, 35 (1): 107–119.

Hopkins, Peter. 2006. 'Youthful Muslim Masculinities: Gender and Generational Relation'. *Transactions of the Institute of British Geographers* 31 (3): 337–352.

Hussain, Yasmin, and Paul Bagguley. 2007. *Moving on Up: Asian Women and Higher Education*. Stoke-on-Trent: Trentham.

Kundnani, Arun. 2009. Spooked! How Not to Prevent *Violent Extremism*. London: Institute of Race Relations. www.irr.org.uk/pdf2/spooked.pdf. Accessed December 15 2012

McDonald, Paula, Barbara Pini, Janis Bailey and Robin Price. 2011. 'Contested Terrain: Youth's Aspirations for Education, Work, Family and Leisure'. Work, Employment and Society 25 (1): 68–84.

McDowell, Linda. 2002. 'Masculine Discourses and Dissonances: Strutting "Lads", Protest Masculinity and Domestic Respectability'. *Environment and Planning D: Society and Space* 20:97–119.

Mirza, Heidi. 1992. *Young, Female and Black*. London: Routledge.

Mirza, Heidi, and Diane Reay. 2000. 'Spaces and Places of Educational Desire: Supplementary Schools as a New Social Movements'. *Sociology* 34 (3): 521–544.

Mirza, Heidi, 2009. *Race, gender and educational desire: Why black women succeed and fail*. Taylor and Francis US.

Modood, Tariq. 2006. 'Ethnicity, Muslims and Higher Education Entry in Britain'. *Teaching in Higher Education* 11 (2): 247–250.

Modood, Tariq, and Tony Acland, eds. 1998. Race and Higher Education: Opportunities, Experiences and *Challenges*. London: Policy Studies Institute.

Modood, Tariq, and Michael Shiner. 1994. *Ethnic Minorities and Higher Education: Why Are There Differential Rites of Entry?* London: Policy Studies Institute.

Mythen, Gabe. 2005 'From "Goods" to "Bads"? Revisiting the Political Economy of Risk'. *Sociological Research Online* 10 (3). http://www.socresonline.org.uk/10/3/mythen.html Accessed December 15 2012

Parmar, Parminder. 1988. 'Gender, Race and Power: The Challenge to Youth Work Practice'. In *Multiracist Britain*, edited by Philip Cohen and Harwant Bains, 236–275. London: Macmillan.

Raco, Mike. 2009. 'From Expectations to Aspiration: State Modernisation, Urban Policy, and the Existential Politics of Welfare in the UK'. *Political Geography* 28:436–444.

Ramamurthy, Anandi. 2006. 'The Politics of Britain's Asian Youth Movements'. *Race and Class* 48 (2): 38–60.

Reay, Diane, Miriam David and Stephen Ball. 2001. 'Making a Difference?: Institutional Habituses and Higher Education Choice'. *Sociological Research Online* 5 (4). http://www.socresonline.org.uk/5/4/reay.html. Accessed December 15 2012

Renold, Emma. 2005. *Girls, Boys and Junior Sexualities: Exploring Children's Gender and Sexual Relations in the Primary School*. London: RoutledgeFalmer.

Roberts, Ken. 1995. *Youth and Employment in Modern Britain*. Oxford: Oxford University Press.

Rose, Nicholas. 1996. *Inventing Our Selves: Psychology, Power and Personhood*. New York: Cambridge University Press.

Savage, Mike. 2000. *Class Analysis and Social Transformation*. London: Routledge.

Shah, Bindi, Claire Dwyer and Tariq Modood. 2010. 'Explaining Educational Achievement and Career Aspirations among Young British Pakistanis: Mobilizing "Ethnic Capital"'? *Sociology* 44 (6): 1109–1127.

Shain, Farzana. 2003. *The Schooling and Identity of Asian Girls*. Stoke-on-Trent: Trentham Books.

———. 2009. 'Uneasy Alliances: Muslims and Communists'. *Journal of Communist Studies and Transnational Politics* 25 (1): 95–109.

———. 2011. *New Folk Devils: Muslim Boys and Education in England*. Stoke-on-Trent: Trentham Books.

———. 2012. 'Intersections of "Race", Class and Gender in the Social and Political Identifications of Young Muslims in England'. In *Intesectionality and 'Race' Education*, edited by Kalwant Bhopal and John Preston, 138–157. New York: Routledge.

Sivanandan, Ambalavaner. 1982. *A Different Hunger: Writings on Black Resistance*. London: Pluto Press.

Skeggs, Beverley. 1997. Formations of Class *and Gender: Becoming Respectable*. London: Sage.

———. 2004. *Class, Self, Culture*. London: Routledge.

Smart, Carol, and Becky Shipman. 2010. 'Visions in Monochrome: Families, Marriage and the Individualization Thesis'. *British Journal of Sociology* 55 (4): 491–509.

Stafford, Bruce, and Dierdre Duffy. 2009. 'Review of Evidence on the Impact of Economic Downturn on Disadvantaged Groups'. Working Paper No 68, London, Department for Work and Pensions.

Tackey, Nii Djan, Helen Barnes and Priya Khambhaita. 2011. *Poverty, Ethnicity and Education*. London: Institute of Employment Studies/Joseph Rowntree Foundation.

Taylor, Paul. 1992 . 'Ethnic group data and applications to higher education'. *Higher Education Quarterly*, 46, 359–374.

Thapar, Suruchi, and Gurchathen Sanghera. 2010. 'Building Social Capital and Education: The Experiences of Pakistani Muslims in the UK'. *International Journal of Social Inquiry* 3 (2): 3–24.

Vickerstaff, Sarah A. 2003. 'Apprenticeship in the "Golden Age": Were Youth Transitions Really Smooth and Unproblematic Back Then?' *Work, Employment and Society* 17 (2): 269–287.

Wilson, Amrit. 2006. *Dreams, Questions, Struggles: South Asian Women in Britain*. London: Institute of Race Relations.

Wright, Cecile, Penny J. Standen and Tina Patel. 2010. Black *Youth Matters: Transitions from School to Success*. New York: Routledge.

Yosso, Tara J. 2005. 'Whose Culture Has Capital? A Critical Race Theory Discussion of Community Cultural Wealth'. *Race Ethnicity and Education* 8 (1): 69–91.

8 Gendered Surveillance and the Social Construction of Young Muslim Women in Schools

Heidi Safia Mirza and Veena Meetoo

INTRODUCTION: SITUATING 'SURVEILLANCE'

In this chapter we interrogate the ways in which young Muslim women are subject to the highly visible mainstream cultural discourses of gendered surveillance, risk, safety and well-being in school. Drawing on the narratives of seventeen young Muslim women aged sixteen to nineteen we found their gendered subjectivity and experiences in school were lived through Islamophobic discourses that circulated in educational spaces. The official heightened preoccupation with Muslim gendered cultural restrictions and ethno-religious transgressions, such as forced marriage or honour crimes manifested itself in the young women's bodily regulation, which was apparent within the localised school site, and beyond into the wider educational policy discourse.

Employing an intersectional theoretical framework, we identify three dominant narrative constructions of young Muslim women in schools which are located within the cross-cutting modalities of religion, race, class, gender and sexuality. First, the raced, gendered and sexual bodily regulation of young Muslim women was visible through the teachers' narratives on the headscarf.[1] The young women recounted experiences of added surveillance by teachers explicitly linked to their wearing of religious dress in school. Second, we present a gendered, racialised, class narrative that positions Muslim girls at risk of the heightened regulation from their families and community by examining the schools' responses to such issues. We map how the schools intervened in everyday cultural practices by working towards producing the model neo-liberal middle-class student. Here, teachers and parent liaison officers would encourage the young working-class women to actively challenge their culture through discourses grounded in Western feminist ideals of female 'empowerment'. Lastly, we present the raced, gendered, religious narrative construction of Muslim girls in educational policy that—in contrast to Muslim boys—positions them as simultaneously visible and invisible, resulting in the failure of institutions and professionals to effectively respond to their safety needs when issues of risk and personal safety arise in school.

The three narrative constructions demonstrate the way in which Muslim young women have become objects of surveillance in educational spaces. The reification of their cultural/religious difference, and in particular the preoccupation with their over-determined dress, has made them an Islamophobic signifier, symbolic of the 'barbaric Muslim other' that has existed in the Western imagination since the terrorist attacks of 9/11 (Mirza 2012). Discourses in schools and at a policy level attach wider social and political meaning that 'sticks to' the Muslim female body (Ahmed 2004), constructing her as the 'oppressed other' in need of protection and thus open to pastoral intervention. In what Haw (2009) describes as the 'mythical feedback loop', the media's emphasis on signifying stories of 'backward' Muslim practices, such as veiling, impacts on the identity of the wider British Muslim community, which in turn affects the young women's internal world and sense of self. As Sara Ahmed (2004) explains, the figure of the veiled Muslim woman challenges the values that are crucial to the multicultural nation, such as freedom and culture, making her a symbol of what the nation must give up to be itself. Thus being visibly 'non-assimilated' in a multicultural society invites a certain type of benign surveillance as 'standing out' invokes deep feelings of need, rejection and anxiety within the majority 'White other'. The Muslim woman's demand to be 'different' (i.e. wear the veil) is seen as a rejection of the welcoming embrace or 'gift' of the multicultural 'host' society.

The African American feminist writer Patricia Hill Collins (1998) argues surveillance has become an effective means of control when the power of hegemonic whiteness is placed under threat. She shows how Black women are now closely 'watched' as they enter and circulate within desegregated White public environments. She writes, 'surveillance seems designed to produce particular effects—Black women remain visible yet silenced; their bodies become written by other texts, yet they remain powerless to speak for themselves' (1998, 38). Thus bodily surveillance can be seen as a powerful means of gendered/racialised regulation in institutionalised settings such as the school. Foucault argues state surveillance of populations happens not only through the monitoring of births, marriages and deaths, but also through the surveillance of certain groups. The 'problematic behaviour' of such groups becomes the legitimate object of professional observation and policy regulation (Foucault 1979). It is an understanding of the nature of this professional and policy regulation and its effects on the young Muslim women that is our concern within this chapter.

THE SOCIAL CONSTRUCTION OF THE 'YOUNG FEMALE AND MUSLIM' PUPIL IN SCHOOL

This chapter focuses on the ways in which young Muslim women's gendered subjectivity and experiences in school were lived through the powerful

Islamophobic discourses that circulated in educational spaces. Key global events have increased the visibility of Muslim females in schools. Since the 2001 bombing of the Twin Towers on 9/11 in the US and the 2005 7/7 bombings by young British Muslim men in the UK, there has been an overwhelming preoccupation with the 'embodied' Muslim woman in British public spaces (Mirza 2012). Haw (2009) pinpoints the case of Shabina Begum, a young Muslim girl who was excluded from school for wearing the jilbab and the heightened media debate she aroused as having particular significance for educational discourse. A consequence of such heightened visibility is reflected in the ways in which young Muslim women are increasingly constructed in the professional educational imagination as a racialised group, marking a departure from the ethnic categorisation of Pakistani and Bangladeshi girls. In our study, the young Muslim women were commonly referred to by teachers as a distinct category of student with a shared identity that marked them as different from other racialised groups.

Studies that focus explicitly on young Muslim women in secondary schools have emphasised their femininity and oppression by their home culture (as opposed to the freedom of school). This is usually explored through the symbolism of their clothing and choice in marriage (Haw 2009). The representation of these young women as the over-controlled victims of oppressive cultures means 'it is a common experience for Asian (and Muslim) girls to be ignored or marginalised in classroom interaction because it is assumed that they are industrious, hardworking and get on quietly with their work' (Shain 2003, 62). Such representations inform teacher expectations of young Muslim women, who are commonly stereotyped by their teachers as having poor attendance, low self-esteem and on the receiving end of low academic expectations from their parents. Zine's (2006) study of Muslim girls in Canada shows how those who wear headscarves struggle with their teachers' common assumptions that they are oppressed at home and that Islam does not value education for women. These assumptions then get translated into the girls' experiences of 'low teacher expectations and streaming practices where [they] were encouraged to avoid academic subjects and stick to lower non-academic streams' (Zine 2006, 244).

Basit (1997) conducted interviews with fifteen- and sixteen-year-old Muslim girls in the east of England to explore how the dynamics of Muslim family life impact on their identities. Her study reveals interesting insights into the mismatched perceptions of the teachers and the Muslim girls. The teachers believed that British Muslim girls were lacking freedom at home which they had at school, and that this was a cause of tension between them and less restricted (White) English girls. The Muslim girls, on the other hand, wanted more freedom, but not as much as the English girls had because this freedom was perceived as a symptom of parental neglect. Basit identified that the girls were in 'a process of constant negotiation winning more freedom in certain areas, such as education, by behaving in accordance with parental wishes, such as not going out with boys' (1997, 436).

Research with working-class Pakistani, Bangladeshi and Indian girls aged thirteen to sixteen conducted by Shain (2003) shows them actively engaged in producing new identities that draw on both residual cultures of the home and the local and regional cultures they now inhabit. Shain described four strategies for survival employed by her interviewees. First, resistance through asserting their Asian cultural identity, a response in the main to experiences of racism. Second, survival by passivity, working within stereotypes and focusing on academic achievement. Third, rebelling against their parental and community values. Fourth, asserting religious identity. Like Shain, who found the wearing of non-Western clothes to school as an important site for the contestation of school identities, Dwyer (1999) describes young Muslim women as mixing Western and Muslim styles to create new ethnicities. The Muslim girls in Dwyer's study described clothing in oppositional terms as either Asian or English, and articulated an alternative narrative which disrupted dominant representations of Muslim women's oppression through the symbol of the veil. They spoke about veiling as libratory by arguing that the veil offers women protection from the male heterosexual gaze. This is in contrast to Hamzeh's (2011) findings in which the restricted gendering discourses on the 'veil' challenged Muslim girl's opportunities for learning. The young Muslim women in her study contested, or 'deveiled' the visual, spatial, ethical and gendering discourses of the hijab enforced by their parents by questioning and strategically adapting their dress, mobility in public places and physical behaviour around boys.

In the context of the young women's articulation of new and alternative identities, this chapter seeks to understand the nature of Muslim young women's layered experiences of surveillance and regulation in educational spaces. The theoretical possibilities offered by the epistemological concept of intersectionality enables us to analyse the multiple dimensions of race, class, gender, sexuality and religion in the context of macro Islamophobic discourses that circulate in the West and how it is experienced at the micro level of young women's lived lives. It is to a consideration of this theoretical framework which we now turn.

THEORISING MUSLIM YOUNG WOMEN AT THE INTERSECTION OF RACE, CLASS, GENDER, SEXUALITY AND RELIGION

We used an intersectional approach to deconstruct and frame the accounts from the young Muslim women, parents, teachers and policymakers to illuminate how young Muslim women are currently positioned in social discourse at the level of the school. Intersectionality is an evolving approach which is increasingly being applied in understanding inequalities and identities referring to:

The interaction between gender, race and other categories of difference in individual lives, social practices, institutional arrangements,
and cultural ideologies and the outcomes of these interactions in terms
of power. (Davis 2008, 68)

Kimberlé Williams Crenshaw (1994) first coined the term specifically in
relation to violence against women of colour in a legal context, highlighting the nature of problems encountered in the judicial system due to being
a Black woman. She metaphorically drew on the example of a traffic light
at the crossroads where gender and race meet and the implications such
embodiment carries which can further disadvantage the position of the
Black woman. Crenshaw argued that the structural obstacles women of
colour face make them more vulnerable than White women to battery and
rape. Whereas the ideas characterising intersectionality are not new, and
have been engaged with particularly by Black feminists e.g. hooks (1981)
and Collins (1998), an intersectional approach provides a potential space
where a diverse range of experiences beyond being 'Black' and female can
be interrogated.

The focus on interaction between socially constructed categories allows
for an understanding of how divisions are produced and reproduced in relation to one another, rather than as separate categories of difference (Yuval
Davis 2006). It facilitates an examination of individualised and highly contextualised identities and social positioning in terms of time, place and other
intersecting social locations (Phoenix and Pattynama 2006). Moreover, it
is argued that intersectionality enables us to see that different dimensions
of social life cannot be separated out into discrete and pure strands. As
Brah and Phoenix write, 'we regard the concept of intersectionality as signifying the complex, irreducible, varied, and variable effects which ensue
when multiple axis of differentiation—economic, political, cultural, psy-
chic, subjective and experiential—intersect in historically specific contexts'
(2004, 76). In this sense intersectionality draws our attention to the ways
in which identities, as subject positions, are not reducible to just one or
two or three or even more dimensions, such as 'race' or 'gender' or 'class'
layered onto each other in an additive or hierarchical way. Intersectionality,
offers a more complex epistemology referring to the converging and con-
terminous ways in which the differentiated and variable organising logics
of race, class and gender and other social divisions such as sexuality, age,
disability, ethnicity, culture, religion and belief simultaneously structure
the macro material conditions which produce micro everyday 'lived' social
and economic inequalities.

In the case of young Muslim women, an intersectional analysis provides
the scope to examine processes of gendered racialisation in relation to sexuality, class and religion, amongst others such as age. Such an analysis of the
interplay of multiple social positioning provides an opportunity to tease out
the process by which categories are produced, experienced, reproduced and

resisted in everyday life (McCall 2005). For instance, some categories of difference may be troubled in some contexts and not others. For example, the religious identity of Muslim girls in schools can be seen as negative and constraining in contrast to the home, where it is seen as a positive attribute by the family and girls themselves (Ramji 2007). Furthermore, unlike feminist theory or Critical Race Theory, which are both more ideologically situated, an intersectional approach can allow for an understanding of ruptures and signs of resilience or resistance that the girls may demonstrate (Staunaes 2003).

THE STUDY: ACCESSING MUSLIM YOUNG WOMEN IN SCHOOLS

The research on the seventeen young Muslim women discussed here formed part of a larger European Union–funded study, 'Young Migrant Women in Secondary Education—Promoting Integration and Mutual Understanding through Dialogue and Exchange'.[2] The project's overall purpose was to address the gender gaps in European integration and equality policies in schools and investigate the implications of 'gender mainstreaming' for young ethnic migrant women in education. The participating European countries, which included Cyprus, Greece, Spain, Malta and England, adopted a critical gender perspective to evaluate the five national case studies.

In England we selected two inner-city state secondary schools situated in a large urban conurbation in south-east England. The young migrant women (n = 34) were sixteen to nineteen years of age and in the Sixth Form. 'Hazelville' was a large mixed-sex state comprehensive school, with a highly diverse population in terms of class, ethnicity and the migration routes of students and their families. The school was in a 'gentrified' area; however, the majority of students were working class of African Caribbean heritage (approximately 60 per cent), followed by White British (30 per cent) and lastly 'other' ethnic groups, which included the Muslim pupils (10 per cent). The Muslim girls in Hazelville were recent migrants (i.e. three to thirteen years in the UK) and came from many different countries, including Somalia, Burundi, Sierra Leone, Afghanistan and India. In contrast, 'Bushill' was an all-girls state secondary school located in an inner-city borough classified as one of the most economically disadvantaged in the country. The mainly Bangladeshi families of the young women reflected the low socio-economic status of the population that defined the area. Ninety-four per cent of the school's pupils were Muslim. They were mainly second- and third-generation Bangladeshis with a parent or grandparent who had been a migrant. The school achieves highly in national inspection reports and also in academic performance with significant numbers of students going on to higher education.

Access to the schools was facilitated through teacher, research and professional networks. The research team had an established relationship with teaching staff at Hazelville, which was also a partnership school of the

Institute of Education, where the project was based. Through 'snowball-ing' via teacher networks, the team gained access to the second school. To interrogate the policy dimensions of the project, in-depth interviews were also conducted with teachers and pastoral staff across the two schools (n = 7), and with policy actors at both national government (n = 4) and local level (n = 3). Finally one focus group was conducted with migrant parents who were part of a parental involvement group (n = 13) to whom access and translation was facilitated by one of the local policy actors.

The interviews were carried out in English by the research team, Veena Meetoo and Heidi Mirza. Both of us are women of South Asian heritage with migrant parents, enabling us to draw on an insider/in-betweener (Hamzeh 2011) and 'located' positionality (Mirza 2009) in the research process. Ethical approval for the project was sought through the Institute of Education ethics committee, and in keeping with codes of confidential-ity, the identity of the participants, names of students, teachers, govern-ment and local policy actors and the two schools have been changed. An iterative interpretative approach was used to develop the emerging themes from the qualitative narratives elicited from the interviews and focus groups. Ongoing findings were discussed with the other project partners and an agreed coding frame for analysing the data was developed using a critical feminist intersectional framework in order to gain an understand-ing of the ways in which racism, patriarchy, religion and other systems of oppression simultaneously structured the young women's cultural and social space in schools.

The findings on the three dominant narrative constructions of Muslim young women—first, through dress and bodily regulation; second, through the production of the model student; and, third, through their visibility and invisibility in policy—are explored in the sections that follow.

BODILY REGULATION: MUSLIM GIRLS, TEACHERS AND THE HEADSCARF

Muslim women who wear the headscarf or hijab have largely been con-structed as a homogenous group, oppressed and lacking agency (Afshar 2008; Khiabany and Williamson 2008). As Hamzeh (2011) points out, the *hijab* is a socially constructed gendering discourse that has hegemonised women's ways of thinking and acting for centuries. She suggests the *hijab* discourse is not a simplified argument around dress, 'but an unexposed complex pattern of normative values and practices which act as a social force that sets the conditions for the construction of material reality' (2011, 485). It is therefore important to map how Muslim females' bodies become sites through which the cross-cutting modalities of race, class, gender, sex-uality and religion are lived, contested and experienced at the intersection of different social spaces and in different historical times (Brah 1996).

We found wearing the headscarf was reluctantly accepted by many White teachers as a given in a multicultural school context. The young women recounted many negative experiences linked to wearing religious dress. In these cases the headscarf was not taken seriously—seen as merely an outward display of imposed necessary religiosity—a facade behind which the girls hide their 'true self'. It was as if given the opportunity they would relinquish the burden and 'take it off'. As the following extract from one young Muslim woman demonstrates:

> There are a few teachers who, like, I wouldn't say they have a problem with our faith, but they do make a few comments which sometimes I just think are unnecessary. . . . You know like it's been quite hot the past week and stuff, the teacher would say something like—'Are you not so hot with your scarf? Why don't you take it off? I won't tell your mum'. It's like we wear it for our parents, but we don't. Just comments like that. (Focus Group, Bushill)

The headscarf was seen as an annoyance and hindrance by some teachers, often open to blatant disrespect, such as the following example in Bushill involving a young White male teacher demonstrates:

> We had a teacher who was annoyed with a student because she'd been doodling on the table, and the response to that, because he was totally annoyed and vexed, his response to that was—'Why don't you clean it with your headscarf?' (Focus Group, Bushill)

Secretly 'taking it off' or using it 'to clean' were forms of derision used to minimise or undermine the headscarf's (or niqab's) seemingly imposing and threatening physical presence. In the teachers eyes to be proved a 'true Muslim' meant the young women's faith constantly had to be tested. This was no more evident as in the case when one White middle-class teacher saw it as her duty to police the 'correct' wearing of the headscarf. For Jane, the head of inclusion at Hazelville, the Muslim female's authenticity had to be measured through her headscarf:

> My issue is Muslim girls, in particular, wearing a headscarf with big earrings, and actually the two are mutually exclusive, because the headscarf is about being modest isn't it? . . . It's about not drawing attention to yourself, because you are there as a vehicle for God, not as a body yourself, right? I understand that these students are tremendously conflicted about their place within society . . . I think I'm the only teacher in the school . . . the only teacher in the school who actually tells girls off for wearing [a] headscarf and earrings, and I say, 'It's either the headscarf or it's the earrings, it's not both'. And the reason I do that, it's partly because of I want them to be proud of who

they are, and if they are saying—'I'm a Muslim and I am wearing the headscarf'—and I realise they may not be given the choice, right, but if they are saying that, do it, do it; don't send a mixed message. (Jane, Head of Inclusion, Hazelville)

In Jane's view, young Muslim women who wear the headscarf, whether out of choice or not, should perform the fixed utopian Muslim femininity that she 'knew'. For Jane, there is no accommodation; her authoritative gaze was grounded in her 'rightful' knowledge of Islamic religious identification. She continues:

I think they make themselves vulnerable by doing it, because they send a mixed message . . . because I think they are reinforcing stereotypes actually of—they are not really religious, they are, that they are terrorists—or—I know she wears a headscarf, but she 'wants it' really—you know, that's why I think they make themselves vulnerable, because I think they are sending a mixed message . . . I think that reinforces that stereotype of [*whispers*]—they are not really religious. Do you know what I mean? And to me that is unbearable, because I think it's very disrespectful to all the people who actually are Muslim, practicing Muslims, and are very wonderful people, as most people are.

The headscarf, as a signifier of Islam, has become an 'identity site' where some teachers not only feel free to openly contest the young Muslim women's religious identity, but also use it to regulate their emerging sexuality. In these oppositional contexts, the headscarf was used by some teachers as a legitimate means to regulate, punish and control the young women's behaviour in the class (i.e. to use for cleaning), morality on the streets (i.e. no wearing of earrings) and test their inner faith (i.e. to secretly take it off).

However, there were other less oppositional encounters with Muslim female dress in the schools. Unlike Hazelville, where the headscarf was the exception, at Bushill the hijab was part of the uniform worn by most of the girls. This normalisation of Muslim dress and values within the school was seen as providing a 'safe space' for the Muslim majority, as the deputy head Katie explains:

The girls and their communities themselves are quite marginalised, so it's by sticking together that they get strength, so they look after each other because the world outside isn't necessarily as welcoming and friendly. So we are like a haven for them, and often a haven from their community and their families, actually, as well as from the world outside the family. So they have that to think of (Bushill) as a safe place. (Katie, Deputy Head, Bushill)

However, within this gendered Muslim 'haven', the embodied relationship between sexuality, dress and academic achievement was still feminised and policed in the school.

> There are certainly girls who are cooler than others; you know, there's always the fashionable girls. But I think you have a real sense here of students making choices, so the students, the girls are kind of aware that if they choose to spend endless hours on makeup and clothes, fashion, boys, then they are not going to do as well academically, and you kind of see them making that choice. (Katie, Deputy Head, Bushill)

The young women's subversive expressions of their emerging sexuality through 'choice' of dress and style were seen to be at odds with an academic identity and doing well at school. For Shain, traditional South Asian dress was 'an important site for the contestation of school identities' (2003, 65). Similarly, Claire Dwyer's (1999) interviews with young Muslim women engage with the premise that the veil is a marker of difference and how they use dress to construct identity in a school context. Styles were mixed to create new 'hybrid' ethnicities, as young women explored their identity through clothes and fashion.

However, this focus on fashion could also lead to bullying and victimisation, as Shani, who migrated from Burundi, illustrated. She spoke of how she was picked on and bullied during her years at secondary school and chose to wear the full niqab as her mother, who was depressed and on incapacity benefits, could not afford to buy her nice clothes:

> Everyone used to look down on me and . . . I don't know . . . I think because, like, I don't fit in, because I don't fit in with the trends. I don't have the nice new trainers. I don't fit in with what they do and stuff like that. (Shani, Burundi, Hazelville)

Shani's experience highlights other forms of surveillance and regulation through dress, including peer group sanctions through cruelty and Shani's own self-surveillance expressed in her decision to wear the niqab through despair rather than faith or choice. Here social class is entwined with gender, race and religion as it features in the everyday schooling experience of one Muslim young woman.

Our findings show how Muslim young women are subject to teachers' expectations about what it means to be a 'true' and 'good' Muslim girl, which is particularly manifested through bodily regulation and dress. At the heart of such assumptions lies a preoccupation with the symbolic meaning of the headscarf. Teachers' perceptions of the young women wearing the veil were bounded by popular concerns about their agency and scope for choice. Through their subjection to embodied surveillance prevalent in the cultural and social space of the school, young women's lives were structured by both openly expressed gendered religious racism, as well as the more subtle forms of covert regulation of their sexuality and social class.

GENDERED REGULATION: FAMILY AND COMMUNITY SURVEILLANCE AND THE 'MODEL MUSLIM FEMALE' STUDENT

Muslim young women were often perceived as 'at risk' from the heightened regulation from their family and community by the school. This was not surprising as there is a common perception that Muslim and South Asian young women are heavily controlled by their families and community (Ghuman 2003). With so much focus on family regulation, little is known about the diverse manifestations of gendered surveillance in the school site. Many of the young Muslim women recounted stories of being controlled by community members both in and outside school. Such surveillance was tied to regulation of their sexuality and can be partially understood through notions of honour and shame (*izzat*), which feature highly in public discourses about women of South Asian and Muslim background (Werbner 2007; Haw 2009).

Munizeh from Afghanistan spoke of being policed by other members of her ethnic community on the school site. She explains how a younger Afghan boy watched her and subsequently reported back to her father:

> [He was] saying bad words . . . saying things that are not true, to people, like from in my family . . . They said, 'your daughter is with boys, hanging around with Black boys, and sitting in the car' . . . Thank God my father didn't trust them. Because, I mean, the teacher . . . was involved in this, even went up to my dad and said this was mis-accusations . . . and I never had a relationship with him, he's just a guy from there, and he just keeps on observing every move I make . . . In the beginning, when he used to do it I didn't feel comfortable to come to the school . . . Why would this guy observe you and look at you twenty-four hours and tell bad things about you? (Munizeh, Afghanistan, Hazelville)

Munizeh, whose parents wanted her to marry an older man in Afghanistan after discovering that she had a 'boyfriend', explained that the teachers, who were mainly White and middle-class, did not understand the tensions she faced between family loyalty and personal safety:

> Obviously they don't have the same culture as me. The things I am telling them they kind of get shocked, like the abuse what happened in my parents' family, you know, they took it a bit strict, and they said they had to call the police. I told them because I was in pain, and they told the police, and the police came and said, 'we won't do anything

more'. I had to beg, I had to beg them 'please don't arrest any of my family. I don't want them to know that I am here with you guys'. . . . I had to give the DNA and they took pictures of him and I had to talk to the police in a small room, only me . . . They said if they do forced marriage they take you in a car, or force you, just call the police, or do something, or shout, they told me these things. And, you know, I was actually being prepared for it. (Munizeh, Afghanistan, Hazelville)

In response to Munizeh's case, staff at Hazelville responsibly intervened, calling the police, using guidelines from the Forced Marriage Unit (Brandon and Hafez 2008; Gill and Mitra-Khan 2010). However, Black and South Asian feminist researchers have troubled the bias of simply problematising such sensationalist incidences of community regulation. They highlight the complexities of more subtle forms of surveillance that reach beyond culture and the home (Mirza 2010; Shain 2003; Puwar 2003; Ahmad 2004). Whereas teachers, parental liaison and welfare staff were often involved in cases of forced marriage and other forms of patriarchal gender control, a more subtle form of embodied regulation based on Muslim female empowerment through educational progression and Western values was evident in the production of the 'model Muslim female student'.

The production of the ideal 'model Muslim female student' was encouraged in opposition to what was seen as the backward everyday cultural practices and values within the Muslim community and family. The 'model Muslim female student' succeeds by taking part in mainstream educational opportunities so she, by herself, can rise above the seemingly overbearing familial surveillance and restrictions that hold her back.

The schools intervened in everyday cultural practices by working towards producing the 'model Muslim female student'. Teachers and parent liaison officers would encourage the young women to actively challenge their culture, drawing on Western ideals of female 'empowerment'. Bushill, renowned for its success in raising the achievement of its predominantly nearly all Muslim female population, challenged parental and student 'Eastern' attitudes to education by employing pastoral staff to nurture the young women so they could achieve and behave in ways that are recognised in the wider world of higher education, and subsequently the world of work. For instance, the young women actively participated in country-wide conferences, such as the 'Model UN'. They completed work experience in high-profile legal and banking companies in the neighbouring financial hub of the city. The young Muslim women appeared to be confident speakers and in touch with current affairs concerning themselves as young Muslim women, and with broader international issues, such as global warming and HIV and AIDS. Their competence and confidence was impressive, they made trips to the theatre to see Shakespeare and open days at various well-known universities:

They became enlightened, they talk on a different strata, they talk about different matters, not kitchen sink things. They talk philosophical matters, they talk about international affairs, human tragedy, geographical things, history, politics, how the world is changing, what is their role in it, they come and talk about, and that surprises me. I never think that they have that sort of brain, but they do have that sort of brain. (Ali, Parent Liaison Officer, Bushill)

Neela, the Sixth Form learning mentor, was specifically employed in Bushill to help the young women to secure highly sought-after places at the top Russell Group universities. She explained her role was to challenge the young women's attitudes and cultural boundaries:

It's not really in my job description to say that . . . you must get these girls outside of school, get them to meet who are non-Bengali, who are White, who are Black, who are non-Asian, and even females as well . . . but I felt that when I first started this role, this is something that has to change. So if I give you another job description of mine, this will lead on to what I do in terms of getting the girls to socialise with other people, non-Muslim females. (Neela, Learning Mentor, Bushill)

Neela continues to explain how through work placements with large law firms and banks she allocates mentors to individual students, ensuring that:

There are as many men as possible for these girls to be mentored by . . . Some of them did have an issue at the beginning. When I first started in September . . . I gave them a list of who they were attached to, and they just looked at the list, the male names, they came running back to me and said . . . I can't do this, can you please sort me out somebody. So even though I would want them to . . . I can't go against their wishes, because they are sixth formers, they are independent learners . . . some of them won't even shake a man's hand, if you like. It's not all bad with every single student, some more than others. (Neela, Learning Mentor, Bushill)

The school's approach to empowering the young Muslim women appears to be working at the first hurdle as they gain places at top universities. However, it is not their empowerment but their *routes* to empowerment that remain problematic. Entrenched racist attitudes that prevent the young women from entering top-ranking institutions remain intact and unchallenged. Many of the young women struggled social and educational settings beyond the 'safe haven' of the school. As Ahmed (2004) argues, British multiculturalism is only 'skin deep' and does not welcome 'difference' in all social and educational spaces.

POLICY PATTERNS: THE VISIBILITY AND
INVISIBILITY OF YOUNG MUSLIM WOMEN

Two aspects of policy stand out in relation to young Muslim women in school. First, the young women are largely invisible in the multicultural and community cohesion discourses that frame approaches to minority ethnic pupils. Given the neo-liberal educational emphasis on schools performativity and success (Ball 2010), the official public discourse is one of concern with boys' underachievement (Department for Education and Skills 2007). At a governmental level, this manifests itself through policies aimed at the crisis of masculinity and disaffection for Black boys, alienation and separatism for Muslim boys and whiteness and low self-esteem for White working-class boys.

This preoccupation with boys rather than girls was clearly articulated in frank and open discussions with policymakers at a national level who did not see the absence of a gender perspective as problematic with regard to talking about Muslim pupils. Interestingly (as in the quote that follows), the normative emphasis on boys in policy meant that a 'gender perspective' was perceived as related to only 'girls', simultaneously implying that such targeted measures for boys are not gendered:

> A lot of the work on community cohesion there hasn't been a gender . . . we haven't done anything specifically around gender. Although there's nothing stopping a school . . . this is where the local element comes in, we've said to schools there's nothing stopping you if there's a particular issue around gender, in your school, in your local community . . . but we haven't pushed that. (Gamal, Government Senior Policy Advisor)

Second, when gender does arise in policy discourse in relation to Muslim girls, they are constructed as pathological victims of their culture, where concern is largely focused on their familial and religious practices. Whereas gender equality is integral to school policy, where schools must comply with legislative monitoring of pupils attainment, where Muslim communities are concerned, the issues aimed at girls are almost always organically cultural. When asked what gender policies are in place, the same senior policy advisor explains:

> We did some work with the Home Office a couple of years ago, a big campaign, posters being sent out to all schools . . . the Foreign Office have a Forced Marriage Unit, specifically dedicated to this, educating pupils about their rights, trying to educate the community. So there's quite a bit of work going around, just making young girls aware of their rights, and that they have support . . . You may recall some issues around children missing from education, about three thousand-odd are missing from education, and do local authorities know, we are trying to get local

authorities to improve their information. . . . I know it's done some bit of work around female genital mutilation, because that's quite prominent in . . . Somali communities, and is a growing problem. A little bit of work has been done . . . against the taboo in some of our Muslim community . . . first cousin marriages. . . . And I think, going forward, if we are going to address issues around women these are the issues I think we need to be doing. (Gamal, Government Senior Policy Advisor)

Whereas educational policy must address the human rights violations of young women's bodily rights, it is also crucial that policy perspectives move beyond stereotypical views of the issues and look at violence against all pupils more generically (Womankind 2011). White pupils also suffer cultural domestic violence abuses, and these must be seen not as a cultural matter, but as a gendered issue to be treated in the same way for all groups (Dustin and Phillips 2008; Mirza 2010). However, what we are witnessing here is the way in which Muslim young women are produced as voiceless subjects, open to state surveillance in terms of cultural practice, but yet absent from the mainstream policy discourse (Ali 2003).

Prevention of Violence and Extremism (PVE) as a policy strategy has been the main thrust of central government policy and is now mainly targeted at faith-based migrant groups and at Muslims in particular. When asked if PVE had a gender element to its focus, the senior government policymaker replied:

I think PVE was there to address threats posed to national security . . . it's part of a kind of terrorism strategy . . . I wouldn't say there was, from the outset, it's got to be boys we've got to target, but I think it was, who are the people most vulnerable, at most risk? And it just so happens to be young male Muslims, of a particular age, who are more likely to be radicalised, more likely to, you've only got to look at 7/7, at the bombers there. (Gamal, Government Senior Policy Advisor)

The dichotomy of masculine and feminine identity and behaviour amongst Muslim youth continued to be crudely separated in the PVE discourse and acted as a justification for its male focus:

And the programme that was designed to address some of the issues wasn't really because there are gender issues, there were just more issues around that sort of clash of cultures, you know, lack of identity, their sort of feeling of, you know, alienation, risk posed by their sort of lack of their knowledge, lack of faith, lack of knowledge of their own faith. Those were more the issues, and I think those issues also apply to girls as well, but I think girls were just less likely to then get worked up, probably were radicalised, but were less likely to go on and probably commit, I don't think we've come across any, in our work, any young girls going on and committing a violent extremist act. But I'm sure there are young Muslim girls who are radicalised, with extreme views, but they don't go on and commit violent acts. (Gamal, Government Senior Policy Advisor)

Where a school's policy concerns Muslim young women specifically, it is within the boundaries of cultural/social measures. However, multicultural-ism in Britain has failed to recognise gender difference, with consequences for 'ethnicised' young women (Meetoo and Mirza 2007). In this regard they suffer from a form of counter surveillance—that is, they become invis-ible, not full -protected, and thus vulnerable to oppressive cultural and reli-gious practices, such as forced marriage and 'honour' crimes.

CONCLUSION: INTERSECTIONALITY AND GENDERED SURVEILLANCE

This chapter focused on the ways in which young Muslim women's gen-dered subjectivity and experiences in school were lived through the power-ful Islamophobic discourses that circulated in educational spaces. In the study, gendered surveillance and control exercised by teachers, the wider community and family was a dominant theme in many of the Muslim young women's narratives. The young women's embodied raced and gen-dered subjectivities were shaped by their experiences of surveillance and bodily regulation, which revealed the ways in which racism, patriarchy, religion, class, sexuality and gender and other systems of oppression simul-taneously structured their cultural and social space in schools.

We identified three dominant narrative constructions that legitimated the surveillance and ensuing bodily regulation of the young Muslim women in the schools. Drawing on an intersectional framework these were located within the cross-cutting modalities of religion, race, class, gender and sexuality.

First, the teachers' narratives on the headscarf was immersed within the wider racialised religious public discourse in which the Muslim woman's vulnerable yet over-determined body has become symbolic in the battle against Islam and the Muslim enemy 'within' (Meetoo and Mirza 2007). The wearing of the veil became a key symbol for the young women, invit-ing both unrestrained public comment and open legitimate surveillance. As Kanneh (1995, 347) writes, 'ethnic dress becomes interchangeable with tradition and essentialism and the female body enters the unstable arena of scrutiny and meaning'. Thus the young women's private reasons for wear-ing the veil becomes public property, a 'weapon' used by many different competing interests to control and legitimate their own power and status. For example, we saw teachers who wished to regulate and control the young women's behaviour in the class through ridicule, disrespect, authenticity and choice. There were also parents, brothers and other young men that wished to control their daughters' and sisters' emerging sexuality within the ascendant political patriarchal religious discourse that illegitimately sanctions gendered violence.

Second, the production of the compliant 'model Muslim female student' appeared to be a response to the heroic Western need to 'save' the young women from their backward cultural and religious practices (Mirza 2012). Here young Muslim women at risk of heightened sexual regulation from their family and community would be actively encouraged to draw on Western ideals of female 'empowerment' and neo-liberal values to inspire their journey into educational uplift, which would raise them out of their plight. This approach had many positive effects, but also ironically produced seductive forms of 'gender-friendly' self-regulation (Robinson 2000) among the young women. Bradford and Hey (2007) discuss the ways in which working-class young people from minority ethnic backgrounds are readily inculcated into the neo-liberal educational discourse of performativity and individuated success through acceptable and compliant identity which is 'performed' through embodied practices and credentialist behaviours in school sites. The working-class young Muslim women were thus brought into the trajectory of middle-class neo-liberal individualism through their own newfound gendered and classed desires, aspirations and values for success.

The third narrative construction positioned young Muslim women as simultaneously visible and invisible as gendered and raced objects in educational policy. The official heightened preoccupation with Muslim gendered religious cultural restrictions and ethno-religious transgressions, such as forced marriage or honour crimes, manifested itself in the young women's bodily regulation, which was apparent both within the localised school site and beyond into the wider educational policy discourse. The young women's gendered subjectivity and experiences of education were characterised by the dual multicultural discourse of visibility and invisibility. On one hand, no agenda existed that specifically acknowledged them as a group with particular needs. On the other hand, if they did receive attention they were subject to narrow discourses of gendered surveillance, risk, safety and well-being. As this study has shown, schools and education policy as it plays out has not addressed the needs of young Muslim women, or if it does, it pathologises them in terms of cultural practices, thus locking them into gendered stereotypes as victims of religious and cultural practices.

Within an intersectional understanding, we can reveal the ways in which gendered, raced and classed structures of dominance and power shape Muslim young women's gendered subjectivity and experiences of education. Ultimately, the girls' ability to overcome issues such as parental and school surveillance and survive and flourish in urban inner-city schools depends on their resilience and ability to negotiate the macro-regulatory discourses that framed their experiences at the micro level of the school. To truly decolonise our educational spaces, post-colonial, anti-racist and multicultural educators need to engage in the radical pedagogic project of challenging the ways in which Muslim young women experience schooling through national and community discourses of racism, sexism and Islamophobia (Hamzeh 2011; Phoenix 2009; Smith 1999). This chapter is one step towards illuminating young Muslim women's struggle for voice and agency, which continually rises to challenge and transform the powerful interlocking hegemonic discourses of race, class, gender, sexuality and religion that embrace us all.

NOTES

1. The 'veil' as a term used here encompasses the variety of highly visible female Muslim dress. There are many different types and names for the 'veil' according to the language, culture, custom and country. There is the hijab or head-scarf, the niqab (full-length dress) and the jilbab, burqa and abaya (which covers the whole body including the face).
2. The project, '*Young Migrant Women in Secondary Education—Promoting integration and mutual understanding through dialogue and exchange*', was funded by European Commission European Fund for the Integration of Third-country Nationals: Community Action. It was an 18 month five country transnational EU project (January 2010—July 2011). Partners included, Mediterranean Institute of Gender Studies (MIGS), University of Nicosia, Cyprus; Centre of Research in Theories and Practices that Overcome Inequalities (CREA), University of Barcelona, Spain; Euro-Mediterranean Centre for Educational Research (EMCER), University of Malta; Department of Sociology, Panteion University, Greece; Centre for Rights Equality and Social Justice (CRESJ), Institute of Education, University of London, UK.

REFERENCES

Afshar, Haleh. 2008. 'Can I See Your Hair? Choice, Agency and Attitudes: The Dilemma of Faith and Feminism for Muslim Women Who Cover'. *Ethnic and Racial Studies* 31 (2): 411–427.

Ahmad, Fauzia. 2004. 'Still "In Progress"?—Methodological Dilemmas, Tensions and Contradictions in Theorizing South Asian Muslim Women'. In *South Asian Women in the Diaspora*, edited by Nirmal Puwar and Parvati Raghuram, 43–65. Oxford: Berg.

Ahmed, Sara. 2004. *The Cultural Politics of Emotions*. Edinburgh: Edinburgh University Press.

Ali, Suki. 2003. '"To Be a Girl": Culture and Class in Schools'. *Gender and Education* 15 (3): 269–283.

Ball, Stephen. 2010. 'New Voices, New Knowledges and the New Politics of Educational Research: The Gathering of a Perfect Storm?' *European Educational Research Journal* 9(2): 124–137.

Basit, Tehima. 1997. 'I Want More Freedom, but Not Too Much: British Muslim Girls and the Dynamism of Family Values'. *Gender and Education* 9 (4): 425–439.

Bradford, Simon, and Valerie Hey. 2007. 'Successful Subjectivities? The Successification of Class, Ethnic and Gender Positions'. *Journal of Education Policy* 22 (6): 595–614.

Brah, Avtar. 1996. *Cartographies of Diaspora*. London: Routledge.
Brah, Avtar, and Ann Phoenix. 2004. 'Ain't I a Woman? Revisiting Intersectionality'. *Journal of International Women's Studies* 5 (3): 75–86.
Brandon, James, and Salem Hafez. 2008. *Crimes of the Community: Honour Based Violence in the UK*. London: London Centre for Social Cohesion.
Collins, Patricia Hill. 1998. *Fighting Words: Black Women and the Search for Justice*. Minneapolis: University of Minnesota Press.
Davis, Kathy. 2008. 'Intersectionality as Buzzword: A Sociology of Science Perspective on What Makes a Feminist Theory Successful'. *Feminist Theory* 9 (April): 67–85.
Department for Education and Skills. 2007. *Gender and Education: The Evidence on Pupils in England*. Department for Education and Skills. RTPOI-07. London, HMSO
Dustin, Moira, and Anne Phillips. 2008. 'Whose Agenda Is It?: Abuses of Women and Abuses of "Culture" in Britain'. *Ethnicities* 8 (3): 405–424.
Dwyer, Claire. 1999. 'Veiled Meanings: Young British Muslims Women and the Negotiation of Difference'. *Gender, Place and Culture* 6:5–26.
Foucault, Michel. 1979. *The History of Sexuality*. Volume 1, *The Will to Knowledge*. London: Penguin.
Ghuman, Paul Avtar Singh. 2003. *Double Loyalties: South Asian Adolescents in the West*. Cardiff: University of Wales Press.
Gill, Aisha, and Trishima Mitra-Kahn. 2010. 'Moving toward a Multiculturalism without Culture: Constructing a Victim Friendly Human Rights Approach to Forced Marriage in the UK'. In *Violence against Women in South Asian Communities: Issues for Policy and Practice*, edited by Ravi Thiara and Aisha Gill. London: Jessica Kingsley. 128–155
Hamzeh, Manal. 2011. 'Deveiling Body Stories: Muslim Girls Negotiate Visual, Spatial, and Ethical Hijabs'. *Race Ethnicity and Education* 14 (4): 481–506.
Haw, Kaye. 2009. 'From Hijab to Jilbab and the 'Myth' of British Identity: Being Muslim in Contemporary Britain a Half-Generation On'. *Race Ethnicity and Education* 12 (3): 363–378.
hooks, bell. 1981. *Ain't I a Woman?: Black Women and Feminism*. London, Pluto Press
Kanneh, Kadiatu. 1995. 'Feminism and the Colonial Body'. In *The Post Colonial Studies Reader*, edited by Bill Ashcroft, Gareth Griffiths and Helen Tiffin, 346–348. London: Routledge.
Khiabany, Gholam, and Milly Williamson. 2008. 'Veiled Bodies—Naked Racism: Culture, Politics and Race in the Sun'. *Race and Class* 50 (2): 69–88.
McCall, Leslie. 2005. 'The Complexity of Intersectionality'. *Signs* 30 (3): 1771–1800.
Meetoo, Veena, and Heidi Safia Mirza. 2007. '"There's Nothing Honourable about Honour Killings": Gender, Violence and the Limits of Multiculturalism'. *Women's Studies International Forum* 30:187–200.
Mirza, Heidi Safia. 2009. 'Plotting a History: Black and Postcolonial Feminisms in "New Times"'. *Race Ethnicity and Education* 12 (1): 1–10.
———. 2010. 'Walking on Egg Shells: Multiculturalism, Gender and Domestic Violence'. In *Critical Practice with Children and Young People*, edited by Martin Robb and Rachel Thomson, 43–57. Bristol: Policy Press.
———. 2012. 'Multiculturalism and the Gender Gap: The Visibility and Invisibility of Muslim Women in Britain'. In *Britain's Muslims, Muslim Britain: Making Social and Political Space for Muslims*, edited by Waqar I. U. Ahmad and Sarda Ziauddin, 120–140. London: Routledge.
Mirza, Heidi Safia, Veena Meetoo and Jenny Litster. 2011. 'Young, Female and Migrant: Gender, Class and Racial Identity in Multicultural Britain'. In *Young*

Migrant Women in Secondary Education: Promoting Integration and Mutual Understanding through Dialogue and Exchange. Nicosia: University of Nicosia Press, pp143–182, http://www.medinstgenderstudies.org/wp-content/uploads/Integration_of_young_migrant_women_2011.pdf (accessed 10 May 2013)

Phoenix, Ann, 2009. 'De-Colonising Practices: Negotiating Narratives from Racialised and Gendered Experiences of Education'. *Race, Ethnicity and Education* 12 (1): 101–114.

Phoenix, Ann, and Pamela Pattynama. 2006. 'Intersectionality'. *European Journal of Women's Studies* 13: 87–192.

Puwar, Nirmal. 2003. 'Melodramatic Postures and Constructions'. In *South Asian Women in the Diaspora*, edited by Nirmal Puwar and Parvati Ranghuram, 21–42. Oxford: Berg.

Ramji, Hasmita. 2007. 'Dynamics of Religion and Gender amongst Young British Muslims'. *Sociology* 4 (6): 1171–1189.

Robinson, Jennifer. 2000. 'Power as Friendship: Spatiality, Femininity, and "Noisy" Surveillance'. In *Entanglements of Power: Geographies of Domination/ Resistance*, edited by Joanne. P. Sharp, Paul Routledge, Chris Philo and Ronan Paddison, 67–93. London: Routledge.

Shain, Farzana. 2003. *The Schooling and Identity of Asian Girls*. Stoke-on-Trent: Trentham Books.

Smith, Tuhiwai L. 1999. *Decolonising Methodologies: Research and Indigenous Peoples*. London: Zed Books.

Staunaes, Dorthe. 2003. 'Where Have All the Subjects Gone? Bringing Together the Concepts of Intersectionality and Subjectification'. *NORA* 2 (11): 101–109.

Werbner, Pnina. 2007. 'Veiled Interventions in Pure Space: Honour Shame and Embodied Struggles among Muslims in Britain and France'. *Theory, Culture and Society* 24:161–186.

Williams Crenshaw, Kimberley. 1994. 'Mapping the Margins: Intersectionality, Identity Politics, and Violence against Women of Color'. In *The Public Nature of Private Violence*, edited by Martha Albertson Fineman and Rixanne Mykitiuk, 93–118. New York: Routledge.

Womankind. 2011. *Challenging Violence, Changing Lives.* http://www.womankind.org.uk/what-we-do/legacy/#edproj. (Accessed 10 May 2013)

Yuval Davis, Nira. 2006. 'Intersectionality and Feminist Politics'. *European Journal of Women's Studies* 13 (3): 193–209.

Zine, Jasmin. 2006. 'Unveiled Sentiments: Gendered Islamophobia and Experiences of Veiling among Muslim Girls in a Canadian Islamic School'. *Equity and Excellence in Education* 39 (3): 239–252

9 Politics of Difference, Intersectionality, Pedagogy of Poverty and Missed Opportunities at Play in the Classroom

Carl A. Grant and Annemarie Ketterhagen Engdahl

INTRODUCTION

In the foreword to Ray Rist's *The Urban School: A Factory for Failure* (1977), Lee Rainwater writes: 'one of the traditional sources of American pride has always been the upward mobility afforded its citizens throughout mass public education. Regardless of income, race, or background, all children are supposedly given an equal opportunity to learn and thereby advance into a share of the good life' (ix). Rainwater knew at the time of his writing, very much the same as we know today, based upon educational research, that this expectation has not come to fruition. Immediately following, we note excerpts from research published before and since Rainwater's statement that continue to describe schools as 'factories of failure'.

> What are the elements in the newer curricula that 'stir' the disadvantaged youngster? The literature and courses of study concerning disadvantaged children are filled with such statements as: 'He needs less'. 'The curriculum must be simplified' and 'We must stress the basic skills'. These sentiments are usually reflected in the curriculum. The programs are bland, watered down, and lacking in content. Yet the disadvantaged youngster needs just the opposite of a bland, dull curriculum. He is the one who lives for today, who settles his problems as they come, who seldom plans. He is the one who needs stimulation, motivation, challenging content. He needs exposure, not enclosure. (Loretan and Umans 1966, 66)

> In the 1960s and 1970s, many conservatives blamed Blacks' problems on a culture of poverty that rejected school achievement, the work ethic, and the two-parent family in favor of instant gratification and episodic violence. In the 1980s, conservatives (as well as some liberals) characterized the 'Black underclass' in similar terms. But this description only fits a tiny fraction of the Black population. It certainly cannot explain why children from affluent Black families have much lower test scores than their White counterparts. (Jencks and Phillips 1998, 10)

I do not advocate a simplistic 'basic skills' approach for children outside of the culture of power. It would be (and has been) tragic to operate as if these children were incapable of critical and higher-order thinking and reasoning. Rather, I suggest that schools must provide these children the content that other families from a different cultural orientation provide at home. This does not mean separating children according to family background, but instead, ensuring that each classroom incorporate strategies appropriate for all the children in its confines. (Delpit 2006, 30)

The purpose of this chapter is to discuss how the politics of difference and how inappropriate teaching practices influence students' opportunities to learn. We employ the concept 'politics of difference' as a lens of analysis to point out how consciously and unconsciously, institutional structures in society as well as the ways some people reason lead to students (specifically students of colour, students from low socio-economic families, students whose first language is not English and students who are not heterosexual) not receiving life-enhancing opportunities. In addition, to sharpen this analysis we use the concept of 'intersectionality'. Thus in this chapter, we discuss how the concepts of politics of difference, intersectionality and an understanding of and resistance toward a pedagogy of poverty can be used to help education researchers and teachers to see missed opportunities in the classroom in order to create an instructional environment where all students are academically engaged and have a meaningful classroom experience that leads to a flourishing life.

INTERSECTIONALITY

Intersectionality is not optional. It is not something you can take off and put back on again at will, when you feel like it. An intersectional lens should inform any critical evaluation of a subject, because these connections are key to understanding the web of oppression that weighs down on us all. These interconnections, too, are very weblike in their nature, because when you tweak one string, all the rest vibrate with it. There is no way to separate these things out from each other. (Smith 2011, online)

Smith's statement that 'intersectionality is not optional' is illuminated by Casey's (2011) observation 'if we are to examine Anthony, to say only that he is African American does not at all give us the full scope of his background and lived experiences. By understanding the complexity of his character, questions arise around the concept of what about him has been shaped by his race and what has been shaped by his class?' Casey goes on to say, 'I believe this question is not necessary to answer; what is necessary is the understanding that class and race are linked indefinitely and inform one another' (2011, 9).

Intersectionality is defined as 'the relationship among multiple dimensions and modalities of social relationships and subject formations' (McCall 2005, 190). In social relationships multiple elements of identity and oppression and power are entwined bringing about multiple forms of discrimination and/or privilege (Collins 2000; Ritzer 2007). In addition, intersections are points where elements of power, access, lack of access and missed opportunities collide. Further, educators should note that the theory of intersectionality, although often based in feminist theory, is increasingly being applied to education in general, teachers and students specifically. As local and global markets interact on both a personal and societal level, students are increasingly defined by their identity (e.g. multicultural family students in Korea; see, for example, Kang 2010; Jo, Seo and Kwon 2008 and migrant student status in the US; see, for example, Lundy-Ponce 2010).

Identity markers (and the forces that give rise to them and influence them) are used to mark classroom success. Standardised tests, school report cards and teacher success are all tied to identity markers. For example, a heated debate in the US, especially since the election of an African American president, is that school failure in urban areas where Black and brown students attend school is influenced by socio-economic class more strongly than race. The argument put forth by Duncan and Murnane (2011) in their edited book *Whither Opportunity* to a great extent marginalises the impact of race and the racism in the school district where Black and brown students attend school.

We, too, argue that students cannot be defined by one aspect of their identity (e.g. economic class or race or gender or sexuality). Aspects of identity or students' ascribed characteristics (e.g. race/ethnicity, economic class, gender, religion, sexuality) that make up their identity can better help educators to serve them. However, it is important to note that these identities or ascribed characteristics cross and re-cross. This fact often receives little attention. In 1986 Grant and Sleeter reported that there was little educational research that recognises the crossing (intersecting) of identity markers. Grant and Sleeter argued that too often only one aspect of identity or possibly two were taken into account in education research studies, and this results in a shallow understanding of students. Additionally, Ladson-Billings (2001) recognised that her students were significantly more complex (and their ascribed characteristics crossed) in ways that were much more complicated then she originally thought. She says:

> To the casual observer I was teaching predominantly white, working-class students, along with a number of African American students who were bused from West Philadelphia. I thought that myself. But as the year progressed, I learned that I was teaching white ethnic students—Italian American, Irish Americans, Jewish Americans, Polish

Americans—of varied religious persuasions—as well as African American students. I also learned that these differences mattered in specific ways, and any success I was to have in the school would be tied to my ability to develop a deeper understanding of the groups to which the children felt an affiliation. (2001, 11)

Her understanding of her students was deepened when she began to examine the contexts and impacts of identity markers on her students. It is not just the examination of their ascribed identities that deepened her understanding, but also her examination of the intersections of those characteristics. These intersections provided insight into the influence of society upon her students' lives.

POLITICS OF DIFFERENCE

Whereas it is important to note that intersectionality means that elements of identity, power, privilege and discrimination are played out for each student in complex and multifaceted ways, it is equally important to note that this discrimination takes place within a culture that operates within a 'politics of difference' leading social institutions such as schools to treat brown and Black students and students whose first language is not English differently, read negatively, in comparison to White students (Lippi-Green 1997; Norton and Toohey 2004; Portes and Rumbaut 2006; Walker, Shafer and Iiams 2004). A push back against structural and personal inequality and othering made by some is for equal rights and distributive justice (Rawls 1971; Young 1990) criticises this approach. Young (1990) argues that it can undermine diverse identities and strengthen a dominant culture, and we add the institutions and ways of reasoning that supports and sustain the dominant culture. She contends equal rights and distributive justice are close to being assimilationist and assumes a unitary and homogenous society such as White, European and male. In order not to be trapped in such unitary framing, especially in schools, where education research over the years has noted that quality of teaching is often based on race or gender or social class (Bonilla-Silva 2010; Rist 1970; Nieto 2009; Picower 2009), we contend this using the lens of intersectionality and politics of difference can help teachers to recognise and respond to the multiple forms of structural and personal discriminations that affect them in the classroom.

THE DAILY BEAST OF CLASSROOM LIFE

Fundamental to our discussion is acknowledging that the nature of school, classroom life and pedagogical practices are routinely insufficient in many instructional spaces that serve poor students, students of colour and students whose first language is not English. Each day in the US and many other countries students are faced with issues of power, access, identity and missed opportunities for validation. Each day, students encounter school systems and other societal structures that challenge and minimise their identity and sense of self. Each day, students live through moments when their identity is questioned or they are 'othered'. Whereas our descriptions of such practice are based upon schools in the US, we have no doubt that such practices exist in other countries where poor and minority students attend school (Grant and Lei 2001; Grant and Portera 2011; see also Daniel 1968; Raudenbush and Willms 1991).

Since the rollout of No Child Left Behind (Bush 2001), the federal and state government, local school districts and individual schools in the US increasingly have demanded that teachers differentiate (break down) their classroom achievement test scores and instructional plans by demographics (Grissmer 2000; Leigh 2010). Also teachers are instructed to take more than one identity marker (e.g. race, gender) for students into account when assessing and reporting test results (see, for example, Isensee and Vasquez 2012). Whereas accounting for multiple elements of identity could be a start towards using intersectionality as a lens to better meet the academic and social needs of students, for the most part this is not so. Instead discussions of differentiation often highlight elements of school identity (e.g. slowness or giftedness) that are by and large constructed or influenced by socio-economic class, language or racial oppression. Such discussions do very little to deal with social justice (i.e. cultural justice and fairness) (Hooda 2012; Isensee and Vasquez 2012; Shalash 2012). Rather, there is a discussion of students' test results that reflects the politics of difference as defined by Young (1990) (e.g. comparison between White and Black and brown students) and these discussions often continue on to generate assumptions about how groups of students based on colour, socio-economic class, gender and language perform; this led to the implementing of 'teacher proof' or highly structured curriculum materials for teachers to use, such as (e.g. language programmes for English language learners that transition into English at the expense of students home language) and cutting back on teaching art and music. Such regulations and norming in the classroom fails to engage students in meaningful ways as well as instil in them a robust quest to learn. In New York City and Los Angeles alone, more than thirty-five thousand students dropped out of school in 2008 (Koebler 2011) and the 2011 Conditions of Education states that the US dropout rate is 8 per cent.

Ausubell (2000) argues that student learning must be meaningful and not simply recall. In spite of this body of research noted by Ausubell, educational researchers report that culturally appropriate classroom practices are distributed unequally on the basis of class, ethnicity and college-going plans (Grant and Sleeter 1986; Gay 2011; Kahne and Middaght 2008; Ladson-Billings 2009). In addition, throughout the last century, researchers report that education reform has moved toward an extraordinary sameness of recitation: repeated lecturing, questioning, monitoring and quizzing (Goodlad 1984). In addition, studies of school life report that students of specific groups (boys, students of colour and students from low socioeconomic class families) are subject to classroom activities that do not encourage them to think critically or to question. Instead, rote recitation of material and basic skill and drill are common (Haberman 1991; Kohn 2011). Haberman (1991) refers to such teaching practices as the pedagogy of poverty. Kohn (2011) argues that present-day school reform is damaging poor children and is similarly a pedagogy of poverty that is constant practice in schools serving the poor and students of colour. In addition, Linda Darling-Hammond argues that the 'most counterproductive [teaching] approaches are enforced mostly rigidly in schools serving the most disadvantaged students'. Similarly, Claude Steele (as cited in Kohn 2011) posits 'a skills-focused remedial education . . . virtually guarantee[s] the persistence of the race gap' (Kohn 2011, 30). Further, Deborah Stipek (2012) claims the result from the pedagogy of poverty is that certain children are left further and further behind. The rich get richer while the poor get worksheets. A point also articulated by Meir (as cited in Kohn 2011, 30), who states school has radically different meanings for middle-class kids, who are 'expected to have opinions', and . . . poor kids, who are expected to do what they're told. Schools for the well-off are about inquiry and choices; schools for the poor are about drills and compliance'. The two types of institutions, according to Meir 'barely have any connection to each other' (30). These practices as observed in schools serving poor students, students of colour and students whose primary language is not English exemplifies how the politics of difference is firmly located in school life and how instructional opportunities come to be missed in classroom instruction.

The take-away or lessons learned from the research on school and classroom life where poor students of colour are being served is that teachers need to create learning opportunities where student identity—their race, gender, sexuality, socio-economic class, language and religion—are taken into account as part of their learning experiences. Students, educational research argues, need learning opportunities where they can engage subject matter with a critical lens. Aronowitz (2000) discuss such learning as a 'critical appropriation—the process by which students acquire the means to challenge—if not—reverse the technical divisions that fragment society as well as the higher learning, and perhaps most importantly, by which they are encouraged to become critical intellectuals prepared to swim against the current' (125–126). Critical appropriation is not common in the schools discussed by the researcher in the preceding (i.e. where poor students of colour attend) and as such there are many missed opportunities to promote student learning.

Student learning, we argue, must consider multiple elements of identity and the systems/institutions that influence identity. In addition, as much as possible, they should be experiential and take into account students' life experiences and cultural history in order to promote authentic learning. It is not privileged knowledge or knowledge not available to schools and teachers that there is an intersection of power and privilege at work against poor students of colour (Rist 1970; Grant and Sleeter 1986; Orfield 2004). Yet, there are concerted efforts to minimise attention toward addressing the intersection of, for example, race, socio-economic status, place (e.g. schools) and space (e.g. urban) and acknowledging the influence of the politics of difference. Recognising this lack of attention and the missed opportunities that accompanies them will be essential for teachers looking to validate and affirm their students and to prepare them for a flourishing life.

MISSED OPPORTUNITIES

Simply stated, there are opportunities in classroom to inspire students, to make learning fun and to validate students' history and culture. Also there are missed opportunities for recognising the *play* of intersectionality and politics of difference throughout the school day.

A missed opportunity is a moment during the school day when teachers or staff may operate with positive intentions but fail to take the extra steps in order to provide a more culturally responsive and appropriate environment. A missed opportunity does not need to be a negative moment. It does not need to be a blaring mistake. A missed opportunity may often pass by unnoticed. It is through recognising those fleeting moments or institutional structures when we could have shifted our thinking and actions to a culturally responsive mode that we begin to change our practice and, in fact, change our educational philosophy.

Missed opportunities for individual students are too prevalent and common in our schools as we noted at the introduction and throughout much of this chapter. That said, but to highlight: There are missed opportunities for recognising and validating our students. There are missed opportunities for noting ways that identity influence student learning. There are missed opportunities for acknowledging and recognising intersecting discrimination in the classroom. However, perhaps most notably, there are missed opportunities when we create curriculums and learning opportunities that systematically stifle and restrict access to educational opportunities.

Examples of Missed Opportunities

In the examples that follow, we have noted opportunities throughout a school day that could provide a more inclusive, authentic and rich environment for students if the lenses of intersectionality and politics of difference are applied. We show how missed opportunities can be changed in order to create a more inclusive, empowering and supportive classroom for students—regardless of their identity markers. In particular, the politics of difference is addressed. Each of the examples brings an increased level of rigour and complex thought to the classroom. When comparing the missed opportunity with the fulfilled opportunity, it is easy to see the way that the 'extraordinary sameness' that affects so many Black and brown students can be redesigned in order to create dynamic, thought-provoking classroom opportunities. These examples show that when a lens of intersectionality and an acknowledgement and appropriate counterapproach to the politics of difference are applied, students can experience teachers thinking about them in ways that validate and affirm the many aspects of their identity. It is a chance for teachers to provide an alternative to the dominant discourse created by a politics of difference and instead provide all students with a robust and challenging curriculum regardless of their background or identity markers.

Example 1 illustrates how multiple perspectives on history allow students to investigate the intersectionality of their own identity. Example 2 leads young students to examine the roll of family in their own identity, as well, bolstering their ability to advocate for their needs both in the classroom and in their daily life. Finally, Example 3 directly combats a politics of difference by increasing the rigour and critical thinking in the classroom. These are only examples of how a teacher could enrich their students' educational opportunities. Of course, the changes to the lessons are not exhaustive and other opportunities could certainly be identified. Additionally, there is the risk of identifying a missed opportunity and replacing it with a superficial or reductionist opportunity. We attempt to avoid this pitfall; you must let us know how well we did.

Example 1 (Social Studies)

Missed Opportunity	Fulfilled Opportunity
A middle school, history teacher, Ms. Parker (pseudonym), a White female teacher with three years of experience, notices that the textbook's description of the American Revolutionary War (war between England and the US colonies, 1775–1783) is only told from the perspective of a White American revolutionary. Ms. Parker goes to the library and finds a book outlining experiences of women of the Revolutionary War. She begins each history lesson by reading one of the women's stories.	Ms. Parker notices that the textbook's description of the Revolutionary War is only told from the perspective of a White American revolutionary. Ms. Parker recognises that using only this perspective could stir up a number of problems for her students' learning. First and foremost, the teacher wants to make sure that her students don't think that a White male perspective is the only perspective in history that is valued. Ms. Parker recognises that using only the textbook to look at history does not give students

(*Continued*)

Example 1 (Social Studies) *Continued*

Missed Opportunity	Fulfilled Opportunity
	an engaging and inquiry-based approach to the content. Ms. Parker wants to make sure that students have the opportunity to think critically about this time period and can relate the purpose of the Boston Tea Party. In addition, she wants to give students the opportunity 'to have opinions' and to debate which ride Paul Revere or William Dawes took to alert the colonies that the British were coming. This was more daring. She wants the students to consider the circumstances of history, such as 'Why did the colonists dress up as Indians when throwing the tea off the ship?' And give an opinion about such circumstances, including activating higher-order thinking skills by engaging in discourse and discussion about the events. In order to achieve these goals, the teacher takes a number of steps to supplement the curriculum. 1. She includes artefacts such as statements from letters written by minutemen in the war, reports on the active participation of Native American warriors of the Cherokee tribe during the war and varying reports from both Britain and America of the events that led to the Boston Massacre. This helps to move students away from rote recitation of material and basic skills and drills that we mentioned earlier. 2. She creates thirteen different stations (some with pictures, some with video snippets and

Missed Opportunity	Fulfilled Opportunity
	others with text) that outline experiences of thirteen different groups living in the US during the Revolutionary War. Some of the groups identify by race, others by political affiliation, some by employment and income level and others by region. For example, one station might give the perspective of the Revolutionary War from a White woman whose principal occupation was making clothes at home, who identified with the Federalist Party in Delaware; another might be a perspective of a free, Black man whose parents had been enslaved and who had not seen him since he was a child in Massachusetts.
	3. Students take guiding questions and visit each of the stations. At each station they discuss with their group how this perspective is the same or differs from their current understanding of the Revolutionary War and the purpose and meaning of the war to them.
	4. Ms. Parker creates a Socratic seminar, where students discuss the benefits, hopes and drawbacks of the Revolutionary War from their perspectives and the perspectives of their family member who had they been living in the colonies during that time.
	5. Students are instructed to write an essay that explains their understanding of the purpose of the Revolutionary

(*Continued*)

Example 1 (Social Studies) *Continued*

Missed Opportunity	Fulfilled Opportunity
	War, events that led to the war and how the war influences events today.
	6. The class then debates why these perspectives were missing from the textbook.
	7. Finally, students are asked to compare their understanding of the American Revolution with that of other revolutions throughout the world. Students can choose from one of the following events:
	a. The French Revolution (1775–1783)
	b. The Haitian Revolution (1791–1804)
	c. The Russian Revolution (1917)
	d. The Cuban Revolution (1956–1959)
	e. The Iranian Revolution (1978–1979)

The 'fulfilled' lesson opportunity takes advantage of the missed opportunities and directly addresses intersectionality and politics of difference, and it employs appropriate and engaging teaching strategies. The lesson uses a lens of intersectionality in that it allows students to see historical figures not as just one-dimensional figures with one perspective, and one element of identity but as complex individuals hopeful of a meaningful life. Exposure to multidimensional figures will help the students to have a deeper understanding of themselves and others as complex, multidimensional human beings. Additionally, the lesson addresses the politics of difference in a number of ways. First, students are given the opportunity to see how systematic oppression (e.g. treatment of the colonies by England) affected individuals in history. Perhaps more importantly, the complexity and rigour in these lessons are in direct opposition to the dominant culture created by the politics of difference that stifle opportunities in so many classrooms.

Example 2 (Language Arts)

Missed Opportunity	Fulfilled Opportunity
After reading *Chicken Little*, a fable read in many US kindergarten classes, the kindergarten teacher, Mr. Herrera (pseudonym), with eight years teaching experience, designs a number of comprehension questions that ask students to recall elements of a story, such as rising action, moral of the story and conclusion. Students work in pairs to articulate their summary with a partner in class.	Mr. Herrera recognises that although there is nothing the matter with recalling elements of a story, the fable of Chicken Little provides some additional opportunities in his kindergarten classroom. The version of the story that the class is reading has a happy ending with Chicken Little escaping from the fox den. The fox is the last animal that Chicken Little tells about the 'sky falling'. He escapes from the fox and goes on to warn other animals about the sky falling. In this version, the 'moral' of the story could either be interpreted as 'have courage' or 'be persistent'. The teacher recognises that the story could serve other purposes as well, such as the opportunity for students to discuss the complexity of their family and social structures or think critically about how they can advocate for themselves with the adults around them. In order to achieve those goals, the teacher takes a number of steps to supplement the curriculum. 1. After reading Chicken Little, Mr. Herrera designs a class activity to help students recall and make meaningful elements of the story. Students work in pairs to recall the story with their classmates. 2. After this activity, Mr. Herrera then calls the students together on the rug and asks students to reflect on a time when they tried to tell an adult something and were

(*Continued*)

Example 2 (Language Arts) *Continued*

Missed Opportunity	Fulfilled Opportunity
	3. When kindergarten students are learning story structures, they often start with describing the setting and characters within before they describe the main event. Students share their experiences with classmates and with the teacher. They are encouraged to describe their family dynamics, and the diversity of the family structures is noted and praised within the class. This activity is inclusive as the setting on the rug allows all students to be involved. It allows students to use their home language and lends cultural appropriateness to the classroom.
	4. Mr. Herrera then uses guided questioning to help students to feel validated to express their needs to adults (just as Chicken Little did). He makes sure that the students recognise that even though Chicken Little was not heard the first time, he persisted.
	5. Later in the day, students create a pair of storyboards comparing their experience with that of Chicken Little.

Despite the young age of the children, the 'fulfilled' opportunity lesson still uses a lens of intersectionality as well as addresses the politics of difference. Through the discussion about families, the students are able to see that their classmates relate to different parts of their lives in different ways. Students at this age are just learning to understand other's feelings and perspectives, so this type of activity is an ideal way to help students to recognise their complex personal identities at a later time. The students' home structures and home languages are validated. The complexity, cognitive development and emotional guidance that are offered during this lesson are the types of activities that provide opportunities to think in different, non-dominant ways.

The mathematical example that we illustrate in the following requires a bit of context. We have learned from our work in schools that efforts to provide culturally responsive or culturally relevant teaching in mathematics often seeks to establish connections to students' daily lives, and rightly so. Whereas we believe that home/community/school connections are important, it is also important to use mathematical language or the 'code of power' when teaching Black and brown students instead of the pedagogy of poverty. This is so in order to provide students with opportunities that a knowledge of mathematics offers. Whereas teachers quickly think of ways to apply geometry to students' home lives (e.g. noting simple geometrical figures—circle, square, rectangle—in their life space), a much more sophisticated mathematics vocabulary (e.g. acute angles, equilateral triangles, perpendicular lines) is needed if poor students are to take advantage of educational opportunities. Example 3 uses mathematical language and mathematical reasoning in ways that allow students in a multiracial and bilingual classroom access to the content as well as mastery of the content. In addition, the example pushes against the 'extraordinary sameness' that we noted earlier.

Example 3 (Mathematics)

Missed Opportunity	Fulfilled Opportunity
A maths teacher, Ms. Williams (pseudonym), an African American teacher with five years of experience, decides the best way to assess if students have mastered double-digit multiplication is to have them complete a series of independent practice mathematics problems.	Ms. Williams is wondering about the best way to assess if students have mastered double-digit multiplications. She prepares double-digit mathematics problems for each student to complete independently. In doing so, she recognises that that there needs to be more complex ways of thinking about mathematics to accompany this assessment. In addition, she is careful to repeat, but not to overuse, the mathematical language central to fully understanding the mathematics topic she is teaching. In addition, she wants students to share their way of completing two-digit multiplication using the

(Continued)

Example 3 (Mathematics) *Continued*

Missed Opportunity	Fulfilled Opportunity
	appropriate mathematical language with other students. Furthermore, she wants the students to advocate for themselves by identifying the difficulty that they have with the topic. In order to achieve these goals, the teacher takes a number of steps to supplement the curriculum. 1. When introducing the two-digit multiplication, Ms. Williams presents the topic using multiple visuals, such as plastic manipulatives, videos with representations of multiplication and students' drawings from last year's class. Students are asked to study each resource and other resources that they may identity, and then select the one that helps them to understand the best. 2. Next, students group themselves with other students who are approaching the topic in a similar way. Each group presents their thinking to the class. By expressing their own mathematical thinking and using mathematical language, students clarify the concepts for themselves. In addition, by listening to their peers express their mathematical reasoning, they have an opportunity to listen and learn and to engage other students about their ideas. 3. Avoiding the pedagogy of poverty, (e.g. drill and practice, worksheets and being kept in silence) students are given voice,

Missed Opportunity	Fulfilled Opportunity
	respect and independence. 4. Finally, students are encouraged to select from a number of activities that provide enrichment, including tutoring sessions.

Contextualising students' mathematical thinking in a culturally responsive way and teaching mathematics in ways that also includes using the code of power can be challenging. That said, teachers must continue to approach mathematics in a way that is meaningful and that demands high expectations for students and additionally pushes back against the politics of difference.

CONCLUSION

We believe that the identification of missed opportunities is a unique way of approaching equality for students in the classroom. Whereas there are certainly a plethora of excellent approaches to educational equality, e.g. Culturally Responsive Teaching, Culturally Relevant Teaching, Multicultural Education etc. (Grant and Sleeter 2006; Ladson-Billings 2009; Gay 2010; Lindsey et al. 2011), often, teachers see these approaches as 'all encompassing . . . demanding too much time . . . and new learning' (Gay 2010, 127). By identifying missed opportunities and offering a way to fulfil the opportunities, we seek to gradually but steadily move teachers toward successful teaching of all students.

Finally, we see our contribution to this volume being one that intersects theory and practice. We push away from the claim that scholarship should be one or the other. Few scholarly books and journal articles speak to both constituencies: researchers and teachers. Classroom teachers often resist reading chapters in books or journal articles because they say they are 'too researchey'. Researchers do not usually want to 'soil their hands' with efforts to bring research and practice together. Thus, although far from perfect, we look at two theories/concepts: the politics of difference, which often goes unnoticed as teachers say, 'I am colour blind', and intersectionality, which, too, is silenced as teachers say, 'I treat all my students the same'. The identification of missed opportunities and a willingness to make those opportunities a vibrant, meaningful and appropriate learning experience can help teachers to avoid the pedagogy of poverty in the classroom.

REFERENCES

Aronowitz, Stanley (2000). *The Knowledge Factory: Dismantling the Corporate University and Creating True Higher Learning*. Boston: Beacon Press.

Ausubel, D. P. (2000). *The Acquisition and Retention of Knowledge: A Cognitive View*. Dordrect; Boston: Kluwer Academic Publishers.

Bocking, W. O., Knudson, G., Goldberg, j. M. (2007). 'Counseling and Mental Health Care for Transgender Adults and Loved Ones'. *International Journal of Transgenderism*, 9 (3/4), 36–82.

Bonilla-Silva, Eduardo. 2010. *Racism without Racists: Color-Blind Racism and the Persistence of Racial Inequality in the United States*. Lanham, MD: Rowman and Littlefield.

Bush, George Walker. 2001. No Child Left Behind (NCLB) Act of 2001, Pub. L. No. 107–110, & 115, Stat. 1425. Washington, DC: United States Department of Education.

Casey, Zachary, 2011. 'The Fight in My Classroom: A Story of Intersectionality'. *Practitioner Research, i.e., Inquiry in Education* 2 (1): 2–13. http://digitalcommons.nl.edu/ie/vol2/iss1/3. Accessed January 15, 2013.

Collins, Patricia Hill. (2000). Gender, Black Feminism, and Black Political Economy. *Annals of the American Academy of Political and Social Science*, 568. 41–53.

Darling-Hammond, Linda. 2006. 'Constructing 21st-Century Teacher Education'. *Journal of Teacher Education* 57 (3): 300–314.

Daniel, William Wentworth. 1968. *Racial Discrimination in England: Based on the PEP Report*. New York: Penguin.

Delpit, Lisa. 2006. *Other People's Children: Cultural Conflict in the Classroom*. New York: New Press.

Duncan, Greg J. and Richard J. Murnane. 2011. *Whither Opportunity?: Rising Inequality, Schools, and Children's Life Chances*. New York: Sage.

Gay, Geneva. 2010. *Culturally Responsive Teaching: Theory, Research, and Practice*. New York: Teachers College Press.

Goodlad, John. 1984 . *A Place Called School. Prospects for the Future*. New York: McGraw-Hill.

Grant, Carl A. and Lei, Joy. L. (2001) Editors. *Global Constructions of Multicultural Education*. Mahwah, NJ: Lawrence Erlbaum.

Grant, Carl A. and Portera, Agostino (2011) Editors. *Intercultural and Multicultural Education*. New York: Routledge.

Grant, Carl A., and Christine E. Sleeter. 1986. *After the School Bell Rings*. Philadelphia: Falmer Press.

Grant, Carl A. and Sleeter, Christine E. 2006. *Turning on Learning: Five Approaches for Multicultural Teaching Plans for Race, Class, Gender and Disability*. Indianapolis: Jossey-Bass.

Grissmer, David (2000). 'The Continuing Use and Misuse of SAT Scores'. *Journal of Psychology, Public Policy and Law*, 2000 Mar 6(1), 223–232.

Haberman, Martin. 1991. 'The Pedagogy of Poverty versus Good Teaching'. *Phi Delta Kappan* 73 (4): 290–294.

Hooda, Samreen. 2012. 'Virginia New Achievement Standards Based upon Race and Background'. *Huffington Post*, August 24. Accessed January 17, 2013, at http://www.huffingtonpost.com/2012/08/23/virginia-new-achievement-based-on-race_n_1826624.html.

Isensee, Laura, and Vasquez, Michael. 2012. 'Criticism Follows Florida's Race-Based Student Achievement Goals'. *Miami Herald*, October 13. Accessed January 17, 2013, at http://www.miamiherald.com/2012/10/13/3049005/criticism-follows-floridas-race.html.

Jencks, Christopher, and Meredith Phillips. 1986. *The Black–White Test Score Gap*. Washington, DC: Brookings Institute Press.

Jo, Ho Young, D. H. Seo and S. H. Kwon, 2008. 'An Ethnographic Study on the Academic Performance of Children of Migrants (Damunhwa gajeong janyoui hakopsuhange kwanhan munhwagisuljeok yongu)'. *Korean Journal of Sociology of Education* 18 (2): 105–134.

Kahne, Joseph and Middaugh, Ellen (2008). 'Democracy for Some: The Civic Opportunity Gap in High School'. Circle Working Paper 59. *Center for Information and Research on Civic Learning and Engagement* (CIRCLE).

Kang, Soon-Won. 2010. 'Multicultural Education and the Rights to Education of Migrant Children in South Korea'. *Educational Review* 62 (3): 287–300.

Koebler, Jason. 2011. 'National High School Graduation Rates Improve'. *US News*, June 13. Accessed January 29, 2013, at http://www.usnews.com/education/blogs/high-school-notes/2011/06/13/national-high-school-graduation-rates-improve.

Kohn, Alfie. 2011. 'Poor Teaching for Poor Children . . . in the Name of School Reform'. *Education Week*. Accessed January 17, 2013, at http://www.edweek.org/ew/articles/2011/04/27/29dc.h30.html.

Ladson-Billings, Gloria. 2001. *Crossing over to Canaan: The Journey of New Teachers in Diverse Classrooms*. San Francisco: Jossey-Bass.

———. 2009. *The Dreamkeepers: Successful Teachers of African American Children*. San Francisco: Jossey-Bass.

Leigh, Andrew. 2010. 'Estimating Teacher Effectiveness from Two-Year Changes in Students Test Scores'. *Economics of Education Review* 29 (3): 480–488.

Lindsey, Delores B., Kikanza J. Nuri-Robins, Raymond D. Terrell and Randall B. Lindsey. 2011. *Culturally Proficient Instruction: A Guide for People who Teach*. Thousand Oaks, CA: Corwin Press.

Lippi-Green, Ros. 1997. *English with an Accent: Language, Ideology, and Discrimination in the United States*. New York: Routledge.

Loretan, Joseph, and Shelley Umans. 1996. *Teaching the Disadvantaged: New Curriculum Approaches*. New York: Teachers College Press.

Lundy-Ponce, Giselle. 2010. 'Migrant Students: What We Need to Know to Help Them Succeed'. *Colorin Colorado on the Web*. Accessed January 22, 2013, at http://www.colorincolorado.org/article/36286/.

McCall, Leslie. 2005. 'The Complexity of Intersectionality'. *Signs* 30 (3): 1771–1800.

Nieto, Sonia (2009). *Language, Culture, and Teaching: Critical Perspectives*. New York: Taylor & Francis.

Norton, Bonny, and Kelleen Toohey, Editors. 2004. *Critical Pedagogies and Language Learning*. Cambridge: Cambridge University Press.

Orfield, Gary. 2004. *Dropouts in America: Confronting the Graduation Rate Crisis*. Cambridge, MA: Harvard Educational Publishing Group.

Picower, B. (2009) The Unexamined Whiteness of Teaching: How White Teachers Maintain and Enact Dominant Racial Ideologies. *Race Ethnicity and Education*. 12 (2): 197–215.

Portes, Alejandro, and Ruben G. Rumbaut. 2006. *Immigrant America: A Portrait*. Berkeley: University of California Press.

Raudenbush, Stephen, and Jon Douglas Willms. 1991. *Schools, Classrooms, and Pupils: International Studies of Schooling from a Multilevel Perspective*. Waltham, MA: Academic Press.

Rawls, John. 1971. *A Theory of Justice*. Cambridge, MA: Harvard University Press.

Rist, Ray C. 1970. 'Student Social Class and Teacher Expectations: The Self-Fulfilling Prophecy in Ghetto Education'. *Harvard Educational Review* 40 (3): 411–451.

————. 1977. *The Urban School: A Factory for Failure*. Boston: MIT Press.

Ritzer, G. (2007). Contemporary Sociological Theory and Its Classical Roots: The Basics. Boston: McGraw-Hill.

Shalash, Samieh, Va. 2012. 'Black Caucus Protests State's New Achievement Goals for Different Groups'. *Daily Press*, August 16. Accessed January 17, 2013, at http://articles.dailypress.com/2012–08–16/news/dp-nws-subgroup-discontent-20120816_1_new-achievement-goals-black-students-asian-students.

Smith, S. E. 2011. 'Interscetionality Is Not Optional'. December 6. Accessed January 13, 2013, at http://meloukhia.net/2011/12/intersectionality_is_not_optional.html.

Stipek, Deborah. 2012. 'Education Is Not a Race'. *Science* 332 (6037): 1481.

Walker, Anne, Jill Shafer and Michelle Iiams. 2004. '"Not in My Classroom": Teacher Attitudes Towards English Language Learners in the Mainstream Classroom'. *NABE Journal of Research and Practice* 2 (1): 130–160.

Young, Iris Marion. (1990). Justice and the Politics of Difference. Princeton, NJ: Princeton University Press.

Part III

Educational Inequalities

Identities, Inclusion and Barriers

10 'I Want to Hear You'

Listening to the Narratives, Practices and Visions of a Chuj Maya Teacher in Guatemala

Alexandra Allweiss

> For me education is much more than just reading, than just looking at a book . . . it's knowing your self-esteem. (Juana María)

INTRODUCTION

Hearing and recording the narrative for this study began on a cool morning as sunlight streamed through the open door. The clear August sky invited us to look out the window to a picturesque view of the sacred Mayan temple that stood at the edge of the valley far below. The knowledge that I was in a special place, with a special person who had an important story and that she was willing to share it, washed over me. Laughter and friendly talk with Juana María before the start of her narrative added to the tranquillity of the morning.[1] Sipping hot coffee relieved the morning dampness. We smiled at one another and I said, 'Are you ready?' She replied, '*Lista. Empecemos*'. I turned on my recorder and asked Juana María to describe herself to begin the conversation that is significant to what is to follow. She responded:

Pues, para decirle yo me identifico como una indígena o una maya . . . pertenezco a una etnia Chuj . . . El año pasado me graduée de maestra bilingüe intercultural. Entonces, yo vivo aquí en Xantin. Estudié [aquí] . . . Estoy muy orgullosa de ser maya. Estoy bien orgullosa de mi pueblo, de la gente de Xantin, un lugar de orgullo para mi . . . Me gusta vivir la vida tal como presenta, pero también me gusta pensar muchas cosas, mejorar lo que Dios me da . . . Prefiero pensar, 'quizás esto no debe ser asi' . . . Las dificultades no son obstáculos

Well to tell you, I identify as an Indigenous person or a Maya . . . I pertain to an ethnicity, Chuj . . . Last year I graduated as a bilingual intercultural teacher. So, I live here in Xantin. I studied [here] . . . I am very proud to be Maya. I am very proud of my pueblo, of the people of Xantin, a place of pride for me . . . I like to live life as it comes, but I also like to think about a lot of things, to improve the things God gives me . . . I prefer to think, 'maybe this shouldn't be like this' . . . Difficulties are not obstacles for me, but rather challenges that I

para mi, sino desafíos que debo solucionar algo. Entonces a mi me gusta ser solidaria con las personas. Me gusta ayudar ... ayudar a mi familia, ayudar a mi comunidad, y también a todas las personas que están a mi alrededor.

should solve. So I like to be in solidarity with people. I like to help ... to help my family, to help my community and also all the people that are around me.

Juana María is a proud Chuj Maya woman and teacher, whose narrative serves as the foundation and guide for this chapter.

Across the globe educational reform is under way. In many countries, classroom teachers are on the front line of the reform effort. These education policies, however, are generally devised, implemented and evaluated using a top-down approach. Yet, there is much more that can be learned about the effects of such education policy by discussing these reform efforts with teachers. This chapter will document the experiences of one middle school teacher, who is representative of a sample of thirty-two educators in Xantin,[2] Guatemala, participating in a larger research project designed to shape instructional practices to be responsive to the Intercultural and Bilingual Education (IBE) reforms in Guatemala. At the heart of the teacher's work is the goal of teaching students in a manner that fosters academic, social and personal success.

A narrative inquiry approach is used to frame this chapter,[3] and it is used to investigate the intersections and influences of 'cultural racism',[4] gender inequities and place-based classism on education policy and practice through a teacher's experience. Voices of educators working within the framework of the national reforms provide powerful critiques and visions for change that are not always visible through a top-down approach. Narrative inquiry allows us to view the challenges and possibilities of these reforms using the experiences and insights from one Chuj teacher, Juana María.

BACKGROUND

To understand the context of Juana María's insights, it is important to look at the way the reforms in Guatemala set out to address a cluster of social inequality issues as well as the critiques from this perspective. The Guatemalan Ministry of Education began a process of educational reform in 1997, a year after the signing of the Peace Accords following thirty-six years of state-sponsored violence and conflict. The aim of the reform is to improve the quality of education in Guatemala so that it reflects the needs of the country's multicultural population and in so doing will be in accordance with international standards (such as UNESCO's Education for All Framework, 1990). The Ministry's reform policies call for IBE opportunities for students and the creation of a new national curriculum (CNB). The

CNB was put into effect in 2004 after years of planning and consultation with national and international 'experts' and organisations. The primary goal of the CNB is 'respecting and responding to the characteristics, needs and aspirations of a multicultural, multilingual and multiethnic country'.[5] In addition the curriculum aims to address social inequalities and gender and cultural discrimination through formal schooling.

The CNB provides a guiding framework for teachers at different grade levels (preschool, primary school, middle school) and for high school students with different career focuses, given the diversification of Guatemalan high schools into career paths (e.g. education, accounting, secretarial, nursing). Students receive a degree and certificate according to what they study; for example, students graduating from the three years of *Magisterio* (teacher education) receive a high-school-level diploma and an elementary teaching degree that allows them to work in the primary schools. The CNB has separate documents for these different levels and career focuses.

The pre-K and primary school CNBs lay out the goals of the national educational reforms:

> The Education Reform proposes to satisfy the need for a better future. That is to achieve a society that is pluralistic, inclusive, solidarity, just, participatory, intercultural, pluri-cultural, multiethnic and multilingual. A society in which all people participate consciously and actively in the construction of a common good and in the improvement of the quality of life for each person and, as a result, that of the *Pueblos* without any discrimination for political, ideological, ethnic, social, cultural, linguistic or gender reasons.[6]

The CNB states that it is seeking to transform central aspects of the curriculum to 'positively impact the whole educational system: especially, to bring solutions to problems that have traditionally affected Guatemalan education'.[7]

The organising documents state that the national government's Ministry of Education is to establish the general curriculum to be used in schools. Yet, this general curriculum is also designed as flexible, so it can be 'contextualised' according to regional and local contexts. This demonstrates that there are spaces to adjust the curriculum to meet needs, abilities and epistemologies of the students, teachers and families.[8]

Both scholars within the country and international scholars have critiqued the educational reforms in Guatemala. Collectively they argue that the multicultural reform the country has adopted has been taken up through 'strategic essentialism' in that it emphasises a certain way to 'be Maya'.[9] The reform also ignores the intersectionality of identities at play for individuals,[10] and it solidifies the polarising classifications of Ladino[11] and Maya.[12] In addition, Hale argues that the legal recognition of many cultures does not challenge the neo-liberal model and structures that perpetuate inequalities.[13] Esquit also argues that the state's multicultural reform efforts are a way for the state and those in power to continue to 'discipline' and control the Indigenous population and hinder their efforts to achieve self-determination and political awareness.[14] These notions of multiculturalism limit the possibilities of the educational reforms.

Several scholars, including Hale and Sieder, also contend that racist power structures continue to be entrenched in the political, social and economic structures of Guatemala. These power structures perpetuate inequalities and serve to disadvantage non-dominant groups in Guatemala.[15] Mayas, for example, continue to be pushed to learn Spanish and Ladino culture in order to gain access to social, political and economic opportunities that are unavailable to those who only speak their native Mayan language. Whereas these studies have explored the flaws inherent in Guatemala's national education policy and curriculum, few studies have focused on how these reforms are put into practice by the educators charged with enacting them.

WHO ARE THE CHUJ?

There are twenty-two distinct Mayan language groups recognised by the Guatemalan government. The four largest groups are Quiche, Kaqchikel, Qeqchi and Mam, which have recently been the focus of national projects and have historically had greater access to educational services and opportunities. The privileging of these four groups has created and entrenched a hierarchical social relationship among Guatemala's Mayan groups. Xantin, as a Chuj Maya community (the ninth largest Mayan group in Guatemala) faces great marginalisation as a 'minority' Mayan community. Xantin has not received priority in national education initiatives, including those directed at Mayan communities.[16] Similarly, the experiences of 'minority' Maya communities have been excluded in much of the literature on education. As López (cited in Herdoíza-Estévez and Lenk) argues, educational 'efforts have focused on the four most-used Maya languages—Kaqchikel, Mam, Qeqchi and Quiche—to the detriment of the other 19 linguistic communities'.[17]

Language here and throughout this chapter is conceptualised through its deep connection to culture. Ngũgĩ Wa Thiong'o argues, 'language . . . is both a means of communication and a carrier of culture'.[18] And Freire and Macedo similarly attest, 'language is also culture. Language is the mediating force of knowledge; but it is also knowledge itself'.[19]

In addition to few studies being conducted that explore teachers' efforts and experiences, there are few studies of the Chuj Maya, a linguistic group of about forty thousand to fifty thousand speakers, who live in the north-western region of Guatemala. The Chuj have suffered from state-led violence and historic marginalisation. The few published studies of the Chuj have focused on anthropological explorations[20] and historical narratives.[21] Also, there has been an exclusion of Chuj voices from political and educational decisions on the national level. At the national level there is a deficit framing of Chuj people as 'unqualified' for making curriculum or policy decisions.[22]

Xantin, Guatemala

Xantin is a semi-urban Chuj Maya town situated high in the mountains of Guatemala. This research focuses on the experiences and views of those living in the *cabecera municipal* (municipal centre) and the schools that they attend. However, participants' experiences are not exclusive to the *cabecera* as many were born, raised, travelled or have worked in *aldeas* (villages) throughout Xantin. The *cabecera* is home to an estimated seven thousand to ten thousand inhabitants, the majority of whom (an estimated 98 to 99 per cent) identify as Chuj. Some teachers and students come from nearby municipalities to study and work; the teachers from other municipalities most often identify as Ladino and the students are often Maya (Chuj or Q'anjobal).

Historically, Xantin has been marginalised and suffered from direct and indirect repression from the state. Because of its location and historic oppression, Xantin often has been removed from national policies and regulation and has received only marginal support and access to infrastructure and social services (such as roads, schools, teachers and running water). The few NGOs present in the community are focused on education and health services. Access to formal national schooling has been historically limited. An estimated 30 per cent of the population in Xantin is considered literate.[23]

THE LARGER PROJECT

This research draws on my two and a half years of teaching experience in Xantin, which allowed for a level of familiarity with the people and the place and gave me access to schools and community spaces. The interview with the teacher, Juana María, was conducted during four weeks of structured ethnographic research in August 2011. The overall study included thirty-two individual ethnographic interviews with teachers, student-teachers, school principals and community leaders. Classroom observations and participant observations were also conducted.

For the larger project I used inductive and deductive coding methods to analyse the data. Inductive coding was used to identity recurring themes about how educators in Xantin discuss their educational experience, how they put the reform effort into practice and how they viewed the IBE reform in general. After coding all the data collected, Juana María's interviews emerged as particularly salient. Juana María, along with other interviewees, offered comments about language, cultural discrimination, educational changes and discrimination inherent in national policies. Deductive coding was used to draw out further themes that were prevalent in the relevant literatures. Data were coded multiple times and member checking was used to confirm the conclusions reached and to mitigate the risk of misrepresentation. I use intersectionality as a framework to explore multiple social issues, especially braided notions of place, gender and culture that influence educators' experiences of formal education structures. [24] And whereas intersectionality can serve as a useful framework, Juana María makes sense of these issues in her own way that at times shows them as intersecting and at other times sees them as distinct.

RESEARCHER POSITIONALITY

As a White female from the US my cultural frame of references and life experiences differ from many people in Xantin. As Smith states, this can cause points of tension, because 'Western' research 'brings to bear, on any study of indigenous peoples, a cultural orientation, a set of values, a different conceptualization of such things as time, space and subjectivity, different and competing theories of knowledge, highly specialized forms of language, and structures of power'. [25] Language represents a particular source of tension in this research because the language used in the interviews was Spanish, the language imposed on the Chuj and one that continues to represent domination. Spanish, unlike Chuj, is not able to fully represent Chuj cosmovision or worldviews. This issue is further complicated through the process of translation into English for this chapter, because it is another language that represents domination and imperialism in Guatemala.

To make sense of and navigate my positionality as a researcher I use Narayan's notion of 'quality of relations' rather than polarising notions of insider–outsider or native–non-native researchers. [26] Narayan argues that the researchers' positionality is multiple and shifting. Because of my years of experience teaching in Xantin and relationships within the community, I am neither an outsider nor am I an insider. The relationships I developed with members of the community allowed for more nuanced insights. That said, my positionality calls for a deep reflexivity of the possible tensions with representation and my research goals. It is important to me because of my focus on the quality of my relations to put forth an honest, and respectful representation of Juana María, whose knowledge and insights inform this study.

JUANA MARÍA

Using a narrative inquiry approach, this chapter focuses on Juana María, who attended school in Xantin from elementary through high school and currently teaches at her former middle school and high school. She is also studying education at the university on the weekends. Listening to a teacher's voice speaks back to and adds to the top-down policy critiques presented earlier. Her experience allows certain issues to be brought into focus that are often excluded and/or not with through top-down approaches.

At the time of the interview, Juana María and I had known each other for three and a half years, so our conversations were free and open. We spoke on two separate occasions for the interview. Our first conversation took place at my apartment early in the morning over coffee. The second interview took place at her school during one of her free periods. In between, we spent time watching the local schools compete in soccer and basketball. And one morning we went to her parents' house to visit her mom and enjoyed a long talk about her family and local events over coffee and sweet bread. Throughout the time I have known her, Juana María is always teaching me.

THE CENTRALITY OF PLACE AND THE CURRICULUM

Xantin has a deep place-based historical memory and is considered a 'sacred place' to those who live there.[27] But because of its historical marginalisation from the central government, its history, although tied to national policies, has developed in a unique way that has led to varied understandings of and feelings about formal schooling and national policies. These understandings are deeply situated within the local culture and place-based historical memories. Escobar states, 'place continues to be an important source of culture and identity'.[28]

One of the major issues many educators discussed was that the CNB, despite its efforts to be more inclusive, was created in the capital by people who had and have very little knowledge of the reality of lives of people in Xantin. As one school principal stated: 'You must understand that the CNB is created in the cities where they have completely different expectations, here the reality is different. Here we could make a curriculum and send it to the capital and it wouldn't work there, because things are different'. Thus, many in Xantin believe that the national curriculum, established to be more inclusive and foster a greater sense of unity, neglects their own culture and reality. That said, educators in Xantin discussed different ways they were making sense of the national curriculum using their own social and cultural location and knowledge.

Teachers in Xantin engage with the government policy in unique ways that take into account the needs and values of the students and community. Juana María argued that the responsibility of contextualising the curriculum lies with individual teachers, and some teachers that are more invested than others. She stated:

Sí, está contextualizando la educación. Pero aunque el CNB o la reforma quiere eso, si de uno mismo no nace eso, si sigue siendo tradicionalista, ¿caso se va a vivir eso? No. Pero si uno sigue en lo que es la reforma, trata de investigar y trata de ponerse de conciencia de que si hay que un tema contextualizarlo con la cultura ... Porque algunos profesores, hablando de la preprimaria por ejemplo, ¿para qué le sirva que les enseñes lo que es el semáforo si no hay un semáforo aquí? Entonces, ¿eso para qué? Mejor buscar ... temas que sí estén adecuados para los alumnos.	Yes, education is being contextualised. But even if the CNB or the reform wants that, if this doesn't come from oneself, if one continues to be traditionalist, is there any way one is going to live that? No. But if one continues with that which is the reform, tries to investigate and tries to be aware that you have to contextualise each theme with the culture ... because some teachers talking about preschool, for example, what's it worth to teach them about what a stoplight is if there is no stoplight here? It's better to look for ... topics that are appropriate for the students.

Juana María stressed the importance of teachers 'living' the curricular changes and being committed to contextualising their teachings to meet the needs and understandings of their students. She argued that it is not valuable to teach students about things they cannot relate to or do not have around them, i.e. teaching about a stoplight when Xantin does not have a stoplight. Thus, teachers are responsible for making decisions that help their students connect to what is taught in schools.

Other educators similarly argued that it was their responsibility to make sure their teachings met the needs of their students' lives and context. They felt that the government's major contribution was to open up these spaces. They contend that if the curriculum calls for students learning about stoplights and there are no stoplights in the community, they need to find ways to make the learning goals apply to their students. However, some educators argued that such inapplicable lessons do not meet the needs of their students and demonstrate that the current curriculum is a carry-over from past overt marginalising and discriminatory educational policies. For these educators, the government is responsible for incorporating and centring the Chuj's (and all cultural groups') realities and ways of knowing into the official curriculum. Fundamentally, however, the majority of the teachers questioned the ability of the national curriculum to reflect the realities of the students they teach and combat social inequalities; teachers have the task of filling these spaces and fostering quality culturally relevant teaching practices.

Chuj educators' ideas and practices push back against the notion that those in power know what is best for Indigenous communities and that the government and outside educational 'professionals' can foster educational models that meet the needs of marginalised groups without taking into account their knowledge and experiences. As Juana María argued, learning about things that are not present in Xantin or a part of the community and culture may not be relevant; it is important to make sure the students are reflected in the curriculum. To make her teaching relevant, Juana María works hard to connect her teaching with issues present in Xantin. She explained her practice:

Hablando de ciencias naturales, yo síi trato la manera de buscar, investigar . . . ¿cómo es que debo someterme a eso lo que está viviendo los alumnos? Hay mucha desnutrición en Xantin, muchísimo. Entonces, ¿cómo es que debo pasarme o contextualizar mi tema con eso? Yo relaciono eso. Buscar enfermedades o ver la enfermedad y la salud. Y pongo ejemplos de lo que están viviendo en Xantin.	Talking about natural sciences, I try to find a way to find, to research . . . how should I present things that the students are living? There is a lot of malnutrition in Xantin, a lot. So how can I use or contextualise my topic with that? I relate it. I look for diseases or look at disease and health. I give examples of what they are living in Xantin.

Thus, Juana María, like many of her peers, makes slight changes in the curriculum to ensure that what she is teaching reflects what students have seen and/or experienced. She stays true to the main standards laid out in the curriculum while also connecting it to the local context.

This notion of relating classroom teachings is not just about making teaching relevant to students, but it is also focused on providing students with a sense of self through learning about their culture. Juana María believes education is more than just teaching students to read and write. She believes it is also about knowing oneself, reflecting Freire's concept of 'reading the word and the world'.[29] She asserted her vision of education as follows:

Para ser profesor es mucho más amplio que sólo enseñar, pasar y explicar letras, números. Es mucho más que eso . . . ¿Por qué recibimos la educación? Para mi la educación es bastante más que sólo leer, que sólo ver un libro. Es mucho más que esto; es conocer tu autoestima. Yo sí de la educación he aprendido mucho y de los profesores, muchísimo.	To be a teacher is much more comprehensive that just teaching, passing and explaining letters, numbers. It is much more than that . . . Why do we get an education? For me education is much more than just reading, that just looking at a book. It is much more than this; it is knowing your self-worth. From my education I have learned a lot and from the teachers even more.

Thus, Juana María argued that the official curriculum that fosters reading and writing skills is only part of what education is about. This argument is consistent with how she situates Chuj culture and knowledge in her notion of education.

LEARNING FROM A TEACHER'S EXPERIENCE

Juana María drew from her own experiences as a student, student teacher and teacher in Xantin to discuss formal schooling in her community. Britzman argues that teachers' use their own educational experiences to inform their teaching practice.[30] Britzman states, 'Teachers bring to their work their own idiomatic school biography, the conflicted history of their own deep investments in and ambivalence about what a teacher is and does'.[31] Thus, insights in Juana María's educational experiences and background helps add to the understanding of how and why policies are implemented as they are and why she chose to resist or accept aspects of the national policy. Juana María described her own educational history as inconsistent and disconnected, especially throughout her years in elementary school.

Voy a hablar un poco sobre mi historia, como he pasado. Entonces, cuando yo empecée la primaria me enseñóo una profesora [ladina] . . . era bien estricta . . . sólo nos dejaba deberes en caligrafía . . . y después salía afuera y no nos enseñaba. Aunque, como éeramos niños pequeñitos ,como empezamos en los 6 anos, 7 años en la preprimaria . . . nos enseñaba con su idioma que es el castellano. Pero como nosotros éramos niños no podíamos entender . . . Después que pasée en primero me enseñóo un profesor [chuj] . . . Sóolo nos enseñaba y hablaba en Chuj. Y asi pasó primero . . . segundo . . . Hasta tercero . . . Entonces cuando llegué ahí, una profesora [laadina] nos enseñó. Ya era muy diferente, muy . . . Pero no sabía . . . solo sabía hablar bien el Chuj. Entonces cuando ella nos decía, nos hablaba, casi no la entendíamos ¿Por qué? Porque solo nos hablaban Chuj.. Pasé en que en cuarto . . . La profesora era [ladina]. Era bien estricta, entonces si no podíamos hablar bien el castellano nos pegaba. Nos pegaba. Entonces si hablábamos

I will talk a little about my history, how it has been. So, when I started primary school I had a [Ladino] teacher . . . she was very strict . . . she would just leave us with calligraphy work . . . and then she would go outside and she didn't teach us. However, we were small kids, we start primary school at six years, seven years old, [and] . . . she taught us with her language, which is Spanish. But since we were kids we couldn't understand . . . After I passed to first grade I was taught by a [Chuj] teacher . . . He only taught and spoke to us in Chuj. And that is how I went through first grade . . . second grade . . . Until third grade . . . So when I got there [Ladina] teacher taught us. It was very different, very . . . I didn't know . . . I could only speak Chuj well. So when she spoke to us we could barely understand. Why? Because they had only spoken to us in Chuj . . . I got to fourth grade . . . The teacher was [Ladina]. She was very strict, so if we couldn't speak Spanish she hit us. She hit us. So if we talked in Chuj, for example, we asked a classmate for

en Chuj, por ejemplo, pedíamos
un lápiz a un compañero si hablábamos nos castigaba. 'Es que
tienen que aprenderme,' nos decía.
Pero uno tenía la razón; y ella pen-
saba que ya sabíamos porque nos
enseñaba, ya estaba en cuarto.

a pencil, if we talked she punished
us. 'It's just that you have to learn',
she would tell us. On the one hand,
she was right and she thought that
we already knew [Spanish] because
they taught us. I was in fourth
grade after all.

Juana María shows how each year she faced teachers who had different
expectations and cultural and linguistic orientations. Whereas her classes
had been taught solely in Chuj from first through third grade, in her fourth
grade classroom language was rigidly controlled. A number of other teachers recalled this practice, which made them feel that their language had no
place in school; Chuj was even worthy of corporal punishment. Only Spanish language was 'valuable' for schooling.

With the official move to bilingual education and the freedom to develop
materials in Mayan languages, a major source of tension that emerged
throughout the interviews was what language students should be taught in
the Chuj language to provide students with a strong knowledge base from
which to navigate Spanish and 'school knowledge'. Yet, whereas Spanish
language dominance in schools often undermines the Chuj language and
ways of knowing, it also provides students with dominant cultural capital
and a position to speak back from. As Freire and Macedo argue:

> The notion of emancipatory literacy suggests two dimensions of literacy.
> On the one hand, students have to become literate about their histories,
> experiences, and the culture of their immediate environments. On the
> other hand, they must also appropriate those codes of the dominant
> spheres so they can transcend their own environments. There is often
> an enormous tension between these two dimensions of literacy.[32]

In Xantin, Chuj students are expected to learn the dominant culture and
language (Spanish) to be 'successful'; however, the values and structures
underlying these practices often come into opposition with the values
pointed to as important in the community as a whole. Juana María highlighted this tension with language in schools.

[Los profesores] nos explicaban
mucho en español entonces casi
nos olvida un poco [el chuj] ... Y
uno es que nosotros pensamos que
es mejor aprender más el español
porque así nos dice. Por ejemplo,
'es que ustedes deben hablar en
español para que síi lo vamos a

[The teachers] explained a lot to us
in Spanish, so we almost forgot a
bit [of our Chuj] ... And for one
thing we think that it is better to
learn more Spanish, because that's
what we are told. For example, 'you
should speak Spanish, so we will
understand it, to communicate

entender, a comunicarnos y lo van a aprender máas'. . . . Bueno yo pienso, uno es mejor para nosotros por ejemplo. ¿Quée tal si llega una persona y te pregunta algo y no sabes hablar? Simplemente te vas a quedar mudo. Entonces, eso si tiene su ventaje y desventaja. Es que aprendemos y estamos olvidando de nuestroa idioma.

ourselves and we will learn more'. . . . Well, I think that on the one hand it is better for us, for example, what if someone comes and asks you something and you don't know how to speak? You will simply be left mute. So that has its advantage and disadvantage; we are learning and we are forgetting our language.

Juana María pointed out the value of knowing Spanish to communicate with people outside Xantin and to not be left without a voice. Nevertheless, she notes how learning Spanish without incorporating Chuj promotes a sense of language loss. As she states, 'we are learning and we are forgetting our language'.

Juana María argued that the privileging of Ladino language and culture has its historical roots in colonial power structures that taught Mayas to 'respect' Ladinos.

Nos enseññaron así, que nosotros debemos de escuchar a ellos [los ladinos], que nosotros debemos de respetar a ellos. Uno es que hablando más de la colonización, desde eso se vino que hay que respetar a ellos que solo hay que respetar a ellos. Es que nosotros somos indios y nosotros debemos aprender lo que ellos dicen.

They taught us that, that we should listen to them [the Ladinos], that we should respect them. One thing is that talking about colonisation, from there came [the notion] that one must respect them, only respect them. It's that we are indios and we should learn what they say.

Juana María's statement highlights how 'cultural racism' is experienced in Xantin through education. 'Cultural racism' is used by Hale to describe the 'subtle fusion' of biological and cultural precepts in Guatemala.[33] As Juana María argues, these structures act to marginalise Mayan students and show them that their culture, language and knowledge and not the most valuable or the most worthy of respect. This is highlighted in her statement, 'they are the only ones to be respected. It's that we are *indios* and we should learn what they say'.

THE VALUE OF CULTIVATING CHUJ IDENTITY

Like many of her counterparts, Juana María argued that it was important to teach students about themselves and their culture, to foster a strong sense of their own identity and to use that as a base to navigate other cultures and languages. She stated,

> Que uno no olvide de su origen, de su cultura. Está bien también porque mire estamos comunicándonos en español. Está mejor que aprendemos tres cuatros idiomas. Pero uno principal que no nos olvidemos de lo nuestro. Porque lo nuestro es más importante que los otros ... es importante aprender de otros pero que no se olvidemos de lo nuestro.

> One should not forget his origin or culture. It's also good, because look we are communicating in Spanish. It is better that we learn three, four languages. But the principal thing is that we don't forget what is ours. Because what is ours is the most important ... it is important to learn from others, but we should not forget what is ours.

Thus with a strong sense of their own culture and language, Juana María argued that students would be better situated to learn and navigate other cultures and languages. Freire and Macedo argue a similar point in their assertion that:

> Literacy can only be emancipatory and critical to the extent that it is conducted in the language of the people. It is through the native language that students 'name their world' and begin to establish a dialectical relationship with the dominant class in the process of transforming the social and political structures.[34]

Thus, students' language and culture is important not only in its own right, but also for engaging with the dominant language and constructions of knowledge.

Place and Class

Class, much like other social constructs such as race and ethnicity, is understood and constructed differently in different contexts. In Xantin, experiences of place and culture are deeply intertwined with socio-economic class; the majority of the Chuj population in Xantin lives at or below the poverty line (approximately 92 per cent of the population of the municipality).[35] Bourdieu argues that capital extends beyond economic capital to social and cultural capital, which are all linked. Thus, capital accumulation is not only what people have, but also how, because of it, they are able to access power structures and utilise that accessibility to both establish new networks and connect with existing networks.[36] As Bourdieu states:

> The volume of the social capital possessed by a given agent thus depends on the size of the network connections he [sic] can effectively mobilize

and on the volume of the capital (economic, cultural or symbolic) possessed in his own right by each of those to whom he is connected.[37]

Because Xantin is geographically and socially isolated, many people's social networks are generally concentrated within the community and municipality. Thus, social class emerged in interviews with Chuj educators in relation to other communities and not as much between individuals living in Xantin. Ladino teachers and student teachers were the only ones who explicitly brought up class inequalities as a social concern (possibly because of their connections and in many cases roots outside Xantin and their social locations within a dominant cultural group). Place-based and classed struggles were a part of every interview and intersected with notions of race as well as gender. In each interview with a Chuj educator, a reference was made to the economic struggles that either the interviewee or his/her parents went through to ensure they received an education. Juana María spoke with me about her 'struggles' with education and her parents' (especially her mother's) efforts to raise money to support her.

Gender

Points of reference from place, class and race were complicated with discussions of gender in regards to the education of girls. Several educators argued that educating a girl is generally seen as a losing economic investment for a family, because the girl is expected to leave the family when she gets married and live with her husband's family. Thus, many parents of girls believe that educating a girl works to the economic gain of her husband's family rather than bringing them any direct economic benefit. Juana María highlighted this issue on numerous occasions throughout the interview:

Además pienso que los hombres antes eran muy machistas como que las mujeres no valían nada . . . los papáas casí no dejaban ir a sus hijas a estudiar. Uno es porque se van a casar, la mentalidad es así, y quizás no se ha cambiado todavía, porque así sigue dando . . . [L]os hombres por ejemplo [dicen a las mujeres] . . . 'no, te vas a casar, te vas juntar' y todo eso . . . Yo conozco a una familia cerca a la casa de mi mamá, que sólo el hombre está estudiando y hay 4 niñas y no están estudiando. Y es que les dice el papá, 'es que ustedes deben

Moreover I think that the men before were very machistas as though the women weren't worth anything ... parents didn't really let their daughters go study. One is because they are going to get married, the mentality is that way, and maybe it hasn't changed yet, because that is how it continues to be ... [T]he men for example [say to women] ... 'no, you are going to get married, you are going to juntar' and all that ... I know a family close to my mom's house that only the boy is studying and there are four girls and they are not studying. And the father says *estar en la casa cocinando, limpi-ando, teniendo la casa bien limpia. Es que él después se va a graduar y les va a dar dinero, les va a com-prar la ropa para que ustedes va a vivir mejor'. Entonces ¿quée es eso? . . . Porque hay mujeres que se siguen separando de los hom-bres porque les pegan, les mal-tratan, no les dan su lugar como mujer; en la casa simplemente es como una sirvienta. Y también en la educación, no les mandan a su hijas . . .*

to them, 'it's that you all should be in the house cooking, cleaning and making the house very clean. He will graduate later and he will give you money, he will buy you clothes so you all will live better'. What is that? . . . There are women that continue to get separated from the men because they beat them, they abuse them, they don't give them their space as a woman in the house simply she is simply like a servant. And also in education they don't send their daughters . . .

Juana María shows the ways girls continue to be excluded from educational opportunities and how boys are privileged in the access to formal school-ing. By stating that girls are just going to get married, parents and class-mates tell girls that they are not worth investing in and that they are not worthy of receiving an education. Part of this argument is the belief that once girls are married they are responsible for the housework and taking care of the children (which they are expected to start having once they are married). Formal schooling does not always fit with this concept of the role of a married woman. Later in the interview, Juana Maria outlined the flaws in thinking of girls' education as a losing economic investment given there are possibilities for them to continue to study even after they are married:

Pero yo pienso que eso no es algo lógico de hacerlo. Aunque sea que la mujer se case, pero es para su superación, puede seguir estudiando, puede seguir luch-ando aunque tenga un hombre a su lado, pero no quiere decir que esto se va a quedar y ya no puede seguir, no.

But I think that that isn't logical to do. Even if the woman gets mar-ried, but [studying] is for her own improvement. She can continue studying, she can continue fighting, even if she has a man by her side, but that doesn't mean that she is going to stay where she is and she can't continue, no.

A number of educators argue that this perception is shifting and a number of girls' parents are starting to see education as an investment in a woman's future opportunities and success in life. By shifting the focus from an eco-nomic investment for the family to an investment in the individual girl's future, education is coming to be seen as a way to provide girls and women with greater autonomy, so they will not feel forced to remain in abusive relationships and can support themselves and their families.

Thus, gender inequities are a central concern in Xantin and in Guatemala as a whole. As Juana María continued her education, she talked about how her experiences were increasingly influenced by her gender, which also intersected with cultural and linguistic marginalisation. The view of schools as male-dominated spaces affected her relationship with her classmates. In her middle school and high school she was one of three girls in a class of fifteen students. She described her experience as follows:

JM: Ya no nos pegaban además nos enseñaban muy bien ... así de la aprendizaje bien, pero así con confianza o relaciones entre compañneros no fue bien ... cuando pasée en ese etapa [los compañeros] no nos ayudaban, nos maltrataban, fue un poco horrible. A mi síi me molestaron bastante. ¿Por qué? Porque me defendíia de ellos. Hablaba también ... Además varias veces fui con el director para decirle ... después me odiaban bastante.

AA: ¿Y el director te ayudó?

JM: Síi, me ayudó. Fue a hablar con ellos. Una vez me lastimé. Uno me empujó y después me lastimé la pierna ... y después me lastimé aquí en mi frente. No sé, un compañero me agarró la cabeza y me empujó en la pared, pero no sé porquée me empujaron y después aunque sea fue a hablar con el director y después soy la que molestaba a ellos y no sé quée.

JM: They didn't hit us anymore and they taught us very well ... The learning [was] good, but [the] trust or relationships among classmates ... wasn't good ... when I was in that stage [the compañeros] didn't help us, they said mean things to us, it was a bit horrible. They really harassed me a lot. Why? Because I defended myself against them. I spoke too ... Moreover I went to the principal many times to tell him ... then they really hated me.

AA: And did the principal help you?

JM: Yes, he helped me. He went to talk to them. One time I got hurt. One of them pushed me and then I hurt my leg ... and then I got hurt here on my forehead. I don't know, one compañero grabbed my head and pushed me against the wall, but I don't know why they pushed me and afterwards he went to talk to the principal and then [the story was that] I am the one that molestaba them and I don't know what.

Juana María felt that her male classmates targeted her for being a woman who was not submissive in a male-dominated class. In their attempt to control her, male members of the class blamed her for causing their violent behaviour directed toward her. Women who stood up for themselves or were more vocal were accused of *molestando* (roughly translated to disturbing or being bothersome or annoying). Framing female students as *molestando* gave male students cover to mistreat them. Many of the women

I interviewed for the larger project expressed similarly being described as bothersome, thereby giving male students 'reason' to act against them. Girls described feeling unsafe and marginalised because of the actions and attitude of male students.

Many times the female students did not believe teachers or administrators would understand or support them if they brought up the issues they were experiencing. That being said, a number of female students did seek help from teachers and administers and were not surprised but disappointed that very little change occurred. Because of the actions of the male students and the ineffectiveness of teachers and administrators to eliminate the violence toward them, girls learned that schools are male-dominated spaces; they are not sites for gender-equitable learning and often not safe spaces. In addition, they learned that if they were to succeed in school they had to be 'seen and not heard'.

TO SPEAK OF CHANGE IS NOT CHANGE

Ever since I met her, Juana María has been a passionate advocate for Indigenous women's rights, especially for the women in Xantin. Thus, during the interviews she spoke a lot about discrimination against women that she herself has experienced and witnessed throughout her schooling. In the majority of the other interviews, however, when asked about gender discrimination, the educators generally responded that there is no longer any discrimination because there are now as many girls in primary school as boys. Increased access and gender parity in elementary schools was immediately cited as proof of gender equality. This discourse mirrors both national and international priorities to increase girls' access to education and satisfies the argument of Western liberal feminists that gender equality is about equal access to opportunities. Most of the respondents stated that, yes, there was gender discrimination in Xantin five to ten years ago, but now that has changed because there are equal numbers of boys and girls studying.

When I mentioned this argument to Juana María and asked her if she felt that there was still gender discrimination, she responded:

JM: Sími todavía hay, porque yo veo con mis propios ojos, porque yo síi lo vivo, si hay. Aunque profesores, ay dios, siguen discriminando a las mujeres. Y ya que tienen una professióon, y síi todavía hay. Y ¿por quéque no lo quieren decir? Porque les duele. No quieren decir la verdad.

JM: Yes, there still is, because I see it with my own eyes, because I live it; there is. Even though they are teachers, oh God, they continue to discriminate against the women. And they are professional . . . Why don't they want to talk about it? Because it hurts them. They don't want to say the truth.

AA: *¿Y y me puedes hablar un poco sobre los profesores discriminando a mujeres?*

JM: *Bueno, yo vi un caso en [mi práctica] . . . El profesor sóolo escuchaba a un alumno . . . Entonces, yo lo víi cuando llegué. Entonces, él [dijo], 'Quiero escucharles, ¿quée es lo que me van a hablar sobre tal tema?, Oquiero escuchar lo que entienden . . . ', les decía a los niños. Entonces la niña respondió, levantó la mano y explicó. [Entonces el profesor dijo], 'Quiero escucharte Jorge . . . te escucho a ti'. Entonces el niño explicaba. Pero yo pienso que fue la respuesta máas explicativa lo que dijo la niña . . . Ella respondió bien lo que yo pienso. Entonces después el niño explicó, entonces [el profesor respondió], 'Es cierto lo que dice Jorge'. Entonces aunque no lo dijo, 'lo que dijo ella no está bien' [con] 'es cierto lo que dijo JorgePedro', entonces todos los niños van a pensar que ella no [sabía]. Igual seguía así hasta que un día yo les pregunté si es mejor echar de menos a una niña . . . Lo que dijeron los dos, 'sí, está perfecto'. Asi se pudiera decir [el profesor] que ella sí tiene razón y él también. Pero, 'es cierto lo que dijo Pedro'Jorge'. Yo pienso que no. Con poquitas cosas aunque decimos que no seguimos pensando, no seguimos discriminando a las mujeres, pero con poquitas cosas se demuestra que si.*

AA: And can you tell me a little about the teachers discriminating against women?

JM: Well, I saw a case in [my student-teaching] . . . the one teacher only listened to a male student . . . So, I saw this when I got there. He [said], 'I want to hear you all. What are all of you going to tell me about this topicheme? I want to hear what you all understand . . . ' he said to the kids. So the girl responded, raised her hand and explained. [The teacher then said], 'I want to hear you, Jorge . . . I listen to you'. So the boy explained. But I think that more explanatory answer was the one the girl gave' . . . She responded well, I think. Then after the boy explained, then [the teacher responded,] 'What Jorge says is true'. Even though he didn't say, 'what she said wasn't good'[with] 'it's true what Jorge said . . . ' then all the children will think that she didn't [know]. It continued the same way there until one day I asked if it is better to bring down a girl . . . What the two said, 'yes, it's perfectly fine'. What [the teacher] could have said was that she was right and he as well, but 'what Pedro says is true'. I don't think so. With the little things even if we say that we don't continue thinking about it, we don't continue to discriminate against women, but with the little things it shows that yes [we do].

Juana María highlighted the way subtle and constant discrimination acts to reinforce gender biases and she points to how teachers' actions can also be biased against female students. This 'hidden curriculum' sends messages to students that girls are inferior to boys.[38] Juana María argued that even though a girl gave a good answer, the teacher dismissed her response in favour of the boy's response. She contended that these actions continue to privilege boys in formal schooling. Throughout the interviews, many of the women related experiencing similar situations in the classroom and a number of male educators discussed seeing girls similarly treated.

Gender is also a central issue in multicultural education and explicitly addressed in the CNB, because gender and culture are deeply intertwined and dually constructed Anzaldúa tells us:

> Culture forms our beliefs. We perceive the version of reality that it communicates. Dominant paradigms, predefined concepts that exist as unquestionable, unchallengeable, are transmitted to us through culture. Culture is made by those in power—men. Males make the rules and laws; women transmit them . . . The culture expects women to show greater acceptance of, and commitment to, the value system than men.[39]

Thus, it is important to recognise the multiple ways gender and culture are connected and intersect. This affects girls' and women's experiences and opportunities. Whereas Anzaldúa argues that education offers new opportunities for women, it does not necessarily mitigate the socio-cultural pressures, such as marriage and childbearing, that women experience and are forced to negotiate.[40]

Juana María, like a number of educators I interviewed, talked about how the gendered issues experienced in the classroom are connected with social issues in the community and families. Through their example, Juana María argued that parents teach their sons to discriminate against girls. This mentality often carries into the classroom and affects the gendered relationships among peers. If the men do not show respect to their wives and daughters, their sons will learn to do the same, both to the girls and women in their home and outside their homes in the community and in the schools.

Uno es que quizás sus papás por le dan ejemplos. Por ejemplo,el papá, diríamos, no le espera mucho a la mamáa . . . no tiene valor ante éel . . . Entonces obviamente el niño va creciendo con esa mentalidad, y cuando va a llegar en clase simplemente que él vio lo que es su papá, mucho peor que él va a ser con su compañera. Entonces eso es desde al familia también que el niño no le respeta a su hermana, mucho peor en la clase.

One is that maybe their parents provide the examples. For example, the father let's say doesn't expect a lot out of the mom . . . she doesn't have value for him . . . So obviously the child is going to grow up with that mentality and when he gets to class he's just seen how his father acts and he's going to be much worse with his compañera. So that is from the family that the boy doesn't respect his sister, much worse in the class.

The participants interviewed, as part of the larger project, differed in their opinions regarding where gender discrimination was situated. A number of Ladino interviewees argued that gender inequalities and *machismo* was an inherent component of Mayan culture, whereas many Mayan respondents argued that it was a legacy of colonial repression that imposed multiple systems of oppression including patriarchy. Juana María historicised this pointing to the violence of colonisation.

Uno porque no sabemos la historia que de desde hace mucho se descriminó mucho a las mujeres cuando hubo la colonización cuando llegaron a conquistar y empezaron a violar a mujeres. Y yo pienso que desde ahí vino lo que es la raíz de la descriminacióon de todo eso. Y obviamente los mayas los vivieron ya como que les hicieron eso delante de ellos. ¿Cómo que no es que no lo van a hacer?	One thing is that we don't know the history of the ways that since long ago women have been very discriminated against since there was colonisation when they came to conquer and started to rape women. And I think that from there came the root of discrimination and all that. And obviously the Mayas lived this and since they did this in front of them, how is it that they aren't going to do it?

Juana María argued that gender discrimination either began with or was reinforced by the gender violence of colonisation. This analysis counters the ahistoricising of gender inequalities often done by national and international groups that situates gender inequality as an inherent part of Mayan culture. Juana María's statement echoes Mohanty's argument that imposition of colonial power structures both consolidated and entrenched existing inequalities and created new ones.[41] This explanation highlights the way racist and gendered power structures have been historically interconnected and the potential for classroom experiences to reinforce structural discrimination through the perpetuation of such power inequities.

Juana María argued that any attempts to address gender inequalities in schools needs to be done with the support and investment of the community and families. She argues that if change does not take place in the families, then the efforts of the schools and teachers cannot make much of an impact. Thus, she envisioned combating gender inequality as a joint effort.

Uno es que aunque un profesor trata de hacerlo si los papás no lo hacen ¿de qué sirve? ¿De qué sirve hacer eso si los papáas no lo van a hacer? Entonces, ¿cómo es que los niños van a cumplir? ¿Cómo es que los niños van a tomar conciencia	One is that even if the teacher tries to do it if the parents aren't doing it, what's the point? What's the point of doing that if the parents don't do it? So, how are the kids going to comply? How are the kids going to gain awareness if the

si ni los papás han tomado la mano para decirles? Entonces, uno es el trabajo del padres, la madre, y los profesores

parents are not taking them by the hand to tell them? So, one thing is the job of the father, the mother and the teachers

Building off her argument for the importance of collective change, Juana María discussed how she envisioned fostering this community-wide change. She argued that boys and girls and women and men all need to be a part of this process with everyone working together and teaching one another how to value themselves as well as those around them.

Formaría a todas la niñas de aquí en la escuela por ejemplo y les imparto sobre la autoestima, los derechos, las obligaciones también y que ellas también piensan, '¿Qué hacemos?' Hagamos grupos entonces y llamamos a los compañeros; un grupo de ellas hablen con ellos y otro grupo de ellas hablen con otros y así. Y si vemos el resultado de que los hombres pasen de exponer, por ejemplo, delante de las mujeres que por ejemplo un hombre y una mujer dicen, 'Tú vales, yo también, hagamos conciencia de que nosotros podemos salir adelante. Aunque somos diferentes de sexo, pero somos inteligentes por naturaleza y todo lo sabemos'. Buscar, tratar la manera de hacerlo si los muchachos por ejemplo toman la conciencias entonces hacer grupitos y con otras comunidades hablando. Quiero que los hombres también estén delante de las señoras por ejemplo, las señoras, ah sí, las mujeres también y que las mujeres estén delante de los hombre también. Y así podemos promover, ese que hoy y mañana no, poco a poco, pero si podemos hacer.

I would form a group with the girls here at the school, for example, and I would teach them about self-esteem, rights, and obligations, too, and so that they also think, 'what should we do?' Let's make groups and call the compañeros; a group of the girls talks to a group of the boys and another group of the girls talk with others and so on. And we can see the result when the men come up to speak, for example, in front of the women that, for example, a man and a woman say, 'You are valuable, me too; let's raise awareness that we can move forward. Even if we are different sexes, but we are intelligent by nature and we all know it'. Looking, trying to find a way to do it; if the boys become aware then make groups and talk with others in the community. I want the men to be in front of the older women, for example, the señoras, ah yes, women, too, and that the women are in front of the men, too. And in this way we can promote it, not today or tomorrow, little by little, but we can do it.

Juana María's vision is situated within a larger discourse on human rights and women's rights in particular. In Xantin, the mayor's office is working to foster women's access to services and support as well as an understanding of their rights as women and citizens of Guatemala. Juana María's educational vision builds off these efforts in a way that makes it more inclusive and collaborative with all members of the community involved in promoting greater equity.

JUANA MARIA'S VISION OF A SOCIAL JUSTICE EDUCATION

Juana María pushes for a locally based social justice orientation in her education vision. She imagines all members of the community being involved in her educational vision for change that advocates for gender-conscious community building through mutual affirmation and support. Her goal is to have boys and girls learning from one another and learning how to respect one another. She then imagines this teaching branching out to the adults and elders in the community. Her vision mirrors that of many other educators I spoke to, who seek to push beyond the national curriculum to foster locally based models that have the potential to facilitate real change by being situated within the culture and reality of the community itself. Like Juana María's narrative demonstrates, the insights of local educators can push past ahistorical framings of gendered disparities that fail to examine structural and systemic issues with a discussion of how colonisation influenced both cultural and gender discrimination. This brings into question the ability of top-down educational models to address social inequities, because teachers like Juana María are able to see issues and propose solutions that are not always visible through top-down policy initiatives and/or studies where educators' voices are often absent.

ANALYSING THE INTERSECTIONS

Juana María's experience is illustrative of the degree to which formal schooling in Xantin can be both colonising and decolonising. It is colonising in the way that it undermines Chuj culture. And it is decolonising as formal schooling provides students with access to dominant cultural capital, which gives them the tools and language with which to navigate and push back against oppressive power structures. Juana highlighted the challenge of the struggle to make education decolonising.

Through Juana María's narrative, it is apparent how multiple social categories are at play and influence Chuj educators' experiences and understandings. Educational experiences, as discussed by Juana María, highlight how culture/race, place and gender intersect in formal schooling in complex and meaningful ways. Policies that seek to address one form of oppression fail to recognise how social categories are interconnected and mutually reinforcing in very complex and interlocking ways.[42]

Thus, it is important to consider how educators' insights can be used to create richer and more complex ways of honouring people's lived experiences and promoting equity in education in ways that cannot be envisioned through a top-down approach. This added understanding brings into question notions of qualifications and expertise, and *who* is 'qualified' to make policy and curriculum decisions for formal schooling. 'Minority' Mayan communities that have been historically marginalised and excluded from formal schooling systems are generally presumed not to possess members who are qualified to make these decisions.[43] Formal schooling and language requirements continue to silence members of 'minority' communities and perpetuate the privileging of knowledge connected with the dominant culture even within a national framework of 'multiculturalism'.

Evidence that the state's model of multiculturalism reinforces the status quo and reinforces social hierarchies in turn raises questions about the goals of the state's multicultural initiatives and how decisions regarding education of 'minority' children are made, as well as *whose* voices are heard and how power and structural inequalities are addressed or concealed. By highlighting the knowledge and experience of a Chuj educator, this chapter calls attention to the tensions and exclusions experienced by Chuj students and educators within the formal schooling system.

Exploring the experiences of educators, who have on-the-ground experiences in schools in communities, illuminates the complexity of these issues and calls for the development of solutions that are locally based and build off of community strengths, knowledges and realities. As researchers, it is our responsibility to listen to these insights. By highlighting the knowledge and experience of a Chuj teacher, this chapter calls for the consideration of teachers as policymakers rather than simply enactors of curriculum. The teachers who are making decisions on a daily basis regarding what education in their classrooms, schools and communities will look like are concurrently being silenced by exclusion from current power structures and those considered 'qualified' to create educational policies and curricula *for* local communities. Hearing from and centring the voices of local, on-the-ground teachers is crucial to the understanding of educational policies in a manner that is sensitive to local language, culture and ways of knowing. Individual teachers' insights and practices enhance the understandings of both national policies and local educational realities. This chapter seeks to open the discussion of education reforms and multicultural education and centre the knowledge and visions of all teachers towards new models, which foster greater equity.

NOTES

1. All names are pseudonyms.
2. Pseudonym.
3. For this analysis, I draw on tools from narrative inquiry methodologies: Linde (1993); Clandinin and Connelly (2000); Coles (1989); Mishler (1999).

4. 'Cultural racism' is a term used by Charles Hale (2002, 2008) to describe the way structural racism is manifested in Guatemala and grounded in a 'subtle fusion' of biological and cultural precepts.
5. MINEDUC, DICADE, DIGEBI (2005).
6. MINEDUC (2005, 13), author's translation.
7. Ibid, 15.
8. Ibid.
9. Sieder (2008).
10. Dietz and Córtes (2008).
11. Guatemala's 'mestizo' and Spanish-speaking population and the country's dominant cultural group.
12. Rodas (2008).
13. Hale (2002).
14. Esquit (2008).
15. Hale (2008); Sieder (2002).
16. Herdoíza-Estévez and Lenk (2010).
17. *Ibid*, 205–206.
18. Wa Thiong'o (1986, 12).
19. Freire and Macedo (1987, 53).
20. Piedrasanta (2009).
21. Melville (2005); Maxwell (2001).
22. Personal correspondence with individual in the Ministry of Education, April 2012.
23. FUNCEDE (2011).
24. Crenshaw (1991); Collins (1998); McCall (2005); Bhopal and Preston (2012).
25. Smith (1999, 42).
26. Narayan (1993).
27. Piedrasanta (2009).
28. Escobar (2008, 7).
29. Freire (1970); Freire and Macedo (1987).
30. Britzman (2003).
31. Ibid, 2.
32. Freire and Macedo (1987, 47).
33. Hale (2008).
34. Freire and Macedo (1987, 159).
35. FUNCEDE (2011).
36. Bourdieu (1986).
37. Ibid. (249).
38. Apple and King (1983); Aikman and Unterhalter (2007).
39. Anzaldúa (1987, 38).
40. Anzaldúa (1987).
41. Mohanty (1991).
42. Roth (2004).
43. Personal correspondence with individual in the Ministry of Education, April 2012.

REFERENCES

Aikman, Shelia, and Elaine Unterhalter. 2007. *Practising Gender Equality in Education*. Herndon, VA: Oxfam GB.
Anzaldúa, Gloria. 1987. *Borderlands/La Frontera: The New Mestiza*. San Francisco: Aunt Lute Books.

Apple, Michael, and Nancy King. 1983. 'What Do Schools Teach?' In *The Hidden Curriculum and Moral Education*, edited by Henry Giroux and David Purpel, 82–99. Berkeley: McCutchan Publishing Corporation.

Bhopal, Kalwant, and John Preston. 2012. *Intersectionality and 'Race' in Education*. New York: Routledge.

Bourdieu, Pierre. 1986. 'The Forms of Capital'. In *The Handbook of Theory and Research for the Sociology of Education*, edited by John G. Richardson, 241–258. New York: Greenwood Press.

Britzman, Deborah. 2003. *Practice Makes Practice: A Critical Study of Learning to Teach*. Rev. ed. New York: SUNY Press.

Clandinin, D. Jean, and F. Michael Connelly. 2000. *Narrative Inquiry: Experience and Story in Qualitative Research*. San Francisco: Jossey-Bass.

Coles, Robert. 1989. *The Call of Stories: Teaching and the Moral Imagination*. Boston: Houghton Mifflin.

Collins, Patricia Hill. 1998. 'The Tie That Binds: Race, Gender and US Violence'. *Ethnic and Racial Studies* 21:917–938.

Crenshaw, Kimberlé. 1991. 'Mapping the Margins: Intersectionality, Identity Politics, and Violence against Women of Color'. *Stanford Law Review* 43:1241–1299.

Dietz, Gunther, and Laura Selene Mateos Córtes. 2008. 'El discurso internacional ante el paradigma de la diversidad: estructuraciones subyacentes y migraciones discursivas del multiculturalismo contemporáneo'. In *Multiculturalismo y futuro en Guatemala*, edited by Santiago Bastos, 23–54. Guatemala City, Guatemala: FLACSO/OXFAM.

Escobar, Arturo. 2008. *Territories of Difference: Place, Movements, Life, Redes*. Durham, NC: Duke University Press Books.

Esquit, Edgar. 2008. 'Disciplinando al subalterno. Vínculos de violencia y de gobierno en Guatemala'. In *Multiculturalismo y futuro en Guatemala*, edited by Santiago Bastos, 123–148. Guatemala City, Guatemala: FLACSO/OXFAM.

Freire, Paulo. 1970. *Pedagogy of the Oppressed*. New York: Continuum.

Freire, Paulo, and Donaldo Macedo. 1987. *Literacy: Reading the Word and the World*. New York: Bergin and Garvey.

FUNCEDE. 2011. *Comportamiento Electoral Municipal in Guatemala: Elecciones Generales 2007*. Guatemala City, Guatemala: FUNCEDE.

Hale, Charles. 2002. 'Does Multiculturalism Menace? Governance, Cultural Rights and the Politics of Identity in Guatemala', *Journal of Latin American Studies* 34:485–524.

———. 2008. *Más que un indio/More than an Indian: Racial Ambivalence and Neoliberal Multiculturalism in Guatemala*. Santa Fe: School of American Research Press.

Herdoíza-Estévez, Magdalena, and Sonia Lenk. 2010. 'Intercultural Dialogue: Discourse and Realities of Indigenous and Mestizos in Ecuador and Guatemala'. *Interamerican Journal of Education for Democracy* 3:196–223.

Linde, Charlotte. 1993. *Life Stories: The Creation of Coherence*. New York: Oxford University Press.

Maxwell, Judith. 2001. *Textos Chuj de San Mateo Ixtatán*. Palos Verde: Fundación Yax Te'.

McCall, Leslie. 2005. 'The Complexity of Intersectionality'. *Signs: Journal of Women in Culture and Society* 30:1771–1800.

Melville, Thomas. 2005. *Through a Glass Holocaust: The US Holocaust in Central America*. Bloomington, IN: Xlibris.

MINEDUC, DICADE, DIGEBI. 2005. *Curriculum Nacional Base*. Guatemala City, Guatemala: DICADE.

Mishler, Elliot. 1999. *Storylines: Craftartists' Narratives of Identity*. Cambridge, MA: Harvard University Press.

Mohanty, Chandra. 1991. 'Introduction'. In *Third World Women and the Politics of Feminism*, edited by Chandra Mohanty, Anne Russo and Lourdes M. Torres, 1–50. Bloomington: Indiana University Press.

Narayan, Kirin. 1993. 'How Native Is a "Native" Anthropologist?' *American Anthropologist* 95:19–32.

Piedrasanta, Ruth. 2009. *Los Chuj: unidad y rupturas en su espacio*. Guatemala City, Guatemala: Armar Editores.

Rodas, Isabel. 2008. 'El rol de las emociones en las identidades narrativas de los grupos e individuos en desplazamiento'. In *Multiculturalismo y futuro en Guatemala*, edited by Santiago Bastos, 157–171. Guatemala: FLACSO/OXFAM.

Roth, Benita. 2004. *The Separate Roads to Feminism: Black, Chicana, and White Feminist Movements in America's Second Wave*. New York: Cambridge University Press.

Sieder, Rachel. 2002. 'Recognising Indigenous Law and the Politics of State Formation in Mesoamerica'. In *Multiculturalism in Latin America: Indigenous Rights, Diversity and Democracy*, edited by Rachel Sieder, 184–207. New York: Palgrave MacMillan.

———. 2008. 'Entre la multiculturalización y las reinvindicaciones indentitarias: construyendo ciudadanía étnica y autoridad indígena en Guatemala'. In *Multiculturalismo y futuro en Guatemala*, edited by Santiago Bastos, 69–96. Guatemala: FLACSO/OXFAM.

Smith, Linda Tuhiwai. 1999. *Decolonizing Methodologies: Research and Indigenous Peoples*. London: Zed Books.

Wa Thiong'o, Ngũgĩ. 1986. *Decolonising the Mind: The Politics of Language in African Literature*. Portsmouth: Heinemann.

11 What Does It Mean to Be the 'Pride of Pinesville'?

Opportunities Facilitated and Constrained

Amy Johnson Lachuk, Mary Louise Gomez and Shameka N. Powell

INTRODUCTION

Researchers who understand literacy from a contextual perspective agree that looking closely at how persons practice literacy can shed insight into the intersections of their race, gender, cultural, language and social class identities (e.g. Barton and Hamilton 1998; Brandt 2001; Finders 1997; Heath 1983; Hicks 2002; Street 1995, 1984). Specifically in the case of African American people, literacy scholars have described how education and literacy are viewed culturally as being synonymous with one another, the only means for upward social mobility (Harris 1992; McAdoo 2007), and as a valuable commodity that can serve emancipatory functions (e.g. Gadsden 1992; Harris 1992; Williams 2007). Such perspectives on education and literacy are rooted in the shared cultural history of oppression and enslavement that persons of African descent have endured in the US. However, the focus on literacy within African American people's lives largely has been situated in urban communities (e.g. Ballenger 1998; Compton-Lilly 2003; Cushman 1998; Mahiri 1998, 2004; Morrell 2004; Paratore 2001; Rogers 2003). Few studies, other than Edwards (1993), Gadsden (1992) and Heath (1983), have considered literacy practices within the lives of African Americans living in rural communities. This lack of focus on the rural South is noteworthy given the increasing number of African Americans who are 'return migrating' from northern urban centres to rural southern communities (Morris and Monroe 2009; Stack 1996). Because of such return migration, the rural south-eastern US has three times the percentage of African Americans living elsewhere in the US (Morris and Monroe 2009).

Life history and narrative inquiry are promising methods for understanding such intersections of literacy and cultural identity because they focus on situating a person's story within a broader social and cultural milieu. Whereas literacy scholars have sought to document how diverse people use literacy across their everyday contexts, only a handful (e.g. Barton and Hamilton 1998; Brandt 2001) have sought to understand how persons' uses of literacy are embedded in their narratives and life histories. In response,

Amy developed a study where she asked participants to share their life histories, focusing specifically on their education and literacy experiences as a means of exploring these questions:

- What insights does the life history of one African American woman living in a rural southern town reveal about educational opportunities and barriers she and other African American citizens encounter?
- How does an intersectionality framework highlight the ways she navigates educational landscapes and sees herself as successful?

In engaging with these questions, we highlight how intersecting dimensions of race, class, gender and other aspects of identity afford one African American woman's attainment of higher education while limiting the education of others.

THEORETICAL FRAMEWORK

'Intersectionality' is a term coined by Kimberlé Crenshaw (1989, 1991) to highlight the overlapping nature of various axes of identity such as race, class, gender, ethnicity, age, sexual identity and/or disability that often work together and simultaneously to oppress females. Crenshaw (1989) critiqued legal cases heard under the Civil Rights Act of 1964 and showed how the courts ultimately denied female African Americans' claims of discrimination grounded in what were not seen as exclusive categories of race-based or sex-based discrimination. She argued that injuries otherwise invisible can be recognised through a lens that incorporates multiple dimensions of people's categorical memberships. Sometimes called 'vectors of privilege' (Ritzer 2007, 206), these individual factors can work together limiting people's access to jobs, health care, child care, housing and/or safe neighbourhoods.

Drawing on such understandings, Patricia Hill Collins (2000) explains 'intersectionality' as operating within what she terms a 'matrix of domination', intersecting systems of oppression that are organised through the domains of structural, disciplinary, and interpersonal power. These four domains of power: (1) govern social interactions among people through the organisation of power via regulating, for instance, who can vote, eat at certain restaurants and/or ride public transportation; (2) manage notions of oppression as a means of hiding racism and sexism as, for example, natural outcomes of the sorting and distribution of knowledge (as in whose stories are told) in institutions such as schools; (3) legitimate oppression working through our language, values and ideas; and (4) manage personal relationships that allow the subordination of some people via others' thoughts and actions. Collins understands intersectionality as breaking open seemingly static social boundaries and as developing a questioning stance regarding, for instance, what it means to live simultaneously in multiple worlds.

In educational research, Gillborn and Youdell (2000) engage with understandings of intersectionality to assert that schooling institutions increasingly select and sort based on particular dimensions of students' racial, ethnic, gendered and class backgrounds—effectively rationing available educational opportunities. As Gillborn and Youdell explain, 'teachers' judgments of [one's] ability [is] shaped by wider social forces, such as gendered, classed, and racialized notions of appropriate behavior, motivation, and attitude' (2000, 200). Stated differently, teachers' selections of pupils who are 'worthy' to be labelled 'gifted', who have potential for the ability to test well and who deserve entry into higher education often are based on comportment. We suggest such ideas about who students are and their potential for success shaped how one African American woman was able to squeeze through a rather narrow pipeline on the route to higher education while most of her classmates were denied this opportunity.

METHODOLOGY

We investigate the intersections between peoples' identities and education through life history inquiry. In life history research, the stories people tell are used to create detailed portraits that emphasise the interplay between individuals' social lives and the structures in which they live (Bertaux and Bertaux-Wiame 1981). Such portraits create more complicated understandings of the relationships between an individual's life and its respective and collective contexts, between the self and place and between the individual's identities and historical change (Cole and Knowles 2001, 11). In so doing, life history can provide a theoretical touchstone that helps to improve existing social theories (Becker 1970). Furthermore, life history focuses on the narratives and experiences of individuals who traditionally have been marginalised from the social science or historical research enterprise. In this way, life history can create 'points of contact' between readers of this article; exposing people to individuals they might not otherwise meet. In this case, life history is seen as useful to areas of study that have grown somewhat stagnant because it can give new perspectives on issues such as race, gender, place and social class (Becker 1970).

One limitation of life history research relates to representation of an entire life. Although life histories are generated through extensive interviewing, it is unrealistic to assume that any researcher can represent the entirety of another person's life. Many life history inquirers report on 'landmark events' or events that distinguish an aspect of a person's life, such as 'one's marriage, divorce, major illness, religious conversion, or death of a parent, sibling, or child' (Gomez, Rodriguez and Agosto 2008, 1647). As persons recount major life events, certain themes emerge that bring cohesion to their tellings (Linde 1993). Although the data in this chapter capture the range of data collected, we follow the example of Viernes Turner (2007), who, instead of trying to portray the entire lives of her participants, emphasised critical life factors that led to their present situations.

Our discussion is focused on the life history of one African American female participant, Anca Myers Monroe (all names of persons, places and institutions are pseudonyms). Her life history is part of a larger ethnographic study that investigated literacy and educational practice in a small rural community called Pinesville.

STUDY CONTEXT

Pinesville, US (population 572) (US Census Bureau 2000) is a predominantly African American community located ninety miles east of a major metropolitan area in the south-eastern US. It has been identified as a community with persistent intergenerational poverty (Carl Vinson Institute of Government 2003). The effects of such poverty are exacerbated by an explicit and intentional social structure undergirded by an oppressive White supremacist history (Tickamyer and Duncan 1990). Pinesville was created during the height of cotton production, a time when the area was at its most prosperous. And like so many of the communities that surround it, Pinesville represents 'the old planter-dominated region of the South Atlantic, with its high Black population [. . .] aristocratic leadership, and cotton monoculture' (Schultz 2005, 1). When Pinesville was created, it had more African Americans than European Americans, a trend that is consistent today. Before the Civil War, nearly all Pinesville's African American residents were enslaved. Such a history lurks within Pinesville, where the rebel flag still waves above the residences of some of Pinesville's European American families. And, although African Americans are in the majority, European Americans politically and economically control Pinesville.

Pinesville is located in a county ranked last in its state for adults completing high school—43.8 per cent (Carl Vinson Institute of Government 2003). Currently, Pinesville only has one school. Pinesville Community School (PCS) is a pre-K–12 public charter school that was founded in 2001 after Pinesville ended a school district unifying agreement with Grey County School District, a neighbouring county and school district. With one classroom teacher and one teaching assistant per grade level, PCS is the largest employer in the county.

However, people who live in rural places like Pinesville confront specific challenges not only related to lack of employment, but also related to lack of child care, health care and educational resources (e.g. Carl Vinson Institute of Government 2003; McLaughlin and Sachs 1988). Pinesville has a small medical clinic with limited hours but no hospital; only a few childcare centres; and a community college satellite centre that offers a GED programme, but there are no options for higher education in the community.

The story of Pinesville could be the story of many communities located within the Black Belt region, a crescent-shaped area that spans eleven southern states and where one-third of the nation's poor live (Carl Vinson Institute of Government 2003). This area of 'the rural south historically has been marked by high poverty rates and characterized by low education levels, poor economic conditions, and a poor quality of life for many individuals of all ages' (Carl Vinson Institute of Government 2003, 1). With a per capita income of $5,500 less than the national average and a high unemployment rate, education has been suggested as being imperative for generating economic growth within the region (ibid.). Because social class and race play such prominent roles in Pinesville's history, a life history study situated within the community highlights salient aspects of intersectionality.

DATA GENERATION

In December 2005, Amy began working with twenty teachers at PCS as part of a state-funded project focused on teaching science through literacy (see Johnson and Cowells 2009, 410). In January 2007, after having spent two years as a participant observer in the community and working on a professional development project at PCS, Amy began the life history portion of this study. In all, Amy spent approximately five hundred hours recording field notes and making observations on social life, literacy practices, education and employment within Pinesville. Drawing on the work of Brandt (2001) and Thompson (2000), Amy crafted a semi-structured interview protocol and conducted life history interviews with thirteen persons who live and work in Pinesville. Each interview was audio-recorded, ranged in duration from two to four hours and took place at a location of the participant's choice. To supplement observational and interview data, Amy conducted historical research on Pinesville, particularly focusing on civil rights activities within the community during the 1960s. These were retrieved through archived copies of the weekly local newspaper. Collecting and reviewing these sources enabled Amy to understand better how a history of racial segregation and White supremacy circulated within education, literacy and employment.

Participants

To select the thirteen life history participants, Amy turned to the work of Michele Foster (1997) and Gloria Ladson-Billings (1997), who both used community nomination techniques for enrolling participants. For example, after interviewing one person, Amy asked the participant to nominate another person whom she believed would be interested in being interviewed. This process continued between January 2007 and May 2008, during which time Amy interviewed twelve African Americans and one European American.

Several study participants nominated Anca Myers Monroe as a suitable interviewee for Amy, describing her as the 'pride of Pinesville'. They saw her as a suitable interviewee as she had left the community to acquire an education but had returned to teach and to 'give back' to those in Pinesville. Anca's return signalled for other community members the power of education to transcend geographic constraints and local barriers. Additionally, Anca, as 'the pride of Pinesville', shaped other participants' notions of what it means to be successful. It is for these reasons that we focus on Anca's life history alone.

DATA ANALYSIS

Data analyses began with the life history interviews, which were analysed using methods of qualitative inquiry. First, Amy read through all the life history interviews, using a combination of external and internal codes. External codes were ones Amy brought to the data: people, places, things and practices. Internal codes were codes that Amy saw emerging from the data: being from Pinesville, leaving Pinesville, staying in Pinesville, staying in school, access to education, inequity, opportunity and employment. Amy then composed analytic memos for each participant; in these she highlighted how such factors as staying in Pinesville, for example, played out in participants' lives. Mary Louise and Shameka contributed to the chapter via their theorising of Anca's life history. Drawing on Amy's codes and memos, Mary Louise and Shameka also developed an intersectional coding scheme through which we located themes featuring braided elements of race, class, gender and place in the data.

OUR POSITIONS

Relationships are at the heart of life history inquiry (Goodson and Sikes 2001). To ensure that persons felt comfortable sharing the details of their lives with Amy, she cultivated a relationship with participants. Amy is a European American woman from a small rural community in the midwestern US, which has helped connect her with some of the complexities of life in a small town. Amy's grandparents and family members were farmers, working-class, and had limited access to secondary and postsecondary education. That Amy's mother had to travel great distances away from home in order to pursue postsecondary schooling has enriched her insights into the lengths to which people will go for educational opportunities. Mary Louise is a Latina from New England. Mary Louise grew up in a working-class family whose limited economic means prevented her parents from seeking postsecondary education. Her father lived with and economically supported his widowed mother (who did not speak English) through his early thirties. Both of Mary Louise's parents achieved high school graduation and worked full-time at low-paid clerical positions throughout their lives. Mary Louise's understandings of what individuals must sacrifice to contribute to a family's well-being enabled her understandings of Pinesville residents' collective sense of responsibility for others. That we are cultural and racial outsiders to Pinesville has required us to draw on our own life experiences and family histories to enrich data analyses.

Finally, Shameka is an African American female who grew up in a rural southern town similar to Pinesville and was reared in a closely knit working-class family who lived in the same town. Shameka was the fourth generation of her family raised there. Very much like Anca, Shameka is an only child but was raised in an extended family environment in which three of her cousins were like siblings to her. In spite of such understandings, we acknowledge that data generation and interpretation might have a different texture if all of us were African American or any of us were from Pinesville.

A LIFE HISTORY

LaTasha Bianca ('Anca') Myers Monroe

LaTasha Bianca ('Anca') Myers Monroe (b. 1978) is the 'pride of Pinesville' as she earned a bachelor's and master's degree and returned to teach in the community. Anca credits her mother, Brenda Myers (b. 1956), for much of her success in school. Brenda did not complete high school and worked in a factory and then a nursing home while Anca was growing up. In Anca's earliest years, her mother was a single parent. According to Anca, high school graduation rates within the community must be understood within the social, economic and historical context of Pinesville:

> My generation is pretty much the first that have completed education. Because before then, coming from sharecroppers to cotton pickers, my mom didn't graduate high school. At the time, you know with sisters and brothers, and my grandmother struggling, she quit school to help work. And that's what happened to a lot of people in the community [. . .]. That is something that is just very prevalent amongst a lot of people here [in Pinesville].

In saying this, Anca was observing how the economic well-being of entire families was tied to reliance on every individual's contribution, and that sacrifices, such as Brenda's not continuing her schooling, were made by many people. This especially was true for African Americans who only recently had become wage labourers in the cotton fields rather than as enslaved persons or sharecroppers.

Anca described how Brenda created an environment in which structure, discipline and opportunity were emphasised. Brenda was very determined that her daughter would not be denied the schooling and literacy opportunities that had eluded her—she saw how her race, social class and gender would pose obstacles to her daughter's education. As Anca explained it, her mother explicitly warned her against the dangers of becoming pregnant before completing her education. In Brenda's generation, many of her female classmates discontinued their high school education because they had become pregnant as teenagers. Unlike their wealthier counterparts, Pinesville students often had to choose between school and a pregnancy because they did not have access to the financial resources necessary for doing both simultaneously.

When she entered school at age four, Anca recalled being able to read: 'Even before going to school, I remember reading . . . I loved reading books'. Anca could not recall her mother explicitly teaching her how to read, yet she explained that she had absorbed reading through her mother's own practices. Because Pinesville had no bookstores, her mother would order reading materials via mail order catalogues and other means such as the county public library or the grocery store. Brenda took advantage of available resources to be certain that Anca had engaging texts at hand.

Anca remembered that she often would read books with her cousins, who, because they lived nearby, were her childhood playmates. Within this extended family configuration, Brenda was positioned as the disciplinarian. Anca described how Brenda provided a very structured upbringing for her, stating: 'I couldn't do things that they [my cousins] could do. When it was dark, I was in the house getting ready for bed. I had a bedtime, eight o'clock, and I didn't get to ten o'clock until I was in high school. So I wasn't staying up until twelve or one o'clock the way some kids do'. However, in spite of Brenda's reputation, Anca's cousins always wanted to spend time at Aunt Brenda's house, because there they encountered structure and discipline: '[My cousins] said my mother was mean, but they always wanted to come to my house. Because we always did stuff and there were rules. And so they say they don't really want it [rules], but kids really do'. What also made Aunt Brenda's house appealing were the opportunities she offered the children. Anca recounted how every weekend they would take a trip somewhere:

> I remember having cousins who would come over and we would just do things, go places. We always went somewhere on the weekends. Like we were always up at six in the morning. There's nothing here [in Pinesville] but we'd always be . . . somewhere else, shopping on the weekends or just doing things together.

Brenda's attention to structure, discipline and opportunity demonstrate her acumen concerning how people achieve and succeed in US schools as these elements mirror the expectations that schools often privilege. Polite student comportment, a regular daily schedule that allows for adequate time for rest and studying and a knowledge base including the world outside one's community all contribute to school success. It was this alchemy of structure, discipline and opportunity that Anca credits with her academic, personal and professional successes. Heath (1983) points out that when home and school expectations match, the likelihood of school success increases, and when home and school expectations fail to match, the likelihood of such success diminishes. Indeed, Brenda's child-rearing practices fostered the behaviours and knowledge that provided a platform for Anca's recognition as a good student.

Similar to how she describes Brenda, Anca describes having teachers who combined structure, discipline and opportunity to support her academic goals. Unlike people who attended school in the 1960s or before, Anca recalls having a mixture of European American and African American teachers, and states that most of her teachers 'were not community people'. Nonetheless, Anca remembers having teachers 'who didn't play' and held high expectations for her learning. Because she was tall for her age and looked more mature than her classmates, as well as being academically accelerated, Anca explains that she was frequently 'bumped up' to complete lessons with students in higher grade levels. Such experiences gave Anca confidence in her academic abilities and made her believe she always could learn more. Anca said that such high expectations were paralleled at home, where Brenda helped her with her homework and expected Anca to place school as a priority. Known throughout the community as Anca Myers (short for 'Bianca', her middle name) she attended Pinesville Elementary School and then Grey County Middle and High Schools, where she excelled academically.

In seventh grade, Anca began attending school in Grey County when the school districts merged. She explains that at first 'it seemed strange because I didn't know people'. Pinesville Elementary School was a small school, with one class per grade level, and Anca knew all her classmates and teachers. There, she was in a sixth grade class with twenty students. At Grey County Middle School, she entered into a seventh grade class with over 150 students: 'So, you sort of get lost in it'. What made a difference for Anca and what probably kept her from 'getting lost' was that upon entering middle school, she was placed in 'an accelerated programme'. The accelerated programme was smaller in size than the regular education classes, yet it required Anca to be split apart from her Pinesville classmates: 'I wasn't with the people that I had been with for all those years [at Pinesville Elementary School]. So I was sort of thrown into this whole new group of people'.

Anca described how she literally and metaphorically took on a new identity at Grey County Middle School. For example, it was the first time that people used her first name, LaTasha. In Pinesville, she always was called her by her middle name, Bianca: 'If you were to go ask [any of the teachers here] what my name is, they will say Anca Myers. Myers is my maiden name. Because that's what everybody here in Pinesville called me. They had such a hard time with my name in kindergarten. From then on, I was L. Bianca Myers'. Transitioning to Grey County presented tensions in her identity exemplified by her name change.

> It's sort of an analogy for the change that came with it. Because living in Pinesville and then going to school in Grey County, it was completely different. And the things that I was exposed to being there were completely different. So it sort of analogises what happened in my life. It was a name change but also an identity change because I was exposed to so many things.

In the bigger school system, she encountered more resources to support her academically: 'Resources—the types of things that we did in class—because I know being a bigger system, especially, there on the lake, they had lots more money than we did here in Pinesville'. She also was exposed to people who represented a wider range of backgrounds: 'The types of different people that I was exposed to. Like, I had never gone to school [before] with people who didn't speak the same language that I did'.

Other students, not as fortunate to be seen as warranting 'acceleration' were left behind in middle school classes with far fewer resources. These enhanced opportunities for learning in a special programme stretched Anca's confidence and her social and academic horizons—she knew people who lived 'on the lake' in Grey County and in her own rural Pinesville. She knew people linguistically similar to and different from herself and developed a wider repertoire of speech patterns that would serve her well over the course of her schooling.

However, a drawback of attending school in Grey County was that the teachers were more lax in their expectations for students from African American and low-income backgrounds. For, in Pinesville, 'it was really no nonsense in every teacher I had. It was strict. You came to class, you did what you were supposed to do, and that was it'. The same was not true in Grey County, where teachers did not have the same sense of discipline or control over the students that Anca was used to: 'We had a teacher in seventh grade and one of the classes literally ran her off and she literally got sick. And that was something I wasn't used to'. If the same teacher had been in Pinesville, the school's principal would have stepped in to bring order to the classroom:

> If I had a teacher here who wasn't as strong, Mr. Chapman, the principal, would have said, 'No'. If he did this [fingers to lips] then that means mouths are closing. You don't say a word. And nobody said a word. So, that was different in Grey County, where the principal did not intervene to restore order in the classroom.

It is these different expectations for students' behaviour that Anca believes led to so many of her Pinesville classmates dropping out of high school in Grey County. Anca feels that when the students entered a school district in which teachers were unfamiliar to them and did not enforce a culture of strictness that Pinesville students were able to slip through the cracks. Anca sees that if students' behaviours did not match teachers' expectations, they were viewed as not warranting the time and attention given others, like herself, who were deemed 'ready to learn'.

Being enrolled in accelerated classes also made a difference for Anca because, unlike many of her Pinesville peers, Anca was on the college preparatory track and encountered rigorous courses. At Grey County High School her opportunities only expanded. Not only did she encounter curricular engagements that she might not have encountered in Pinesville, but she was given more opportunities through her relationships with some of her wealthier classmates: 'At Grey County, I had classmates who lived out on the lake, who knew lots of people who wrote recommendations for scholarships and colleges and things for me that I never would have known had I been here'. When she graduated from high school, she was valedictorian, challenging the popular misconception that 'nothing good comes from Pinesville'. Anca received a full scholarship to a large state university, where she followed a pre-med course of study and conducted original research at the state's medical college. Similar to conflicting goals that Crockett, Shanahan and Jackson-Newsom (2000) have identified other rural youth experiencing, she was torn between earning a medical degree and fulfilling her more immediate goals of getting married and returning to raise a family in Pinesville. Deferring her dream of becoming a doctor, Anca changed her college major to biology to accommodate her more immediate hope to return to her community, marry and have children. And after earning her degree, she accepted a job at PCS as the high school science teacher, where she began teaching with a provisional credential while earning her master's degree in education. She said:

> I came home for the summer. I was getting married in August and somebody said, 'They have a part-time science position at the school'. So I came and applied for it. I got a call back and accepted it, and I said 'Okay, I'll do this for a year until I figure out what I'm going to do with the rest of my life'. After the first nine weeks, I was hooked.

Anca commented that at PCS she sees herself as so much more than just a high school science teacher. She values the relationships she has developed with students over the years. In fact, when she started teaching, she recounted: 'I was part-time middle school and high school. So I taught the sixth grade, which is the graduating class this year [2008]. They were my first class in sixth grade. So I don't know what I'm going to do when they leave'. An important part of her teaching focuses on mentoring students for success:

They ask questions all the time [about college]. We've been working on scholarships. They've sent off applications and financial aid. We've done all of it together. Whatever paperwork they need to get done, we've been working on it and they ask questions and sometimes I just tell them things like, 'watch out for this', and 'don't do this and don't do that'.

As a teacher, Anca fills many different roles for her students. On one hand, she is the teacher, 'Mrs. Monroe [who] is not playing and you're going to be doing what you're supposed to do'. On the other hand, she is a counsellor or big sister who offers advice to her female students about boys and relationships: 'there are times when I will have a girl and [her boyfriend] he has three girlfriends and I say, "Come here, girl, let me talk to you because this doesn't work for me. I'm not going to watch you allow yourself to be used like that"'. She has strong relationships with parents and works with them to meet the social and emotional needs of her students. For instance, she often has female students who ask her questions about sex and physical intimacy. Anca conveyed that in such situations she has called the parent and said, 'I have your child who wants to talk about such and such, maybe she doesn't feel comfortable talking to you, do you mind?' Like her mother, Anca recognises that pregnancy likely will deny future opportunities for schooling to young, rural African American females who are from low-income families. Through these multiple roles, Anca demonstrates how her teaching is her way of giving back to Pinesville: 'One of the reasons I stay teaching in Pinesville, is just doing for my community, from where I came'.

In her teaching, Anca can be seen as 'paying it forward' or helping those in her community whom she has eclipsed in education, social status and income. Anca recognises that she has been rewarded for her disciplined dedication to schooling imbued in her by her mother Brenda, by her recognition as talented by her teachers and through her placement in small, accelerated classes in middle school. She also sees that those who had not been viewed as having special academic gifts were left on their own to flounder in larger classes led sometimes by lax teachers who failed to identify their talents and promise as students. Anca aims to use that which she has learned to infuse her teaching with the knowledge, skills and hope that her students can acquire and succeed as she has. She did not want the young women and men who studied with her to be left behind because their teachers did not perceive them as having academic gifts or potentials. Unlike most of her Pinesville peers, she was able to resolve the pursuit of higher education and a career in her home community (Hektner 1995; Rojewski 1999). She was able to generate what Farmer et al. (2006, 3) refer to as 'community social capital' or the caring concern of family members and other significant adults in the community to sustain her goals.

In mentoring her students for success, Anca is supporting their college and career aspirations with help in scholarship and college applications and is ensuring that they are prepared for the scholastic rigours of college-level science courses just as she has been supported. In consulting with students' parents when she is uncertain of their boundaries with regard, for example, to questions students ask concerning sexual intimacy, she is extending a community of concern for herself and her students beyond the classroom walls. In doing so, Anca is practicing reciprocity—returning the structure, discipline and opportunity that has been given her to her students and their families.

DISCUSSION

In the next paragraphs, we share themes interweaving race, class, gender and place that emerged from our data analyses. These include: attention to how socio-economic status, gender and community social capital are linked in fostering Anca's successful experiences with school, and also how 'bringing our children home' to be schooled in Pinesville is both a community investment in education and a tribute to the resources that Pinesville attempts to provide all its residents. Finally, we discuss how living in and being from Pinesville provides both encouragements and constraints to postsecondary education and remaining linked to one's rural community.

Dreams Deferred

Langston Hughes (1951) asked, 'What happens to a dream deferred?' The hopes and dreams family members had for Anca could have been derailed in numerous ways. With that in mind, it is not surprising that she constantly was admonished by family, friends and teachers to 'stay clear of boys' because of the potentially limiting effects that teenage pregnancy might have on her educational goals. Family members were aware of a large number of teenage pregnancies and single mothers that have historically existed in Pinesville. The threat of teenage pregnancy and the sexual vulnerability of girls in particular are widely understood as intersecting with one's life chances and educational goals. Failure to heed this advice could derail or defer their (dreams of) success.

When we view Anca's life history through an intersectional lens, we come to a better understanding of how cautions about teenage pregnancy and sexual vulnerability are informed by an astute awareness of geographic contexts. Anca's story illuminates how for many Black females, especially those living in rural contexts, their dreams may be deferred by the very system [school] that is there to benefit them. Scarce educational resources may come together with a depressed rural economy to create nearly insurmountable odds for those who are not deemed the pride of the town. To put it another way, receiving a good education could help one obtain success, but certain threats, in this case teenage pregnancy, could jeopardise all that.

Whereas Anca did not have to defer her dream of an education because of pregnancy, she did defer other dreams. Anca's longing to return to her roots in Pinesville, marry and have children caused her to defer her dream of attending medical school. She sees living in Pinesville as fulfilling another dream—that of raising a family in the small town she loves and also of investing her capital in the education of students in her community.

'Bringing Our Children Home': A Community Engagement in Education

Anca was fortunate to have a mother who rallied others in her family and community to support her daughter's literacy development and educational outcomes. Such a communal investment in education is reflected in the efforts to open a pre- K–12 public school in Pinesville. In interview after interview, persons recounted how when the agreement with Grey County Schools finally ended and PCS had opened, that they finally would be able to 'bring their children home' or let them 'go to school at home'. In Pinesville, community members describe feeling an investment in the educational outcomes of all people within their community and not just those within their own families.

Historical evidence tells us that such investments in schooling and the power of knowledge are rooted deeply in the African American community. Franklin (1990) has written that African American educators in the nineteenth and first half of the twentieth centuries 'always moved out into the community to provide leadership for organizations and movements aimed at the social, economic, and political advancement of the entire African American community' (59). Just as Anca Myers Monroe sees her job as more than teaching, but as serving her community and its families, so did other African American educators across time and places see their obligation as passing 'knowledge onto others in their family, community, and cultural group' (ibid., 40). In what Franklin calls an 'ethos of service' (ibid), Anca Myers Monroe has taken up such a 'paying it forward' obligation and embracing it for and with her students at PCS. Anca sees how her investment in her middle and high school students enables them potentially to succeed. She also sees how their rural and isolated location also may bar their eventual success unless they are viewed as 'exceptional' or 'gifted' as she has been. Anca also envisions her successes in education and career as tied to her students' future successes.

Living in Pinesville/Being from Pinesville

What does it mean to be from the place called Pinesville? For Anca and her Pinesville neighbours, community membership is a metaphor for caring for one another, especially through education—ensuring that all the children in the community achieve at the highest levels. Anca spoke of Mr. Chapman, her Pinesville principal, who believed that all students should pay attention in class and comport themselves with dignity, and that these attributes would help them in succeeding. It also was clear to Anca that all students do not benefit equally from attributes of 'good' comportment as she was elevated to higher-level classes for those seen as most gifted, whereas other classmates were left behind in courses where teachers had lower expectations for academic and personal performance. These were conflicting messages—that one should work hard and be well behaved, yet not necessarily reap the rewards of those assets.

It was incumbent on Anca, as for many rural residents, to leave her community if she was to pursue the postsecondary education that would enable her career success. Whereas Anca was able to continue her college education due to her academic talents and homilies of persistence her family had bestowed on her, many other Pinesville students have been unable to do so. Many students believe that they do not belong in such collegiate sites, or they develop an intense longing for home and community. Others believe that such an education is not attainable due to costs of tuition and room and board, transportation issues or all of these. Through Anca's experiences, we can see how being an extraordinary female African American student can propel a person towards success, even when one is from an economically depressed community and resources are sparse. However, such success does not seem available to all as leaving the community currently is tied to postsecondary education and community social capital. Until higher education is available in or near Pinesville, many will continue to be denied access to it and the economic and social rewards that it brings. Anca's life history is a poignant one as her personal success may vindicate those who believe that 'nothing good comes from Pinesville' and that rationing education to many while one succeeds is acceptable.

All three of the themes we identified in participants' conversations—deferring one's dreams, bringing children home to be schooled in a community invested in their education and living in and being from the small, rural community of Pinesville—are intertwined one with another. They allow us to see how all are tied together in both affording and constraining opportunities for education. A woman may avoid teenage pregnancy and gain a postsecondary education, yet also give up other dreams of alternate careers she might have pursued because the pull of the place one calls home is so strong. Thus, one succeeds, but also defers other goals and dreams. Likewise, one may 'pay it forward' and provide leadership for the good of the whole community but be unable to help many youth because of the isolation and absence of services in the place from which she comes.

IMPLICATIONS

So, what implications does Anca's life history have for researchers? Our exploration of the life of one African American woman who lives in the rural South suggests that researchers need to be aware of how axes of identity such as race, class, gender and the place from which one comes work together in complex ways to influence educational and economic opportunities. First, the meaning of success differs according to who is asked and the contexts in which they live and work. For Anca, becoming a doctor and having a lifestyle characterised by potential wealth and prestige were trumped by the pull of family, community and the rural landscape from which she came. How success is viewed in rural communities may be characterised by what some researchers have termed 'educating out and giving back' (Farmer et al. 2006), or the strategy of going out of the community to attain an education and then returning to work and live, or returning regularly for community events and special occasions. Key to 'giving back' is the continuing connection to place—where one's family and relationships reside.

Second, in seeking to understand how to ameliorate social conditions in southern rural communities like Pinesville, scholars must look to the broader social and historical context of Pinesville and the region in general rather than factors that locate the social issues within the individual or the economic context. For example, the 'Study of Persistent Poverty in the South' concluded: 'The economy of the rural South is at risk because it lacks an *able workforce* and the tools with which to build wealth' (Carl Vinson Institute of Government 2003, 8; emphasis added). Such a statement about the quality of the workforce in the rural South can be disconcerting and problematic as it neglects attention to the institutional and contextual factors that have contributed to such an assertion. An infrastructure that includes programmes and activities designed to enrich the lives of youth, postsecondary educational opportunities and promising local jobs to which African American youth can aspire must be present if an able workforce is to be developed (Farmer et al. 2006).

Third, as previously stated, it is important to note that all study participants believe education *can* help one transcend poverty and is a given good in and of itself. Furthermore, study participants believe that being educated can lead to improved life chances for themselves and their children as well as for *everyone* in Pinesville and the region in general. It seems, however, that fulfilment of dreams seems highly connected to access to local and regional education opportunities. These educational opportunities are contingent upon the allocation of funds for public transportation, provision of a capable teaching force and the availability of good jobs—those occupations that allow one to care for one's family as well as caring for the community. It is through these actions that all people can become the 'pride of Pinesville'. Without such local resources, as well as attention to the interrelationships between elements such as White economic dominance, education, race, class, gender and place, few people in Pinesville and other rural locations will have an opportunity to succeed.

REFERENCES

Ballenger, Cynthia. 1998. *Teaching Other People's Children: Literacy and Learning in a Bilingual Classroom*. New York: Teachers College Press.

Barton, David, and Mary Hamilton. 1998. *Local Literacies*. New York: Routledge.

Becker, Howard S. 1970. *Sociological Work: Method and Substance*. Chicago: Adline.

Bertaux, Daniel, and Isabel Bertaux-Wiame. 1981. 'Life Stories in the Bakers' Trade'. In *Biography and Society*, edited by Daniel Bertaux, 169–189. Beverly Hills: Sage.

Brandt, Deborah. 2001. *Literacy in American Lives*. New York: Cambridge University Press.

Carl Vinson Institute of Government. 2003. *Dismantling Persistent Poverty in Georgia*. Athens, GA: Carl Vinson Institute of Government.

Cole, Ardra L., and J. Gary Knowles, eds. 2001. *Lives in Context: The Art of Life History Research*. Walnut Creek, CA: AltaMira Press.

Collins, Patricia H. 2000. *Black Feminist Thought: Knowledge, Consciousness, and the Politics of Empowerment*. 2nd ed. New York: Routledge.

Compton-Lilly, Catherine. 2003. *Reading Families: The Literate Lives of Urban Children*. New York: Teacher College Press.

Crenshaw, Kimberlé. W. 1989. 'Demarginalizing the Intersection of Race and Sex: A Black Feminist Critique of Antidiscrimination Doctrine, Feminist Theory and Antiracist Politics'. *University of Chicago Legal Forum*, 1989: 139–167.

———. 1991. 'Mapping the Margins: Intersectionality, Identity Politics, and Violence Against Women of Color'. *Stanford Law Review* 43 (6): 1241–1299.

Crockett, Lisa J., Michael J. Shanahan and Julia Jackson-Newsom. 2000. 'Rural Youth: Ecological and Life Course Perspectives'. In *Adolescent Diversity in Ethnic, Economic, and Cultural Contexts*, edited by Raymond Montemayor, Gerald R. Adams and Thomas P. Gullota, 43–74. Thousand Oaks, CA: Sage.

Cushman, Ellen. 1998. *The Struggle and Tools: Oral and Literate Strategies in an Inner City Community*. Albany: SUNY Press.

Edwards, P. A. 1993. 'Before and After School Desegregation: African-American Parents' Involvement in Schools'. *Educational Policy* 7 (3): 340–369.

Farmer, T. W., Kimberly Dadisman, Shawn J. Latendresse, Jana Thompson, Matthew J. Irvin and Lei Zhang. 2006. 'Educating Out and Giving Back: Adults' Conceptions of Successful Outcomes of African American High School Students from Impoverished Rural Communities'. *Journal of Research in Rural Education* 21(10): 1–12.

Finders, Margaret J. 1997. *Just Girls: Hidden Literacies and Life in Junior High*. New York: Teachers College Press.

Foster, Michelle. 1997. *Black Teachers on Teaching*. New York: New Press.

Franklin, V. P. 1990. '"They Rose and Fell Together": African American Educators and Community Leadership, 1795–1954'. *Journal of Education* 172:39–64.

Gadsden, V. 1992. 'Giving Meaning to Literacy: Intergenerational Beliefs about Access'. *Theory into Practice* 31 (4): 328–336.

Gillborn, David, and Deborah Youdell. 2000. *Rationing Education: Policy, Practice, Reform, and Equity*. Buckingham: Open University Press.

Gomez, M. L., Terri L. Rodriguez and Vonzell Agosto. 2008. 'Life Histories of Teacher Candidates'. *Teachers College Record* 110:1639–1676.

Goodson, Ivor, and Patricia Sikes. 2001. *Life History Research in Educational Settings: Learning from Lives*. Buckingham: Open University Press.

Harris, Violet J. 1992. 'African-American Conceptions of Literacy: A Historical Perspective'. *Theory into Practice* 31 (4): 276–286.

Heath, Shirley Brice. 1983. *Ways with Words: Language, Life, and Work in Communities and Classrooms*. Cambridge: Cambridge University Press.

Hektner, Joel M. 1995. 'When Moving Up Implies Moving Out: Rural Adolescent Conflict in the Transition to Adulthood'. *Journal of Research in Rural Education* 13:131–138.

Hicks, Deborah. 2002. *Reading Lives: Working-Class Children and Literacy Learning*. New York: Teachers College Press.

Hughes, Langston. 1951. *Montage of a Dream Deferred*. New York: Holt.

Johnson, Amy S., and Lauren Cowles. 2009. 'Orlonia's Literacy in Persons: Expanding Notions of Literacy through Biography and History'. *Journal of Adolescent and Adult Literacy* 52 (5): 410–420.

Ladson-Billings, Gloria J. 1997. *The Dreamkeepers: Successful Teachers of African American Children*. San Francisco: Jossey-Bass.

Linde, Charlotte. 1993. *Life Stories: The Creation of Coherence*. Oxford: Oxford University Press.

Mahiri, Jabari. 1998. *Shooting for Excellence: African American and Youth Culture in New Century Schools*. New York: Teachers College Press.

———. (2004). *What They Don't Learn in School: Literacy in The Lives of Urban Youth*. New York: Peter Lang.

McAdoo, Harriette, Pipes. (2007), *Black families*. Thousand Oaks, CA: Sage.

McLaughlin, Diane K., and Carolyn Sachs. 1988. 'Poverty in Female-Headed Households: Residential Differences'. *Rural Sociology* 53:287–306.

Morrell, Ernest. 2004. *Becoming Critical Researchers: Literacy, Empowerment, and Urban Youth*. New York: Peter Lang.

Morris, Jerome E., and Carla R. Monroe. 2009. 'Why Study the US South? The Nexus of Race and Place in Investigating Black Student Achievement'. *Educational Researcher* 38:21–36.

Paratore, Jeanne R. 2001. *Opening Doors, Opening Opportunities: Family Literacy in an Urban Community*. Needham Heights, MA: Allyn and Bacon.

Patton, Michael Q. 2001. *Qualitative Research and Evaluation Methods*. 3rd ed. Thousand Oaks, CA: Sage.

Ritzer, George Y. 2007. *Contemporary Sociological Theory and Its Classical Roots: The Basics*. Boston, MA: McGraw-Hill.

Rogers. Rebecca R. 2003. *A Critical Discourse Analysis of Family Literacy Practices: Power in and out of Print*. Mahwah, NJ: Lawrence Erlbaum Associates.

Rojewski, Jay W. 1999. 'Career-Related Predictors of Work-Bound and College-Bound Status of Adolescents in Rural and Non-Rural Areas'. *Journal of Research in Rural Education* 15:141–156.

Schultz, Mark R. 2005. *The Rural Face of White Supremacy: Beyond Jim Crow*. Champaign: University of Illinois Press.

Siddle Walker, Vanessa. 1996. *Their Highest Potential: An African American School Community in the Segregated South*. Chapel Hill: University of North Carolina Press.

Stack, Carol B. 1996. *Call to Home: African Americans Reclaim the Rural South*. New York: Basic Books.

Street, Brian V. 1984. *Literacy in Theory and Practice*. Cambridge: Cambridge University Press.

———. 1995. *Social Literacies: Critical Approaches to Literacy in Development, Ethnography, and Education*. London: Longman.

Thompson, Paul. 2000. *The Voice of the Past: Oral History*. 3rd ed. New York: Oxford University Press.

Tickamyer, A. R., and Cynthia M. Duncan. 1990. 'Poverty and Opportunity Structure in Rural America'. *Annual Review of Sociology* 16:67–86.

US Census Bureau. 2000. *American Fact Finder.* Washington, DC: US Census Bureau.

Viernes Turner, Caroline S. 2007. 'Pathways to the Presidency: Biographical Sketches of Women of Color Firsts'. *Harvard Educational Review* 77 (1): 1–38.

Williams, William H. A. 2007. *Self-Taught: African American Education in Slavery and Freedom.* Chapel Hill: University of North Carolina Press.

12 A Place to Hang My Hat On

University Staff Perceptions in Multiethnic New Zealand

Edwina Pio, Ali Rasheed, Agnes Naera,
Kitea Tipuna and Lorraine Parker

INTRODUCTION

A rich extensive literature exists on inclusion and exclusion in the workplace (Brief, Butz and Deitch 2005; Corsun and Costen 2001; Greenhaus, Parasuraman and Wormley 1990). Over the last few decades, this literature has initially focused on women in the workplace (Maranto and Griffin 2010; Roos 2009; Van den Brink, Benschop and Jansen 2010), with subsequent research highlighting the complexities that ethnic minority people face at work (Aguilera 2003; Aguirre Jr. 2000; Alesina and La Ferrara 2000; Chugh and Brief 2008a; McClain, Schrader and Callahan 2008). In the slowly burgeoning literature on ethnic minority staff at work (Fearfull and Kamenou 2006; Jones, Wilson and Jones 2008), there continues to be limited literature on minority staff in higher education, specifically universities (Rosser 2004; Stucki et al. 2004). There is also limited research in New Zealand (NZ) or Aotearoa, the Māori name for New Zealand, on the perceptions of ethnic minority staff working in a university culture. Our study seeks to shed light on how ethnicity shapes the lived experience of Māori, the Indigenous people of NZ and Pasifika staff in universities. In particular, we are interested in understanding minority perceptions of staff engagement in universities. Minorities are not part of the mainstream ethnic group and hence we are also interested in the unspoken negotiation process of how such staff adapt to institutionalised practices while simultaneously maintaining their own cultural ethnic characteristics.

Boyd and Halfond (2000) argue for the need to approach diversity with openness in tandem with a university's traditional quest for truth and to create a climate conducive to the substantive scrutiny of race, ethnicity and prejudice. In fact, aspects of ethnicity abound in sensitivity, consequently creating a relative silence around challenging these issues (Chugh and Brief 2008a), in universities. Our focus on ethnicity outlines the importance and continuing relevance of ethnicity in its various manifestations in higher education.

Our empirical study contributes to the existing research on minority staff in universities in three respects. Firstly, it develops a more sophisticated understanding of the experiences of ethnic minority staff and the process of decolonising inquiry as a lived-through performative experience. Secondly, it adds a more nuanced layer to our understanding of how inclusion and exclusion are played out in the ethnicity equation within a university. Thirdly, it troubles neat conceptual packages by interweaving post-colonialism with decolonising inquiry in what is considered legitimised behaviour for minority academic and administrative staff in universities.

STUDY CONTEXT

Ethnicity is a complex and challenging variable and is a measure of cultural affiliation, as opposed to race, ancestry, nationality or citizenship. In NZ, ethnicity is self-perceived and self-identified and individuals can belong to more than one ethnic group at one time (Statistics New Zealand 2006a). The NZ census defines an ethnic group as: one or more elements of common culture which need not be specified, but may include religion, customs or language; unique community of interests, feelings and actions; a shared sense of common origins or ancestry; a common geographic origin (Statistics New Zealand 2006a). Hence besides biological ancestry, the focus is on shared worldviews in defining ethnic groups in NZ. However, with an influx of migrants over 150 years in NZ, it is important to acknowledge that ethnicity is fluid and inter-marriages over the decades have resulted in mixed ancestry and culture (Callister 2006; Pearson, 2000). Therefore, on the NZ census form, an individual can tick more than one ethnicity, e.g. NZ European, Māori, Samoan, Tongan, Chinese and Indian.

The 2006 census counts show ethnic groups of Māori at 14.9 per cent and Pasifika at 7.2 per cent, in the approximately 4.1 million people in NZ (Statistics New Zealand 2006d). Yet NZ was primarily inhabited by Māori before the arrival in NZ of Captain Cook in 1769. With Cook's arrival extensive European/Western settlement followed, forever changing the demography of the country. Since then, NZ has increasingly become a diverse nation with its foundations resting on the Treaty of Waitangi and the interaction of peoples identifying with more than two hundred ethnicities. The image of a clean, green and nuclear-free country together with its idyllic lifestyle has attracted more people from around the globe. Currently, almost a quarter of the NZ population were not born in the country (Statistics New Zealand 2006d) and the prevalence of the 90 per cent of exclusively European heritage New Zealanders three decades ago has been reduced to 67 per cent (Te Ara 2009). Table 12.1 indicates the percentages of ethnic groups based on the NZ census classification for 2006 and projected numbers for 2021.

NZ's history of colonial administration in the Pacific resulted in the movement of Pasifika peoples to NZ after the Second World War, and subsequently in the 1970s as contract workers (Pearson 1990). The Pasifika people's ethnic group is now a significant portion of the NZ population.

Table 12.1   Ethnic Groups Based on NZ Census Classification (Total Percentages)

Ethnic Group	2006	2021
European/Other	76.8%	71.3%
Māori	14.9%	16.2%
Pacific	7.2%	9.1%
Asian	9.7%	14.5%
Middle Eastern, Latin American, African (MELAA)	0.9%	0.9%

Source: Statistics NZ, Census 2006 and projections.

The 2006 census recorded 265,974 individual Pasifika people, composing 6.9 per cent of the total NZ population. The number of people identifying with the Pasifika ethnic group was up 14.7 per cent from the 2001 census, which was the second-largest increase among all ethnic groups. In 2006, 60 per cent of the Pasifika population were NZ born (Statistics New Zealand 2006c). Samoans formed the largest Pasifika ethnic group in NZ in 2006 and made up 131,103 or 49 per cent of the Pasifika population, with Samoans born in NZ accounting for 60 per cent (77,247) of the total Samoan population. Cook Island Māori were the second largest Pasifika ethnic group in NZ, making up 58,011 or 22 per cent of NZ's Pasifika population. Tongans were the third-largest Pasifika ethnic group in NZ, making up 50,478 or 19 per cent of NZ's Pasifika population. Niueans, Fijians, Tokelauans and Tuvaluans are some of the other Pasifika peoples in NZ (Statistics New Zealand 2006c).

NZ became a part of the British Crown in 1840 and whereas NZ was never a colonised nation like, for example, India and parts of Africa, the changing demography to a European majority has resulted in colonialism which continues to linger in higher education. Elsewhere, despite the fact that the geographical influence of the West has changed with the politics and independence of nations, there remain hints of colonialism (Young 2001) which serve as pervasive conditions within organisations, including universities. Such discourses have resulted not only in ideas of discursive institutionalisation of the West as 'superior', but also in cultural practices and institutions such as that of the law and legal systems, medical and health care practices, universities, education curricula and journalism (Prasad 2006). Thus colonialism has become deeply embedded not only in ideas and images of the 'less informed', but also in the systems and institutions of many parts of the world (Swadener and Mutua 2008).

In NZ, increasing importance is being placed on the implications of staff issues in universities, in particular, alignment to the NZ Vice Chancellor's Committee (NVCC) study 'The Academic Workforce Plan: Towards 2020', as well as equal employment and diversity issues more generally (NVCC

2008, 2009). This plan is a collaborative project across the Vice Chancellors' Committee which acknowledges that universities will face significant difficulties in maintaining an effective and efficient academic workforce, given the ageing and diverse NZ academic workforce.

Academic Māori staff are under-represented across all tertiary institutions in NZ (Massey University 2009; Ministry of Education [MOE] 2004, cited in Durie 2009). In terms of profiling the average Māori academic in a tertiary institution, they are more likely to be female, younger on average than their non-Māori colleagues and in more junior academic positions (Tertiary Education Commission [TEC] 2008). In more senior roles, Māori are further under-represented; with only 3 per cent as associate professors and 4 per cent as professors (Statistics NZ 2006b;TEC 2008). Overall Māori and Pasifika staff are under-represented in academia, though the number of administrative staff is higher than that of academic staff (Davidson-Toumu'a and Dunbar 2009; MOE 2003, 2005).

Even though the relevance of anti-discrimination legislation is recognised as a barrier against unfair practices in the workplace, an absolute guarantee can only be assured by a change in attitudes, perceptions and behaviours of employers, colleagues and team members (Durbin, Lovell and Winters 2008). Smith et al. (2004) highlight the role of special-hire interventions as an effective tool to promote under-represented ethnic minorities in faculties. McClain, Schrader and Callahan (2008) found that despite recruiting high levels of women and under-represented groups, both groups are consistently under-represented at certain levels of faculty administration. Nevertheless the need to transform higher education staffing and culture has informed strategic plans of action for increasing opportunities for advancement and job satisfaction.

The university that is the site of our study is similar to all the eight universities in NZ, in having a majority Pakeha/European staff. This chapter unpacks the lived experiences of ethnic minority professionals, specifically Māori and Pasifika academic and administrative staff, in a university setting in order to understand how ethnicity impacts their engagements at work.

THEORETICAL FRAMEWORK

Decolonising inquiry is based on the notion that non-Western forms of knowledge are excluded and/or kept on the periphery of research resulting in the silence of non-Western voices (Pitama, Ririnui and Mikaere 2002; Smith 1999; Swadener and Mutua 2008). Colonisation is deemed responsible for relegating the non-Western and Indigenous voices and subjects to the margins and legitimising oppression. Decolonising inquiry seeks to 'highlight and advocate for the ending of both discursive and material oppression' (Swadener and Mutua 2008, 34). Such inquiry seeks to affirm and reclaim Indigenous epistemologies and is also more than a spatial-temporal phenomenon, but inquires into the mechanisms which silence specific groups in the 'ways it constructs and consumes knowledge and experiences of such groups' (Swadener and Mutua 2008, 35). For example, there are a number of reasons why depending on the organisational setting, the work environment and the role, Whites and non-Whites can have very different employment trajectories (Bielby 2008; Pio, 2008, 2010).

Over the last few centuries, colonialism in its various forms has influenced countries both within and outside the various empires and has served to dichotomise and institutionalise various forms of discourse upon which knowledge was/is created and constructed. Often such knowledge was created with the purpose of putting in place a hierarchy which served to mutually impact the colonised and colonisers (Bhabha 1994; Chakarabarty 2000; Gandhi 1998; Said 1978). Such a hierarchy was constructed with Western knowledge/colonisers as 'superior' and the non-West/non-Western knowledge as 'inferior'. Whereas such dichotomies are no doubt simplistic they serve to highlight the hierarchical system of colonialist binaries where, for example, the West was active, in the centre, in areas they considered civilised, developed, superior, scientific, modern and liberated, and which were/are predominated by White people. In contrast, the non-West was deemed passive, on the margin or periphery, primitive or savage, backward and developing, archaic, and comprising Black, brown or yellow peoples (Prasad 2006).

Universities are expected to have a 'culture of free and open inquiry that encourages and supports academics to hold ideas that may differ from those of their colleagues' (Openshaw and Rata 2007, 407). Yet it is possible that the discourses of colonialism continue to impact upon the university and its actions in terms of the implementation of policies. Such impacts can lead to constructive policies which seek to 'destabilize the binaries' of colonialism, so that there is 'less repair and maintenance work' (Prasad 2006, 136) to keep the binaries enshrined. Prasad (2006) utilises the notion of 'soft-power', which is the unwritten, unquestioned understanding of what constitutes legitimate understanding and behaviour. Such soft-power can serve as a powerful nexus in preserving the binaries of colonialism as it links with hard power in the control of resources, including who deserves such resources and how they can access it. Soft-power can be likened to micro-politics, which are the formal and informal ways in which individuals and groups achieve their goals in organisations, and these can be conflict and/or collaborative laden (Morley 2006; Van den Brink, Benschop and Jansen 2010). Thus universities can serve as a 'discursive site of resistance, where the marginalized oppose the dominant and contest asymmetries of power' (Prasad 2006, 139). Such sites of resistance can be part of the performative actions towards decolonising inquiry. 'Decolonization of the mind demands a firm departure from the temptation of solitary identities and priorities' (Sen 2006, 99) on the part of the employer and employee in order to make the experiences, skills and qualifications of minority staff truly matter in the workplace.

Research indicates perceptions of bias, lack of networking opportunities and dissatisfaction with racial/ethnic diversity as factors of an institution's diversity climate that need to be addressed if a university is to succeed in the competitive job market of the future (Rosser 2004; Sabharwal and Corley 2009). Gateways into the workplace refer to recruitment and getting hired, whereas pathways refer to being listened to, getting credit and getting a 'fair shot once in the door': These are more difficult to obtain for ethnic minorities (Chugh and Brief 2008b, 318). Jackson (2008) characterises the faculty of colour or ethnic minority experience as involving: lack of support (e.g. being subject to differential evaluation mechanisms and inappropriate questioning relating to non-scholarly matters), the revolving door syndrome (where retaining ethnic minority staff is an issue—though policies may be in place, there is a lack of collegiality among staff members), tokenism (e.g. token hires), typecasting (e.g. only ethnic minority people can research and teach ethnic minority courses), one minority per pot (unwanted quota system from no minorities allowed to one in each department) and a brown-on-brown taboo (White-on-White research is given legitimacy, but brown-on-brown research is questionable).

Universities in NZ all have equal opportunities policies and processes to encourage inclusion in the workplace. However, research findings may well parallel the situation in universities internationally, where despite affirmative action policies and research providing evidence of the economic and student learning benefits of having multiethnic staff, there may be gaps between rhetoric and reality, so that some ethnicities have more spaces to hang their hats on, whereas others struggle to find a space. The main aim of the research reported in this chapter was to explore the lived-in and lived-through experiences of minority ethnic staff in a university in NZ. The expectation is that this study on staff ethnicity in a NZ university will serve as a medium of awareness and sensitization for the macro and micro worlds of work in a university.

METHODOLOGY

This project is situated within the broad framework of qualitative inquiry and emerges from the interpretive and post-positivist genres. A qualitative approach was used in order to explore the perceptions of ethnic minority staff employed in universities in NZ. In this context, the task of the researcher is 'to appreciate the different constructions and meanings that people place upon their experience' (Vignali 2004, 750), for the individual's lived experience forms their reality. Furthermore, there is both an intellectual and political purpose in making linkages between history, structures and individual lives, as researchers who are also committed to connecting scholarship to social struggle and transformation (Mir and Mir 2002). The epistemological underpinnings of this study are anchored in hermeneutics and the situatedness of the context and meaning in constructing reality (Patton 2002).

The research team consists of individuals who identify with Māori, Asian and Pakeha/European ethnicities. For the Pasifika ethnic group, consultation was undertaken in order to make the research culturally and professionally appropriate. We believe that this identification of ethnicity facilitated a layered understanding and richer life-experiences of the participants, whilst at the same time acknowledging the tension in research as a site of struggle. We identify the positionality that our ethnicity provides through visual and audial markers as information sources for those with whom we interact (Katzew 2009). Thus by acknowledging who we are as researchers and how this affects our research, we identify with scholars of colour, as we bring 'ourselves through the door and support others in doing so as well, so we can define ourselves and claim unambiguous empowerment, creating discourses that address our realities, affirm our intellectual contributions and seriously examine our worlds' (Turner 2002, 89). In this quest for cognizance, as the voiceless gain voice, based on the writings of scholars of colour and minority group perspectives, 'the stories we tell one another will change and the criteria for reading stories will also change' (Denzin 2004, 468).

Data Collection

Information was gathered through semi-structured in-depth *kanohi ki te kanohi* (face-to-face) interviews which were audio-recorded and supported with note taking (following each interview) and informal conversations. We sought to emulate a *korero mai* (discussion/conversation) approach (Pitama, Ririnui and Mikaere 2002; Smith 1999) with sixteen participants who took part in individual interviews which ranged between thirty minutes to two hours, averaging approximately sixty minutes per participant. The participants consisted of eight Māori and eight Pasifika individuals in one NZ university. In each of the two ethnic groups, there were four females and four males of which two each were academics and two each were administrative staff (see Table 12.2 for participants interviewed). Potential participants were contacted through the research team's contacts based on ethnicity—Māori/Pasifika—and a minimum of two years' work experience in the university sector in NZ. All the interviews were conducted by the research team and Māori researchers, with ethical approval for the study obtained from the university.

University documents pertaining to Māori and Pasifika staff were accessed to understand university policies that related to ethnicity as well as to locate the numbers of Māori and Pasifika staff employed at the university.

Table 12.2 Participants Interviewed

Ethnicity	Gender	Academic	Administrative	Total Participants
Māori	4 male 4 female	2 male 2 female	2 male 2 female	8
Pasifika	4 male 4 female	2 male 2 female	2 male 2 female	8

Data Analysis

Transcriptions were carried out either immediately after the interviews, or within four weeks of the interview taking place. Notes made immediately after the interviews were also incorporated into the final transcripts, along with a concise summary of each of the participants. Analysis of the transcripts involved a search for salient themes and elements, which were coded using two broad categories: institutional structures and professional experiences. Repeated readings of the transcripts led to identification of key events, relationships between categories and a more multifaceted understanding of minority voices. Therefore, the two broad categories were further subdivided into career entry/progression, ethnic epistemologies, university polices, and country of origin.

Member checks (Lincoln and Guba 1985) were used to ensure that the stories accurately represented the participants experiences and hence participants were involved in their transcriptions and summaries. Peer debriefings (Mertens 2005) with discussions on the findings and conclusions were resorted to, by discussing the summaries, transcripts and interpretations with university colleagues, for increasing accuracy in the representation of the participants. University documents pertaining to Māori and Pasifika staff and trends in numbers of these staff were also analysed.

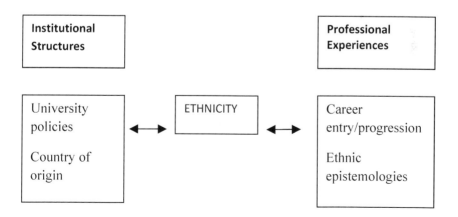

Figure 12.1 Minority staff engagement in universities.

EMERGENT THEMES AND DISCUSSION

Based on our data analysis, a model of minority staff engagement in universities has been developed. The model, displayed in Figure 12.1 is discussed and interwoven with participant extracts and theoretical reflections to explicate the findings.

Institutional Structures

Our data indicated that institutional structures were dependent on university policy and the country of origin of staff, for example, if staff were from minority ethnicities such as Māori or Pasifika. In its strategic plan, the university in this study identifies key strategic objectives which focus on strong engagement with Māori, Pasifika and new settler communities, and on recruiting staff and students internationally (University Documents 2007). These developments align with the university's strategic objective to ensure that the staff and student profile better reflects the population it serves. This commitment to equal opportunity employment recognises the significance of being relevant to the diverse communities of a twenty-first-century city where the university is located and adjusting the profile of staff in order to support changes in student, teaching and research profiles.

This university's strategic plan 2007–2011 has a number of objectives, of which three objectives specifically refer to ethnicity (University Documents 2007—confidentiality maintained about the university under study). One of the objectives focuses on Māori and includes building effective relationships with Māori communities, conducting research that benefits Māori, including Māori pathways in the curriculum, promoting access, success and advancement for Māori staff and students and valuing and promoting Māori language and values.

Māori participants in our study had a number of comments with reference to this university objective. A Māori male academic was very positive about the university's creation of a Māori context and said:

> I am fortunate I work in a Māori context so I don't need to explain myself and I am reminded of my good fortune when I step outside this context, it would be very hard for me at this stage of my career and at my age to work in an environment that did not value Māori.

A female Māori academic had the following to say:

> I become very frustrated when there are Māori in leadership roles who have the ability to make a significant difference at a much wider level and that would give greater effect to the work that is done at lower levels but who for whatever reason choose not to . . . There are days when it is easier to deal with institutional ignorance; on the hard days I

seek out other Māori to feed my *wairua* [spirit]; always works I go back recharged to do another day.

These two quotes show the impact of soft-power and micro-politics in the everyday functioning in a university and the yawning gaps that exist between university policies and how they are acted out. Thus although Māori staff work at the university, what constitutes legitimate understanding and behaviour for Māori people does not seem to be understood outside of a Māori environment, or the formal and informal ways in which some people are insiders and others outsiders (Morley 2006).

Another objective of this university is to encourage access and success in university education for students from the diverse communities within the region. Priorities include becoming the university of choice for Pasifika communities by building effective relationships with Pasifika communities, encouraging access, success and advancement of Pasifika staff and students, conducting research that benefits Pasifika and their communities, including Pasifika pathways in the curriculum and developing a culture of inclusion and celebrating diversity in all the university's activities.

The following quotes from Pasifika participants, male and female, as well as academic and administrative staff, indicate a positive experience in the university. For example: '[Back in the Islands they say] . . . let's have a look for a university so that we can send our kids there . . . they'll think hey . . . let's send our kids there or make contact with this guy'. Such statements reinforce the search for better futures for their children by Pasifika Island peoples, as the education in NZ is considered 'superior' to that in the Islands, but there is some fear associated in sending their children to NZ due to possible changes in value systems, hence a role model in the form of a Pasifika academic is considered positive. Another participant said: 'I really enjoy my [. . .] role as well and being able to support our Māori and Pasifika students . . . I feel very privileged taking that role'. Or this extract: 'after spending seventeen years here you feel ingrained in the wood . . . you are part of the university community' and finally: 'I am very satisfied with my job because I have a feeling that this is a way I can give back to my own community'.

It seems evident from these extracts that Pasifika staff seem more satisfied than Māori staff in this specific university and this is an accolade to the implementation of the university's institutional structures. It is possible that Māori as original inhabitants of the land want a greater stake in decision making at the university and thus a greater stake in the future of NZ. This was in evidence in what all the Māori participants expressed, particularly as they self-identified as *tangata whenua* (meaning original inhabitants or people of the land). Decades of colonisation led to loss of land and influence (Treaty of Waitangi 2006) and in the current century, Māori assert the right to be in charge of their futures. Such a stance can serve as the performance of resistance in a university (Prasad 2006).

Table 12.3   Percentage Distribution of Academic and Administrative (Admin) Staff in a University 2007–2010

Ethnicity	2007		2008		2009		2010	
	Academic	Admin	Academic	Admin	Academic	Admin	Academic	Admin
Māori	5.4%	8.3%	5.1%	8.8%	4.8%	8.4%	4.5%	8.0%
Pasifika	2.3%	8.1%	2.1%	8.2%	2.0%	7.5%	2.1%	7.3%

The final example of institutional structures in this university's objectives is to ensure the university provides a challenging, stimulating and rewarding work environment for all staff. Priorities include ensuring the staff and leadership profile reflects the communities the university serves, providing staff with opportunities and providing students and staff with inspirational models. Yet, when we explored the trends in staff employment between 2007 and 2010, we note hardly any improvement in the numbers of Māori and Pasifika employed. Please see Table 12.3, which indicates the percentage distribution of academic and administrative staff. For example, in 2007 there was 5.4 per cent Māori academic staff and in 2010 it was 4.5 per cent. In 2007 the percentage for Pasifika non-academic staff was 8.1 per cent and in 2010 it was 7.3 per cent. Thus whereas this university's strategic policies clearly spell out its commitment to inclusion of Māori and Pasifika, the numbers tell a different story. Although numbers never tell the entire story, and they could be due to a number of factors, including reasons external to the university, it is worrying that over a four-year period, despite espoused policies, there is hardly any real change.

Professional Experiences

Two subthemes emerged when analysing the data pertaining to professional experiences—career entry/progression and ethnic/Indigenous epistemologies. The university in this study seeks to be the university of choice for Māori and Pasifika students, and to this end it seeks to employ Māori and Pasifika staff. Hence participants did not see problems in their entry into the university; however, moving to higher levels within the university was not easy. This experience falls in line with the research of Chugh and Brief (2008b), who write about gateways into employment or career entry, where minority members are often at the start of these paths, but many continue to remain at lower levels within the university. Remaining at lower levels or blocks to pathways to higher levels (Chugh and Brief 2008b) are sometimes offset by minority staff being given senior designations—yet these senior roles do not have much decision-making power and thus represent a bow to tokenism (Jackson 2008).

Minority ethnic/Indigenous epistemologies or minority ethnic/Indigenous ways of knowledge making and worldviews are an expression of one's ethnic self at work. Regarding ethnic epistemologies or ways of seeing and acting in the world from a particular point of view, the extracts that follow indicate difficulties that non-Māori have with Māori staff in terms of understanding, for example the meaning of silence. As a Māori female academic said: 'I am always amused that non-Māori take silence as an acknowledgement of agreement, but I suppose because we know this we should respond in a way that will communicate what we want'. This indicates the need for enhanced understanding of various modes of communication that may not be Western and hence perhaps the need to educate the university in non-Western and Indigenous ways of communication which need to be legitimised (Chakarabarty 2000). This would encourage a free flow of 'different' ideas which constitute a critical aspect of free and open inquiry in a university (Boyd and Halfond 2000; Openshaw and Rata 2007). Silence could also be viewed as a site of resistance. Decolonising inquiry seeks to interrogate and explore the colonial encounter and the notions, images and material encounters of Eurocentrism or the West and the resistance to such accepted ways of thinking and being. Gandhi (1998) refers to post-colonial voices as a cacophony, where various subalterns are now speaking and being allowed to speak. However, we acknowledge that silence cannot always be equated with powerlessness (Morley 2006), and in some contexts silence serves as a modus operandi for resistance.

A Māori female administrator stated: 'I think some non-Māori staff try to understand us, but they simply view the world differently and so our stories get filtered to where sometimes who we are becomes less visible. We've been with [these] people for two hundred years and even after two hundred years of contact we have to explain ourselves every step of the way; that hurts, as a Māori person that hurts me'. This quote illustrates the need for communication that displays various worldviews or the need for information and education on ethnic epistemologies, so that ethnicity when expressed can be understood in its various nuances. Such understanding can reaffirm and reclaim ethnic epistemologies, which would go a long way in fracturing both discursive and material oppression (Swadener and Mutua 2008).

A female administrator refused to be classified as Kiwi (the more common way of referring to people from NZ although often denoting those of Pakeha/European stock): 'I'm not a Kiwi. I don't even apologise for that because I'm not. I'm Māori, and that's what I want to be identified as. When I travel overseas if they say to me, 'Are you a Kiwi?' I say, 'No I am a New Zealand Māori, I am Māori', and I don't want people to give me a look that somewhat tries to diminish that because that is where my strength comes from, that is everything I am; that's what I'm about'. Such quotes are a clear expression of the university as a site of resistance and the need for a greater impact of university policies in the micro-politics and soft-power that abounds in everyday interactions. The quotes also express the desire for the creation of *mana* (honour/respect) through ethnicity. Hence there is a need for more emphasis on what a Māori participant refers to as: 'the way we form relationships and the importance of "kanohi ki te kanohi", that is, face-to-face relationship, and an honest approach'.

Yet, there is a legacy of a long history of colonisation, and in the move towards decolonisation, persistence in the replication of stereotypes in the thinking of the majority culture continues, which appears to impact on communication between Pakeha/European and Māori staff. This illustrates the need for a more concerted effort into decolonising inquiry and performative action (Prasad 2006; Smith 1999) which will help in understanding why, for example, a Māori participant said: 'Look, at the end of the day I'll go to anyone who will listen to me, anyone who will help me'.

Although Pasifika participants were happy with the institutional structures at the university, some felt that their professional experiences were problematic. A Pasifika male academic said: 'As a Pasifika person my voice does not get heard, and also people tend to blame and shame me because of my ethnic origin'. This view was echoed by a Pasifika female academic who said: As a Pasifika community we are not a homogenised group we have our own differences and sometimes we get marginalised in social circles since we are not from the dominant group'. In the first quote, marginalisation of Pasifika staff appears to occur in the university because of their perceived difference to White staff, whereas in the second quote, marginalisation seems to be more within the Pasifika community, which consists of many island nations with varying levels of soft-power and micro-politics displayed at work among these communities, with country of origin achieving dominance. This is perhaps the reason why a Pasifika female administrator said: 'As an (. . .) ethnic person my beliefs and my culture, that is my strongest challenge, because you know cos [my discipline] is Black and White is White, and that's it. My research is gonna be on that . . . how to integrate culture in [my discipline]'. In other words, there is a need to connect scholarship to culture which includes social struggle and transformation (Mir and Mir 2002).

In the professional experiences of participants in our study, we note that decolonising inquiry can unfold the patterns of thinking and imagining which have been institutionalised in representing the other, i.e. Māori and Pasifika or the colonial native (Bhabha 1994; Said 1978). In fact the 'general psychological attitude toward the subject people often generated a strong sense of humiliation and an imposition of perceived inferiority' (Sen 2006, 85). Our study has sought to open up the landscape of such colonial baggage and unpack the amazing psychological tenacity in universities, even years after the political and geographical demise of colonialism (Gandhi 1998). Arguably, the participants' lived experiences in engagements at work consist of strands of domination and resistance along with behavioural manifestations which may be seen in organisational life through the recognition of the colonial imprint or the historical coloniser (Ahluwalia 2001). Prasad (2005, 280) writes that 'the post-colonial tradition compels recognition of global (frequently imperialist) dynamics into management and organization studies, thus contextualizing contemporary workplaces within wider political situations . . . restores a stronger sense of historical cultural awareness to our understanding of contemporary organizations and is useful in identifying patterns of hierarchical reproduction that are grounded in colonial dynamics'.

CONCLUSIONS

This chapter has investigated how ethnicity shapes the lived-in and lived-through experiences of academic and administrative minority staff, specifically Māori and Pasifika staff in a NZ university. Whereas educational inequality is impacted by the intersectionality of race, gender and class and although both men and women participated in our study, we have highlighted 'race'/ethnicity in our analysis of our empirical data as the gender and class differences were negligible in comparison with those pertaining to ethnicity. However, it must be noted that there exist persistent socio-economic disparities between the Māori and Pasifika populations in NZ as compared with other ethnic groups. Thus relative to European/Pakeha people, both Māori and Pasifika peoples tend to have lower incomes and higher rates of unemployment as well as lower educational levels. Whereas there has been a certain amount of 'catch-up' in employment, education and income, inequality is still omnipresent. Reducing such inequalities with urgency and speed will take concerted action from both majority and minority groups in NZ, to increase the number of postgraduate and doctoral degrees in this population along with identification of career academics and their recruitment in the tertiary sector. Multiple educational pathways, institutional reforms with accountability for targeted goals pertaining to these populations, staff development opportunities to engage with Māori and Pasifika peoples and greater community involvement and partnership, in conjunction with nurturing research capacities, are key to reducing educational inequality and addressing the voices from these communities. Our findings indicate that although there is a good deal of progress made in terms of university policies that are written and articulated, there is much work to be done in the actual performance and implementation of these policies. Thus there is need for renewing and revitalising the university diversity climate and the implementation of policies (Rosser 2004; Turner 2002) with specific reference to ethnicity. In NZ, government policies specifically mention Māori and Pasifika peoples, thus rendering them visible. The university under study also makes visible these ethnic groups, keeping in mind the census projections and a younger age profile for these specific groups (MOE 2010; Statistics New Zealand 2006d). However, there is still a very large gap between the positioning of government and university policies and their real-life real-time implementation in multiethnic NZ.

There is thus a greater need to disseminate worldviews of minority ethnic peoples such as, for example, notions of culture for Pasifika (translation of Tongan/Samoan): *Lotoma'ulalo/Fa'amaualalao* (humility), *Faka'apa'apa/ Fa'aaloalo* (respect) and *Ofa/Alofa* (love) embedded within a sense of community and family; and notions of culture or *Māori tanga* for Māori such as *Aroha* (care/love), *Kaitiaki* (caretakers/trustees/stewards of resources), *Mana* (respect), *Manaaki* (respect/kindness) and *Mauriora* (well-being). This study suggests such worldviews or Indigenous and minority ethnic epistemologies, which are ways of knowing and acting, continue to serve as the core of behaviour among minority ethnic staff in universities, and these ways of knowing can further inform the actions of policy makers, as well as staff, in seeking to make the university truly diverse in its rhetoric and actions.

This chapter is a call to a deeper understanding of minority staff, in particular Māori and Pasifika staff in universities in NZ. Furthermore, it alerts universities to be more vigilant in the translation of policies into equality practices/actions which ensure that all staff have a place to hang their hat on!

ACKNOWLEDGEMENTS

Our deep thanks to the participants for their sharing, to Dr. Pare Keiha for his guidance, to our families for their constant faith in our work and to the editors of this book, Kalwant and Uvanney, for their helpful suggestions.

REFERENCES

Aguilera, Michael Bernabe. 2003. 'The Impact of the Worker: How Social Capital and Human Capital Influence the Job Tenure of Formerly Undocumented Mexican Immigrants'. *Sociological Inquiry* 73:52–83.
Aguirre Jr., Adalberto. 2000. *Women and Minority Faculty in the Academic Workplace: Recruitment, Retention and Academic Culture*. Vol. 27. San Francisco: Jossey-Bass.
Ahluwalia, Pal. 2001. 'When Does a Settler Become a Native? Citizenship and Identity in a Settler Society'. *Pretexts: Literary and Cultural Studies* 10 (1): 63–73.
Alesina, Alberto, and Eliana La Ferrara. 2000. 'Participation in Heterogeneous Communities'. *Quarterly Journal of Economics* 115:847–904.
Bhabha, Homi. 1994. *The Location of Culture*. London: Routledge.
Bielby, W. T. 2008. 'Promoting Racial Diversity at Work: Challenges and Solutions'. In *Diversity at Work*, edited by A. P. Brief, 53–86. Cambridge: Cambridge University Press.
Boyd, David P., and Jay Halfond. 2000. 'Higher Education's Role in the Dialogue on Race'. *International Journal of Value-Based Management* 13:35–46
Brief, Arthur, R. Butz and E. Deitch. 2005. 'Organizations as Reflections of Their Environment: The Case of Race Composition'. In *Discrimination at Work: The*

Psychological and Organizational Bases, edited by R. Dipboye and A. Colella, 119–148. London: Lawrence Erlbaum Associate Publishers.

Callister, Paul. 2006. 'Ethnic Measurement as a Policy Making Tool'. In *Public Policy and Ethnicity: The Politics of Ethnic Boundary-Making*, edited by E. Rata and R. Openshaw, 142–55. Basingstoke: Palgrave Macmillan.

Chakarabarty, Dipesh. 2000. *Provincalizing Europe*. Princeton, NJ: Princeton University Press.

Chugh, Dolly, and Arthur P. Brief. 2008a. 'Introduction: Where the Sweet Spot Is: Studying Diversity in Organisations'. In *Diversity at Work*, edited by Arthur P. Brief, 1–12. Cambridge: Cambridge University Press.

———. 2008b. '1964 Was Not That Long Ago: A Story of Gateways and Pathways'. In *Diversity at Work*, edited by Arthur P. Brief, 265–317. Cambridge: Cambridge University Press.

Corsun, D., and A. Costen. 2001. 'Is the Glass Ceiling Unbreakable? Habitus, Fields, and the Stalling of Women and Minorities in Management'. *Journal of Management Inquiry* 10 (1): (2001): 16–25.

Davidson-Toumu'a, R., and K. Dunbar. 2009. 'Understanding the Experiences of Pacific Students and Facilitating Socio-Cultural Adjustment into Higher Education in Aotearoa New Zealand'. *Journal of the Australian and New Zealand Student Services Association* 33:69–88.

Denzin, Norman. 2004. 'The Art and Politics of Interpretation'. In *Approaches to Qualitative Research*, edited by Sharlene Hesse-Biber and Patricia Leavy, 447–472. New York: Oxford University Press.

Durbin, Susan, Lin Lovell and Janet Winters. 2008. 'Diversities in an Organisational Context'. *Equal Opportunities International* 27:396–400.

Durie, Mason. 2009. 'Towards Social Cohesion: The Indigenisation of Higher Education in New Zealand'. Accessed September 29, 2009, at http://www.17ccem. com/upload/Prof_MasonDurie-.

Fearfull, Anthias, and Nicolina Kamenou. 2006. 'How Do You Account for It? A Critical Exploration of Career Opportunities for and Experiences of Ethnic Minority Women'. *Critical Perspectives on Accounting* 17 (7): 883–901

Gandhi, Leela. 1998. *Postcolonial Theory*. New York: Columbia University Press.

Greenhaus, Jeffrey, Saroj Parasuraman and Wayne M. Wormley. 1990. 'Effects of Race on Organizational Experiences, Job Performance Evaluations and Career Outcomes'. *Academy of Management Journal* 33 (1): 64–86.

Jackson, Jerlando. 2008. 'Race Segregation across the Academic Workforce: Exploring Factors that May Contribute to the Disparate Representation of African American Men'. *American Behavioral Scientist* 51. Accessed January 20, 2012, at DOI:10.1177/0002764207312003.

Jones, James. R., David C. Wilson and Peggy Jones. 2008. 'Toward Achieving the "Beloved Community" in the Workplace: Lessons for Applied Business Research and Practice from the Teaching of Martin Luther King Jr.'. *Business and Society* 47:457–483.

Katzew, A. 2009. 'Hello Professora: Teaching as a Chicana at a Predominantly White University'. *Latino Studies* 7:252–261.

Lincoln, Yvonne, and E. Guba. 1985. *Naturalistic Inquiry*. Beverly Hills, CA: Sage.

Maranto, Cheryl, and Andrea Griffin. 2010. 'The Antecedents of a "Chilly Climate" for Women Faculty in Higher Education'. *Human Relations*. Accessed January 20, 2012, at DOI: 10.1177/0018726710377932.

Massey University. 2009. 'Academy to Address the Dearth of Māori Academics'. Accessed October 21, 2009, from, http://www.massey.ac.nz/massey/about-us/

news/article.cfm?mnarticle=academy-to-address-dearth-of-Māori-leaders-02-06-2009.

McClain, Lisa, Cheryl Schrader and Janet Callahan. 2008. 'Improving Campus Climate for Faculty from Underrepresented Groups'. Paper presented at the ASEE Annual Conference and Exposition, Conference Proceedings.

Mertens, Donna. 2005. *Research and Evaluation in Education and Psychology*. Thousand Oaks, CA: Sage.

Mir, Raza, and Ali Mir. 2002. 'The Organizational Imagination: From Paradigm Wars to Praxis'. *Organizational Research Methods* 5:105–125.

Ministry of Education [MOE]. 2003. *Review of the implementation and Effectiveness of Special Supplementary Grants for Māori and Pasifika Students in Tertiary Education Institutions from 2001–2002, Māori Report*. Wellington: MOE.

———. 2004. *Tertiary Education Strategy 2002–2007: Baseline monitoring report*. Wellington: MOE

———. 2005. *Māori in Tertiary Education: A Picture of Trends*. Wellington: MOE.

Morley, Louise. 2006. 'Hidden Transcripts: The Micropolitics of Gender in Commonwealth Universities'. *Women's Studies International Forum* 29:543–551.

New Zealand Vice Chancellors Committee [NVCC]. 2009. *Request for Proposal: Academic Workforce Planning*. Wellington: NZVCC.

New Zealand Vice Chancellors Committee [NVCC]. 2008. *Briefing for the Incoming Government*. Wellington: NZVCC.

Openshaw, Roger, and Elizabeth Rata. 2007. 'The Weight of Inquiry: Conflicting Cultures in New Zealand's Tertiary Institutions'. *International Studies in Sociology of Education* 17:407–425.

Patton, Michael. 2002. *Qualitative Research and Evaluation Methods*. Thousand Oaks, CA: Sage.

Pearson, David. 1990. *A Dream Deferred: The Origins of Ethnic Conflict in New Zealand*. Wellington: Allen and Unwin.

———. 2000. 'The ties That Unwind: Civic and Ethnic Imaginings in New Zealand'. *Nations and Nationalism* 6:91–110.

Pio, Edwina. 2008. 'Ethnic Imprint? Career Conversations with Indian Women in New Zealand'. Paper presented at the career practitioners association of New Zealand conference, Auckland, February.

———. 2010. *Longing and Belonging*. Wellington: Dunmore.

Pitama, Di, George Ririnui and Ani Mikaere. 2002. *Guardianship, Custody and Access: Māori Perspectives and Experiences*. Auckland: Ministry of Justice.

Prasad, Anshuman. 2006. 'The Jewel in the Crown: Postcolonial Theory and Workplace Diversity'. In *Handbook of Workplace Diversity*, edited by Alison M. Konrad, Pushkala Prasad and Judith K. Pringle, 121–144. London: Sage.

Prasad, Pushkala. 2005. *Crafting Qualitative Research*. New York: M. E. Sharpe.

Roos, Patricia. 2009. 'Subtle Mechanisms: Reproducing Gender Inequity in Academia'. In *Equality, Diversity and Inclusion at Work: A Research Companion*, edited by Mustafa Ozbilgin, 27–40 Cheltenham, UK: Edward Elgar.

Rosser, Vicki J. 2004. 'Faculty Members' Intentions to Leave: A National Study on Their Worklife and Satisfaction'. *Research in Higher Education* 45:285–309.

Sabharwal, Meghana, and E. A. Corley. 2009. 'Faculty Job Satisfaction across Gender and Discipline'. *Social Science Journal* 46:539–556.

Said, Edward. 1978. *Orientalism*. New York: Vintage Books.

Sen, Amartya. 2006. *Identity and Violence: The Illusion of Destiny*. London: Allen Lane, Penguin.

Smith, Daryl. G., Caroline S. Turner, N. Osei-Kofi and S. Richards. 2004. 'Interrupting the Usual: Successful Strategies for Hiring Diverse Faculty'. *Journal of Higher Education* 75:133–160.

Smith, Linda. 1999. *Decolonizing Methodologies: Research and Indigenous Peoples*. London: Zed Books.

Statistics New Zealand. Ethnicity. 2006a. Accessed January 20, 2012, at http://www.stats.govt.nz/surveys_and_methods/methods/classifications-and standards/classification-related-stats-standards/ethnicity/definition.aspx.

———. 2006b. 'Iwi by Qualification (Highest)'. Accessed January 20, 2012, at http://wdmzpub01.stats.govt.nz/wds/TableViewer/tableView.aspx.

———. 2006c. 'Pacific Profiles 2006'. Accessed January 20, 2012, at http://www.stats.govt.nz/Census/about-2006–census/pacific-profiles-2006.aspx.

———. 2006d. 'Quick Stats about NZ Population and Dwelling'. Accessed December 19, 2009, at www.stats.govt.nz/ . . . /statistics/ . . . /2006 . . . /quickstats . . . /qstats-about-nzs-population-and-dwellings-2006–census.aspx.

Stucki, P., A. Kahu, H. Jenkins, P. Bruce-Ferguson and R. Kane. 2004. 'Narratives of Beginning Māori teachers: Identifying Forces That Shape the First Year of Teaching'. Accessed January 31, 2012, at http://www.tlri.org.nz/pdfs/9214–summaryreport.pdf.

Swadener, Beth B., and Kagendo Mutua. 2008. 'Decolonizing Performances: Deconstructing the Global Postcolonial'. In *Handbook of Critical and Indigenous Methodologies*, edited by Norman K. Denzin, Yvonna S. Lincoln and Linda T. Smith, 31–43. Thousand Oaks, CA: Sage.

Te Ara. 2009. *Multicultural New Zealand*. Accessed January 11, 2010, at http://www.teara.govt.nz/en/the-new-zealanders/13.

Tertiary Education Commission. 2008. *Baseline Trends in Research in the Tertiary Sector: A Working Paper Contributing to the Independent Strategic Review of the Performance-Based Research Fund*. Accessed October 21, 2009, at http://tec.govt.nz/Documents/Reports and other documents/pbrf-baseline-trends-in-the-PBRF-v2.pdf.

Treaty of Waitangi. 2006. Accessed January 31, 2006, at www.treatyof Waitangi.govt.NewZealand/story/treatydebated.php.

Turner, Caroline Sotello. 2002. 'Women of Colour in Academe'. *Journal of Higher Education* 73:74–93.

University Documents. 2007. *University Strategic Plan*. New Zealand.

Van den Brink, Marieke, Yvonne Benschop and Willy Jansen. 2010. 'Transparency in Academic Recruitment: A Problematic Tool for Gender Equality?' *Organization Studies* 31:1459–1483.

Vignali, C. 2004. An Action Research Approach for Internationalization. In Dana, Leo Paul (Ed.). *Handbook of Research on International Entrepreneurship*, 748–764. UK: Edward Elgar.

Young, Robert. 2001. *Postcolonialism: An Historical Introduction*. Oxford: Blackwell.

13 Intersectional Pedagogy
From Movies to the Classroom

Elżbieta H. Oleksy

To Marine

METHODOLOGICAL CONCERNS

Intersectionality

In her article 'The Complexity of Intersectionality' (2005), Leslie McCall wonders why 'despite the emergence of intersectionality as a major paradigm of research in women's studies and elsewhere, there has been little discussion of how to study intersectionality; that is, of its methodology' (1771). In response to her question, she puts forward three methodological perspectives: 'anticategorical complexity', 'intracategorical complexity' and 'intercategorical complexity'.

By the time McCall formulated her proposition, intersectionality research had been practiced (sometimes under other names) for over twenty years. With antecedents in critical race studies (Anthias and Yuval-Davis 1983; hooks 1984), it was employed in a number of disciplines, such as law and legislation (Crenshaw 1989; Grabham et al. 2009; Burri and Schiek 2009; Kantola and Nousiainen 2009), sociology (Collins 1998b; McCall 2005; Dill and Zambrana 2009), economics (Brewer, Conrad and King 2002), political science (Hawkesworth 2003), literature (Brah 1996; Oleksy 1994), film (May and Ferri 2002; Oleksy 2007), psychology (Cole 2009) and in other areas. Yet it has been argued that intersectionality defies disciplinary placement, even though it inspires thinking in various disciplines. Although very influential, McCall's scheme, which is squarely placed within social science, does not constitute a response to an assumed need for *one* intersectionality methodology. But should it? As has increasingly become evident, methodology in social and cultural studies has not responded to the growing need of interdisciplinary work. In particular, the many functions of the Internet have altered our understanding of the empirical with its demand to address diverse social networks and audiences. As I have argued elsewhere (Oleksy 2011), recent developments in social computing technologies, in giving people the tools to join diverse social networks, create niches for 'living' intersectionality, for voicing specific forms of 'lived experience'.

Nevertheless, I find McCall's proposition useful for my purposes here. My research into intersectional critical pedagogy is poised between two of her categories, the second and the third: 'intracategorical complexity' and 'intercategorical complexity'. The use of the third category is confusing in McCall's text, because she also calls it 'categorical'; for clarity I will use her preferred wording: 'categorical approach'. As I draw the results of my research from classroom situations over a lengthy period of time, I deal with both 'single social groups' and 'multigroup'.

'Intracategorical complexity' contests universalising essentialism in identity politics and approaches inequalities through lived experience at—heretofore—neglected axes of social stratification such as, for instance, the interlocked categories of gender, race, ethnicity, dis/ability and sexuality. Through ethnography, the method works with a single social group methodically untangling the discrete categories of oppression permeating one another. As I have argued before (Oleksy 2011), the subtle line that advances McCall's methodology in this category beyond previous research based on identity politics is what she calls unravelling 'one by one the influences of gender, race, class, and so on' (2005, 1787) and showing how they route through one another. 'Categorical approach', argues McCall 'focuses on the complexity of relationships among multiple social groups within and across analytical categories. . . . The subject is multigroup, and the method is systematically comparative' (2005, 1786).

I follow this logic in my research into pedagogy. I have been working with groups of graduate and postgraduate students from different geographic locations, spanning Asia, Europe, North America and South America, different levels and fields of prior education, who also embody a host of intersections. I use the term 'single social group' in a loose sense, even though—in my research experience—a 'single' group is diversified in terms of race, ethnicity, nationality, gender, sexuality, dis/ability, etc. It is still a single group whose pedagogic experience is methodically compared with knowledge produced by other single social groups. Thus, a multigroup comparative knowledge is and will have been produced and dealt with comparatively at the end of each cycle: annually, biannually and—in the final analysis—at the closure of the project.

Pedagogy and Ethnography

There has been general consensus that contemporary free access to higher education has created major inequalities worldwide. The paradox of this statement is that although mass higher education should be hailed, it has consequences that were not fathomed by the architects of this reform: increased dropout rates, lower quality of instruction, unprofessional competition for students by public and private schools, oversized class populations, etc. Most importantly, however, 'massification' of education has made it impossible to cater to students' special needs. This is especially detrimental to students with disabilities.

Concurrently, recent debates on inclusive schooling have emphasised the necessity to employ the concept of intersectionality in order to contest the neoliberal discourses of education (Liasidou 2012; Campbell 2005; Makkonen 2002)—an approach which treats on a par the categories of race, disability, gender, socio-economic standing and, possibly, many others. Concepts such as 'racialising disability' and 'disabling race' have burgeoned in criticism (e.g. Dossa 2009; Nelson 2011). Such intellectual jugglery renders critical language obscure and should be used with care. This is escalatory lingo of oppression, not liberation. As Rosemarie Garland Thomson implores, disability as a bodily problem should not be addressed by normalisation rhetoric, but rather 'as a socially constructed identity and a representational system similar to gender' (2005, 1559). It is important to note that, on the subjective level, people with impairments may identify as disabled or nondisabled, and people without visible disfigurements may identify as disabled, as I will demonstrate, on specific examples, later in this text.

In this chapter I will use insights from critical pedagogy to build links with the movement of educational inclusion. My teaching practice is rooted in a conviction that pedagogy should be organised in such a way as to allow pedagogical subjects to construct themselves and their place in the world in the best possible way. With Susan Gabel I share the view of pedagogy as 'a living, breathing text of experience that allows the narration of pedagogical stories to take any turn and possess any value as long as they are the turns and values of the pedagogical narrators' (Gabel 2002, 179). I endorse participatory, engaged pedagogy, which is open to resistance and dissent and therefore anticipates vulnerability of all pedagogical subjects (students and teacher). Consequently, I believe in pedagogy that should not pre-conceptualise pedagogical subjects in terms of the intersections they embody, such as nationality, ethnicity, race, sexuality or dis/ability, but rather 'let them emerge within interactions in the pedagogical community' (Gabel 2002, 181). I thus follow the route delineated initially by David Lusted's (1986) emphasis on interactive creativity in a pedagogical situation, Patti Lather's (1991) emancipatory/liberating pedagogy and bell hooks's notion of caring for students and seeing them as 'whole human beings' (1994, 15). All of these postmodernist approaches to teaching counter a pedagogy of assimilation and standardisation with its rigid categories of curriculum, instruction and evaluation, without the spontaneous interactive moments and exchanges of all pedagogical actors.

Investigating audiences presents a host of methodological and ethical concerns in terms of subjects under study, collected material which may often contain ethically sensitive content, methods of analysis and the conclusions. Drawing on my experience with an intersectional classroom, I present here the early findings as regards the process and the outcome of a course, 'Intersectionality and Audience Analysis in the Feminist Class-room', in the fall and spring terms of 2010–2011 and the fall term of 2011–2012 at the Women's Studies Centre, University of Łódź. Most of my material comes from classes with international students enrolled in the Erasmus Mundus Master Program in Women's and Gender Studies in Europe (GEMMA)—an enclave of racially and ethnically diverse students. GEMMA comprises seven European institutions: universities of Granada, Bologna, Hull, Łódź, Oviedo, Utrecht and Central European University in Budapest, as well as the State University of New Jersey, Rutgers. Students choose a host and a mobility university and, having successfully finished the programme, receive a double degree.

Conjointly in this text, I discuss the outcome of the class with the same syllabus, voluntarily chosen by students of film studies, gender studies and psychology at the University of California, Berkeley, in the spring semester of 2010–2011. Differences in age, class, race, ethnicity, dis/ability, sexual-ity and gender characterised both communities of students. The language of instruction at both locations was English. The majority of students were women. Both GEMMA and Berkeley students were fully aware of the proj-ect at hand and authorised me to disclose information about them and quote them under their first names. Their ages ranged from twenty to forty-four. Before enlisting for GEMMA, most of the students had completed undergraduate studies in various fields of the humanities and social sci-ences, whereas some of them already held MA or PhD degrees in areas as diverse as philosophy, political studies, literature, media studies and medi-cal studies. Such intimate information as sexuality is not provided in this text except for the cases when students permitted me to disclose it or when it is included in particular narratives.

In my pedagogical project, students first gain knowledge of intersec-tionality as theory, methodology and policy option through prior reading and discussion in class. Subsequently, we view a selection of films (one per class), and we discuss each of them. These discussions are recorded and transcribed. At the end of the course, students deliver journals and per-sonal narratives, interlacing their intimate accounts with their choice of film/films. The logic of my scheme is discussed in the next section.

STUDYING AUDIENECS

Initially, film studies research was modelled on literary criticism. It was a purely aesthetic discipline, whose study methods, such as textual analysis, were likewise borrowed from literature (e.g. Haskell 1973).When audience research re-emerged in the late 1970s,[1] it also appropriated literary meth-ods of analysis: semiotics and psychoanalysis. One of the major figures of this movement was Laura Mulvey (1975), who championed psychoanalytic feminist film theory and the voyeuristic male gaze, which garnered both applause and criticism.[2] Towards the end of the twentieth century, scholars turned their interest from the semiotics of static textual meanings and the 'implied' or 'ideal' viewer (Livingstone 1998) to the actual audiences. Early spectatorship theory, pioneered by Jackie Stacey (1994), adopted ethnography as a research instrument used, at that time, primarily by anthropologists.[3] Diversification of viewers as study objects constituted the next step, and changing the focus from 'audience' to 'audiencing' (Fiske 1992) neatly captured the process of generating and circulating meanings.

Increasingly, people's involvement in audiencing has become a critical way in which they experience their citizenship. Their social status as citizens of a particular race, ethnicity, sexuality, dis/ability, gender and class is 'mediated through their audiencehood' (Livingstone 1998, 197).[4] As Livingstone argues:

> While people obviously exist prior to any particular engagement with media, this position seems crucially to underplay the extent to which the media are implicated in the formation of contemporary discourses, both directly in people's media-immersed lives and indirectly in the sense that cultural discourses are fundamentally formed within a mediated environment. (1998, 212)

Martin Barker furthers this viewpoint by indicating that audiencing is a:

> process that begins *in advance* of the actual encounter, as people gather knowledge and build expectations. . . . audiences bring their social and personal histories with them . . . which continue after the 'event' as the audiencing encounter is given a place . . . sometimes providing the (cognitive, affective, emotional, sensual, imaginative) resources for conceiving self and the world. (2006, 124)

Reinforcing these opinions, I propose a novel approach to the empirical investigation of the visual. So far, it has not been documented how interconnections between various social differentials, such as gender, race, ethnicity, nationality, dis/ability and sexuality intersect in a particular lived experience and shape the reception of visual texts, as well as providing audiences with a standpoint to query the dominant hegemony and actively oppose it. My goal in this chapter is to document how a critical analysis of films empowers students and gives them incentive to oppose 'normalizing power effects' (Sholle 1991, 87).

FILMING DIFFERENCE

Of the many films which my students and I decided to discuss in class, I have selected four for a brief analysis: *Passion Fish* (John Sayles, 1992), *The*

Sweet Hereafter (Atom Egoyan, 1997), *Antonia's Line* (Marleen Gorris, 1995) and *A Single Man* (Tom Ford, 2009). The classes discussed intersections therein: disability, gender and race in *Passion Fish*; disability and sexuality in *The Sweet Hereafter*; diverse ability and sexuality in *Antonia's Line*; and gender and sexuality in *A Single Man*.

Passion Fish portrays relations across difference. A soap opera actress, May-Alice Culhane (Mary McDonnell), turns paraplegic after a spinal cord injury suffered in a street accident. Sayles's picture is a postmodern collage of soap opera and feature film. In this composition of stylistically diverse narrative orders, the main role is performed by the same woman. May-Alice returns to her native Louisiana, to the old, run-down house on the bayou and, after many failed attempts at hiring a nurse, she employs Chantelle (Alfre Woodard). She spends her time watching television and drinking to excess. But seemingly calm, composed Chantelle also undergoes a crisis. Addicted to drugs in the past, she was involved in criminal activities in Chicago's Black ghetto and lost custody of her young daughter. The film traces the convalescence of the two women, who discover the meaning of life in friendship.

Discussing *Passion Fish* in class, students differed on the meanings the film offered. Whereas they pointed out the parallelism of the two women's situations, they also indicated that the intimacy between May-Alice and Chantelle was restricted solely to the house and not beyond. Outside the house both women related to the people of their own race. Gloria, a Cuban American student of African descent, argued that *Passion Fish* is 'America [the United States] in the wheelchair [that] needs to be provided for by . . . minority groups; you know: let's get together because America is getting disabled'. Jerzy, a Polish student who has lived most of his life in a dysfunctional and disabled family, focused on the scenic beauty of the film because, as he said, 'disability films are not so rare anymore'. Be that as it may, *Passion Fish* was conceived of as a satire on commercial productions about illnesses ('sickness of the week films'). Sayles's film criticises the images of women propagated by American mass culture. In television series', women have accidents, lose sight and memory, are deprived of their reproductive organs—in a word, they are manipulated by the apparatus of mass culture.

Although the topics addressed by Sayles's film would suffice as material for several soap operas, what makes it unique (and non-commercial) is the absence of sentimentalism and a consistent avoidance of situational pathos.

The Sweet Hereafter likewise concerns the issue of disability. On an icy winter day in a close-knit village in British Columbia, a school bus full of children slides off the road and onto a frozen lake, where it sinks. All the children but one die; the oldest girl, Nicole Burnell (Sarah Polley), who survives the accident, turns paraplegic and will be confined to a wheelchair for the rest of her life.

As the despairing parents have been healing after the tragedy, a lawyer, Mitchell Stevens (Ian Holm), arrives with a hidden agenda. He goes from house to house to goad the people towards a class-action lawsuit to compensate them for their loss. If he wins the case, and he is sure he will, Stevens will receive one-third of the settlement money. However, Stevens is not interested in the remuneration of his efforts. In his twisted way, he needs a culprit to answer for his own tragedy. His only daughter, whose life he once saved when she had been bitten by a baby widow spider, is a drug addict and—possibly—HIV positive. Stevens wants the state to pay for his and the parents' tragedies.

However, his attempts are fruitless. Nicole, who is the key witness of the deposition, offers a false testimony: the driver, Dolores Briscoll (Gabrielle Rose), drove too fast on the frost-laced, slippery road and thus caused the accident. Earlier, before she and her father drive to the deposition, Nicole, who before the accident was involved in an incestuous relationship with her father, casually says 'I'm a Wheelchair Girl now'.

Students found *The Sweet Hereafter* the source richest in meanings among the choice of films we discussed in class. Fareed, a French Arab American student, noted 'a detached quality of an afterlife' in the film and commented that 'unlike other films [we watched in class] where people were consciously playing different roles—you know, at the same time I was George [*A Single Man*], I was also the real me; at the same time that I was a married Turk [*Head-On*, Fatih Akin, 2004], I was also a liberated female. Here there's that interesting disconnect between the different facades of their identity'. Focusing on Nicole as the only child who survived the accident (and was thus left behind other children like the lame child in Robert Browning's 'The Pied Piper of Hamelin' [1888], which is an intertext for *The Sweet Hereafter*), Fareed saw Nicole as a character that 'captures the powerlessness of the children brought to the cave, the cave being here the barn [where] her father brings her to do the quasi-incestuous relationship. . . . Even though the film lacks the usual horror toward incest, it's presented very lightly and maybe that's what makes it all the more horrifying'. He added that, compared with *Antonia's Line*, *The Sweet Hereafter* differs in 'almost lamenting the ephemerality of identity formation through the community'.

Antonia's Line (original *Antonia*, 1995), directed by Dutch feminist Marlene Gorris, is a fable on what could be perceived as feminism beyond the waves. In it, a spectator will not find the austerity of the second wave or the frivolity of the third generation. Unlike Sofia Coppola's *Marie-Antoinette* (2006), designed, among other things, as an allusion to the emptiness and shallowness of the chick culture, *Antonia's Line* presents a world in which joyful, affirmative feminism is appropriated by all. A feminist utopia, one might say? Perhaps. But, in the words of one reviewer, how different from the 'po-faced, airbrushed, body-double business of the Hollywood feature' (Spencer 1996, 35).

Antonia's Line begins as the title character (Willeke van Ammelrooy) is about to die but first scans her past. In retrospect, she arrives with her daughter, Danielle (Els Dottermans), at her native village, after World War II, as her mother lies dying. Soon they settle down, and Antonia begins gathering around her all kinds of eccentrics: a farm labourer, Looney Lips (Jan Steen); a village philosopher, Crooked Finger (Mil Seghers); a fertile 'fallen woman', Letta (Wimie Wilhelm); a rape victim, Deedee (Marina de Graaf); and Russian Olga (Fran Waller Zeper), whose red hair makes her look like a Toulouse-Lautrec prostitute (Jaehne 1996). By the film's end, there will be four generations of Antonia's line and a sizeable community gathered at her deathbed. Considered as an intertext for paintings from Brueghel, Bosch, Van Eyck to Rembrandt and Vermeer (Jaehne 1996), time in *Antonia's Line* is measured by cycles of nature with crops, sex, births and deaths.

Early on in the film, Danielle wants to have a baby without having to marry. She and her mother go to a neighbouring town and meet Letta, a 'fallen woman', who suggests that Danielle and her brother have sex. In due time, Danielle's daughter, Thérèse, is born. In a film which disrupts all categories, where almost every episode brings new intersections, the only character who is explicitly labelled is Thérèse. She is a prodigy child.

Much of the discussion in class centred on disability; which is only lightly touched on in the film, but somehow resonated for my students. Jules (a Philippine) focused on three characters, Looney Lips, Deedee and Thérèse:

> By the mainstream standards they are disabled social outcasts. . . . But the way Antonia treated them and made them part of the family, you would choose to go for the other side, which is diversability. Because you see how functional they are, how helpful with harvesting, farming, and they were never treated differently. . . . In a normal setting they wouldn't really find each other. They would just be, you know, social outcasts in separate parts of the place, scattered all over the city. But when they were brought together, they could function normally, they could be a couple, they could just be like normal people in a working relationship. . . . and Thérèse of course! It's also difficult, not being normal, having superior IQ at a very young age. . . . She's into philosophy, mathematics, music, it's . . . wow! Those are really difficult fields to master, and she's able to do them like they're just play, she's playing with music and math.

The last film I have chosen for the present discussion is *A Single Man* (Tom Ford, 2009). It is loosely based on Christopher Isherwood's novella (1964) under the same title, and depicts a single day, November 30, 1962, in the life of George Falconer (Colin Firth), a middle-aged professor of a small college in Los Angeles. Bereft by his partner's death eight months earlier in an accident and desperately longing for him, George plans to end his life. On that day, George goes about his habitual activities: teaches a class, goes to the bank, talks with a student, stops at a bar and visits an old friend and former lover, Charlie (Julianne Moore). However, the day is far from ordinary because George takes steps to get ready for suicide.

Notwithstanding comments on Colin Firth's admirable acting, the film received mixed reviews. Critics complained that it did not match the prototype, Isherwood's novella, which was one of the first oeuvres of the gay liberation movement. Mixed also was my students' reception of the film. They noted the constructed nature of the film and the affinity between its cinematography and Ford's sexist, misogynist advertisements. Barbara, a lesbian activist from Italy, criticised the 'normativity of the gay culture' promoted in the film and added: 'I see the upper class represented every day and I'm not interested in what they feel because they are the minority of the minority of the minority'. Conversely, Zoran, a gay activist from Serbia, pointed out that:

> we have to give a possibility for homosexual couples to be upper class, to be . . . as Tom Ford showed. What I really dislike in the gay community which I come from is particularly that if you're gay, you have to listen to this music, to listen to that. . . . We have to allow diversity. I mean, why not have upper-middle-class gay couples? Why not have design[er] houses? . . . There's a whole psychological theory about why the perception of gayness is like 'they have to have everything structured'. It explained that the shame they are taking with them has to be structured to some kind of excellence in life,[5] so either you will have to be successful in your business or you will have perfect sense of art.

This short exchange of opinion is but one of many—often conflicting—discourses of criticism and resistance that I have experienced while teaching this course. The wealth of personal experience also characterises students' personal narratives, fragments of which are presented in the next section.

Intersectional Classroom

In this section I present fragments of four personal narratives, which draw on the films discussed under the previous heading. Fareed's personal narrative, 'On Disempowerment and Empowerment of the Wheelchair', begins characteristically:

> The circumstance of my birth is the stuff of movies. Just a day after my mother had a routine ultrasound confirming that the new baby was going to be a girl, she went into labor. Amid pus and blood, I was born on March 6, 1987—a boy, it turned out, and three and a half months premature. I weighed a deathly two pounds, and my prognosis was not good. In between moments where my heart stopped, the doctors informed my parents to prepare for the worst. There was no way, they thought, that under such conditions, a child could live. Well, my body had other ideas, and I pushed through. The celebration of survival was quickly tainted, however, by the harsh reality of my mental

disability. I had cerebral palsy and over 40 percent of my brain was not just underdeveloped, but absent entirely. If I were to live, which seemed increasingly likely, I would be burdened mentally as well as physically. Would I be a vegetable? If I spoke at all, would I be able to form complex ideas? It could be years before my family understood the depths of my paralysis. The odds were decidedly against me, but like any good underdog story, I proved the numbers deliciously wrong. From high school valedictorian to Princeton University undergrad to Berkeley graduate student, I left the incubator and death's touch far behind, and have reveled in language, delighted in ideas and relied most firmly on my mind, unimpeded by the physical limitations I was born with.

Subsequently, Fareed comments on the scene in *Passion Fish* in which Sayles skilfully introduces the viewer to the gothic atmosphere of the old mansion, evocative of such classic images of the South as the thriller *What Ever Happened to Baby Jane?* (Robert Aldrich, 1962), in which one of the characters is disabled. Fareed writes:

> After being invited to come enjoy the movie, Chantelle enters the living room and casually sits on May Alice's wheelchair. Law concerning the rights of disabled people often emphasizes a person's sovereignty over his wheelchair, framing it not only as an assistance device but as an extension of his body. It is not to be touched or manipulated without the express permission of its owner; anything less is akin to assault. As a disabled viewer, I was shocked when without asking, Chantelle took her place on May Alice's wheelchair. Amplifying this takeover of May Alice's personal territory, Chantelle holds onto the invalid's 'umbilical cord', the remote control. The scene thus presents May Alice's tacit subordination to fully mobile individuals like Chantelle. As an injury-free actress, she was in complete control of her stage and her audience. Disabled, she must relinquish all, even her wheelchair, to the able-bodied. That her eventual soul mate so effortlessly commits such an invasion clearly illustrated to me how the body of a disabled person can be broken and taken over on a *whim*.

Here, Fareed inverts from Sayles's film to Atom's Egoyan's *The Sweet Hereafter*:

> At the very moment where [Nicole] challenges her father for his objectification of her able-bodied self, she refers to herself as 'wheelchair girl'. She recognizes how she outwardly appears, but this does not prevent the girl from declaring her personal strength in front of the man who left her so broken. If anything, the fact pushes Nicole to grow ever more intellectually savvy in her progression into a person in total control of who she is. She inverts a supposed conceptual and physical

limitation into a source of liberation. This empowering gesture is ultimately what we remember of the fiercely willed Nicole. In that sublime moment of the cross examination [at the deposition], where her eyes never break away from her abuser's, we forget her wheelchair. How she so establishes that strength of her singular identity pinpoints how my disability motivates my personal drive. Although Chantelle's co-option of May Alice's wheel chair reminds me of how I might be perceived as purely handicapped, Nicole's astonishing transformation in court cinematically frames my intention to prove that my disability remains but a part of who I am. These heroines reveal how the medium can effortlessly frame an identity faced with a domineering intersection, and the possibility that an arm brace and a not-so-subtle limp can be rendered invisible.

At this point I must disrupt the flow of narrative and briefly return to the discussion on pedagogical autobiography. In Susan Gabel's article, referred to previously, she records a conversation over the phone with a social worker and, subsequently, with her disabled daughter, Tiffany. When she informs the social worker that Tiffany is disabled, the daughter violently protests: 'No! Not me!' (Gabel 2002, 180). Afterwards, Gabel attempts to establish why her daughter, who suffers from *spina bifida*, which limits her movements, her ability to read and count and affects her speech, and who answers positively to her mother's question 'Is it OK that [her mother and other children] have disabilities?', does not see *herself* as a disabled person. At the end of these exchanges, the mother reluctantly says: 'OK, Tiffy. I will have to agree. You are not disabled' (180). Even though, as Gabel later explains, she adhered to the view that social and cultural construction of disability resulted from discrimination against people with impairment/s rather than 'innate individual deficit' (181), her reaction to her daughter's revelation exposed her 'tacit conceptual dissonance' (181).

Disability may signify a self-selected identity or set of meanings. But disability is also a status of oppression, a cultural and social aversion to people with unique embodiments and not an innate deficit. As Gabel aptly points out, 'ability diversity should be considered among other diversities (e.g., race, ethnicity, gender, sexual orientation, culture, etc.)' (2002, 183). In my research, such was the case of a French student, Marine, who draws on *Antonia's Line* and thus begins her narrative:

> First day of high school. As a long repeated choreography, students go around, looking for their class, meeting their friends, talking, laughing . . . the usual. I am among them, without being really part of it, looking around, curious. How is it going to be this year? Finally, the teacher arrives, takes this new group of children to their class. I follow. We enter the class. I sit alone. The traditional welcoming discourse. And the dreaded moment: the list. Checking information, each student

answering the call. A, B, C. . . . M arrives. First language. Second language. '24th of November 1991'. I raise my hand. '91? There must be a mistake'. 28 pairs of eyes look at me. I blush. My tiny voice breaks the silence: 'Euuuhh, no. No it's correct'. Frowning. I have to explain, to justify my presence here. 'I . . . I skipped three classes'. Whispering. If my new classmates had not found some topic to talk about yet, they have now. Just like that I became 'the girl who skipped three classes'. I hate this girl. Of course, she did not arrive out of nowhere, she had evolved. She had skipped one class, first, a second later, and now the third. But this third one made my status as a 'prodigy' official. All year long, I was an outsider within.

Subsequently, she draws an analogy between herself and Thérèse from *Antonia's Line*:

> From her infancy, people repeated [to] her that she was different, that she needed a special treatment. She was 'a prodigy'. At first I was angry to see such a depiction of 'intelligence'. Her will to study, her philosophical aspirations, her gift for mathematics, her difference . . . Therese is what people expected me to be. I was angry because such a depiction comes to strengthen stereotypes. As I grow older, the age difference matters less and less, but I still feel like I need to compensate for it. In my case, my IQ played the role of the ability/disability category, I received special care and attention while I just wanted to be 'normal'.

Out of the selection of films, *A Single Man* garnered most attention as the background material for students' personal narratives. Several of them felt rapport with the movie because of its rendition of sexuality and of the fear that George Falconer talks about when he lectures to his students on his personal rendition of Aldous Huxley's *After Many a Summer Dies the Swan* (1939). He gives a nuanced and very personal monologue about the politics of fear, which has been triggered by the daily news on the Cuban missile crisis. He discusses the theory of invisible people (like himself), the fear of the Jews, and the Communist scare.

Ignacio, a Spanish student, felt a particular rapport with George's situation. He wrote:

> My family is very conservative; they are Catholic with an ancestrality in Opus Dei. The fact of thinking of something sexual was a sin; I grew up with this ideology in my head. It seemed that I was the black sheep of my family. I was afraid that my parents really knew of my sexual orientation. In my town with 20,000 inhabitants at the time, gays or men with feathers were very badly regarded. I remember a guy whom people threw stones at for having ladies manners. In this context, I dared not say anything. . . . The fact of not being lady-mannered has helped me to

pass unnoticed in one of the toughest stages of life, such as childhood
and adolescence. . . . I was 19 when I moved to Granada and I began to
meet many kids who were like me, some still trapped in their homes, in
their villages, and others who had gone out of the closet and lived their
sexual orientation with full normality.

Towards the end of *A Single Man*, just before George Falconer is about to
die of a heart attack, he thinks:

A few times in my life I've had moments of absolute clarity. When for
a few, brief seconds the silence drowns out the noise and I can feel.
Rather than think. Things seem so sharp and the world seems so fresh.
It's as though it had all just come into existence. I can never make these
moments last. I cling to them. But like everything, they fade. I've lived
my life on these moments. They pull me back to the present. And I real-
ize that everything is exactly the way it's meant to be.

These thoughts resonated for a Dutch student, Annemijn. They triggered
memories of a vacation in Spain:

I think that is what the film really was about. . . . [it] gained significance for me personally in that I realized the importance of circumstance, but more importantly of other people as an intersection. . . .
They are the encountering moments with others when I intersect with
them rather than meet them. And the world really does look different,
more colorful, more alive, more beautiful, more in movement than it
does in other moments. . . .

I think that is the reason the moment on top of the hill in Spain came
to me when I was thinking about *A Single Man*, because even though
in that moment I became aware of the insignificance of my life to the
world, my life does have significance for the people around me. And as
a matter of fact, the love of my life . . . was standing behind me looking
at the same view. And she most of the time makes my world turn from
grey to colorful. . . .

George Falconer says that he's lived his life on those moments, that
they pull him back to the present. Even though they fade. I think it is
inevitable that they fade, because as I turned around on the hilltop in
Spain I could see the cars passing by with people in them. And it wasn't
the world anymore, but the cars that were moving. And rather than
both me and the world moving and becoming as I was walking back to
the car it felt like the earth was solid and standing still again and 'I' was
the center of my universe again. For a split second as I am writing this
I think: it would not be so bad to die like George, in a moment when
the silence drowns out the noise and everything is exactly the way it's
meant to be.

These personal accounts narrate very different forms of exclusion and inclusion. While doing this, they challenge prevailing discourses which construct and stigmatise individuals in relation to intersections they embody. It is especially pronounced in reference to disability, but also race, ethnicity, sexuality, etc. Drawn on lived experience, the stories presented here are both personal and political. When pursuing his undergraduate study at Princeton and attending a philosophy course with Peter Singer, Fareed was for the first time in his life 'forced to grapple with who [he was/is] and more disquietingly, with [his] expendability'. Especially gifted Marine had to cope with loneliness and the spotlight that accompanies child prodigies. Ignacio spent his adolescence in fear of disclosure of his sexuality. Although diverse, these are very laden political issues.

CONCLUSION

While writing this chapter I became acutely aware of the difficulties of bringing together the different goals that I had set for myself in terms of theory, methodology, teaching practice and narrative. Most contemporary research is non-narrative and grounded in 'quantitative data and positivist assumptions about cause, effect and proof' (Pinnegar and Daynes 2007, 3). And even when research does use narrative, it is often second-hand and reflects not the voice of the subject (teller) but of the listener (researcher). This poses an epistemological concern with the ethics of representation. Even though my students author their narratives, I am also aware of these pitfalls.

My intention in this chapter has been to demonstrate the ways in which students give structure and value to their lived experience at the time they compose their personal narratives. Writing a personal narrative provides a reflexive realm where we 'show ourselves to ourselves' as we engage in our own dramas (Myerhoff 1982, 104). As Marine writes, 'intersectionality can be used in a positive way, not only as an "interlocking system of oppression" but playing with categories and choosing new ones'. Ignacio ends his narrative on a positive note by appreciating the 'dynamics of [intersectionality] classes because films are a very good avenue to connect to people; music, images and dialogues interact to make people identify with the characters. The fact of writing a personal narrative is also very enriching for the person itself, as it's a social expansion of what you've been silencing for a long time'.

This chapter has addressed subjectivity as lived experience in its physical, political and socio-cultural contexts. The narratives which my students wrote initially as a requirement for the course constituted, as some of their later feedback suggested, manifestos of the diverse ways that culture has permeated their lives. They have made subjectivity more intelligible, and their stories demonstrated awareness of the power of writing. Above all, through their performance of narration they have revealed a dynamic interplay between self and experience.

ACKNOWLEDGEMENT

I am grateful to all the graduate students who participated in my intersectionality classes for their invaluable discussions and written work. I also appreciate their permission to use their insights in this chapter. For financial support during the initial writing of this chapter, I thank the Kościuszko Foundation and Polish Ministry of Science and Higher Education.

NOTES

1. Commercial audience research, which was initiated in Great Britain in the 1930s and 1940s and restricted mainly to participant observation, has now been criticised on several counts, one of them being that it reveals very little about why and how people use mass media. Neither does it analyse the consequences of that use. See Webster, Phalen and Lichty (2006).
2. In Laura Mulvey's scheme, classical American cinema prefers the male perspective of reception both on the narrative level (male plots, strong male characters) and the visual level. The woman in classical film is the object of the 'male gaze'; she constitutes a coded convention—a signifier, and, as such, she represents an ideological meaning only for men. The 'woman as woman' equals visual void, absence, lack (Mulvey 1975).
3. Unlike the usage of ethnography by anthropologists who observe/work with their subjects over a lengthy period of time, Stacey uses the method as it is practiced in audience analysis, i.e. through interviews, letters and questionnaires. I also follow this method in my work with students.
4. See also Sholle (1991, 80–89) and Meers (2001, 134–144).
5. The student refers to a Freudian concept of 'anal personality . . . in connection with gayness. The character of prof Falconer showed by Tom Ford is precisely pedantic, ordering the things in the house in that manner, preparing himself for the suicide with such pedantry and accuracy. Tom Ford directed that brilliantly'. See Freud (1948).

REFERENCES

Anthias, Floya, and Nira Yuval-Davis. 1983. 'Contextualizing Feminism: Ethnic, Gender and Class Divisions'. *Feminist Review* 15:62–75.
Barker, Martin. 2006. 'I Have Seen the Future and It Is Not Here Yet . . . ; or, On Being Ambitious for Audience Research'. *Communication Review* 9 (2): 123–141. Accessed August 23, 2011, at http://cadair.aber.ac.uk/dspace/bitstream/handle/2160/2224/I%20HAVE%20SEEN%20THE%20FUTURE%20AND%20IT%20IS%20NOT%20HERE%20YET.pdf?sequence=1.
Brah, Avtar. 1996. *Cartographies of Diaspora, Contesting Identities*. London: Routledge.
Brewer, Rose M., Cecilia A. Conrad and Mary C. King. 2002. 'The Complexities and Potential Theorizing Gender, Caste, Race, and Class'. *Feminist Economics* 8 (2): 3–18.

Browning, Robert. 1888. *The Pied Piper of Hamelin*. London: Frederick Warne and Co.

Burri, Susanne, and Dagmar Schiek. 2009. 'Multiple Discrimination in EU Law. Opportunities for Legal Responses to Intersectional Gender Discrimination'. European Commission. Directorate General for Employment, Social Affairs and Equal Opportunities.

Campbell, Fiona K. 2005. 'Legislating Disability, Negative Ontologies and the Government of Legal Identities'. In Tremain, S., ed. *Foucault and the Government of Disability*. Michigan, IL: University of Michigan Press.

Cole, Elizabeth R. 2009. 'Intersectionality and Research in Psychology'. *American Psychologist* 64 (3): 170–180.

Collins, Patricia Hill. 1998a. *Fighting Words: Black Women and the Search for Justice*. Minneapolis: University of Minnesota.

———. 1998b. 'It's All in the Family: Intersections of Gender, Race, and Nation'. *Hypatia* 13 (3): 62–82.

Crenshaw, Kimberlé Williams. 1989. 'Demarginalizing the Intersection of Race and Sex: A Black Feminist Critique of Antidiscrimination Doctrine, Feminist Theory, and Antiracist Politics'. *University of Chicago Legal Forum*: 139–167.

Dill, Bonnie Thornton, and Ruth Enid Zambrana, eds. 2009. *Emerging Intersections: Race, Class, and Gender in Theory, Policy, and Practice*. New Brunswick, NJ: Rutgers University Press.

Dossa, Parin. 2009. 'Racialized Bodies, Disabling Worlds'. *Social Science and Medicine* 60 (1): 2527–2536.

Fiske, John. 1992. 'Audiencing: A Cultural Studies Approach to Watching Television'. *Poetics* 21:345–359.

Freud, Sigmund. 1948. *The Standard Edition of Complete Psychological Works of Sigmund Freud*. Translated and edited by James Strachey. London: Hogarth Press.

Gabel, Susan. 2002. 'Some Conceptual Problems with Critical Pedagogy'. *Curriculum Inquiry* 32 (2): 178–201.

Garland-Thomson, Rosemarie. 2005. 'Feminist Disability Studies'. *Signs* 30 (2): 1557–1587.

Grabham, Emily, Davina Cooper, Jane Krishnadas and Didi Herman, eds. 2009. *Beyond Intersectionality. Law, Power and the Politics of Location*. New York: Routledge and Cavendish.

Haskell, Molly. 1973. *From Reverence to Rape. The Treatment of Women in the Movies*. Chicago: University of Chicago Press.

Hawkesworth, Mary. 2003. 'Congressional Enactments of Race-Gender: Towards a Theory of Race-Gendered Institutions'. *American Political Science Review* 97 (4): 529–550.

hooks, bell. 1984. *Feminist Theory. From Margin to Center*. Cambridge, MA: South End Press.

———. 1994. *Teaching to Transgress: Education as the Practice to Freedom*. New York: Routledge.

Huxley, Aldous. 1939. *After Many a Summer Dies the Swan*. New York: Harper & Brothers.

Isherwood, Christopher, 1964. *A Single Man*. Methuen & Co. Ltd.

Jaehne, Karen. 1996. 'Antonia's Line'. *Film Quarterly* 50 (1): 27–30.

Kantola, Johanna, and Kevät Nousiainen. 2009. 'Institutionalizing Intersectionality in Europe'. *International Feminist Journal of Politics* 11 (4): 459–477.

Lather, Patti. 1991. *Getting Smart. Feminist Research and Pedagogy with/in the Postmodern*. New York: Routledge.

Liasidou, Anastasia. 2012. 'Inclusive Education and Critical Pedagogy at the Intersections of Disability, Race, Gender and Class'. *Journal for Critical Education Policy Studies* 10 (1): 168–184.

Livingstone, Sonia. 1998. 'Audience Research at the Crossroads: The "Implied Audience" in Media and Cultural Theory'. *European Journal of Cultural Studies* 1 (2): 193–217.

Lusted, David. 1986. 'Why Pedagogy?' *Screen* 27 (5): 2–14.

Makkonen, L. L. M. Timo, 2002. *Multiple, Compound and Intersectional Discrimination: Bringing the Experiences of the Most Marginalized to the Fore.* Institute For Human Rights, Åbo Academi University.

May, Vivian A., and Ferri, Beth A. 2002. '"I'm a 'Wheelchair Girl Now"'. Abjection, Intersectionality, and Subjectivity in Atom Egoyan's *The Sweet Hereafter'. Women's Studies Quarterly* 30:131–150.

McCall, Leslie. 2005. 'The Complexity of Intersectionality'. *Signs: Journal of Women in Culture and Society* 30 (3): 1771–1800.

Meers, Philipe. 2001. 'Is There the Audience in the House?: New Research Perspectives on (European) Film Audiences'. *Journal of Popular Film and Television* 26 (3): 138–144.

Mulvey, Laura. 1975. 'Visual Pleasure and Narrative Cinema'. *Screen* 16 (3): 6–18.

Myerhoff, Barbara.1982. 'Life History among the Elderly: Performance, Visibility, and Re-Membering'. In *A Crack in the Mirror: Reflexive Perspectives in Anthropology*, edited by J. Ruby, 99–117. Philadelphia: University of Pennsylvania.

Nelson, Camille A. 2011. 'Racializing Disability, Disabling Race: Policing Race and Mental Status'. *Berkeley Journal of Criminal Law* 15 (1): 1–63.

Oleksy, Elżbieta H. 1994. 'The Structure of Kinship. Ellen Glasgow and Zora Neale Hurston'. In *Studies in Literature and Language: In Honour of Adela Styczyńska*, edited by I. Janicka-Świderska, 111–116. Łódź: Łódź University Press.

———. 2007. 'Intricate Interdependencies and Female Buddy Movies'. In *Walking on a Trail of Words. Essays in Honor of Agnieszka Salska*, ed. J. Maszewska and Z. Maszewski, 345–356. Łódź: Łódź University Press.

———. 2011. 'Intesectionality [*sic*] at the Cross-Roads'. *Women's Studies International Forum* 34:263–270.

Pinnegar, Stephinee, and Gary Daynes. 2007. 'Locating Narrative Inquiry Historically: Thematics in the Turn to Narrative'. *Handbook of Narrative Inquiry: Mapping a Methodology*, edited by J. Clandinin. Thousand Oaks, CA: Sage.

Sholle, David. 1991. 'Reading the Audience, Reading Resistance: Prospects and Problems'. *Journal of Film and Video* 43 (1–2): 80–89.

Spencer, Liese. 1996. '*Antonia's Line/Antonia*'. *Sight and Sound* 6 (9): 34–35.

Stacey, Jackie. 1994. *Star Gazing: Hollywood Cinema and Female Spectatorship.* London: Routledge.

Webster, James G., Patricia F. Phalen and Lawrence W. Lichty. 2006. *Ratings Analysis. The Theory and Practice of Audience Research.* Mahwah, NJ: Lawrence and Erlbaum Associates.

14 Intersecting Identities
Young People's Constructions of Identity in South-East Europe

Alistair Ross

INTRODUCTION

This chapter examines a different kind of intersection than that considered elsewhere in this volume: that between potentially conflicting territorial or political identities of the self that arise as young people in Bulgaria and Romania attempt to reconcile their potential memberships of a national community, a regional Balkan identity, and a European identity. The educational implications of this analysis relate to young people in a much wider context than these two south-eastern European countries. At the time of writing, they are the most recent members of the European Union, joining in 2007, but they will have been joined by Croatia by the time this book is published, and very likely within the next four to six years by six or seven other Balkan states. Some of the implications will resonate much more widely than the Balkan peninsular: The tensions of multiple membership of different and nesting political entities, and of being a 'global citizen' are becoming more common and pressing across Europe and beyond.

McCall (2005) describes intersectionality as 'the relationship among multiple dimensions and modalities of social relations and subject formations' (1171). She also interprets the term as encompassing 'perspectives that completely reject the separability of analytic and identity categories' (1171, footnote 1). The traditional axes of identity used in intersectionality (e.g. Crenshaw 1991; Collins 2000; Siltanen and Doucet 2008) were gender and race, to which social class, ethnicity and ability have often been added. Intersectionality theory suggests that social oppression is not based on these factors in a way that is independent of each other, but that they inter-relate and intersect to create multiple forms of oppression and discrimination (e.g. Ritzer 2007).

In this chapter, other potentially intersecting dimensions are added to this. The constructions of identity by young people in south-eastern Europe—in particular in the two Black Sea states of Bulgaria and Romania—are structured in part by dimensions of nationality, regionalism and Europeanisation. These shape, and are shaped by, each other to create a tangled and complex nexus of suppressed or oppressed identities. This 'multidimensional conceptualisation' (Browne and Misra 2003) may help explain how socially constructed categories of difference interact to create a hierarchy of social identities in these young people. Following McCall's (2005) categorisation of approaches to intersectionality, I am here using both intercategorical and intracategorical stances: I both use the existing categorical distinctions of nationality, regionality and Europeanism and at the same time question their utility and relevance in the contemporary context. In doing this, I am simply reflecting the constructions advanced by the young people themselves who, while readily employing these categories, at the same time struggle with the distinctions and contradictions between them. They appear to recognise that they, and their generation, cross the boundaries of constructed categories.

The two countries analysed in this chapter are part of a much larger study of young peoples' constructions of identity in the newer states of Europe that I am conducting. This one-person study, under the aegis of Jean Monnet chair, is an investigation of how young people between twelve and eighteen conceptualise themselves in the changing political circumstances of Europe, and about how they see themselves as different to older generations. I am working in the string of countries that have either joined the European Union in the 2004–2008 expansion (Bulgaria, Cyprus, the Czech Republic, Estonia, Hungary, Latvia, Lithuania, Poland, Romania, Slovakia and Slovenia) or are currently candidate countries to become members (Croatia, Iceland, Macedonia and Turkey). The political status of many of these countries has changed over the past twenty years, from being behind the Iron Curtain to being part of the European Union, or about to join the Union—and in these particular countries, such as Bulgaria and Romania, young people in their teens will be the first generation to be born, and thus wholly socialised, within these new polities.

An individual's civic identity and citizenship has usually been singular, traditionally associated with a defined and exclusive area (Mackenzie 1978). However, this has in many cases become partially eroded through processes such as globalisation, large-scale migration and the development of dual citizenship (Jopkke 2010). Those countries in the European Union now have a citizenship additional to the citizenship of their own country: they are also citizens of the European Union, and this gives them some rights and privileges that are superior to those given by their own country. Identities are increasingly recognised as being both multiple and constructed contingently, and may include a range of intersecting dimensions, including gender, age and region (Lutz, Kritzinger and Skirbekk 2006). How do young people manage to construct these related but different identities? Are there tensions between these constructions, or can they be reconciled (Licata, 2000)? Young people in these countries are attempting this in very different conditions to those experienced by their parents or their grandparents at the same age: Are they conscious of this? Does it make them feel different in any way?

METHODOLOGY

These are complex questions. Rather than use questionnaires or interviews, both of which impose direction and meaning on the subject, I am using focus groups to stimulate discussions on these topics between small groups of young people (Marshall and Rossman 1999). Because this study is of how young peoples' ideas are socially constructed, and because social constructions are created through interaction in a social context, focus groups have the advantages of being able to allow the investigator a modest degree of access to the discourses they may use between themselves, and allowing the young people to an extent to set an agenda for what appears to them to be relevant to their own lives. They are not, of course, wholly free in this: I try to steer the conversation to cover the topics on which I am focusing, although they only discuss and reveal what they choose. I cannot always be sure of the meaning of the terms that they use, and to continually demand explanations would turn the discussion into an interrogation and vitiate the purpose of the focus group. Questionnaires pre-construct conceptualisations, putting words into the mouth of the respondent: I want to hear their own constructs. The discussions I have had are not simply a dialogue, but an interchange that is largely between the young people themselves, in which they use their own vocabulary and structures, not mine. A focus group is not simply a serial semi-structured interview, in which the same question is put in sequence to each member of the group. It is more of a discussion— primarily between the young people themselves—into which I put a number of issues on which to focus. They may be in the form of questions, but they are questions that are clearly structured to indicate that I do not know what the answer might be. I participate in the discussion—sometimes with phatic expressions or with gestures, to keep the conversation going, sometimes with naive requests for explanations, occasionally with a challenge or an assertion that one of them has contradicted themselves—but always in ways that show that I am listening to and respecting their opinions.

I have now conducted almost 160 focus groups, with over 970 young people in fifty different locations in these countries. In each of these locations one to three schools were selected in areas with different social backgrounds, and in most schools there was a group of twelve-to fifteen-year-olds and one of fifteen-to eighteen-year-olds. Permission was sought from the young people and, for those under sixteen, from their parents. The sample is not representative, nor was it intended to be, but it illustrates the diversity of views expressed.

In some countries I have to do this with simultaneous interpretation, particularly with younger age groups. This requires particularly sympathetic translators, well acquainted with the ideas I am seeking to explore: I have been particularly fortunate in having built up a network of colleagues in many of these countries who have helped me do this. The project would not have been possible without help from many people.[1] Schools and parents

Table 14.1 Locations of Focus Groups in Bulgaria and Romania

Bulgaria

Locations	Population	Number of Schools	Number of Groups	Number of Students	Dates of Interviews
Veliko		2	2	12	April 22–23, 2010
Tarnovo	69,000	2	2	15	March 15, 2012
Blagoevgrad	71,000	1	3	19	March 14, 2012
Sofia	1,292,000	2	4	26	March 16, 2012
3		*6*	*11*	*72*	

Romania

Locations	Population	Number of Schools	Number of Classes	Number of Students	Dates of Interviews
Timişoara	307,000	2	4	26	October 11–12, 2011
Oradea	206,000	2	4	25	October 13–14
Iaşi	317,000	2	4	30	October 17–18
Bucureşt	1,930,000	4	4	24	October 19–20
4		*10*	*16*	*105*	

have been recruited, arrangements made for visits and, critically, help given in translating many of the transcripts. With many older groups in both of these countries I was able to work most of the time in English, accompanied by interpreters who help translate particular phrases or vocabulary that presents difficulties. It is not perfect; but it is practical.

I worked in seven locations in these two countries, as shown in Table 14.1.

IDENTITIES IN CONTEXT

I have used two particular frameworks in my analysis of the construction of identities in this analysis of these two countries. Michael Bruter (2005), analysing the emergence of mass European identity, describes territorial identities as having two component elements, the 'civic'—identification with 'the set of institutions, rights and rules that preside over the political life of the community' (12)—and the 'cultural'—identification with 'a certain culture, social similarities, values' (12). This potential dichotomy between civic and cultural Lynn Jamieson and Sue Grundy (2007) describe how some young people 'come to present themselves as passionate utopian Europeans, while for many being European remains emotionally insignificant and devoid of imagined community or steps towards global citizenship' (663).

In addition to these frameworks, I will also raise a couple of specific themes that arose in Bulgaria and Romania that pervaded much of their talk: firstly, a tension between a sense of powerlessness and an assertion of agency in terms of their ability to participate effectively in Romanian society; and, secondly, a profound ambivalence about Romania's location within Europe. Liminality emerges as a defining theme. Many young people in both countries professed elements or quality of ambiguity or disorientation (Turner 1967): they appear conscious of 'standing at the threshold' between their own nationality and Europe, and in some ways to be oppressed, or at least isolated by each of these. The intersection of national identity and European identity created tensions and alienation.

BULGARIA AND ROMANIA: A BRIEF BACKGROUND

It might for some readers be useful at this point to provide a very brief outline of the development of these two states—much of this informs contemporary constructions of identities. The two countries, although neighbours with broadly similar economies, have had very different histories.

Bulgaria has a population of about 7.5 million people and, with a per capita GDP of about €11,200 a year, is the poorest country in the Union—the purchasing power per capita is about 45 per cent of the EU average. Romania has, in European Union terms, a large population of 21.4 million, and with a per capita GDP of about €11,700, it is the second poorest EU country: but it has a large territory (ninth in size in the EU). Both joined the EU in 2007, but neither is a member of the Schengen area or in the Eurozone. Both largely agricultural countries with a predominantly rural population in the late 1940s, by the 1980s had become industrial economies. Following the end of the Communist period (1989–1990) the shock of entering a market economy caused a sharp drop in industrial and agricultural production and economic collapse in the late 1990s. Growth in both countries was strong in the early 2000s, but contracted in 2009; since when growth has been positive, but low. Unemployment is at 7 per cent in Romania and 12 per cent in Bulgaria.

In the tenth century Greater Bulgaria was a large and substantial Balkan power, but then became provinces of the Byzantium Empire. The restored second Bulgarian Empire fell to the Ottomans at the end of the fourteenth century, and it remained part of that empire till 1876, when a poorly organised revolt was easily crushed by Ottoman troops: tens of thousands were massacred. The Russians, considering themselves champions of the Slavs and seeking to expand their hegemony toward the Mediterranean coast, declared war on the Ottomans, liberating most of Bulgaria by early 1878. The consequent Treaty of San Stefano established a large autonomous Bulgarian principality, but the other Great Powers resisted the creation of a Russian client state of this size. The Treaty of Berlin, later in 1878, scaled back the Bulgarian frontier, and carved part of Bulgaria proper into a principality of Rumelia, leaving many ethnic Bulgarians outside the new country and setting Bulgaria on a militaristic approach to foreign affairs.

In 1885 they absorbed Rumelia, and in 1911 they allied with Greece and Serbia to jointly attack the Ottomans and partition Macedonia and Thrace between them. In the First Balkan War of October 1912 these allies took most of Turkey's European territory. Bulgaria tried to seize the largest share, but the Serbs refused to vacate Macedonia: Serbia and Greece formed a new alliance against Bulgaria, who lost the Second Balkan War of 1913 and had to relinquish most of Macedonia to Serbia and Greece. Maps of the boundaries before and after these wars are still on classroom walls in many schools in the Balkan states. In World War I the Bulgarians aligned themselves with Germany and Austria-Hungary (in return for a promise of acquiring Macedonia): they won military victories against Serbia and Romania, and in 1917 defeated Britain, France, Russia and Romania. But anti-war and anti-monarchist sentiment led to the proclamation of a republic in 1918. In the post–World War I settlements, Bulgaria ceded its Aegean coastline to Greece, recognised Yugoslavia (nearly all of Macedonia went to the new state), reduced its army to 1.5 per cent of its previous size and had to pay reparations exceeding $400 million. Bulgarians generally refer to the results of the treaty as the 'Second National Catastrophe'. In the Second World War initial hopes of remaining neutral ended when the German forces demanded passage through Bulgaria in their attack on Greece in 1941. The Bulgarians formally joined the fascist bloc until August 1944, when the Romanians left the Axis Powers and declared war on Germany and allowed Soviet forces to cross its territory to reach Bulgaria.

The Soviet Union occupied the country, which became the People's Republic of Bulgaria, ruled by the Bulgarian Communist Party. After an oppressive Stalinist phase there was from the early 1950s a degree of liberalisation and economic development. Standards of living began to rise, but there was also an assimilation campaign directed against ethnic Turks in the 1980s: some three hundred thousand Bulgarian Turks left for Turkey, and agricultural production slumped. The collapse of Communist regimes in Eastern Europe after the summer of 1989 led to demonstrations in Sofia that became a campaign for political reform. Free elections held in the summer of 1990 were won by the Communist Party, ridden of its hardliner wing and renamed the Bulgarian Socialist Party. In 1991 a new constitution created a parliamentary republic with a directly elected president and a prime minister accountable to the legislature. The 1990s saw several changes of government and massive unemployment as uncompetitive industries failed and the backward state of Bulgaria's industry and infrastructure were revealed (Spirova 2010).

Romania, although like Bulgaria largely Orthodox Christian, has a Romance language that marks the inheritance of the Roman Empire in the second and third centuries. Three principalities of Wallachia, Moldova and Transylvania emerged in the middle ages. Transylvania became an autonomous part of the Hungarian kingdom—there is a substantial Hungarian population still there—whereas Wallachia and Moldavia had a greater degree of independence. By the mid-sixteenth century, all three, and most of Hungary, became Ottoman provinces. But the provinces maintained a large degree of internal autonomy. Transylvania was absorbed by the Hungarians in 1700, and the Russians annexed eastern Moldavia in 1812. Nationalist uprisings in the first half of the nineteenth century against the Ottomans led to the new United Provinces of Wallachia and Moldova in 1859: Transylvania remained with the Austro-Hungarians, who were seen by the Great Powers as a more powerful bulwark against Russian expansion. Romania sided with the Russians in the Russo-Turkish War in 1878 that liberated Bulgaria, gaining some territory as a consequence. Romania joined the Allied forces in 1916 in return for a promise that it would be given Transylvania, which was subsequently agreed at the Treaty of Trianon in 1920, creating *România Mare*: 'Greater Romania'. In the Second World War Romania also initially attempted neutrality, but first Soviet and then Nazi pressures led to Romania joining the Axis powers (loosing Transylvania to the Hungarians and southern Dobruja to the Bulgarians). Romania was a major source of oil for the Axis powers, but the Soviet army moved into Romania in August 1944, and a coup led to Romania changing sides.

The Soviet occupation led to the establishment of a Communist government, and Romania was under direct military occupation and economic control till the late 1950s. The Romanian government used the *Securitate* to eliminate state enemies. Nicolae Ceauşescu came to power in 1965 and pursued policies more independent of the USSR—condemning the invasion of Czechoslovakia in 1968, for example. This led to substantial Western investment, but pressure from the World Bank and International Monetary Fund then led to Ceauşescu reimbursing all foreign debt through policies that impoverished the Romanian people—and reinforced the powers of the police state and his own personality cult. Stan (2010) observed 'of all communist Central and Eastern European countries, Romania remained the least reformed, the most likely to deny basic human rights, and the only one with a sultanist-cum-totalitarian regime right up (to the moment when communism collapsed)' (380).

In December 1989 the Romanian Revolution became the most violent and forceful overthrow of a Communist regime. There were over eleven hundred deaths, including the execution of Ceauşescu and his wife on Christmas day. However, the leaders of the revolution were essentially Communist leaders who were disaffected with Ceauşescu's personality cult. The National Salvation Front took some partial 'original democracy' and liberal marketisation measures, but did not renounce Communism. Romania developed closer ties with Western Europe, joining NATO in 2004, and the European Union in January 2007. Romania has a growing diaspora of about two million people (in Spain, Italy, Germany, Austria, the United Kingdom, Canada and the US) (Stan 2010).

HOW DO YOUNG PEOPLE CONSTRUCT THEIR IDENTITIES?

These histories have a continuing effect on the narratives recounted in school curricula. For the purposes of this study, these events have meant that these young people have had radically different experiences to those of their grandparents and parents. Do young people identify with the cultural and civic aspects of Europe? Do they use the same components in their identification with their country? Are they passionate or indifferent about each? Do they acknowledge a multiplicity of identities, or is their identity singular and essentialist? Does their sense of identity require the construction of 'the Other', an alien identity held in juxtaposition to their own identity? This question is of particular significance to the subjects of this study: As the borders of the European Union continue to demonstrate their flexibility, are there (in the minds of these young people) limits to Europe? Where does the frontier lie?

Focus groups offer a powerful way to address these questions. My opening question challenged them to describe themselves and their identity. What did it mean to them to be Bulgarian or Romanian? How else might they describe themselves, and did they think their parents and grandparents feel this in the same way as them? Did everyone in the country feel the same? I then asked if they sometimes felt European, and how they might describe the characteristics of a 'European'. Finally, I asked them to consider the possible advantages and disadvantages of particular other countries joining the European Union. Could, for example, Russia or Turkey or Serbia become a member of the same club? These countries, as will have become clear, had various historical relationships with each of these two countries.

Analysis of the discussions showed a wide variety of responses, but there were some particularly interesting trends evident. The ways in which they expressed their identification with their own country were often qualified: There were reservations about what were sometimes seen as shortcomings in their compatriots. These in turn made them uncertain about having a sense of European identity: Europeans were thought to have behavioural characteristics that were not (or could not) be matched by Bulgarians or Romanians. They might be members of the European Union, but nevertheless felt that they were accepted on sufferance, and that they were not *really* European—or, at least, not European *yet*. Neither nationals nor Europeans, they were in a liminal borderland situation, neither one thing nor the other. Asking if Russia or Turkey might be thought of as European produced further confusion and possible marginalisation. The intersections of national identity and European identity produced uncertainty.

National Identities

In both countries there was certainly evidence of pride in the country by many young people. This was sometimes simply seen as a natural response to having been born and brought up in the country. For example, Basia K (BG ♀ 17¾) described Bulgaria as 'my native country, it's my home. I feel like I'm in the right place. I want to be here' (her father was a construction worker and her mother unemployed). In Romania, Oana N (♀ 13½) said, 'I have been in many countries, and here I feel like home. There, when I am on the street, I feel very strange'. But Erika I (♀ 16¾), in Timisoara, was not unusual when she said, 'Being Romanian doesn't mean that much to me. I mean this is the country where I was born—but I don't feel related to it. This is my house, but not my home'. Nationality was simply an ascribed characteristic—and not the most important one. Two Bulgarians put this succinctly: 'I think it doesn't matter if we are Bulgarian, or if someone is Turkish . . . the nation doesn't matter, we are all human, and we have to be open to other countries, other nations' (Pavlina P, ♀ 15¾); 'I am proud of being Bulgarian, too, but in these days the nation is just a formality. It doesn't matter where you are born, or where you come from' (Gavril D, ♂ 15½).

These feelings of pride in one's country were related to both history and culture, rather than political institutions and the structures of the state. Particularly in Bulgaria there were references to pride at having survived the 'five centuries' 'under the Turkish yoke'. Borislav T (♂ 16¾) said, 'We have been five hundred years under Turkey, but we had the power to rise and take our country again, after five hundred years, which I think is pretty good thing to do—because five hundred years, for you to keep your nationality alive—this is something big'. But the references to Bulgarian culture sometimes included implicit or explicit recognition of the Ottoman elements within this, as when Vladislav P (♂ 12½) talked of 'Bulgarian traditions are some of the most colourful—their songs and their food—and *ayran* is very good',[2] or when Valentin P (♂ 16½) referred to the culture as 'really interesting, because we're right on the border of Europe and Asia, and we have something from both cultures'. There were as many references to historical pride in Romania, such as Daniela D (♀ 17½): 'Being Romanian means having a certain respect for the historical people, and I'm very proud that, after several wars and fights with other powers, we managed to be all right in the end, even if we are not as good as the other countries'.

The second major area of national pride in both countries was in the natural landscape and the flora and fauna. But this was frequently qualified with references to how some of their compatriots' disregard the environment, and pollution and littering were often mentioned. In Bulgaria, Arnost M (♂ 12¾) said, 'Pollution is everywhere—all the people throw their waste on the roads. In the forests they cut down trees, and they just destroy the nature in Bulgaria'. And in Romania Silvia P (♀ 16) said, 'We do not know how to appreciate [the country]—to preserve this, not to throw garbage on the streets'.

In parallel to expressions of positive feelings for the country were widespread criticisms of the way in which Bulgarians and Romanians behaved. In both countries there were many ad hominem comments that 'people' (a term that apparently did not include the young people in the discussion groups) had ways of thinking (often 'a mentality') that was selfish, anti-social or simply old-fashioned. Thus Mircea D (♀ 16¼), a worker's daughter in western Romania, said, 'Sometimes you are ashamed of being Romanian, because other people do all kinds of unpleasant things'. Fellow citizens often behaved badly, especially those working abroad, and the Roma minority were particularly criticised in Romania (less so in Bulgaria). In both countries, politicians were criticised as self-serving and often corrupt. These factors, they said, led to their countries being perceived badly by members of other European states. The following paragraphs examine each of these assertions in turn.

In both countries there were complaints that people were inclined to talk about problems, rather than actively seek solutions. In Bulgaria, Branimir B (♂ 16¾) said he was 'not proud that Bulgarians talk, but they don't take action when they . . . don't like something'. People were selfish, and there were popular expressions about this: in Romania, Ionut M (♂ 14¼) said, 'They care only if my dog dies, the neighbour's dog should die, too', whereas in Bulgaria, Borislav T (♂ 16¾) said that 'we look at the other [person]'s plate. If I have a problem, I want my neighbour to [have one], too. . . . There is a pot in hell full of Bulgarians—nobody can get out of it, because each person pulls down the others'.

There was, they claimed, a common disregard for civil rights: Nikolai C (BG ♂ 15½) said, 'We don't search for our rights—in other countries, you see something that you don't like, you . . . tell the police and they take the case—problem solved. But in Bulgaria you just close your eyes to it, and don't pay any attention to what happened'. Izabela U (RO ♀ 16) said (in a rare reference to gender equality) that 'in Romania that the men are seen as more important than the women—the man defines the place'.

Several Romanians said that their compatriots were feckless. Ionut M (♂ 14¼): 'my country . . . has people who are like sheep. They follow each other, they do as their neighbours'. Gabi B (♂ 11½) said, 'People in

Romania . . . want to finish work too soon, to work less'. Bulgarians were said to have antiquated patterns of thinking: When Daniel B (♂ 16½) said, 'I think our thinking is old. We are not open-minded enough', Ventsislav K (♂ 16½) offered an explanation 'about old-fashioned thinking . . . this is because we have been slaves for about five hundred years—this is why we are not so modern and open-minded'.

In Romania, the Roma minority in particular were criticised, and there was some indignation that this community had appropriated the term 'Roma': Several said that the Roma were not Romanian. Lucian S (♂ 12¾) asserted that 'the Gypsies are harsh and they mug you and try to do a lot of bad things'. Nina A (♀ 14¾) said that they 'were not Romanian, they are different from the Romanian people—they are their own nationality. Europeans make this confusion, that Romanians and Gypsies are the same'. 'Our reputation is very low because the Gypsies who are born in Romania have Romanian passports—they are not really Romanians', Dumitru D (♂ 14¼) explained. Even expressions of sympathy were constructed through terms of 'othering' and blame: Jean R (♂ 17½) 'the Gypsies . . . don't realise that they are the ones who trigger that attitude from us, because they are the ones who have misconduct'. In Bulgaria, attitudes appeared rather different: speaking of minorities within the country, Nikola A (♂ 16) said, 'Some ethnic groups which are isolated from the social life of Bulgarian . . . society—they won't feel as patriotic as the not-isolated Bulgarians—Gypsies, Turkish, [those] kind of people'. Anti-Roma feeling was associated with older generations: Aleksandar C (♂ 13¾) said his 'grandfather thinks that all the problems in Bulgaria come from the Gypsies and marginal groups', to which Teodor T (♂ 13½) added, 'the Roma are not bad people—I [think] . . . that it's people from all groups who make problems—the problem isn't just in this group'.

In both countries, politicians were criticised as self-serving and often corrupt. In Bulgaria, Toma S (♂ 12½) said, 'Politicians are liars. . . . most Bulgarians don't like Bulgaria because of the government'. Anton L (♂ 17¾) said, 'they stole assets', and Bogdan G (♂ 13) that 'the president or the prime minister . . . say they will do something about the problems, but do nothing, just get votes and take the money'. In Romania, Cosmin L (♂ 13¾) claimed, 'The government simply destroys everything. The people . . . hate the government, but they keep voting for the same rubbish leaders, again and again'. Corruption was mentioned frequently: Marian T (♂ 15¾) was 'very concerned about corruption—in Romania there is a lot . . . especially at a high level'. And Ana P (♀ 13½) said, 'President Băsescu has I don't know how many houses! All our money is in their pockets, and nobody does anything about it'. In Bulgaria, Sergei S (♂ 16) complained, 'What pisses me off is that we see corruption at the lower levels—there is a corruption everywhere, but in other countries it's at the higher levels and people don't see it'.

These behavioural characteristics were all seen as contributing to the poor perception of their countries by members of other European states.

This was sometimes based on personal experiences, or those of family members: Abela F (♂ 14¾), from Romania, said she 'went to France for a summer vacation—I spoke with my parents in Romanian, and everyone was looking at us in the metro like this [arms crossed across front to guard wallet, bags, etc]—with their bag and that—being Romanian these days isn't very nice, because we are seen as thieves, Gypsies and so on'. Milenka P (BG ♀ 13¾) described how her brother 'has been living in Germany for about seven years, and he says that when he says he's a Bulgarian he's treated not as a person'. Some were aware of negative media attention: In Bulgaria there were references to a recent right-wing Netherlands political party's website that had been making derogatory comments about Bulgarians: Toma S (♂ 12½) said that as a consequence, people in the Netherlands 'when they hear Bulgarian they think "Oh, this is rubbish", because our reputation in Europe is very, very bad'.

These comments were frequently tinged with expressions of a sense of powerlessness, that they lacked the agency to affect society and politics. In Romania, Olga M (♀ 16) said, 'We don't have the power to change . . . we've tried to change the president and to encourage our parents to vote for someone else—but it's still the same—men want power, and when they have it, they make use of it'. And Amelia S (♀ 16.0) felt, 'We cannot make any changes because of the bad things, and the bad systems have very deep roots'. There were also assertions that they could make an impact: Amelia S also said, 'We are responsible, being Romanian. We have our rights and responsibilities, and we have to improve the situation—not only ours, but the others around us', and Basia K (♀ 17¾) said, 'The future of Bulgaria is in our hands, our generation's'—to which Ivana P (♀ 17¾) retorted, 'Yes—but if you go abroad, you will not change anything'. This issue, of young people wanting to migrate from Bulgaria or Romania, was divisive. Borislav T (BG ♂ 16¾) explained that 'there are two types of people of our age now—people who want to leave, who don't want to live here and think that if they go abroad they will have a better life—and people who are proud of being Bulgarian, who love the country and want to stay. I think the first kind is bigger—a lot of people want to leave'. This group was exemplified by the comments of Fidanka M (♀ 16)—'I don't think that Bulgaria will provide me with a good job, because the payment is very low . . . I have ambitions to work in Europe. Or in America', and of Anelie V (♀ 16¾)— 'maybe in the future I won't live here—I don't like the country'.

These young peoples' identification with Bulgaria and Romania respectively appears to be strong on the cultural side: There were many expressions of affection for the country. But this was a feeling of warmth, rather than of chauvinism. There were very few remarks that could be construed as nationalistic, and a number that were explicitly non-nationalistic or showing sympathy for a more global identification. But there was also a pervasive critical element about aspects of Bulgarian and Romanian behaviour, and references to outdated 'ways of thinking' and to conduct that they thought inappropriate. Generally there were few references to the institutions of either state, apart from historical references to independence.

European Identities

This sense of uncertainty and diffidence about their construction of a national identity was paralleled in the European sphere. A European identity was acknowledged by some, but a sense of distance, of hesitancy, about 'being part of Europe' was more commonly articulated. Most saw European identity as distinctly subordinated or secondary to their sense of being Romanian or Bulgarian. Thus Mihail B (RO ♂ 15¾) said he felt 'more Romanian than European—I don't really have the thought of being European that often'. Others said that they were European simply in the geographical sense: Nikola A (BG ♂ 16) said that 'every country that is in the territory of Europe, every nationality, should feel European . . . it doesn't matter if it's in the European Union or not—we're all European, even though some countries aren't as advanced as Germany, Italy, those kind of countries'. Vladimär M (BG ♂ 13½) said, 'I don't think we *should* feel European—we *are* in Europe, on the continent'. For others, it was simply a consequence of European Union membership that made them European: so Todor R (BG ♂ 14) asserted, 'We are surrounded by Europe. We are part of the European Union, and we became [a member] in 2008'.

But many of these and similar expressions concerned Bulgaria or Romania as a country being European, rather than being individual feeling of a European identity. Many suggested that they might, as Romanians or Bulgarians, be European in a titular sense, but that in reality this was not accepted by 'the Europeans' themselves. Others said that they did include a European dimension in their identity, but they were also aware of being rebuffed in this. 'They' were constructed as something different from 'us' and Europeanism was to be defined on 'their' terms. Consequently, some of these young people felt that Europe had rejected them—or at least, had not accepted them (as in the example of the Netherlands in the preceding). So Abela F (RO ♂ 14¾) said, 'In the registers, they say we are, we are Europeans—but I don't feel like it', and Loredana Z (♀ 13¼) said, 'I feel European, but the other people in Europe discourage us'. How could Romanians feel European, asked Anatolie U (♂ 13½), if everyone in the other European countries 'says that we shouldn't be in the European Union, and that we don't deserve to be?'

There was a sense that 'being European' meant either belonging to a more developed economy or to having a different culture and mentality. In Bulgaria, Rada V (♀ 15½) simply said that 'the other countries in Europe are much more advanced than us', and Fidanka M (♀ 16) said she found it 'a little hard to feel like Europeans, because there are some big differences between the Bulgarians and some European countries'. In Romania, Mirela B (♀ 16¾) claimed that to be European 'means being part of a developed country, being respected'. Being a European meant behaving in a particular (and non-Bulgarian) way for Teodor T (♂ 13½): 'I feel Bulgarian when I see someone throwing trash in the streets; I feel European when I make him pick it up and put it in the bin'. Europeans were in some way better able, or more likely, to follow social rules. Although the examples often given were of throwing litter on the street, there was a sort of bystander response (Darley and Latané 1968): Bulgarians and Romanians would not follow rules (the young people said) unless everybody else followed them. Vladimär M (BG ♂ 13½) suggested that 'maybe their [i.e. European's] rules make them different from other people . . . they are actually trying to do something', and Elisaveta M (♀ 16½) said, 'It's a question of our thinking . . . maybe they [Europeans] keep with the rules, because here in Bulgaria we are always saying, "why should I do it, because the person next to me isn't doing it?"'

In particular, 'Europeans' were held to have a different mind-set, a different 'mentality' to the Bulgarians and Romanians. Anelie V (BG ♀ 16¾) said, 'I don't feel like a European person . . . everyone thinks only for themselves, out of self-interest'. For Elisaveta M (BG ♀ 16½), 'it's not about how we feel; it's about our thinking'; Borislav T (♂ 16¾) echoed this—'our thinking is not like theirs. . . . people from Europe [are] better in the things [they] do . . . much better mannered . . . better-educated people'. Olga M (♀ 12) talked at length about striving to be European and to be different: 'Bulgaria in some ways doesn't let me be a European, because I don't always think before I act . . . that's why I want to be a European someday. . . . Europe is different because of its culture and its heritage—people in Europe are more self-aware'.

Europe was 'over there' in the West, a different place where they behaved differently and in what was seen as a more 'civilised' way. Vladislav P (BG ♂ 12½) explained that 'to be European . . . you must behave like a European, and Bulgarians don't behave like this . . . Europeans behave very well, they are polite to shop assistants—some Bulgarians are rude to them; and in European countries everyone has manners'. Dumitru D (RO ♂14¼) also felt that 'they [Europeans] are not too different from us, but they have a higher intelligence level than we have—and they are more civilised'.

It seems that what ran through many of these comments was a sense of not feeling fully European, or fully European *yet*. For some, this was simply a matter of material progress: Borislaw A (BG ♂ 12½) said that in Greece he had seen little pollution and well-made streets—'it makes people have a European sense. In Bulgaria we have the opposite—so we are not Europeans'. Gala I (♀ 13¾) said she 'would feel European if we could end the problems that are affecting our parents; the lack of work'. Europe was thus, in a sense, elsewhere, not to be found in this part of the world. Vlad P (♂ 17¼) spoke of Romanian culture as Eastern European: 'in the Balkan regions there are very powerful Slavic influences'; for him, the heart of Europe was in Western Europe—'the bedrock of Europe, so to speak—it has achieved some degree of cultural dominance'. Madalina B (RO ♀ 16¼) referred to Europe as 'in Finland and those countries, they are more civilised and organised'.

There was a sense of liminality, of being on the border of being European and perhaps of anticipation of the potential to cross that frontier. Toma S (♂ 12½) said, 'I don't think we are Europeans *yet*. . . . The country is not really European, because it's not improved to a European level, so it's not European yet'. Nikolai C (♂ 15½) put it this way: 'We've been through bad times . . . that's why it's a bit harder for us to accept ourselves as part of Europe'. Valentin P (BG ♂ 16½) said, 'I think that in five, ten years' time we will say that we are European'. Both Romanian and Bulgarian young people had a view that their countries were marginal to Europe and marginalised by Europe. They seem aware that they may be on the threshold of some new, European way of political and cultural expression (Thomassen 2009). In a period of liminality social hierarchies are in flux, traditions may become indeterminate and the future of these young people see for themselves is fluid and uncertain (see Horvath, Thomassen and Wydra 2009).

A few instead—or as well—asserted an alternative Balkan identity: Sergei S (♂ 16) is typical of these: 'I mostly feel like a man from the Balkans, not so much a European because we have a different structure here, in our thinking. I don't feel like a person of my age from England or France, for example—we have a lot of differences—but a guy from Serbia or Montenegro, I think I'd be similar to him'. Europe was somewhere else, said Gogu G (RO ♂ 14¼)—it was 'Germany, France, Italy, Spain—a lot of countries. I guess it's about us, and maybe the Bulgarians—we didn't take advantage of being in the European Union until now. . . . They have another way of thinking—they think differently to us'.

Europe was thus for some of these young people a problematic construct. It was in some senses a desirable attainment, but as yet not achieved, and at the same time had an exclusiveness that meant that they felt rejected. Europe was thus seen partly as cultural—something that Bulgarians and Romanians 'ought' to share, but of which there was some uncertainty, and also to do with something described as 'behaviour', which seemed to encompass activities from financial probity to being conscious not to litter the streets, where it was felt that they fell short. But Europe was seen also as institutional, and here there was a greater sense of focus and of anticipation. Yet Europe, in an emotional sense, remained distant, cut off partly by the attitude of 'other' Europeans to them, partly by their own distrust of their 'mentality'.

Constructions of European Identities and of the Boundaries of Europe

These constructions were given a different twist when groups were asked to consider the possibility of particular other potential partners in the European Union. I asked them first to consider the possibility of Russian membership and then Turkey: Both countries have played significant roles in their countries' histories. Instead of presenting short quotations from different groups, I now present some longer extracts from a single group in Iaşi, Romania.

Asked if they felt that they might consider themselves as European, Cristian T ($\male$ 16½), son of a builder and a postal delivery worker, said:

> No, I don't think so. Because we can't compare ourselves to European countries like Germany, England, France, Spain, maybe—we aren't in the same bracket.

I asked if Romania was part of the European Union:

Cristian T: Technically. On paper.
Beryx D ($\male$ 16, parents booksellers):
                 Up till now, I've never felt that I'm European . . . and if I felt it, I never got help from anybody—nothing changed.

Several minutes later, I asked how Europeans were different from other people:

Cristian T: A sort of breed of efficient people—and wealthy countries—that's about it. Yes, you must have something in common to create a union. You don't have a culture in common, so what remains in the industry? The economy.
Beryx D: In Europe, most countries are at the same level—for example, in Germany, if someone has a problem—let's say an incurable disease—the state helps him—gives him money, gives him a place to stay . . . In Romania, no one helps you, you remain on the streets. It's not the same, even if we are in Europe. No one helps us.

And then, further into the discussion, I introduced the idea of Russian membership of the European Union.

Cristian T: I think they can't [join] because if we look at the history, they always did different. While we have economic downturns, they register 400 per cent increases, and being such a big country—sort of hungry for more land, for more power—they wouldn't cooperate well with the European Union. They . . . I don't see them as people who can obey rules very easily, and have common sense.
Andrei M ($\male$15¾ , father an engineer):
                 I also think that it's not possible . . . countries that [become] a member of the European Union should be those on the European continent.

AR:	I'm interested in what you said about Russia being different from. . . . . from whom? From Europe, or from Romania?
Cristian T:	I think from Europe because we try to be sort of politically correct here, and they don't really—they have a sort of—We, we Europeans as well—especially you British people—have a history, a habit, of exploiting underdeveloped countries, colonies and so on. But they have a bigger habit of doing this, and a more recent habit of doing it.
AR:	Do you agree with what Cristian T says?
Several:	Yes, yes.
AR:	I'm going to press you on this—because you're now talking about 'we Europeans'—
Cristian T:	Aghr! [exasperation at being caught out, and recognition of what he's said]
AR:	But before you said that you didn't feel European. Can you explain this sort of thinking?
Cristian T:	Yes, yes, I know . . . as a mentality, as a country, I think of us being exactly in the middle—I think we incline to be more European-ish than Russian. We, we evolved towards the European, I think.

When the possibility of Turkish membership was introduced, Andreai M was in favour, despite it being located on two continents, but now Cristian T argued that 'Russia is much more European' [geographically]. Andreai T agreed: 'Well, yes, Russia is much more European because their people are more like us, they even look more like us—Turkish people, they have a different colour of their skin'; to which Emil V ($\male$ 14½) retorted, 'The culture isn't that different'.

Identities at this point become contingent and multiple. Compared with the European Union states, Romania (and, to a lesser extent, Bulgaria) are seen as outside the group. Compared with Russia, both countries moved across the border and became European. Many in Bulgaria were less opposed to potential Russian membership: Some felt that all countries that were in Europe, or even partly in Europe, should become members, whereas others perceived Russia as a rich and powerful state that would help the Bulgarian economy. But there were also references of cultural and historical affinities and divergences: Violeta G ($\female$ 12¼) said, 'We have almost a common language', whereas Olga ($\female$ 12) thought, 'Russians and Europeans are different, maybe that difference would make them feel uncomfortable. . . . Not only the culture, but the way the people think, the way the people act'.

For some of the Bulgarians, Turkey was a particular issue: Ventsislav K ($\male$ 16½) argued, 'I don't think I would like it if Turkey joined—I don't really like them that much, because we've been their slaves for five hundred years'—to which Vladimära G ($\female$ 16¾) replied, 'It's a different generation, and we are not slaves any more, and it doesn't matter that we have been under them for five hundred years'. Similarly, Petar S ($\male$ 13¾) argued, 'What happened between Turkey and Bulgaria was a long time ago—in the same way it happened in World War II with Germany and the whole world—nowadays Germany and the other countries are friendly with each other, and so, I think Turkey and Bulgaria should be the same'. Several Bulgarians argued that Turkey was too different culturally, and in doing so (as with Cristian T in Romania) re-orientated their own sense of being European. Thus Valentin P ($\male$ 16½, parents own a small company) initially said that when he went to other European countries, 'I feel a bit different from them, and not like [a] typical European', but later he said, 'When I went to Turkey, I felt European; when I saw their culture and how they live—the culture is different than ours, and I felt European there, because it was different . . . For Turkey to become a member of the Union—their culture is very different, and I don't know how they will reconcile their culture and religion . . . I don't think they will feel European'. There appeared that, particularly in comparison to Turkey, that there *was* a European culture and one that Bulgarians might possibly share. A European culture was initially questioned, and sometimes denied, but sometimes followed by a recognition that—when Turkey could be 'othered'—there was a common culture with other Europeans.

SOME TENTATIVE CONCLUSIONS

Bulgaria and Romania present an interesting paradigm in studies of the new Europeans. These young people present not just multiple identities, but a confusion of multiple identities: proud of Bulgaria or Romania, but sometimes rejecting it—their country could be modern, prosperous and 'European', but also had a people whose 'ways of thinking' condemned the country to be marginalised, relatively impoverished and unchanging. Theirs was a country in which they could perhaps think that they might live and work in for the future, but also a country that they should leave, perhaps permanently; marginalised in Europe, but also integral to Europe and at one with it in terms of modernity and outlook; in close cultural harmony with their parents and grandparents, but also on the threshold of a new generational attitude. They were insiders and outsiders.

These constructions strain both Bruter's (2005) and Jamieson and Grundy's (2007) models of European identity. Were they attached to cultural or to institutional aspects of their country or of Europe? In some ways, they were detached from both. Neither Bulgarian nor Romanian institutions of government were a focus for identification: but there was also a sense of bipolarity about the culture of their country. Aspects like the natural beauty, the history and the past were strong themes around which rapport was established, but there was ambivalence about the cultural traits of the respective peoples, a sense of distancing themselves from the way that 'Bulgarians thought' or 'Romanian thinking'. Passionate enthusiasm or indifference? Both were evident, often expressed by the same individual. There were similar paradoxical relationships with Europe: Whereas the institutional structures were welcomed—the mobility, the prospects of study abroad, the financial support for the country and sometimes the emphasis on rights—the degree to which there was an *identification* with this is less clear. The same is true of the cultural and behavioural aspects of Europeans. In both cases these were admired, but not fully participated in: partly because of their compatriots own behaviour. Romania and Bulgaria became liminal, territories on the border of Europe. But when the lens was shifted to examine states beyond the European Union, then institutional and cultural affinities with Europe moved to the fore: Indifference became sometimes a more ardent attachment.

The implications of this for educational settings will become increasingly important for Western European countries, as these two countries join the Schengen area in 2014. From that year there will be free movement of labour from these countries, and there are anticipations that, as in the European expansion of 2004, there will be reasonably substantial numbers of workers and their families arriving in Britain, France and Germany in particular. Romania in particular has a relatively large population. Many schools will have pupils from these countries: Young people who will feel a strong sense of inferiority when they compare themselves with the 'real' Europeans who constitute their classmates. Unlike many previous children who have migrated from other European backgrounds, these young people will have no strong sense of national identity, other than an affection for the natural beauty of their countryside. This ambivalence may make itself apparent in various ways, but they are likely to be particularly vulnerable to criticisms or aspersions about their country of origin, being conscious of being stereotyped disadvantageously. At the same time, they will be disorientated by the diversity of the societies they now find themselves in: With a well-developed sense of social and national gradations and hierarchies, they may try to position themselves above some other migrant groups (and perhaps particularly to Roma or Traveller peers), using terms and attitudes that many teachers and other pupils will find difficult and problematic, even racist. It will require particular sensitivity to understand and react positively to their constructions of themselves as liminal beings, uncertain of how their mix of identities socially positions them in their new home.

NOTES

1. I am particularly grateful to (Bulgaria): Katia Christova, Evelina Kelbetcheva, Katya Simeonova, Galia Slavcheva and Mirela Vasilva, and (Romania) Ciprian Ceobanu, Carmen Ceobanu, Magda Ciubancan, Magda Danicu, Carmen Dutu, Alin Gavreliuc, Aurora Goia, Tudor Iordachescu, Simona Laurian, Elena Mazareanu, Eleana Mitu, Monica Oprescu and Monica Secui; also the

heads/principals of the schools and the students, and at London Metropolitan University, colleagues in IPSE, particularly Angela Kamara.

2. *Ayran*: a cold beverage of yogurt mixed with cold water and sometimes salt;
it is popular in many Central Asian, Middle Eastern and south-eastern
European countries.

REFERENCES

Browne, Irene, and Joya Misra. 2003. 'The Intersection of Gender and Race in the
Labor Market'. *Annual Review of Sociology* 29:487–513.

Bruter, Michael. 2005. *Citizens of Europe? The Emergence of a Mass European
Identity*. London: Palgrave Macmillan.

Collins, Patricia. 2000. 'Gender, Black Feminism, and Black Political Economy'.
Annals of the American Academy of Political and Social Science 568:41–53.

Crenshaw, Kimberlé. 1991. 'Mapping the Margins: Intersectionality, Identity
Politics, and Violence against Women of Color'. *Stanford Law Review* 43 (6):
1241–1299.

Darley, John & Latané, Bibb. 1968. 'Bystander intervention in emergencies: Dif-
fusion of responsibility'. *Journal of Personality and Social Psychology* 8:
377–383.

Horvath, Agnes, Bjørn Thomassen and Harald Wydra. 2009. 'Introduction: Liminality and Cultures of Change'. *International Political Anthropology* 3:3–4.

Jamieson, Lynn, and Sue Grundy. 2007. 'European Identities: From Absent-Minded
Citizens to Passionate Europeans'. *Sociology* 41 (4): 663–680.

Joppke, Christian. 2001. *Citizenship and Immigration*. Cambridge: Polity.

Licata, Laurent. 2000. 'National and European Identities: Complementary or
Antagonistic?' Paper presented at the ID-NET conference, European University
Institute, Florence, Italy, June 9–10.

Lutz, Wolfgang, Sylvia Kritzinger and Vegard Skirbekk. 2006. 'The Demography
of Growing European Identity'. *Science* 314: 425.

Mackenzie, William. 1978. Political Identity. Harmondsworth: Penguin.

Marshall, Catherine, and Gretchen Rossman. 1999. *Designing Qualitative
Research*. 3rd ed. London: Sage.

McCall, Leslie. 2005. 'The Complexity of Intersectionality'. *Journal of Women in
Culture and Society* 30 (3): 1771–1800.

Ritzer, George. 2007. *Contemporary Sociological Theory and Its Classical Roots:
The Basics*. Boston, MA: McGraw-Hill.

Siltanen, Janet, and Andrea Doucet. 2008. *Gender Relations in Canada: Intersectionality and Beyond*. Oxford: Oxford University Press.

Spirova, Maria. 2010. 'Bulgaria since 1989'. In *Central and Southeast European
Politics since 1989*, edited by Sabrina Ramet, 401–420. Cambridge: Cambridge
University Press.

Stan, Lavinia. 2010. 'Romania in the Shadows'. In *Central and Southeast European Politics since 1989*, edited by Sabrina Ramet, 379–400. Cambridge: Cambridge University Press.

Thomassen, Bjørn. 2009. 'The Uses and Meanings of Liminality'. *International
Political Anthropology* 3:51.

Turner, Victor. 1967. *The Forest of Symbols*. Ithaca, NY: Cornell University
Press.

15 Conclusions

Uvanney Maylor and Kalwant Bhopal

> It is through intersectionality that we may be able to consider our intersubjectivities; that the categories through which we are defined are interlocked in constant negotiation; and that who we are is never a pre-given reality, but constructed, performed, enacted, and filtered through structured discursive formations. (Collins 2000, 1)

Educational inequalities and oppression are inherent in capitalist and post-colonial societies (Brah and Phoenix 2004; Mirza and Joseph 2012). Through the three themes—difference, diversity and inclusion—this book has aimed to examine new insights and widen understanding about the different and complex ways in which educational inequalities are encountered by students and staff employed in schools and higher education institutions in Australia, Europe, Guatemala, New Zealand, the UK and the US. The collection highlights difficulties and challenges in understanding the dynamics of educational inequalities in schools and higher education experienced in national, international and cross-national contexts.

New insights and knowledge about student and teacher narratives are informed by critical race, feminist, postcolonial, community and narrative theories/discourses. These critical theoretical frameworks/methodologies allow us to:

i). examine the tensions between educational (in)equality,

ii). examine the struggles encountered amongst marginalised groups in gaining a voice and recognition in schools and higher education, and

iii). challenge the taken-for-granted Western normative assumptions about minority ethnic groups and their perceptions of and approach to education.

The collection has shown how staff and student experiences are differently configured in relation to multiple identity positionings ('race', gender, sexuality, dis/ability, class, sexuality, local and national) and along complex configurations of culture, community and historical and socially located power relations, unequally experienced by majority and minority communities. These identity positions are further interconnected by location (the rural and the urban), a sense of place and notions of belonging at community, local, national and international levels.

Clearly, educational inequalities (impacted by identities unknown, ignored and/or excluded) are experienced not just along the axes of gender and ethnicity/'race' or 'race' and class, or gender and class, but through the intersectionality of gender, 'race', class, sexuality, disability and culture at macro and micro levels in particular contexts. The collection recognises that identity differences (including those which are sometimes invisible and hidden, e.g. sexuality) need to be considered together, rather than as disparate factors. It is the nature of how diverse intersectionalities collide and interact with educational structures, policies, practices and discourses and the effects of such collisions/interactions, which need to be understood, otherwise, as Crozier suggests, 'hierarchies of oppression and racialised, classed and gendered antagonisms' will be used to account for the continuing educational inequalities encountered by students and increasingly ethnically diverse staff in schools and higher education globally.

The text illustrates how schools and higher education institutions at a global level are informed by and operate through 'whiteness' (the lens of White middle-class perspectives), and through which educational inequalities are reinforced. It is this worldview (of those already privileged) which is 'taken as the only reality' (Delpit 1995, xv) in educational discourses. What this collection shows is that there are other equally salient realities which are often overlooked (sometimes through ignorance rather than blatant disregard) in educational institutions and discourses, through the policies and practices adopted in normalising, naturalising and underlining White middle-class privilege and power. This is clearly demonstrated amongst upper middle-class White (Swedish) male students as outlined by Nyström's chapter, which demonstrates those who are doubly if not triply privileged have the ability to access and negotiate educational resources through contentions of 'superior ability' and normalised 'effortless high achievement'.

In order to understand educational inequalities and how they differentially affect majority and minority ethnic groups, we need to foreground an understanding of whiteness, White privilege and power and how such power masks the extent of inequalities suffered by minority ethnic groups, but also serves to strengthen and maintain educational inequalities in schools and higher education. For Leonardo, interrogating the category of whiteness and White power becomes essential if minority ethnic communities are to be included in educational settings and discourses, and if inequalities are to be effectively addressed, and eradicated.

As there is a lack of understanding of how White 'race' privilege and power (in reinforcing privilege) as Leonardo, Crozier, Henderson, Pio et al. and other writers in the collection have argued, the influences on educational inequalities for students and staff from ethnically diverse backgrounds are often misunderstood, let alone recognised. The same is true of White minority identities. Regardless of class background, White students are assumed to have White privilege (although in the case of the White working class this may be less recognised or acknowledged) and because the majority of teachers in school (e.g. in the UK, the USA and Europe) are White, they homogenise White students, so that White minority identities can also become invisible and/or unintentionally marginalised (see Maylor 2010). Such complexity is conveyed by Ross's examination of the local, national and 'European' identities of Bulgarian and Romanian youth, who themselves are hesitant about their own (and changing) racial identities, and the place/value of those identities in Europe which is itself constantly being redefined with new meanings and notions of belonging attributed. Their situated liminal identities (Balkan, non-European and a future European identity as yet to be defined) characterised by tradition, history, generationalism, current experiences, conflicts and contradictions aptly illustrates Hall's (1993) contention that identities rather than being fixed are 'a matter of "becoming" as well as of "being"' (394). With the expansion of European borders leading to more ethnically (but less visibly) diverse classrooms, teachers may fail to acknowledge such difference and/or be unwilling to acquire relevant knowledge to support students with different identities; it is probable that such classroom settings will result in the amplification of White minority students experiencing further educational inequalities. Whereas this particular example focuses on White minority ethnic identities, Ross's chapter provides a useful way to think about the ways in which non-White student identities and the intersectionality of those identities, are homogenised in the classroom, and as a consequence are either ignored, undervalued or undermined in teaching and learning, resulting in further educational inequality experienced by non-White students.

Henderson demonstrates how even though Australian teacher discourses acknowledge the interrelationship between ethnicity, gender and itinerancy, they nevertheless reduce itinerant children's lower performance in literacy to one of class, whilst ignoring teacher discourses and school processes which serve to undermine the literacy attainments of children with itinerant lifestyles. Similarly, it is class as articulated by Bourdieu and Passeron (1994) which is considered to account for both the under/achievement of Black students in the UK; an argument more recently challenged by Strand (2012) and Vincent et al. (2012).

Rhamie draws attention to the possibility (and reality) of Black educational success (Wright, Standen and Patel 2010), and provides a more nuanced understanding of the ways in which Black identities are not only complex, but intersect to produce successful educational outcomes for Black students, particularly in relation to the intersection of class and success. Rhamie's chapter is a reminder for educators and researchers alike to look beyond a child's ethnicity and class background—and the dominant stereotyped notions of under/achievement attached to different ethnic groups—to recognise individual abilities, and at the same time, understand the factors that contribute to, reinforce and/or sustain negative attainment stereotypes. Once these factors are understood it will become easier for educators and researchers to shift from a negative to a positive lens, and uncover, nurture and realise Black educational success in its varying forms (e.g. literacy, mathematical/scientific ability etc.). Ultimately, what this will require is a repositioning of students designated as *'underachievers'* to one of *'achievers'*.

Through her analysis of the influence of class, religion, culture and tradition on Muslim boys' aspirations beyond compulsory schooling, Shain outlines the contradictory positioning between low and high aspirations amongst Muslim young men. She refers to an 'added layer of cultural complexity that challenges dominant theorising on risk and individualisation' amongst working-class Muslim male youth, which is invariably obscured by class analyses and deficit perceptions of Muslim identity. This layer of 'cultural complexity' in challenging the contemporary demonization of Muslim male youth demonstrates the complex interrelationship between religion, 'race', gender, class, community and culture, and the ways in which traditional and modern aspects of Muslim culture (including views on marriage) are (re)negotiated and mediated by Muslim boys both in and outside the school. These in turn, work to challenge educational inequalities. Contrary to teacher assumptions, Shain argues that religion and cultural expectations of marriage do not limit Muslim students' educational choices. Their choices are, however, shaped by complex intersections of 'race', ethnicity, gender, sexuality and religion, as well as culture, structure and individual agency.

Similarly, Mirza and Meetoo in their chapter highlight how negative perceptions of being Muslim in educational discourses inform teacher approaches and interactions with Muslim girls in schools. They outline how the lack of joined-up thinking in schools and wider education policy making about Muslim girls' educational experiences result in an absence of teacher and policy understanding of how 'racism, patriarchy, religion, class, sexuality and gender' complexly intertwined 'structured their cultural and social space in schools' and influenced their experiences of (gendered and cultural) surveillance (both by school and their parents) and bodily regulation from teachers (see also Duits and Zoonen 2006).

Shain and Mirza and Meetoo reveal a dearth of understanding of how culture and racialised identities are multifaceted and fluid (Hall 1996), and how culture and religion are adapted and mediated by young people themselves. The authors contend that an emphasis favouring patriarchal and Western notions of protecting Muslim girls from supposedly 'backward cultural and religious practices' do not distract teacher discourses from recognising Muslim girls' agency rather than their sense of victimhood, as well as nurturing Muslim girls' educational and career aspirations. It is equally important that perceptions of Muslim boys' disinterest in education (influenced by Muslim fundamentalism—see Archer 2003) does not influence teachers and their attitudes towards the educational aspirations of Muslim boys.

In this text an intersectional approach acknowledges how 'minority' communities (e.g. Mayan, Māori Pasifika, African American and itinerant Australians) and their knowledge(s) have been historically marginalised and excluded from White dominant educational discourses. The centrality of minority ethnic knowledge(s) and educational resilience influenced through culture, 'race' and place (in local rural communities) is evident in the chapters by Allweiss and Lachuk, Gomez and Powell. Without an unpicking of the intersectional experiences at a community level, it is difficult to understand how the notion of (rural) community impacts on African American and Mayan students and teachers from impoverished backgrounds. These 'minoritised' narratives demonstrate a desire to achieve and emphasise the struggles minority ethnic individuals/communities engage in to achieve educational success. Added to this, the insights offered by Pio et al., about Māori staff negotiation of university practices and policies while maintaining their own cultures/values, further illustrates the depth of knowledge/capitals/resources and resilience prevalent in minority ethnic communities (Yosso 2005),

Allweiss's research with Mayan teachers raises interesting questions about the framing of intersectional subjectivities in rural and urban contexts and their influence on engendering minority ethnic access to equitable education. Allweiss's study encourages us to consider how dominant communities understand the educational achievements acquired by minority ethnic groups. It also assists us in questioning *who* is 'qualified' to make policy and curriculum decisions, which suggests that minority ethnic teachers are not always considered 'qualified' or indeed capable of teaching (Maylor et al. 2013). This is similar to current UK policy whereby those teachers who are qualified to teach outside of the UK and European Economic Area are required to undergo further training/development in the UK before they can be considered and recognised as 'competent' to teach in UK schools.[1]

Through an intersectional lens, we can examine how local, national and international socio-cultural communities can affect the educational experiences of students and staff. The concept of intersectionality helps us to realise the value placed on knowledge and the meaning of 'success' for students and teachers from diverse communities. Without an understanding of intersectionality, it becomes difficult to address educational inequalities (Crenshaw 1995) in schools and higher education. As Crozier states, 'the struggle for a socially just and fair education system therefore, has to get to grips with the 'race', class and gender discrimination in and oppression by the system, through this interrelationship of the broader structural and policy issues and more localised and individual concerns; redistribution of resources and opportunities is essential but only if this process is related to contextualised identities'.

The various experiences highlighted throughout this collection indicate the importance of comprehending intersectional identities not just at an individual or community level, but through the curriculum. Oleksy, for example, uses intersectional critical pedagogy to illustrate how socially constructed identities lead to both the inclusion and exclusion of higher education students identifying, for example, as White, gay, Black, dis/

abled, upper middle-class. If intersectional pedagogies are used positively, students can appreciate the 'dynamics of intersectionality' and connect with different curricula to engage in intersectional dialogue in local and cross-national/cultural contexts. Similarly, Grant and Ketterhagen Engdahl propose intersectional culturally relevant pedagogy as a means for school teachers to seize/exploit opportunities for enhancing ethnically diverse student inclusion and participation in the curriculum and raising their attainment.

With increasing globalisation, cultural and ethnic diversity among students and staff in schools and higher education (Banks 2004; Ryter 2012), an intersectional approach provides opportunities for generating wider understanding of more diverse intersectional identities—including those previously suppressed—through an acknowledgement and a valuing of difference. Drawing on Grant and Ketterhagen Engdahl's intersectional curriculum with teaching opportunities realised to deliver a student-centred school curriculum, the potential is there for educators, senior mangers and policymakers to encompass a wider range of educational approaches and teaching styles to effectively recognise, include and teach students with intersectional identities. If higher education institutions were to adopt a similar approach (i.e. view themselves as institutions of possibilities), it would be possible for the intersectional identities of diverse students and staff to be viewed as opportunities rather than challenges, and in ways which allow both groups to feel included rather than excluded as 'other' (Tuhiwai Smith 2012).

Finally, this edited collection has revealed the ways in which intersectional identities inter and disconnect with local and national educational approaches and policies. Moreover, it highlights the salience of understanding, as argued by Allweiss, how 'policies that seek to address one form of oppression [often] fail to recognise how social categories are interconnected and mutually reinforcing in very complex and interlocking ways'.

If educational inequality is to be truly transformed and replaced with a socially just education system this will require the 'giving up . . . of a White dominated privileged position' and sharing of educational resources, as argued by Crozier. In addition, the process will require a new conceptualisation of knowledge which is valued and not based on a hierarchy in which some knowledge is valued more than others. For this to happen, it is essential for educators, and policymakers, to 'critically examine the cultural backgrounds and social formations out of which . . . students [and teachers] produce the categories they use to give meaning to the world [and how their] readings of the world are inextricably related to wider social and cultural formations and' [power] (Giroux 1987, 177). Ultimately, it will be incumbent on educationalists, researchers and policymakers to recognise that identities are not homogeneous and that 'beliefs systems, education, and many other factors, both specific and general produce, diversity, [similarities] and division within' (Fawcett and Hearn 2004, 215–216).

NOTES

1. Through the Overseas Trained Teacher Programme, non-EU overseas quali-fied teachers 'may be eligible to work in England as a temporary, unqualified teacher for up to four years while [they] achieve [UK] qualified teacher sta-tus' (Department for Education: Teaching Agency—http://www.education. gov.uk/get-into-teaching/teacher-training-options/experienced-teachers/ overseas-trained-teacher-programme; accessed February 6, 2012).

REFERENCES

Archer, Louise. 2003. *Race, Masculinity and Schooling: Muslim Boys and Educa-tion*. Maidenhead: Open University Press.

Banks, James. 2004. 'Teaching for Social Justice, Diversity, and Citizenship in a Global World'. *Educational Forum* 68:289–298.

Bourdieu, Pierre, and Passeron, Jean-Claude. 1994. *Reproduction in Education, Society and Culture*. 2nd ed. London: Sage.

Brah, Avtar, and Ann Phoenix. 2004. 'Ain't I a Woman: Revisiting Intersectional-ity'. Journal of International Women's Studies 5 (3): 75–86.

Collins, Patricia, Hill. 2000. *Black Feminist Thought*. 2nd ed. London: Routledge.

Crenshaw, Kimberlé. 1995. 'Mapping the Margins: Intersectionality, Identity Politics, and Violence against Women of Color'. In *Critical Race Theory. The Key Writings That Formed the Movement*, edited by Kimberlé Crenshaw, Neil Gotanda, Garry Peller and Kendall Thomas, 357–383. New York: New Press.

Delpit, Lisa. 1995. *Other People's Children: Cultural Conflict in the Classroom*. New York: New Press.

Duits, Linda, and Leisbet Van Zoonen. 2006. 'Headscarves and Porno-Chic: Dis-ciplining Girl's Bodies in the European Multicultural Society'. European Jour-nal of Women's Studies 13 (2): 103–117.

Fawcett, Barbara, and Jeff Hearn. 2004. 'Researching Others: Epistemology, Expe-rience, Standpoints and Participation'. *International Journal of Social Research Methodology* 7 (3): 201–218.

Giroux, Henry. 1987. 'Critical Literacy and Student Experience: Donald Graves' Approach to Literacy'. *Language Arts* 64:175–181.

Hall, Stuart. 1993. 'Cultural Identity and Diaspora'. In *Colonial Discourse and Post-Colonial Theory*, edited by Patrick Williams and Laura Chrisman, 392–403. New York: Harvester-Wheatsheaf.

———. 1996. 'Introduction—Who Needs Identity?' In *Questions of Cultural Iden-tity*, edited by Stuart Hall and Paul du Gay, 1–17. Thousand Oaks, CA: Sage.

Maylor, Uvanney. 2010. 'Notions of Diversity, British Identities and Citizenship Belonging'. *Race Ethnicity and Education*13:233–252.

Maylor, Uvanney, Anthea Rose, Sarah Minty, Alistair Ross, Tosun Issa and Kuyok A. Kuyok. 2013. 'Exploring the Impact of Supplementary Schools on Black and Minority Ethnic Pupils Mainstream Attainment'. *British Educational Research Journal* 39 (1): 107–125.

Mirza, Heidi, Safia, and Cynthia Joseph, eds. 2012. *Black and Postcolonial Feminisms in New Times: Researching Educational Inequalities*. New York: Routledge.

Ryter, Di. 2012. 'Improving Participation in a Pluralistic Democracy through a Cosmopolitan Approach to Social Studies Education'. *Journal of International Social Studies* 2 (1): 2–13.

Strand, Steve. 2012. The White British-Black Caribbean achievement gap: Tests, tiers and teacher expectations, *British Educational Research Journal*, 38 (1): 75–101.

Tuhiwai Smith, Linda. 2012. *Decolonising Methodologies: Research and Indigenous Peoples*. London: Zed Books.

Vincent, Carol, Nicola Rollock, Stephen Ball and David Gillborn, 2012. Being strategic, being watchful, being determined: Black middle-class parents and schooling. *British Journal of Sociology of Education*, 33 (3):337–354

Wright, Cecile, Penny Standen and Tina Patel. 2010. *Black Youth Matters: Transitions from School to Success*. London: Routledge.

Yosso, Tara. 2005. 'Whose Culture Has Capital? A Critical Race Theory Discussion of Community Cultural Wealth'. *Race, Ethnicity and Education* 8 (1): 69–91.

Contributors

Alexandra Allweiss worked for two years as a middle school and high school teacher in Guatemala and is currently a PhD candidate in Curriculum and Instruction and Educational Policy Studies at the University of Wisconsin-Madison. Her research interests include Comparative and International Education and Multicultural and Social Justice Education.

Kalwant Bhopal is Reader in Education at the University of Southampton. Her research examines aspects of social exclusion for marginalised minority ethnic groups. She has conducted research on the experiences of Asian women in higher education and Gypsy, Roma and Traveller groups in primary and secondary schools. Her recent publications include *Asian Women in Higher Education: Shared Communities* (Trentham, 2010), *Intersectionality and 'Race' in Education* (Routledge, 2011, with John Preston) and *Identity and Pedagogy in Higher Education: International Comparisons* (Continuum, 2013, with Patrick Alan Danaher). She has been an elected member of the British Education Research Association Council since 2009.

Gill Crozier is Professor of Education in the School of Education, University of Roehampton, London. She is a sociologist of education and has researched and written extensively on 'race' and education and its intersection with social class and gender. Specific areas of her work include: issues relating to parents and schools, young people and higher education. Her work is also concerned with education policy and the sociocultural influences upon identity formation and learner experiences. Her research projects include: The Socio-Cultural and Learning Experiences of Working-Class Students in Higher Education; Identities, Educational Choices and the White Urban Middle Classes; Parents, Children and the School Experience: Asian Families' Perspectives. Her books include: *Parents and Schools: Partners or Protagonists?* (Trentham, 2000); *Widening Participation through Improving Learning* (Routledge, 2009, edited by M. David); *White Middle Class Identities and Urban Schooling* (Palgrave, 2011, with D. Reay and D. James).

Annemarie Ketterhagen Engdahl is a graduate student at the University of Wisconsin-Madison, where she is studying teacher education. She has worked as a teacher, principal and literacy coach and provided district support to students living in urban areas throughout the US.

Mary Louise Gomez is Professor of Literacy Studies and Teacher Education at the University of Wisconsin-Madison, where she teaches graduate courses concerning narrative inquiry and life history and undergraduate courses concerning critical aspects of teaching and learning. Her publications include texts in: the *Teachers College Record*; *Teaching and Teacher Education*; *Race, Ethnicity, and Education*; the *Urban Review*; and *Teacher Education Quarterly*. Currently she is engaged in two research projects— one focused on the experiences of faculty and staff of color with White undergraduate students, and the other around her teaching of a course for university freshmen and sophomores concerning the intersections of race, class, gender, socio-economic status and language background.

Carl A. Grant is the Hoefs-Bascom Professor at the University of Wisconsin-Madison. His research interests as reflected in his scholarship are: multicultural education, social justice and teaching and teacher education. Professor Grant has written/edited forty books and over 120 journal articles. His latest book is *The Moment: Barack Obama, Jeramiah Wright and the Firestorm at Trinity United Church Christ*.

Robyn Henderson is an Associate Professor (Literacies Education) and works in the Faculty of Education of the University of Southern Queensland, Australia. She is based at the Toowoomba Campus, which is situated in a regional city on the edge of the Darling Downs, a large farming and beef area. Robyn researches in the fields of literacies, multiliteracies and literacy education, family mobility and its effects on schooling and the student learning journey in higher education. She is interested in the nexus of literacy learning and student mobility in school contexts, particularly in relation to itinerant farm workers' children who move from place to place as their parents follow the work that is available during summer and winter harvesting seasons. Themes related to pedagogies, diversity, social justice and capacity building are evident in her research. Robyn has published widely and she has edited and co-edited several research books. With a teaching career that has spanned early childhood, secondary and tertiary contexts, Robyn is passionate about bringing research, teaching and learning together. This is highlighted in her recent edited book, *Teaching Literacies in the Middle Years: Pedagogies and Diversity*, which is used as a teacher education text in several Australian universities.

Amy Johnson Lachuk is an Associate Professor in the Department of Curriculum and Teaching at Hunter College, City University of New York. She earned a bachelor's degree in English, and master's and doctoral degrees in Curriculum and Instruction at the University of Wisconsin-Madison. A Teach for America programme graduate, she taught elementary school in two urban school districts. Amy is a former faculty member at the University of Georgia and the University of South Carolina. Amy's work has appeared in the *Journal of Teacher Education*; *Race, Ethnicity, and Education*; *English Education*; the *Journal of Early Childhood Education*; and the *Journal of Adolescent and Adult Literacy*.

Zeus Leonardo is Associate Professor of Education and Affiliated Faculty of the Critical Theory Designated Emphasis at the University of California, Berkeley. He has published several dozen articles and book chapters on critical educational theory. His articles have appeared in *Educational Researcher*; *Race Ethnicity & Education*; and *Teachers College Record*. Some of his essays include: 'The Souls of White Folk', 'Critical Social Theory and Transformative Knowledge' and 'After the Glow: Race Ambivalence and Other Educational Prognoses'. His recent books are *Race, Whiteness and Education* (Routledge), *Handbook of Cultural Politics and Education* (SensePublishers), the forthcoming *Racial Frameworks* (Teachers College Press) and, with Norton Grubb, *Education and Racism* (Routledge).

Uvanney Maylor is Professor of Education and Director of the Institute for Research in Education at the University of Bedfordshire. She is a member of the UK-wide Higher Education Funding Council for Education Research in Excellence Framework Education panel (2014). She is committed to educational equity, inclusion and social justice. Her research interests include issues pertaining to 'race', ethnicity, gender and culture as they impact on educational practice and student and staff experience and identities. She has conducted extensive research including government-commissioned studies about the education and institutional experiences of potentially marginalised and discriminated against groups (including staff and students in schools, further and higher education).

Veena Meetoo is Research Officer at the Thomas Coram Research Unit, Institute of Education, University of London. Her research interests are focused around young people, social justice and inequalities, with particular attention to the intersections of gender, race and migration. She has conducted qualitative research on projects exploring Black and Minority Ethnic Women and Generational Change (Nuffield Foundation), Family Migration and Skilled Migration (European Union), Tackling the Roots of Racism (Joseph Rowntree Foundation) and Young Migrant Women in Secondary Education (European Union), as well as government-funded projects such as a review of the Sexualisation and Commercialisation of Childhood. Veena's current research explores the experiences South Asian and Muslim girls in secondary schools in relation to identities, multiculturalism and gender-based violence. Her latest publication is *Respecting Difference: Race, Faith and Culture for Teacher Educators* (2012, co-authored with Heidi Mirza).

Heidi Safia Mirza is Professor of Equalities Studies in Education at the Institute of Education, University of London. She is known internationally for her pioneering research on race, gender and identity in education. She uses post-colonial and Black feminist theoretical frameworks to explore social justice, human rights and equality issues for Muslim, Black and minority ethnic women, including Islamophobia and gendered violence. She was British director of the European Union project Young Migrant Women in Secondary Education: Promoting Integration and Mutual Understanding through Dialogue and Exchange. She is author of several best-selling books including, *Race, Gender and Educational Desire: Why Black Women Succeed and Fail.* Her most recent book, co-authored with Veena Meetoo, is *Respecting Difference: Race, Faith and Culture for Teacher Educators.*

Agnes Naera (Ngā Puhi) has worked at AUT in a number of roles, but has always been committed to equal educational and equal employment opportunities for Māori and Pasifika peoples. Agnes holds an MBA and is currently the director of Equity Programmes in the Faculty of Business and Law at AUT University, where she seeks to increase the participation, success and achievement of students and staff from under-represented communities across all levels and disciplines in the faculty.

Anne-Sofie Nyström is a Lecturer at the Department of Sociology at Uppsala University. Her research interests are educational inequality and feminist theory, with a focus on (young) men, masculinities and identity processes in peer groups. Her PhD thesis 'Att synas och lära utan att synas lära (To be seen and to learn, without being seen to learn)' (Acta Universitatis Upsaliensis, 2012) on identity negotiation among privileged young men, schooling and underachievement, was well received in Swedish news media and policy debates when it was published in 2012. Nyström's publications include: 'Mellan empati och kritisk granskning—forskningsdeltagande som risk (Between Empathy and Critical Scrutiny—Research Participation from a Risk Perspective)' (in Hildur Kalman and Veronica Lövgren, eds., *Etiska dilemma*, Gleerups 2012); and several conference papers on masculinities, schooling and peer group interaction.

Elżbieta H. Oleksy is Full Professor of Humanities at the University of Łódź, Poland. She chairs the Department of Transatlantic and Media Studies and is founding director of Women's Studies Centre. She was Founding Dean of the Faculty of International and Political Studies (2000–2008).

She has authored/co-authored and edited/co-edited twenty-four books and over a hundred chapters and articles in the field of gender studies and visual culture. Her recent publications include two edited books: *The Limits of Gendered Citizenships. Contexts and Complexities* (Routledge, 2011), *Intimate Citizenships. Gender, Sexualities, Politics* (Routledge, 2008) and a review article, 'Intersectionality at the Cross-roads', *Women's Studies International Forum* 34 (2011), as well as 'The Politics of Representing Gender in Contemporary Polish Cinema and Visual Art' (in *East European Cinemas*, ed. A. Imre, Routledge, 2005). She was president of the Association of Institutions for Education and Research in Europe (AOIFE, 2003–2006) and high-level expert of the European Commission and European Court of Auditors (2002–2008).

Lorraine Parker was director, Organisational Development, at AUT University from 2010 to 2011, working with human resources to coordinate the learning, development and training of the university's staff. Her previous role was that of director of AUT University's Centre for Educational and Professional Development, a position she held for eleven years. The Centre was responsible for coordinating academic development services for staff throughout the university. Prior to joining AUT in 1999, Lorraine was deputy director in the Centre for Professional Development at the University of Auckland, where she had established a staff training and development service with an organisational development focus. In 1996, she attained an MPhil (Hons) in Management Studies and Employment Relations from the University of Auckland. She is currently a Professional Member of the Human Resources Institute of New Zealand (HRINZ). Her research interests are focused on management and leadership development in the higher education sector.

Edwina Pio (PhD, BEd, MNZAC) is Associate Professor at the Business & Law School of AUT University, Auckland, New Zealand, and Visiting Professor at Boston College, Massachusetts, US, and Cambridge University UK, with research interests at the intersection of management, migration, ethnicity and pedagogy. Edwina is widely published in international journals. She has also written a number of books including: *Sari: Indian women at Work in New Zealand* (Dunmore); *Longing & Belonging* (Dunmore); and *Caste Away: Unfolding the Maori-Indian* (Office of Ethnic Affairs). She travels extensively to research and disseminate her work and has been invited to Austria (University of Vienna), the Netherlands (Radboud University), Spain (ESADE), Sweden (Jönköping International Business School) and the US (Boston College). She is on the editorial board of a number of journals and has won awards at the Academy of Management US and in Japan at the International Conference of the Society of Global Business and Economic Development. She is on the PhD/M. Phil Committee at her university and a director on the board of the Australia New Zealand Academy of Management (ANZAM). She is a registered counsellor and works on a voluntary basis with migrants.

Shameka N. Powell earned a bachelor's and master's degree in Secondary English Education at the University of North Carolina-Greensboro. She then taught high school English for several years. She now is pursuing her doctoral degree in Curriculum and Instruction at the University of Wisconsin-Madison. Her dissertation focuses on African American student achievement.

Ali Rasheed is a migrant from the Maldives. He and his family came to New Zealand in 2002 in search of better educational opportunities for his three children. His subsequent research into migrant and ethnic communities in New Zealand is motivated and informed by his own experiences, as well as his continuing interest in ethnicity and gender issues. In addition to his research, he has also been a practitioner of equity and diversity at Auckland University of Technology for the last decade. In this role, he has contributed to advancement of Equal Employment Opportunity for staff and Equal Educational Opportunity (EEdO) for students at the university. He has developed policy and strategies to support the participation and success of students and staff from indigenous and disadvantaged backgrounds. Some of these success stories have been presented at conferences and published in the local and international media.

Jasmine Rhamie is Senior Lecturer in Teaching and Learning and Assistant Programme Convenor for the Primary PGCE in the School of Education at the University of Roehampton. Dr. Rhamie is the author of *Eagles Who Soar: How Black Learners Find Paths to Success*. She has a background as a primary teacher in a range of primary schools in the UK and secondary and tertiary education in the Caribbean. She holds an MA in Psychology of Education from the Institute of Education, University of London, with distinction and gained a PhD in Psychology of Education funded by the ESRC in 2004. She has worked as a research consultant to a number of unitary authorities and organisations in Berkshire and as research and senior research officer on a number of large government-funded projects, such as the Primary Behaviour and Attendance pilot, Behaviour Improvement Programme and Skill Force. Dr. Rhamie has experience of supervising doctoral students and has examined theses at the doctoral level. She has published in a number of peer-reviewed journals and presented at national and international conferences. She is a member of the British Psychological Society (BPsS), British Educational Research Association and a fellow of the Higher Education Academy. She holds Chartered Scientist status with the BPsS. Dr. Rhamie has research interests in 'race' and ethnicity in education, pupil's understandings of identity, BME male trainee teachers experiences and African Caribbean academic success factors.

Alistair Ross is Jean Monnet ad personam Professor of Citizenship Education in Europe and Emeritus Professor London Metropolitan University. His background is in educational sociology and policy analysis, and he is a member of the Institute of Policy Studies in Education at London Metropolitan University (where he was the first director, from 2000 to 2009). His particular research interests are in educational equity and justice, in citizenship education and identities, and in making the educational workforce more diverse and representative. He led the European Commission Erasmus Academic Network Children's Identity and Citizenship in Europe (CiCe) from 1998 to 2008; directed the EPASI in Europe (Charting Educational Policies to Address Social Inequalities in Europe) evaluating educational policies from 2007 to 2009; was consultant for the Migration Policy Index 2010 new strand on Education policies and migrants; and was the invited keynote speaker at the 2011 European Commission Consultation Symposium on Measures to Combat Educational Disadvantage. As part of his Jean Monnet professorship, he is currently making a study of how young people construct their identities in the newer member countries of the European Union and in the candidate countries. Recent publications include *Future Citizens: 21st Century Challenges for Young People* (2011, with Beata Krzywosz-Rynkiewicz and Anna Zalewska); *What's Fair? Young Europeans' Constructions of Equity, Altruism and Self-Interest* (2011, with Melinda Dooly); and *Equalities and Education in Europe: Explanations and Excuses for Inequality* (2012, with Melinda Dooly and Nanny Harsmar).

Farzana Shain is Professor of Sociology of Education at Keele University. She has researched and written on leadership, professionalism and managerialism in further education but is more recently known for her work gendered, raced and classed inequalities and identities, especially in education. Her books include *The Schooling and Identity of Asian Girls* (Trentham, 2003 and *The New Folk Devils: Muslim Boys and Education in England* (Trentham, 2011).

Kitea Tipuna (Ngāti Kahungunu Ki Wairoa) has an interest in Kaupapa Māori research with a particular focus on Māori community development, public relations and communications management. Kitea has been employed at AUT for over twelve years and his professional career has also focused on lifting the aspirations of Māori communities. Kitea has led, managed and contributed to policy development and professional practice at AUT as it relates to Equal Employment Opportunities for Māori, Pasifika and women. Workforce development and increasing the number of Māori and Pasifika staff at AUT has been important to Kitea, and he believes that this will also influence the success and achievement of Māori and Pasifika students studying at AUT. Kitea has a master's degree in Communications Management and his thesis looked at the consultation processes that were undertaken with *tangata whenua* in a development case in his home province of Hawkes Bay.

Index